Henry Longueville Mansel

The Limits of Religious Thought

Examined in eight lectures preached before the University of Oxford, in the year MDCCCLVIII; on the foundation of the late Rev. John Bampton. Fifth Edition

Henry Longueville Mansel

The Limits of Religious Thought
Examined in eight lectures preached before the University of Oxford, in the year MDCCCLVIII; on the foundation of the late Rev. John Bampton. Fifth Edition

ISBN/EAN: 9783337034283

Printed in Europe, USA, Canada, Australia, Japan

Cover: Foto ©Lupo / pixelio.de

More available books at **www.hansebooks.com**

THE

LIMITS OF RELIGIOUS THOUGHT

EXAMINED

IN EIGHT LECTURES,

PREACHED BEFORE THE UNIVERSITY OF OXFORD, IN
THE YEAR M.DCCC.LVIII.

ON THE FOUNDATION OF

THE LATE REV. JOHN BAMPTON, M.A.,

CANON OF SALISBURY.

By HENRY LONGUEVILLE MANSEL, B.D.,

READER IN MORAL AND METAPHYSICAL PHILOSOPHY AT MAGDALEN COLLEGE;
TUTOR AND LATE FELLOW OF ST. JOHN'S COLLEGE;
NOW REGIUS PROFESSOR OF ECCLESIASTICAL HISTORY,
AND CANON OF CHRIST CHURCH.

FIFTH EDITION.

LONDON:
JOHN MURRAY, ALBEMARLE STREET.
1867.

THE OBJECTIONS MADE TO FAITH ARE BY NO MEANS AN EFFECT OF KNOWLEDGE, BUT PROCEED RATHER FROM AN IGNORANCE OF WHAT KNOWLEDGE IS.
BISHOP BERKELEY.

NO DIFFICULTY EMERGES IN THEOLOGY, WHICH HAD NOT PREVIOUSLY EMERGED IN PHILOSOPHY.
SIR W. HAMILTON.

EXTRACT

FROM

THE LAST WILL AND TESTAMENT

OF THE

REV. JOHN BAMPTON,

CANON OF SALISBURY.

——" I give and bequeath my Lands and Estates to the Chancellor, Masters, and Scholars of the University of Oxford for ever, to have and to hold all and singular the said Lands or Estates upon trust, and to the intents and purposes hereinafter mentioned; that is to say, I will and appoint that the Vice-Chancellor of the University of Oxford for the time being shall take and receive all the rents, issues, and profits thereof, and (after all taxes, reparations, and necessary deductions made) that he pay all the remainder to the endowment of eight Divinity Lecture Sermons, to be established for ever in the said University, and to be performed in the manner following:

"I direct and appoint, that, upon the first Tuesday in Easter Term, a Lecturer be yearly chosen by the Heads of Colleges only, and by no others, in the room adjoining to the Printing-House, between the hours of ten in the morning and two in the afternoon, to preach eight Divinity Lecture Sermons, the year following, at St. Mary's in Oxford, between the commencement of the last month in Lent Term, and the end of the third week in Act Term.

" Also I direct and appoint that the eight Divinity Lecture Sermons shall be preached upon either of the following subjects—to confirm and establish the Christian Faith, and to confute all heretics and schismatics—upon the divine authority of the Holy Scriptures—upon the authority of the writings of the primitive Fathers, as to the faith and practice of the primitive Church—upon the Divinity of our Lord and Saviour Jesus Christ—upon the Divinity of the Holy

Ghost—upon the Articles of the Christian Faith, as comprehended in the Apostles' and Nicene Creeds.

"Also I direct, that thirty copies of the eight Divinity Lecture Sermons shall be always printed, within two months after they are preached, and one copy shall be given to the Chancellor of the University, and one copy to the Head of every College, and one copy to the Mayor of the City of Oxford, and one copy to be put into the Bodleian Library; and the expense of printing them shall be paid out of the revenue of the Land or Estates given for establishing the Divinity Lecture Sermons; and the Preacher shall not be paid, nor be entitled to the revenue before they are printed.

"Also I direct and appoint, that no person shall be qualified to preach the Divinity Lecture Sermons, unless he hath taken the degree of Master of Arts at least, in one of the two Universities of Oxford or Cambridge; and that the same person shall never preach the Divinity Lecture Sermons twice."

ADVERTISEMENT

TO THE FIFTH EDITION.

THE third and fourth editions of these Lectures were accompanied by a Preface intended to meet some of the objections urged against the argument of the work by various critics. This Preface is now withdrawn, those portions of it which seemed worth retaining having been thrown into the form of additional notes to the several passages in the Lectures to which they relate. To the present edition it has been thought preferable to prefix a brief summary of the argument of the work as a whole, together with a list of authorities, ancient and modern, whose testimony may be cited in support of the principal doctrines maintained in the body of the work. The summary, though the necessity of it was first suggested by the misapprehensions of some critics concerning the purpose of the main argument, has been drawn up in general terms, without any special reference to such criticisms; its object being simply to assist towards a right apprehension of the argument, not to expose the misapprehensions of individuals. The list of authorities has no pretension to be considered as complete, or as the result of systematic search. It is simply a collection of passages which have come before the author in the general course of his reading, whether before or since the first publication of the Lectures; and, as regards the period subsequent to the Reformation, it is intentionally limited to writers in the communion of the Church of England.

This list might, no doubt, be considerably enlarged by a more careful investigation, or by one extended over a wider area; but it is hoped that enough, at least, has been done to shew that a doctrine which has been vehemently condemned by some recent critics as an heretical novelty is not without sufficient vouchers in support both of its antiquity and of its Catholicity.

SUMMARY OF THE ARGUMENT.

It is assumed throughout the Lectures that human reason is capable of attaining to some conception of a Supreme Being, and that this conception will vary in intellectual elevation and moral purity according to the intellectual and moral condition of those by whom it is formed. This assumption is implied in the title, "The Limits of Religious Thought," which supposes the existence of a religious thought to be limited, and is expressly asserted in the Second Lecture, p. 30. The further question to be considered is this: Granting that such conceptions exist, in various degrees of approximation to the truth, what is the highest point of elevation to which human philosophy, apart from Revelation, can raise them; and what is the nature of the assistance afforded by Revelation when given? Are such conceptions, in their highest form, exact representations of the absolute nature of God, so that the theological conclusions to which they lead are entitled to be accepted as scientific certainties? or are they merely approximate representations, founded on analogy, not on exact resemblance, and leading to conclusions which, however reasonable as probabilities, and however valuable in the absence of more trustworthy information, are yet but one kind of probable evidence among many, whose exact value cannot be estimated till full account has been taken of all corroborative or conflicting evidences derivable from other sources? Under the former supposition, Reason is the paramount authority in all religious questions and the criterion by which any professed revelation must be tested; whether with the Dogmatist we maintain that Reason is in agreement with Revelation, and that the revealed doctrines are to be received because they can be demonstrated from rational premises, or with the Rationalist assert that Reason and Revelation are in some cases opposed to each other, and that in all such cases the revelation must at once be set aside as intrinsically incredible. Under the latter supposition, Reason, though by no means set aside as worthless, is reduced from a supreme to a coordinate authority: its conclusions must be compared with those derived from other sources; and we are at liberty, when Reason and Revelation come into apparent conflict, to admit at least the possibility that the former may be in error, and that the latter need not necessarily be rejected for conflicting with it.

In order to answer this question, it will be necessary to examine the constitution of the human mind, and the character of the conception of Divine things which the mind, under the conditions of that constitution, is capable of forming. The mental conditions which determine the character of a philosophy of religion must be the same with those which determine the character of philosophy in general; and the limits, if limits there are, of philosophy in general will be the limits of religious philosophy also.

There is a problem which philosophy in all ages has attempted to solve, and the solution of which is indispensable before the conclusions of philosophy can be accepted as scientific certainties and sure guides to religious belief. That problem is, to determine the nature of Absolute and Infinite Existence, and its relation to relative and finite existences. Such an inquiry is not necessarily an inquiry into the nature of God: it was prosecuted of old by Heathen philosophers without any necessary connection with their religious belief: it may be prosecuted now by the Pantheist or by the Atheist, no less than by the believer in a Personal God. But to a Christian, the two inquiries, though in themselves distinct, become necessarily combined into one. If we believe that God made the world, not by a necessary process from all eternity, but by a free act commencing in time, we must also believe that before that creation God existed alone, having no relation to any other being, and therefore as the One Absolute Being. In the words of Bishop Pearson, "Deus in se est ens absolutum, sine ulla relatione ad creaturas: fuit enim ab æterno sine ulla creatura, et potuit, si voluisset, in æternum sine creatura esse."[a] And if in this sense we believe in God as an Absolute Being, we must also believe in Him as an Infinite Being; for the conception of a finite being necessarily involves the possibility of something greater and more perfect than itself, which is incompatible with the idea of God. And finally, if we believe that God made the world, we must believe that, at some point of time, the one absolute and infinite Being gave existence to other relative and finite beings; we must believe that the God who is absolute in Himself is also a First Cause in relation to His creatures.

But when once it is conceded that the Absolute and Infinite Being must be identified with the Deity, two distinct conceptions come into contact and apparently into collision with each other. The God demanded by our moral and religious consciousness must be a *Person*. Does the Philosophy of the Absolute and Infinite lead us to the conclusion that the Being contemplated under those aspects is a Personal Being? and if not, must our belief in

[a] *Minor Theological Works*, vol. i., p. 13, see below, p. xxxi.

a personal God be abandoned in obedience to the dictates of such a philosophy? The first of these questions may be to a great extent answered by History. As a matter of fact, the hardiest and most consistent reasoners who have attempted a philosophy of absolute existence—Parmenides, Plotinus, Spinoza, Fichte, Schelling, Hegel—have one and all attained to their conclusions by dropping out of their philosophy the attribute of personality, and exhibiting the absolute existence as an impersonal abstraction, or as an equally impersonal universe of all existence.[b] Are we then bound to follow the philosophy of the Absolute to a conclusion utterly destructive of all religious relation between God and man? and if not, how are we to dispose of the claims of a philosophy, which, to whatever errors it may have led, has undoubtedly exercised a fascination over the most powerful intellects in various ages, and which, if it is to be met at all, must be met, not simply by the repudiation of certain conclusions, but by pointing out the error of the principles which lead to them?

This is the task attempted in the Second and Third of the following Lectures: the former of which endeavours to shew that the metaphysical conceptions of the Infinite and the Absolute, as postulated by the above philosophy, cannot be applied in thought to any concrete object regarded as the one absolute and infinite being, without involving us in apparent contradictions, and equally so, whether we assert the existence of such a being or deny it; while the latter endeavours to explain these apparent contradictions by shewing that they arise, not from any inherent impossibility in the object contemplated, but from certain conditions in the constitution of the mind contemplating

[b] See below, Lecture II., *Notes* 17, 25, 26; Lecture III., *Notes* 7, 8, 20, 22.

it—conditions which are necessary to all positive and consistent human thought, and the violation of which, in the attempt to conceive the unconditioned, leads not to thought, but to the negation of thought. The conclusions drawn from this portion of the inquiry are, first, that the limits of positive thought cannot be the limits of belief; that we are compelled by the constitution of our minds to believe in the existence of an absolute and infinite being, the existence of such a belief being proved even by the unsuccessful efforts made by philosophy to comprehend the nature of this being: and secondly, that the apparent contradictions in which philosophy is involved in the course of such efforts (contradictions, be it remembered, which, as regards past speculations, are simply matters of fact, which exist independently of any theory) furnish no valid argument against such a belief, because, in the first place, they are common to unbelief equally with belief, and, in the second place, they may be shewn to result, not from the legitimate use of reason within its proper province, but from the illegitimate attempt to extend it beyond that province. If, then, it can be shewn that our religious instincts and feelings necessarily require us to believe in a Personal God, we are not justified in rejecting that belief on account of any apparent difficulties raised by the Philosophy of the Unconditioned. We may *believe that* a Personal God exists: we may *believe that* He is also absolute and infinite as well as personal; though we are unable, under our present conditions of thought, to *conceive the manner in which* the attributes of absoluteness and infinity coexist with those which constitute personality.[c] The conclusion thus arrived at may be literally

---

[c] It should be observed, once for all, that the terms *conceive*, *conception*, &c., as they are employed in the following Lectures, always imply an apprehension of the *manner* in which certain attributes can coexist with each other, so as to form a whole or

stated in the words of St. Chrysostom: "*That* God is everywhere, I know; and *that* He is wholly everywhere, I know; but the *how*, I know not: *that* He is without beginning, ungenerated and eternal, I know; but the *how*, I know not."

It has next to be shewn that, as a matter of fact, those elements in the human consciousness which form the basis of religion, and from which positive religious ideas are originally derived, require, as their indispensable complement, the belief in a Personal God. This is attempted in the Fourth Lecture, where it is maintained that the two fundamental feelings on which religious thought is based, the *Sense of Dependence* and the *Sense of Moral Obligation*, necessarily point to a Personal Being, who as a Free Agent can hear and answer prayer, and as a Moral Governor is the source and author of the moral law within us. These are the immediate and positive sources

complex notion. It is not sufficient for conception that we should understand the meaning of each separate term which the notion contains: we must also apprehend them as existing in a certain manner, possible in imagination if not in actual experience. In this sense of the term, the test of conceivability of a complex notion is the coexistence of the component ideas in a possible object of intuition, pure or empirical. This I have endeavoured to explain at greater length in my *Prolegomena Logica*, p. 23, *seqq.*, and in my *Metaphysics*, p. 204, *seqq.* It is similarly explained by Sir W. Hamilton, *Reid's Works*, p. 377. Thus when it is said that the nature of God as an absolute and infinite being is inconceivable, it is not meant that the terms *absolute* and *infinite* have no meaning—as mere terms they are as intelligible as the opposite terms *relative* and *finite*—but that we cannot apprehend *how* the attributes of absoluteness and infinity coexist with the personal attributes of God, though we may believe *that*, in some manner unknown to us, they do coexist. In like manner, we cannot *conceive how* a purely spiritual being sees and hears without the bodily organs of sight and hearing; yet we may *believe that* He does so in some manner. Belief is possible in the mere fact (τὸ ὅτι). Conception must include the manner (τὸ πῶς).

of our knowledge of God; and as such they cannot be set aside by the mere negative abstractions of the so-called Philosophy of the Unconditioned. Yet the consciousness of a Personal God is not in itself an intuition of the Absolute and Infinite, nor does it enable us to conceive the manner in which Absoluteness and Infinity coexist with Personality. We are thus led to the conviction that behind this positive conception of God as a Person there yet remains a mystery which in our present state of knowledge we are unable to penetrate—the mystery of a personality which is absolute and infinite, and therefore not identical with our relative and finite personality, though the latter among finite things is that which is most nearly analogous to it and its fittest representative in human thought and human speech. We are thus again thrown on the same distinction as before—the distinction between belief in the fact and conception of the manner. We believe *that* the Personal God required by our religious consciousness is also absolute and infinite, but we are unable to conceive *how* He is so. This is the general character of religious mysteries, as described in the words of Leibnitz:—"Il en est de même des autres mystères, où les esprits modérés trouveront toujours une explication suffisante pour croire, et jamais autant qu'il en faut pour comprendre. Il nous suffit d'un certain *ce que c'est* (τί ἐστι); mais le *comment* (πῶς) nous passe, et ne nous est point nécessaire."[d]

[d] See below, Lecture V., *note* 12. By explaining the word *comprendre* as denoting apprehension of the manner in which an object of thought exists, as distinguished from mere belief in the fact, Leibnitz shews that he employs this term in the sense in which I have above explained the term *conceive*. In the same sense, M. Peisse, in his translation of Sir W. Hamilton's *Fragments*, p. 98, says, "Comprendre, c'est voir un terme en rapport avec un autre; c'est voir comme un ce qui est donné comme multiple." In this sense, I prefer, with Hamilton himself, to employ the term *con*-

But if it be once admitted that the Divine Personality, as coexisting with Infinity, is so far mysterious to us that it is not apprehended by reason as existing in a particular manner, but accepted by faith as existing in some manner unknown to us, it follows that the positive knowledge which we have of God in this life, is not a knowledge of Him as He is in His absolute nature, but only as He is imperfectly represented by those qualities in His creatures which are analogous to, but not identical with His own. If we had a knowledge of the Divine Personality as it is. in itself, we should know it as existing in a certain manner compatible with unconditioned action: and this knowledge of the manner would at once transform our conviction from an act of faith to a conception of reason. But, inasmuch as the only personality of which we have a positive knowledge is our own, and as our own personality can only be conceived as conditioned in time, it follows that the Divine Personality, in so far as it is exempt from conditions, does not resemble the only personality which we directly know, and is not adequately represented by it. This characteristic of our positive conceptions of the Divine nature and attributes, namely, that they are not derived from an immediate perception of the objects themselves, but from an imperfect representation of them in the analogous attributes of human nature, is what is intended to be expressed by the assertion that such conceptions are *regulative* but not *speculative*. By a *speculative conception* is meant a conception derived from an

---

ception rather than *comprehension*; the latter being frequently used by theological writers in a very different sense, to denote a perfect cognition of the whole nature and properties of an object. This ambiguity, which forms one of the plausible points in Toland's attempt to shew that there is nothing in Christianity above reason, is pointed out by his antagonist Norris, in his *Reason and Faith*, p. 118, ed. 1697.

immediate perception or other intuition of the object conceived, as when I form a notion of human seeing or hearing, or of human anger or pity, from my actual experience of these modes of consciousness in myself; and a speculative truth is a truth expressed by means of such conceptions. A *regulative* conception, on the other hand, is a conception derived, not from the immediate perception or intuition of the object itself, but from that of something else, supposed more or less nearly to resemble it; and a *regulative truth* is a truth expressed by means of such conceptions. Thus when I speak of God as seeing or hearing, or as feeling anger or pity, I do not mean that He has precisely the same modes of consciousness which are expressed by these terms when applied to man, but I borrow from the human consciousness terms which express indirectly and by way of analogy certain divine attributes of which I have no immediate apprehension in themselves. Regulative conceptions are thus accommodations adapted to human faculties, serving as rules and guides to direct our thoughts in relation to things which we are unable to conceive immediately. The same distinction is expressed in the language of Bishop Pearson in the continuation of the passage quoted on p. ix. "At Deus non potest aliter a nobis naturaliter cognosci, nisi relate ad creaturas, scil. aut sub ratione dominii, aut sub ratione causæ, aut aliqua alia relatione. Ergo non potest per se primo a nobis cognosci, sine interventu creaturarum, per ordinem ad quas cognoscitur."

In the Fifth Lecture, the distinction between speculative and regulative conceptions is further pursued in relation to other questions besides those of Theology. It is shewn that in problems of a purely philosophical character, no less than in those of Theology, the attempt to arrive at an absolutely first and unconditioned principle involves us in apparent contradictions, and we are compelled to acquiesce, as our highest point of positive thought, in principles which we practically assume, and act upon as true without being able to conceive how they are true, and which necessarily imply the existence of a mysterious and inconceivable reality beyond themselves. A parallel is thus established between Natural Theology and Philosophy: the limitations of which we are conscious in our attempts to conceive the absolute nature of God, being shewn to be analogous to those which hinder us from attaining to an absolute first principle in such problems as those concerning Liberty and Necessity, Unity and Plurality, the Intercourse of Soul and Body, and the nature of Space and Time. The difficulties in Theology are thus shewn to arise, not from any peculiar antagonism between theology and human reason, but from conditions to which reason is universally subject, and which necessarily imply the existence of truths which are above reason. The analogy is then extended to Revealed Theology; and the method followed by Scripture in its representations of the Divine Nature is shewn to proceed upon an acknowledgment of the same law of thought, and to be thus adapted to the constitution of the human mind.

In the Sixth and Seventh Lectures, the principles thus established are applied with special reference to those Christian doctrines which have been attacked on the ground of their supposed antagonism to the conclusions of human reason, speculative or moral. The insufficiency of such attacks is shewn, on the ground that the so-called rational representations themselves are liable to similar objections, and naturally so, because the difficulties arise, not from defects peculiar to Revelation, but from the limits of human thought in general. Having arrived at this result, we are entitled to speak of the so-called contradictions between Reason and Revelation as merely apparent, not real contradictions; for in order to know two ideas to be really contradictory, it is necessary to have a positive and distinct conception of both as they are in themselves; whereas we have no such positive conception of divine things *per se*, but only an imperfect representation through their analogy to finite things.

We are now in a position to answer the question proposed at the beginning of these remarks, viz.—What is the value of our rational conceptions of the Divine Nature in their highest development? Are they exact representations of that nature, leading to conclusions of scientific certainty, comparable to those of mathematics or of physical science? or are they merely approximate representations, leading only to probabilities, which may be balanced and modified by counter-probabilities of another kind? It is evident that they are the latter, not the former. For if we cannot attain to a positive conception of the nature of an Absolute and Infinite Being, we are not in a position to deduce with certainty the necessary properties of that nature, so as to establish a deductive science of theology comparable to mathematical demonstration: and if we have not a direct experience of the divine attributes in themselves, but only of human attributes, analogous to them but not identical with them, we cannot construct an inductive science of theology comparable to the physical sciences which are founded on the direct experience and observation of natural objects. We are compelled to reason by analogy; and analogy furnishes only probabilities, varying, it may be, from slight presumptions up to moral certainties, but whose weight in any given case can only be determined by comparison with other evidences. There are three distinct sources from which we may form a judgment about the ways of God—first, from our own moral and intellectual consciousness, by which we judge *à priori* of what God ought to do in a given case, by determining what we should think it wise or right for ourselves to do in a similar case; secondly, from the constitution and course of nature, from which we may learn by experience what God's Providence in certain cases actually is; and thirdly, from Revelation, attested by its proper evidences. Where these three agree in their testimony (as in the great majority of cases they do) we have the moral certainty which results from the harmony of all accessible evidences: where they appear to differ, we have no right at once to conclude that the second or the third must give way to the first, and not *vice versâ*; because we have no right to assume that the first alone is infallible. But if Reason is *fallible* in matters of religion, it does not follow that it is *worthless*. Where no revelation has been given, it is man's only guide: where a real or supposed revelation exists, it may sift the evidences on which it rests; it may expose the pretences of a false revelation; it may aid in the interpretation of a true one. But while acknowledging the services of Reason in these respects, we must also acknowledge that a Revelation tested by sufficient evidence is superior to reason, and may correct the errors to which reason is liable; and, consequently, that *exactly in proportion to the strength of the remaining evidence for the divine origin of a religion is the probability that our reason may be mistaken when it concludes this or that portion of its contents to be unworthy of God.* We are bound to believe that a Revelation given by God can never contain anything that is really unwise or unrighteous; but a fallible Reason may suppose things to be unwise or unrighteous which are not really so.

From this estimate of the relations between Reason and Revelation, one other conclusion necessarily follows. If in proportion to the strength of the evidence for the divine origin of a revelation is the probability that reason may be in error in judging any portion of its contents to be unworthy of God, it will follow that where the divine origin of the Revelation is fully established, the authority of Reason as a criterion is reduced to its lowest point. Hence there is a special inconsistency in the conduct of those who, while admitting the divine origin of Christianity, claim a right, on rational grounds, to select a portion of the teaching of Christ as permanent and essential, and to reject the remainder as temporary or unessential. If the divine authority of Christ's teaching be once admitted, the acceptance of all that can be plainly shewn to belong to that teaching follows as a matter of course: and, on the other hand, if any portion of that teaching be rejected on rational grounds, this can only be legitimately done on the assumption that the whole is of human origin, not a divine Revelation.

This submission of Reason to the authority of Revelation is not, of course, a solution of our rational difficulties: it is only a belief notwithstanding those difficulties, and a trust that there is a solution, though we may be unable to find it. And thus it is that an examination of the Limits of Religious Thought leads us ultimately to rest not on Reason but on Faith; appeals, not to our knowledge, but to our ignorance; and shews that our intellectual trial in this life is analogous to our moral trial, that as there are real temptations to sin which nevertheless do not abrogate the duty of right conduct, so there are real temptations to doubt, which nevertheless do not abrogate the duty of belief.

TESTIMONIES OF THEOLOGIANS

TO THE

PRINCIPAL DOCTRINE MAINTAINED IN THESE LECTURES, IN ONE OF THE FOLLOWING FORMS:

1. That the Absolute Nature of God is unknown to man.
2. That conceptions derived from human consciousness do not represent the Absolute Nature of God.
3. That God is revealed in Scripture by means of relative conceptions, accommodated to man's faculties.

I. CLEMENT OF ALEXANDRIA.—*Strom.*, ii. 16, p. 168, Sylb.: "The Divine Nature cannot be described as it really is. The Prophets have spoken to us, fettered as we are by the flesh, according to our ability to receive their saying, the Lord accommodating Himself to human weakness for our salvation" [Translated by Bishop Kaye, Clem. Alex., p. 141]. *Strom.* v. 12, p. 251. "The first principle of all things cannot be named. And if we give it a name, not properly (οὐ κυρίως), calling it either One, or the Good, or Intellect, or the Very Existent, or Father, or God, or Maker, or Lord, we speak not as declaring its name, but by reason of our deficiency we employ good names, in order that the reason may be able to rest upon these, not wandering around others. For these names are not severally indicative of God, but all collectively exhibit the power of the Almighty: for the names of things are given to them either from the properties belonging to them, or from their relation to each other: but none of these can be received concerning God."

II. ORIGEN.—*De Princ.*, I. i., 5, 6: "Our mind, while it is confined within the barriers of flesh and blood, and by partaking of such matter is made duller and more obtuse, though it be far more excellent than the body, yet when it strives after incorporeal things, and seeks to behold them, scarcely obtains so much as the light of a spark or a lantern. But of all intellectual, that is incorporeal beings, what is so surpassing, what so ineffably and inconceivably excellent as God? whose nature cannot be gazed at and beheld by the sharpsightedness of any human mind, though that mind be the purest and most clear. But to make this thing more manifest, we may not unfitly use another similitude. It sometimes happens that our eyes are unable to behold the very nature of light; that is to say, the substance of the sun; but by beholding his brightness or rays poured in, it may be, through windows, or other small receptacles of light, we are able to consider how great is the nutriment and fountain of bodily light. Thus, then, the works of Divine Providence and the design of this universe are, as it were, rays of the Divine Nature, as compared with His substance and nature. Whereas, then, our mind is unable of itself to behold God Himself as He is, yet from the beauty of His works and the comeliness of His creatures it understands the parent of the universe."

III. CYPRIAN.—*De Idol. Vanit.*, c. 9: "We cannot see Him; He is too bright for our vision; we cannot reach Him; He is too pure for our touch; we cannot scan Him; He is too great for our intelligence; and therefore we but think of Him worthily when we own Him to be beyond our thought." (Sic eum digne æstimamus dum inæstimabilem dicimus.) [Translated in *Library of the Fathers*, Oxford, 1846. The same words are also found in MUNICIUS FELIX, *Octav.* c. 18.]

IV. ARNOBIUS.—*Adv. Gentes*, iii. 19: "If you do not refuse to hear what we think, we are so far from attributing to God bodily lineaments, that we fear to ascribe to so great an object even the graces of the mind, and the very virtues in which to excel is hardly granted to a few. For who can speak of God as brave, as constant, as moderate, as wise? who can say that He is honest, or temperate? nay, who will say that He knows any thing, that He understands, that He acts with foresight, that He directs the determination of His actions towards definite ends of duty? These are human goods, and as opposed to vices deserve a laudable reputation; but who is there so dull of heart and stupid as to call God great in human goods, or to speak of the surpassing majesty of His name as if it consisted in a freedom from the stain of vices? Whatever you can say of God, whatever you can conceive in silent thought, passes into a human sense, and is corrupted thereby: nothing can properly signify and denote Him which is expressed in terms of human speech framed for human uses. There is but one way in which man may understand with certainty concerning the nature of God, and that is, to know and feel that nothing can be expressed concerning Him in mortal speech."

V. ATHANASIUS.—*C. Gentes*, c. 2: "God, the Creator of the universe, and King of all things, who is above all substance and human thought." *Orat. II. contra Arianos*, c. 32: "Such examples and such images are presented in Scripture, in order that, since human nature is unable to comprehend concerning God, we may by means of these be able to understand in small part and dimly, to the best of our capacity." *Ibid.*, c. 36. "We ought not to inquire why the Word of God is not such as ours, since God, as we have said, is not such as we are. Nor is it seemly to inquire how the Word is of God, or how He is the brightness of God, or how and in what manner He is begotten of God. For one would be mad who dared to inquire into these things, as deeming that a thing unspeakable and proper to the nature of God, and known only to Him and to the Son, can itself be expressed in words."

VI. CYRIL OF JERUSALEM.—*Catech.*, vi. 2: "We declare not what God is, but candidly confess that we know not accurately concerning Him. For in those things which concern God, it is great knowledge to confess our ignorance."

VII. BASIL.—Ep. ccxxxiv.: "That God is, I know; but what is His essence I hold to be above reason. How then am I saved? by faith; and faith is competent to know *that* God is, not *what* He is." *Adv. Eunom.* i. 12: "In a word, for a man to think that he has found out the very substance of the supreme God is the height of arrogance and pride; .... for let us inquire of him from what source he claims to have arrived at the intelligence of it. Is it from common thinking? This suggests to us that God is, not what He is. Is it from the teaching of the Spirit? Of what kind is this teaching, and where is it to be found? .... What of Paul, that chosen vessel, in whom Christ spake, who was caught up to the third heaven, and heard unspeakable words which it is not lawful for a man to utter,—what teaching did he proclaim to us concerning the essence of God? Who, when he but looked into the partial relations (λόγους) of God's dispensation, as though giddy at beholding the impenetrable vision, broke forth into the cry, '*O the depth of the riches, both of the wisdom and knowledge of God! how unsearchable are His judgments, and His ways past finding out.*' But if these things cannot be reached by those who have attained to the measure of the knowledge of Paul, how great is the folly of those who boast that they know the essence of God." *Ibid.*, c. 14: "But I think that the comprehension of the Divine essence is not only beyond man, but beyond every rational nature—I mean of created beings."

VIII. GREGORY NYSSEN.—*C. Eunom.*, Orat. xii. (*Opera*, ed. 1615, vol. ii. p. 312): "And as, when we behold the heaven, and by the organs of the sense of sight attain in some sort to that beauty which is on high, we doubt not that that which is seen by us exists, but when asked what it is, we are unable to interpret its nature in speech . . . . . So, too, with regard to the Creator of the world, we know that He is, but deny not that we are ignorant of the definition of His essence."

IX. GREGORY NAZIANZEN.—Orat. xxxiv. (*Opera*, 1630, vol. i. p. 538: "A theologian among the Greeks [Plato] has said in his philosophy that to conceive God is difficult, to express Him is impossible. . . . . But I say that it is impossible to express Him, and more impossible to conceive Him (φράσαι μὲν ἀδύνατον, νοῆσαι δὲ ἀδυνατώτερον)." *Ibid.*, p. 548: "What God is in His nature and essence, no man hath ever yet discovered, nor can discover. Whether he ever will discover it, let those who please inquire and speculate. In my opinion, he will then discover it, when this godlike and divine thing, I mean our intellect and reason, shall have mingled with that which is cognate to itself, and the image shall have ascended to the archetype of which it now has the desire."

X. CHRYSOSTOM.—*De Incompr. Dei Natura*, Hom. i. 3:

"That God is everywhere, I know; and that He is wholly everywhere, I know; but the *how*, I know not: that he is without beginning, ungenerated and eternal, I know; but the *how*, I know not." Hom. iii. 2: "Observe the accuracy of Paul. He speaks of God, not as being an unapproachable light, but as *dwelling in the light that no man can approach unto*, that you may learn that if the dwelling is unapproachable, how much more is God who dwelleth in it. . . . . Nor does he say that God dwelleth in light *incomprehensible*, but *unapproachable*, which is far more than incomprehensible. For a thing is said to be incomprehensible when, having been sought and inquired after, it is not comprehended by those who inquire after it; but that is unapproachable which admits of no inquiry at all, and to which none can draw nigh. Thus a sea is called incomprehensible (unfathomable) into which divers may cast themselves and descend to a great depth without being able to find the bottom; but that is called unapproachable which cannot at all be inquired into or sought." *Ibid.*, c. 3: "But that you may learn that this light is unapproachable, not only to men, but to the higher powers, hear the words of Isaiah: '*I saw the Lord sitting upon a throne high and lifted up: above it stood the Seraphims; each one had six wings; with twain he covered his face, and with twain he covered his feet.*' Why, I ask, do they cover their faces and put their wings before them? Why, but because they cannot bear the lightning that springs out of the throne, and those flashing rays? And yet they saw not the light itself untempered, nor the substance itself in purity, but what they saw was a condescension (συγκατάβασις). And what is a condescension? It is when God is not manifested as He is, but shews himself in such manner as he who can see Him is able to bear, measuring the exhibition according to the weakness of sight of the beholders."

XI. HILARY OF POITIERS.—*De Trinitate*, iv. 2: "But we are not ignorant that neither speech of men nor comparison of human nature can suffice for the unfolding of Divine things. For that which is unspeakable admits not of the end and measure of any significance of words; and that which is spiritual is different from the appearance and example of bodily things. Yet when we discourse of heavenly natures, those very things which are bounded by the understanding of our minds must be expressed by the use of common nature and speech, not certainly as suitable to the dignity of God, but as necessary to the infirmity of our intellectual capacity, which must speak that which we think and understand by means of our own things and words."

XII. AUGUSTINE.—Enarr. in Psalm lxxxv. 8: "God is ineffable; we more easily say what He is not than what He is." Serm. cccxli.: "I call God just, because in human words I find nothing better; for He is beyond justice. . . . What then is worthily said of God? Some one, perhaps, may reply and say, *that He is just*. But another, with better understanding, may say that even this word is surpassed by His excellence, and that even this is said of Him unworthily, though it be said fittingly according to human capacity."

XIII. CYRIL OF ALEXANDRIA.—*In Joann. Evang.*, l. ii., c. 5: "For those things which are spoken concerning it [the Divine Nature] are not spoken as they are in very truth, but as the tongue of man can interpret, and as man can hear; for he who sees in an enigma also speaks in an enigma."

XIV. DAMASCENUS.—*De Fide Orthod.*, i. 4: "That God is, is manifest; but what He is in His essence and nature is utterly incomprehensible and unknown" (ἀκατάληπτον παντελῶς καὶ ἄγνωστον). *Ibid.* i. 9: "It is right, therefore, to think that all those things which are said of God do not signify what He is in His essence, but declare either what He is not, or some relation to one of the things distinguished from Him, or something attendant on His nature, or an operation."

XV. ALEXANDER DE ALES.—*Summa Theol.*, qu. li., memb. i., art. 1: "Therefore we must say that names which are not understood symbolically, that is, according to the property of a bodily form, but which are understood mystically, that is, according to the property of a spiritual form, such as *just, good*, and the like, are not said equivocally nor univocally, because they are not said wholly in a different respect, nor yet in the same; but they are said analogically, according to the relation of prior and posterior, which analogy is drawn from some comparison or proportion of some effect of justice or goodness by which the creature is compared to the Creator. Thus, to give each his own is a point of comparison between the justice of the Creator and the justice of the creature. In like manner, and from this unity of comparison, is derived one relation according to analogy, which relation, however, does not establish agreement in genus or in species, but only in comparison."

XVI. AQUINAS.—*Summa*, pars. i., qu. xiii., art. 1: "We cannot so name God that the name which denotes Him shall express the Divine Essence as it is, in the same way as the name *man* expresses in its signification the essence of man as it is." *Ibid.*, art. 5: "When the name *wise* is said of a man, it in a manner describes and comprehends the thing signified: not so, however, when it is said of God; but it leaves the thing signified as uncomprehended and exceeding the signification of the name. Whence it is evident that this name *wise* is not said in the same manner of God and of man. The same is the case with other names; whence no name can be predicated univocally of God and of creatures; yet they are not predicated merely equivocally. .... We must say, then, that such names are said of God and of creatures according to analogy, that is, proportion."

XVII. DURANDUS.—*In* 1 *Sent.*, Dist. xxii., qu. 1: "A name may be said properly to belong to God in two senses: first, as signifying the Divine Essence according to its proper and perfect nature, as it were by definition, as *rational animal* signifies *man*. And in this manner, we must say that no name properly belongs to God: the reason of which is, that we name God as we understand Him; but in this life we do not understand God according to his proper and, so to speak, specific manner of being."

XVIII. HOOKER.—*Ecc. Pol.*, I., ii. 2: "Dangerous it were for the feeble brain of man to wade far into the doings of the Most High; whom although to know be life, and joy to make mention of His name, yet our soundest knowledge is to know that we know Him not as indeed He is, neither can know Him."

XIX. JACKSON.—*Of the Divine Essence and Attributes*, ch. 4, p. 38, ed. 1628: "From the former definition of absolute infinity (*Infinitum est extra quod nihil est*) we may conclude that unless all Power, unless all Wisdom, unless all Goodness, unless all that truly is or can possibly be supposed to have true being be identically contained in God's essence, He could not be absolutely infinite or unlimited in being. Whatsoever is uncapable of limit is uncapable of division or numerical difference. For wherever it can be truly said, *This* is one and *that* another, or, *This* is, and is not *That*, each hath distinct limits. But, seeing our imagination or phantasy is divisible, and our purest intellectual concepts of infinity but finite, we cannot think of God as infinite in power, infinite in wisdom, and in essence; but we must frame a conceit of power distinct from our conceit of essence, and a conceit of wisdom distinct from both."

XX. USHER.—*Body of Divinity*, p. 31, ed. 1648: "For these over-reaching terms of *thing, being, somewhat, nature,* &c., which seem to contain the word *God,* as well as all other things created by Him, do not express any material cause of God; neither do they contain these words, *God* and *creature,* as the general doth his specials or kinds, but are spoken of them equivocally, so that the term only, and not the definition of the term, doth agree to them." *Ibid.*, p. 32: "For in speaking of God, whom no words of man are able to express, the Holy Ghost oftentimes condescending to the weakness of our understanding, useth such terms as, being known to men, do signify something that is like to that which God indeed is of Himself, that we may understand so much as is expedient for us to know of Him." *Ibid.*, p. 45: "Neither is it [the wisdom of God] communicated to any creature, neither can be; for it is unconceivable, as the very essence of God Himself is unconceivable, and unspeakable as it is."

XXI. SANDERSON.—*Works*, Vol. i., p. 234: "God hath revealed Himself, and His good pleasure towards us in His Holy Word sufficiently to save our souls if we will believe, but not to solve all our doubts, if we will dispute. The Scriptures being written for our sakes, it was needful they should be fitted to our capacities; and therefore the mysteries contained therein are set forth by such resemblances as we are capable of, but far short of the nature and excellency of the things themselves."

XXII. HEYLIN.—*Theologia Veterum*, p. 77, ed. 1673: "God then is, in the first place, a simple or uncompounded essence, without parts or accidents; His attributes not differing from His essence at all, but being of His very essence, nor differing essentially from each other, but only in regard of our weak understanding, which, being not able to know or comprehend the earthly things by one single act, must of necessity have many distinct acts and notions to comprehend the nature of the incomprehensible God."

XXIII. BRAMHALL.—*Works*, Vol. iv., p. 194: "Since we are not able to conceive of God as He is, the readiest way we have is by removing all that imperfection from God which is in the creatures—so we call Him infinite, immortal, independent; or by attributing to Him all those perfections which are in the creatures after a most eminent manner—so we call Him best, greatest, most wise, most just, most holy. But . . . . they who dispute philosophically of God do neither ascribe faculties to Him in that manner that we have them, nor yet do they attribute any proper faculties at all to God. God's understanding and His will is His very essence, which, for the eminency of its infinite perfection, doth perform all those things alone, in a most transcendent manner, which reasonable creatures do perform imperfectly by distinct faculties." *Ibid.*, p. 488: "I ascribe no faculties at all to God, except it be anthropopathetically, as the Scripture ascribes eyes and hands to God; which must be understood as is beseeming the majesty of God."

XXIV. LEIGHTON.—*Theol. Lect.* xxi., Works, Vol. iv.,

p. 327, ed. 1830: "Though in the schools they distinguish the Divine attributes or excellencies, and that by no means improperly, into communicable and incommunicable; yet we ought so to guard this distinction, as always to remember that those which are called communicable, when applied to God, are not only to be understood in a manner incommunicable and quite peculiar to Himself, but also that in Him they are in reality infinitely different [in the original, *aliud omnino, immensum aliud*] from those virtues, or rather, in a matter where the disparity of the subjects is so very great, those shadows of virtues that go under the same name, either in men or angels."

XXV. PEARSON.—*Minor Theol. Works*, Vol. i., p. 13: "God in Himself is an absolute being, without any relation to creatures; for He was from eternity without any creature, and could, had He willed, be to eternity without creature. But God cannot naturally be known by us otherwise than by relation to creatures, as, for example, under the aspect of dominion, or of cause, or in some other relation." *Ibid.*, p. 136: "We have not in this life any names which signify God as He is in His essence (*quidditative.*) This is manifest, because names are of conceptions; but there are not given to us in this life any conceptions of the essence of God (*conceptus quidditativi de Deo.*")

XXVI. BARROW.—*Sermon on the Unsearchableness of God's Judgments*: "As the dealings of very wise men sometimes are founded upon maxims, and admit justifications, not obvious nor penetrable by vulgar conceit, so may God act according to rules of wisdom and justice, which it may be quite impossible by our faculties to apprehend, or with our means to descry. As there are natural modes of being and operation (such as God's necessary subsistence, His production of things from nothing, His eternity without succession, His immensity without extension, His prescience without necessitation of events, His ever acting, but never changing, and the like), so there may be prudential and moral rules of proceeding far above our reach. . . . Some of them we may be uncapable to know, because of our finite nature; they being peculiar objects of divine wisdom, and not to be understood by any creature."

XXVII. PATRICK.—*Works*, Vol. iii., p. 39: "It is an ancient saying of Plato, that 'to conceive God is difficult; to express Him is impossible.' But he should rather have said, in the opinion of a greater man, $\phi\rho\acute{a}\sigma\alpha\iota$ $\mu\grave{e}\nu$ $\grave{a}\delta\acute{v}\nu\alpha\tau o\nu$, $\nu o\hat{\eta}\sigma\alpha\iota$ $\delta\grave{e}$ $\grave{a}\delta\upsilon\nu\alpha\tau\acute{\omega}\tau\epsilon\rho o\nu$, 'it is impossible to express Him, and more impossible to conceive Him.'" [See above, No. IX.] *Ibid.*, p. 50: "As a glass represents not the thing itself, but its image; and he that sees a thing in a glass doth not know it immediately from itself, but from its image; such is the knowledge we have of God in this life. We know Him by the effects of His wisdom, power, and goodness, and by the revelation He hath made of His mind and will in His Gospel. We know Him not immediately and by Himself; but we know, as it were, an image of Him in His works and in His word."

XXVIII. BOYLE.—*Discourse of Things above Reason*, Works, Vol. iv., p. 424, ed. 1772: "But then, when we come to consider, attentively and minutely, what is contained in the notion of omnipotence, omniscience, eternity, and those other divine attributes, that are all united in that great confluence and abyss of perfections, God, we may be sure to find that our faculties are exceedingly surmounted by the vastness and gloriousness of that unlimited and unparalleled object, about which, as we can discover that it exists, and that it possesses all the perfection we can conceive, so we may at the same time discern that it must have degrees of perfection, which, because of the inferiority of our nature, we are not able to conceive."

XXIX. STILLINGFLEET.—*Mysteries of the Christian Faith Asserted and Vindicated*, Works, Vol. iii., p. 352: "We know that either God must have been for ever, or it is impossible He ever should be; for if He should come into being when He was not, He must have some cause of His being; and that which was the first cause would be God. But if He was for ever, He must be from Himself; and what notion or conception can we have in our minds concerning it? .... Here we have, therefore, a thing which must be owned by all, and yet such a thing which can be conceived by none."

XXX. SOUTH.—*Animadversions upon Sherlock*, p. 91, ed. 1693: "Although the Divine Nature be one pure, simple, indivisible act, yet in our conceptions of it, which are always inadequate to it, there is a natural order of *prius* and *posterius*, founded in the universal reason of things . . . . . which, though it can make no *prius* and *posterius* in the Divine Nature, yet is by no means to be contradicted or confounded in our discoursing of God; forasmuch as, without our admitting this rule, it is impossible for any human understanding either to conceive or discourse consistently or intelligibly of Him at all."

XXXI. BEVERIDGE.—*On the Thirty-nine Articles*, p. 16, ed. 1846: "But seeing the properties of God do not so much denote what God is, as what we apprehend Him to be in Himself; when the properties of God are predicated one of another, one thing in God is not predicated of another, but our apprehensions of the same thing are predicated one of another. . . . For as they are in God, they are not really distinct, I say, from one another; and the several denominations of love, goodness, justice, mercy, and the like, are grounded merely upon our several apprehensions of the same thing: which several apprehensions proceed from the finiteness of our understandings, who are not able to conceive of infinitude, or an infinite nature, as it is in itself, but only by piecemeal, as it manifesteth itself to us. And therefore God, whose understanding is infinite, suitable to His nature, doth not apprehend Himself under the distinct notions of good, just, powerful, wise, &c., but only as God; though He doth understand how we give such denominations to Him, according to the several apprehensions that we have of Him."

XXXII. LESLIE.—*Method with the Deists*, p. 63, ed. 1745: "What we call *faculties* in the soul, we call *Persons* in the Godhead; because there are personal actions attributed to each of them. . . . And we have no other word whereby to express it; we speak it after the manner of men; nor could we understand if we heard any of those unspeakable words which express the Divine Nature in its proper essence; therefore we must make allowances, and great ones, when we apply words of our nature to the Infinite and Eternal Being." We must not argue strictly and philosophically from them, more than from God's being said to *repent*, to be *angry*, &c. They are words *ad captum*, in condescension to our weak capacities, and without which we could not understand." *Ibid.*, p. 64: "By the word *Person*, when applied to God (for want of a proper word whereby to express it), we must mean something infinitely different from personality among men."

XXXIII. BURNET.—*Exposition of the XXXIX. Arti-*

cles, art. 1: "Therefore the essence of God is one perfect thought, in which He both views and wills all things: and though His transient acts that pass out of the divine essence, such as creation, providence, and miracles, are done in a succession of time; yet His imminent acts, His knowledge and His decrees, are one with His essence. Distinct thoughts are plainly an imperfection, and argue a progress in knowledge, and a deliberation in council, which carry defect and infirmity in them. To conceive how this is in God is far above our capacity, who, though we feel our imperfection in successive acts, yet cannot apprehend how all things can be both seen and determined by one single thought. But the divine Essence being so infinitely above us, it is no wonder if we can frame no distinct act concerning its knowledge or will."

XXXIV. BUTLER.—*Analogy,* Part II., ch. iv.: "According to our manner of conception, God makes use of variety of means, what we often think tedious ones, in the natural course of providence, for the accomplishment of all His ends. Indeed it is certain there is somewhat in this matter quite beyond our comprehension; but the mystery is as great in nature as in Christianity. We know what we ourselves aim at as final ends, and what courses we take, merely as means conducing to those ends. But we are greatly ignorant how far things are considered by the Author of Nature under the single notion of means and ends; so as that it may be said, this is merely an end, and that merely means, in His regard. And whether there be not some peculiar absurdity in our very manner of conception, concerning this matter, somewhat contradictory, arising from our extremely imperfect views of things, it is impossible to say."

XXXV. WOLLASTON.—*Religion of Nature Delineated,*

p. 169, ed. 1759: "The Divine perfection, then, and manner of being must be of a kind different from and above all that we can conceive." *Ibid.*, p. 213: "As God is a pure, uncompounded Being, His attributes of *mercy, justice*, &c., cannot be as we conceive them; because in Him they are *one*. Perhaps they may more properly be called together *Divine reason*, which, as it exerts itself upon this or that occasion, is by us variously denominated."

XXXVI. SKELTON.—*Deism Revealed*, Works, Vol. iy., p. 81, ed. 1824: "We are relative beings, and our duty arises from the situation we are placed in. But duty and relation cannot be applied to God, who is above all the laws of His creature. . . . The essence of human justice consists in a conformity to the law by which the actions of men ought to be regulated. Who sees not, that when those laws are removed, and the determinations of a Being superior to all law come to be considered, justice cannot be predicated of that Being essentially in the same sense it is of men?" . . . *Ibid.*, p. 341: "In respect of the divine nature, the human is but a faint similitude or shadow, in the faculties and personalities of which, certain attributes and other distinctions in God are dimly represented; yet so as to furnish a basis for all that knowledge of God which is necessary to us in our present condition. When we speak of God, we must use such ideas as the human mind, and such words as human language, afford us. Now man not being of the same, but only of a similar nature with God, we cannot think or speak of God immediately and properly, according to His incomprehensible nature, but only by the analogy of our nature to His: for example, when we say God is wise, we mean He knows all things; but we do not mean that He knows, as man does, by the help of senses and long deductions of reason."

XXXVII. COLERIDGE.—*Aids to Reflection*, p. 149, ed. 1839: "Analogies are used in aid of conviction: metaphors, as means of illustration. The language is analogous, wherever a thing, power, or principle in a higher dignity is expressed by the same thing, power, or principle, in a lower but more known form. Such, for instance, is the language of *John* iii. 6: *That which is born of the flesh, is flesh; that which is born of the Spirit is Spirit.* The latter half of the verse contains the fact asserted; the former half the analogous fact, by which it is rendered intelligible. If any man choose to call this metaphorical or figurative, I ask him whether, with Hobbes and Bolingbroke, he applies the same rule to the moral attributes of the Deity? Whether he regards the Divine justice, for instance, as a metaphorical term, a mere figure of speech."

XXXVIII. COPLESTON.—*Enquiry into the Doctrines of Necessity and Predestination*, p. 133: "It has been before observed, that analogy may be perfect where there is no resemblance, that is, where the corresponding terms are wholly heterogeneous; and that resemblance takes place in proportion as the objects denoted by those terms are of a kindred nature. Because, therefore, the nature of man partakes both of matter and of passions, we instantly discard all such ideas when speaking of God, and look upon the words expressive of *them* as simply analogous. What ground have we then for pursuing a different course with the words expressive of *intellectual* and *moral* attributes, except that we conceive a similarity in the *nature* of man and of God in these respects, and are unwilling to relinquish so exalted a pretension? But whatever ground there may be for this notion in the Scriptural phrase *image of God*, there is surely more than enough, both in reason and in Scripture, to repress the rash supposition, that we are justified in reasoning upon His nature as we would upon our own: that is, in drawing inferences from those attributes in Him which we call wisdom, justice, mercy, with the same confidence that we do from those qualities in ourselves, as if the words were expressive of the *same determinate notion* which we annex to them when speaking of ourselves."

The distinction between Analogy and Metaphor, pointed out by Coleridge, is more fully exhibited, and the principle of its application explained, in the following passage from a work frequently referred to in these Lectures, the *Divine Analogy* of Bishop Browne:—

"We have three ways of thinking and speaking concerning God and His Attributes, as well as all other beings purely spiritual and immaterial: by the parts and members of an human Body, or other things merely material; by the passions and affections of an human Soul; and by the operations and perfections of the Mind or Intellect.

"I. As to the first of these, it is certain there can neither be any bodily parts or members or appetites in beings immaterial; much less in the Divine Being, who is of a nature infinitely above that of any created spirit. Nor can there be any such real similitude and resemblance between mere Matter and pure Spirit, as that the nature and properties of one should of themselves furnish our understanding with any just and useful conceptions of those belonging to the other. So that neither the words or ideas of that sort can with any such aptness and correspondency be transferred to the Divine Being, as the operations and perfections of our minds are. Therefore when we attribute to Him any bodily members, such as *eyes*, and *ears*, and *hands*, and *feet;* or bodily actions, such as *searching*, or *seeing*, or *walking;* the words are purely *figurative* and *metaphorical*. These and such like terms are used to express the *wisdom*, or *knowledge*, or *mercy*, or *power* of God; or some other attributes and perfections for which we are not without words more proper, just, significant, and expressive.

"Besides, the transferring our bodily members, or other things merely material, to God or the Divine Nature of Christ, is purely voluntarily, and not of absolute necessity; as it is in those other words, *power*, and *knowledge*, and *wisdom*, and *holiness*, which are by a true Analogy transferred to the Divine Being, and without which we could neither think nor speak either of Him or His attributes. To which I may add, that if the reader will look inward and think with some intenseness, he will find that in attributing to God our bodily members or movements, or any other things merely material, he transfers the bare *words* only, and abhors the transferring of the *idea;* which shews that all such expressions are purely figurative and metaphorical. But in attributing the operations and perfections of the mind or intellect, he jointly transfers both the *word* and the *conception* without scruple; which is a confirmation of their being truly analogical.

"II. The second way we have of expressing God's Attributes is by the affections and passions of an human Soul. Men have run into two extremes concerning this way of speaking of God. Some contend earnestly for *real passions* in God, and of the same kind they are in us, but more excellent in degree; as the Socinians. Others, in the contrary extreme, allow neither any passions in God, nor any Divine perfections similar and answerable to them, to be a foundation for truth and reality in all our discourses concerning God, where we use the language of human passions.

"That there are, literally speaking, no Passions in God, nor indeed any perfections of the same kind with what these are in man, even when duly regulated, is most true: for all our passions and affections, as well as our thinking and knowledge and will, are the joint operations or properties of matter and pure spirit in essential union; and therefore, when they are under even the strictest government and most exact regulation, cannot be of the same kind with the excellencies or perfections of pure Spirits, who have not only a quite different way of knowing from us, entirely separate from all matter and independent of it; but also of loving and hating, of inclination and aversion. And certainly this must be more eminently true with respect to the infinite perfections of the Divine Nature, which differ vastly more in kind from those of all finite created spirits than theirs do from the most exalted human perfections.

"As the passions and affections, therefore, are attended with natural commotion and disturbance in us, and are more apt to be seduced by material impressions than the pure intellect and will; consequently they cannot be attributed to God so fully and exactly as the operations of these last; but are, however, transferred with a lower and less perfect degree of analogy, after we have removed all the natural and moral irregularities of them as carefully as we can. And accordingly we may observe that whenever we attribute even our commendable passions and affections to God, we do it with some degree of scruple and reluctance at the best; whereas, when we transfer *knowledge, wisdom, power,* and *will* to Him, we do it familiarly and without scruple.

"From hence we may observe, that though our passions are not transferred to the Divine Nature as fully as the operations of the intellect and will, yet God is not so grossly represented by them as by our bodily parts; nor is the language of our passions then purely *figurative* and *metaphorical*, but carries in it a good degree of *Analogy*. For though there are, literally speaking, no such passions in God as love or hatred, joy or anger, or pity, yet there may be *inconceivable perfections* in Him, some way answerable to what those passions are in us, under a due regulation and subjection to reason.

"III. The last way we have of conceiving and expressing the Divine Nature and Attributes is by the operations and perfections of our Intellect and Will; which, being more refined and farthest removed from matter, and but accidentally liable to moral corruption (that is, by voluntarily yielding to the vicious appetites of the body, and the irregular passions of the inferior soul), are the best and most lively representations we have of the Divinity; such as *Wisdom,* and *Knowledge,* and *Thinking,* and *Reason,* and *Will,* with all the various modifications of them: and accordingly in these we familiarly transfer both the *word* and the *conception* annexed to it, to express the Divine Perfections. But because even these in us, as well as our passions, are the joint operations of finite matter and spirit in essential union, and are necessarily transacted by the concurrence of body; therefore they are likewise but *Analogy* when applied to the Divinity. Now though they are so, and, as I have observed, though we are utterly ignorant of part of the real ground of that analogy which runs through these, as well as through those moral virtues and evangelical graces proceeding from the due direction and regulation of our passions; yet that there is a sure and solid foundation for this analogy in the nature both of God and man is evident, if we consider,

"I. That we were originally and in our kind formed to some resemblance and similitude of the Divine Nature. The words of God Himself are thus, *Let us make man in our image, after our likeness;* and the relation of Moses by inspiration is thus, *So God created man in His own image; in the image of God created he him* . . . . Without all doubt the solemn manner of expressing this likeness by such an immediate repetition of the same thing over again, and the reduplication of the words, *image* and *likeness*, do plainly shew that something is intended very remarkable; something so real and solid in the very nature of things, that it is not to be evaded by any supposition of its being only a *figurative* and *imaginary* likeness. Nay, something of no less consequence must be intended at the bottom, than by those sayings to lay a firm and immoveable foundation for truth, in all those sentiments and words and expressions, which through all generations were necessarily to be transferred from the human nature to the Divine.

"II. But this will appear more fully if we consider secondly, that all the perfections of intelligent beings must be greater or less, as they make nearer or more distant approaches in their kind to a resemblance of Him, who is the only source and fountain of all perfection. There can be no perfection in the creature but what is derived from thence, and what is originally of a more transcendent kind in Him; and His very creation of such beings especially was no other than a formation of them after the original archetypal idea of them in the Divine Mind; so that if they are good and perfect in their kind, this must consist in having all the resemblance of the Creator their respective natures are capable of. . . . . All the perfections of our reasonable human nature must have something correspondent and similar to them in the Divine, though infinitely more excellent and transcendent in kind. Hence it is that our whole manner of thinking and speaking of God is from what we find in ourselves, and more especially from the operations of the mind. And this we naturally fall into, as if they were exactly of the *same kind* in Him that they are in us; though upon recollection we know it is impossible they should be so. All our thoughts and words concerning Spiritual Beings, and God in particular, do proceed, though insensibly, upon this presumption; that there is something in the real nature of such Beings correspondent and similar to those attributes we substitute for them, and which we conceive to be most excellent and perfect in human nature. And this is a presumption so well grounded upon that image and likeness of God after which we were created, that there is a natural aptitude in all the operations of the mind, and even in our commendable passions and affections, to represent to us the perfections of the Divine Nature: insomuch that our conceptions and expressions of those perfections, though in their first and strictly proper acceptation they be merely human, are all yet apt and necessary when spoken of God; and there is nothing the less of Truth and Reality in this Analogy because we are not able to discern any exact degree and proportion, or that particular sort of similitude which is the ground and foundation of it. Though we do not apprehend it now, yet there is a reason in the very nature of things divine, why they should be conceived and expressed after that manner they now are, rather than after any other; insomuch that we then think justly, and express our thoughts of them in the greatest aptness and propriety of speech our present condition of infirmity will admit.

"III. Lastly, we are to consider, that if there were not a sure foundation for this Divine Analogy in the very nature of things, we should be under a grand delusion in all our sentiments of Natural as well as Revealed Religion. For since the Attributes of God differ from ours in kind, all the knowledge we have of them and the things of another world, even by the mere light of reason, must be founded upon Analogy. For the proof of which, besides what I have urged already, I shall only desire any person, under the strongest prejudice against this doctrine, to single out any one of the Divine Attributes which he thinks most easy and obvious, and try whether he can form any direct idea of it, or any conception or idea which shall be purely spiritual, and entirely exclusive and independent of ideas of sensation and the conscious operations of his own mind, as parts of the ingredients of it. So that either our Creator has rendered human ages utterly void of any useful knowledge of Him and His Attributes; or else there must be a real ground for this analogical conception of them in His nature and our own. We are entirely incapable of any direct knowledge or idea of them; and therefore must necessarily conclude there is a sure foundation for this method of proceeding; or that we labour under an invincible mistake in all our thoughts of Divine Objects, and can never arrive to more than a merely metaphorical and precarious notion of them."

PREFACE

TO THE FIRST EDITION.

IT has been observed by a thoughtful writer of the present day, that "the theological struggle of this age, in all its more important phases, turns upon the philosophical problem of the limits of knowledge and the true theory of human ignorance."[a] The present Lectures may be regarded as an attempt to obtain an answer to this problem, in one at least of its aspects, by shewing what limitations to the construction of a philosophical Theology necessarily exist in the constitution and laws of the human mind.

The title selected may perhaps require a few words of explanation. In the expression, *religious thought*, the term *thought* is not intended to designate any special mode of acquiring or communicating knowledge; as if truths beyond the reach of thought could be attained by intuition or some other mental process. It is used as a general term, to include all that can be distinctly apprehended as existing in any man's own consciousness, or can be communicated to others by means of language. Those states of mind which do not fulfil these conditions are only indirectly examined in the following pages: but the very circumstance that such states, even granting them to exist, can neither be distinctly apprehended nor intelligibly communicated, renders them, whatever may be their sup-

---

[a] Professor Fraser, *Essays in Philosophy*, p. 281.

posed effects on individual minds, unavailable as instruments for the construction or criticism of any religious doctrine.

Though the need of such an inquiry as is now attempted was suggested to the Author chiefly by the perusal of theological writings of the present generation, he has not, in the prosecution of it, thought it necessary to confine his remarks exclusively to contemporary writers, or to those whose influence is extensively felt in this country. Enough reference will be found to recent publications, to shew, it is believed, that the work is not uncalled for at this time; but the causes of the evil chiefly assailed lie deep in the tendencies of human nature, and are operative, with identity of principle and but little variety of detail, at different times and in different places. In Germany, indeed, it may be said that Rationalism, properly so called, is not at present the predominant phase of theological speculation. Still it is found, in no sparing measure, in its own name and character; and still more, it underlies and leavens the speculations of many writers who are apparently pursuing a different method. Publications whose professed object is historical or critical are often undertaken in the interest of a foregone philosophical conclusion. If a writer commences his inquiry by laying down, with Strauss, as a canon of criticism, that whatever is supernatural is necessarily unhistorical; or if, with Vatke or Baur, he assumes the Hegelian theory of development as the "standpoint" from which to contemplate the history of nations or of doctrines, his researches will be indirectly amenable to any criticism which may affect the philosophical principles on which they are conducted. But, directly, the historical and critical researches of modern theology do not come within the class of inquiries examined in the present work. For, whatever may be their merits or defects in the hands of individual writers, they cannot in themselves be regarded as transcending the legitimate boundaries of human thought; but on the contrary, they are rather to be accepted as legitimate, though often over-estimated, contributions to the general sum of Christian Evidences.

With regard to the philosophical speculations in Theology which are the direct objects of examination in the following pages, the present work may be considered as an attempt to pursue, in relation to Theology, the inquiry instituted by Kant in relation to Metaphysics; namely, *How are synthetical judgments à priori possible?* In other words: Does there exist in the human mind any direct faculty of religious knowledge, by which, in its speculative exercise, we are enabled to decide, independently of all external Revelation, what is the true nature of God, and the manner in which He must manifest Himself to the world; and by which, in its critical exercise, we are entitled authoritatively to decide for or against the claims of any professed Revelation, as containing a true or a false representation of the Divine Nature and Attributes? And if it can be shewn that no such faculty exists, but that the conclusions arrived at in this respect are gained indirectly, by transferring to the region of Theology judgments which properly belong to another province of human thought; there then arises a second inquiry; namely, What cautions are necessary to be observed in the process of transferring, and what is the value of the judgments when transferred? The moral and theological writings of Kant and his followers are so far from furnishing a satisfactory answer to these questions, that they rather seem as if they had been written expressly for the purpose of reversing the method carried out with such good effect in relation to metaphysics.

It is rather to a philosopher of our own age and country that we must look for the true theory of the limits of human thought, as applicable to theological, no less than to metaphysical researches,—a theory exhibited indeed in a fragmentary and incomplete form, but containing the germ of nearly all that is requisite for a full exposition of the system. The celebrated article of Sir William Hamilton, on the Philosophy of the Unconditioned, contains the key to the understanding and appreciation of nearly the whole body of modern German speculation. His great principle, that "the Unconditioned is incognisable and inconceivable; its notion being only negative of the Conditioned, which last can alone be positively known or conceived," has suggested the principal part of the inquiries pursued in the present work; and his practical conclusion, "We are thus taught the salutary lesson, that the capacity of thought is not to be constituted into the measure of existence; and are warned from recognising the domain of our knowledge as necessarily coextensive with the horizon of our faith," is identical with that which is constantly enforced throughout these Lectures.

But if the best theoretical exposition of the limits of human thought is to be found in the writings of a philosopher but recently removed from among us; it is in a work of more than a century old that we find the best instance of the acknowledgment of those limits in practice. *The Analogy of Religion, natural and revealed, to the constitution and course of Nature*, furnishes an example of a profound and searching philosophical spirit, combined with a just perception of the bounds within which all human philosophy must be confined, to which, in the whole range of similar investigations, it would be difficult, if not impossible, to find a parallel. The author of that work has been justly described as "one to whose deep sayings no thoughtful mind was ever yet introduced for the first time, without acknowledging the period an epoch in its intellectual history;[b] and it may be added that the feeling of admiration thus excited will only be increased by a comparison of his writings with the pretentious failures of more ambitious thinkers. Connected as the present Author has been for many years with the studies of Oxford, of which those writings have long formed an important part, he feels that he would be wanting in his duty to the University to which he owes so much, were he to hesitate to declare, at this time, his deep-rooted and increasing conviction, that sound religious philosophy will flourish or fade within her walls, according as she perseveres or neglects to study the works and cultivate the spirit of her great son and teacher, Bishop Butler.

[b] W. A. Butler, *Letters on the Development of Christian Doctrine*, p. 75.

CONTENTS.

LECTURE I.

Dogmatism and Rationalism as methods of religious philosophy — meaning of these terms — errors of the respective systems denoted by each; the one forcing reason into agreement with revelation, the other forcing revelation into agreement with reason. — Both methods may be regarded as attempts, from opposite sides, to produce exact coincidence between belief and thought. — Instances of each exhibited and examined. — Human conceptions are unavoidable in Theology; but there is need of some principle to determine their proper place in it. — Such a principle can only be gained by an investigation of the Limits of Human Thought. — The proper object of criticism is not religion, but the human mind in its relation to religion. — A direct criticism of religion as a representation of God can only be accomplished by the construction of a Philosophy of the Infinite. — It is therefore necessary to inquire whether such a philosophy is possible; and this can only be ascertained by an examination of the laws of human thought in general, which will determine those of religious thought in particular. — Analogous difficulties may be expected in philosophy and in religion, arising from the limitations of thought common to both. — Contrast between two opposite statements of the extent of human knowledge, in the words of St. Paul and of Hegel. — Purpose of the following Lectures, as an Examination of the Limits of Religious Thought .. Page 1

LECTURE II.

Statement of the two opposite methods by which a Philosophy of Religion may be attempted; the Objective or Metaphysical, based on a supposed knowledge of the nature of God, and the Subjective or Psychological, based on a knowledge of the mental faculties of man. — Relation of these methods respectively to the Criticism of Revelation — dependence of the former method upon the latter. — Further examination of the Objective or Metaphysical method. — Two different modes in which man may be supposed to be capable of attaining to a knowledge of God — specimen of each — insufficiency of both to found a Rational Theology. — Examination of the fundamental ideas of Rational Theology, — the Absolute — the Infinite — the First Cause — mutual contradictions involved in these three ideas — conception of an eternal Causation incompatible with the Absolute — conception of a temporal Causation incompatible with the Infinite. — The Absolute cannot be conceived as a necessary and unconscious cause, — nor as a voluntary and conscious cause, — nor as possessing consciousness at all, — nor as containing within itself any kind of relation, — nor as one and simple, out of all relation. — Effect of these counter impossibilities on the conceptions of Theology — apparent contradictions in the conception of the Divine Attributes as absolute and infinite. — Further contradictions involved in the coexistence of the Relative with the Absolute, and of the Finite with the Infinite. Pantheism avoids these contradictions by denying the existence of the Finite and Relative — this solution untenable — self-contradictions of the Pantheistic hypothesis. — Alternative of Atheism, which denies the existence of the Infinite and Absolute — contradictions involved in this hypothesis. — Summary of conclusions. — Necessary failure of all attempts to construct a Metaphysical Theology — alternative necessitated by this failure. — Practical result of the above inquiry .. .. Page 23

LECTURE III.

Recapitulation of the results of the last Lecture. — Necessity of examining the Philosophy of Religion from the Subjective or Psychological side, as dependent upon a knowledge of the laws of the human mind. — General conditions of all human Consciousness. — *First condition of Consciousness, Distinction between one Object and another* — such a distinction necessarily implies Limitation — consequent impossibility of conceiving the Infinite. — Explanation of the contradictions involved in the idea of the Infinite — this idea inadmissible as the basis of a scientific Theology. — *Second condition of Consciousness, Relation between Subject and Object* — consequent impossibility of conceiving the Absolute. — Explanation of the contradictions involved in the idea of the

Absolute. — Impossibility of a partial knowledge of the Infinite and Absolute. — *Third condition of Consciousness, Succession and Duration in Time* — hence all objects are conceived as finite — consequent impossibility of conceiving Creation, and counter impossibility of conceiving finite existence as uncreated. — Attempt to evade this limitation in Theology by the hypothesis of the existence of God out of Time — this hypothesis unavailable for any distinct philosophical conception.— *Fourth condition of Consciousness, Personality* — Personality a limitation and a relation, and hence inadequate to represent the Infinite. — Theological consequences of this condition. — Personality the source and type of our conception of Reality, and therefore the only fitting representation of God. — Necessity of thinking of God as personal, and yet of believing in Him as infinite — apparent contradiction between these representations — hence Thought cannot be the measure of Belief. — Consequent impossibility of constructing a Rational Theology. — Attempt to avoid the above conclusions by placing the Philosophy of the Infinite in a point beyond Consciousness — necessary failure of this attempt. — Summary of conclusions. — Practical lesson from the above inquiry   Page 47

LECTURE IV.

Analysis of the religious Consciousness, reflective and intuitive. — Relation of the reflective Consciousness to Theology; its reasonings sufficient to correct our conception of a Supreme Being, but not to originate it — examination of some current theories on this point — statement of the value of the reflective faculties within their proper limits. — Reflection, as well as intuition, necessary to distinct consciousness; but intuition is first in the order of nature, though not in that of time. — Two principal modes of religious intuition — the Feeling of Dependence and the Conviction of Moral Obligation, giving rise respectively to Prayer and Expiation. — Examination of these two modes of Consciousness. — Dependence implies a Personal Superior; hence our conviction of the Power of God — Moral Obligation implies a Moral Lawgiver; hence our conviction of the Goodness of God.— Limits of the Religious Consciousness — Sense of Dependence not a consciousness of the Absolute and Infinite — opposite theory of Schleiermacher on this point — objections to his view. — Sense of Moral Obligation not a consciousness of the Absolute and Infinite.

—Yet the Infinite is indirectly implied by the religious consciousness, though not apprehended as such; for the consciousness of limitation carries with it an indirect conviction of the existence of the Infinite beyond consciousness.—Result of the above analysis—our knowledge of God relative and not absolute—the Infinite an object of belief, but not of thought or knowledge; hence we may know *that* an Infinite God exists, but not *what* He is as infinite.—Further results of an examination of the religious consciousness—God known *as a Person* through the consciousness of ourselves *as Persons*—this consciousness indispensable to Theism; for the denial of our own Personality, whether in the form of Materialism or of Pantheism, logically leads to Atheism.—Summary of conclusions—our religious knowledge is *regulative*, but not *speculative*—importance of this distinction in theological reasoning—conception of the Infinite inadmissible in Theology.—Office of religious philosophy, as limited to finite conceptions.—Practical benefits of this limitation.—Conclusion.

Page 73

LECTURE V.

Distinction between Speculative and Regulative Truth further pursued.—In Philosophy, as well as in Religion, our highest principles of thought are regulative and not speculative—Instances in the Ideas of Liberty and Necessity; Unity and Plurality as implied in the conception of any object; Commerce between Soul and Body; Extension, as implied in external perception; and Succession, as implied in the entire consciousness.—Illustration thus afforded for determining the limits of thought—distinction between legitimate and illegitimate thought, as determined by their relation to the *inexplicable* and the *self-contradictory* respectively.—Conclusion to be drawn as regards the manner of the mind's operation—all Consciousness implies a relation between Subject and Object, dependent on their mutual action and reaction; and thus no principle of thought can be regarded as absolute and simple, as an ultimate and highest truth.—Analogy in this respect between Philosophy and Natural Religion which apprehends the Infinite under finite forms—corresponding difficulties to be expected in each.—Provinces of Reason and Faith—Analogy extended to Revealed Religion—testimony of Revelation plain and intelligible when regarded as regulative, but ultimately incomprehensible to speculation—corresponding errors in Philosophy and Religion, illustrating this analogy.—Regulative conceptions not therefore untrue.—The above principles confirmed by the teaching of Scripture.—Revelation expressly adapted to the limits of human thought.—Relation of the Infinite to the Personal in the representations of God in the Old Testament.—Further confirmation from the New Testament.—Doctrine of the Incarnation; its practical position in Theology as a regulative truth; its perversion by modern philosophy, in the attempt to exhibit it as a speculative truth.—Instances in Hegel, Marheineke, and Strauss.—Conclusion .. .. .. Page 95

LECTURE VI.

Result of the previous inquiries—religious ideas contain two elements, a Form, common to them with all other ideas, as being human thoughts; and a Matter, peculiar to themselves, as thoughts about religious objects—hence there may exist two possible kinds of difficulties; the one formal, arising from the universal laws of human thought; the other material, arising from the peculiar nature of religious evidence.—The principal objections suggested by Rationalism are of the former kind; common to all human thinking as such, and therefore to Rationalism itself.—Proof of this position by the exhibition of parallel difficulties in Theology and Philosophy.—Our ignorance of the nature of God compared with our ignorance of the nature of Causation.—Doctrine of the Trinity compared with the philosophical conception of the Infinite and the Absolute, as One and yet as Many.—Doctrine of the eternal generation of the Son compared with the relation of an Infinite Substance to its Attributes.—Purpose of such comparisons, not to prove the doctrines, but to shew the weakness of human reason with regard to them—true evidence of the doctrines to be found, not in Reason, but in Revelation.—Further parallels.—Doctrine of the twofold nature of Christ compared with the philosophical conception of the Infinite as coexisting with the Finite.—Reason thus shewn not to be the supreme judge of religious truth; for Religion must begin with that which is above Reason.—Extension of the same argument to our conceptions of Divine Providence.—Representations of General Law and Special Interposition—supposed difficulty in the conception of the latter shewn to be really common to all human conceptions of the Infinite.—Both representations equally imperfect as speculative truths, and both equally necessary as regulative. — Imperfections in the conceptions of General Law and mechanical action of the universe — this conception is neither philosophically necessary nor empirically universal; and hence it is not entitled to supersede all other representations — it is inapplicable to the phenomena of mind, and only partially available in relation to those of matter. — Conception of Miraculous Agency, as subordinate to that of Special Providence — no sufficient ground, either from philosophy or from experience, for asserting that miracles are impossible. — Comparison between the opposite conceptions of a miracle, as an exception to a law, or as the result of a higher law — both these conceptions are speculatively imperfect, but the former is preferable as a regulative truth. — Summary of conclusions — parallel difficulties must exist in Theology and in Philosophy — true value and province of Reason in relation to both .. .. Page 118

LECTURE VII.

Philosophical parallel continued with regard to the supposed moral objections to Christian doctrines. — Error of the moral theory of Kant. — Moral convictions how far necessary and trustworthy, how far contingent and fallible — parallel in this respect between moral and mathematical science, as based on the formal conditions of experience — possibility of corresponding errors in both. — Human morality not absolute, but relative. — The Moral Law cannot be conceived as an absolute principle, apart from its temporal manifestations — Parallel in the idea of Time and its relations. — Morality as conceived by us necessarily contains a human and positive element; and therefore cannot be the measure of the Absolute Nature of God. — Application of the above principles to Christian Theology. — The Atonement — Weakness of the supposed moral objections to this doctrine — such objections equally applicable to any conceivable scheme of Divine Providence. — Predestination and Free Will — Predestination, as a determination of the Absolute Mind, is speculatively inconceivable, and therefore cannot be known to be incompatible with human Freedom — Parallel in this respect between Predestination in Theology and Causation in Philosophy. — Eternal Punishment — rashness and ignorance of rationalist criticisms of this doctrine — the difficulties of the doctrine are not peculiar to Theology, but common to all Philosophy, and belong to the general problem of the existence of Evil at all, which is itself but a subordinate case of the universal impossibility of conceiving the coexistence of the Infinite with the Finite. — Contrast between illegitimate and legitimate modes of reasoning on evil and its punishment — illustrations to be derived from analogies in the course of nature and in the constitution of the human mind. — Extension of the argument from analogy to other religious doctrines — Original Sin — Justification by Faith — Operation of Divine Grace. — Limits of the Moral Reason. — Conclusion .. .. .. Page 141

LECTURE VIII.

Right use of Reason in religious questions — Reason entitled to judge of a Religion in respect of its evidences, as addressed to men, but not in respect of its correspondence with philosophical conceptions of the Absolute Nature of God. — No one faculty of the human mind is entitled to exclusive preference as the criterion of religious truth — the true criterion is to be found in the general result of many and various Evidences — practical neglect of this rule by different writers. — Comparative value of internal and external evidences of religion, the former as negative, the latter as positive. — Cautions requisite in the use of the negative argument from internal evidence — external and internal evidence can only be estimated in conjunction with each other. — Distinction between the proper and improper use of the Moral Sense in questions of religious evidence. — Application of this distinction to facts recorded in Sacred History. — Analogy between physical and moral laws as regards miraculous interventions. — Probable and partial character of the moral argument; error of supposing it to be demonstrative and complete; possibility of mistakes in its application. — General summary of Christian Evidences — alternative in the case of their rejection — Christ's teaching either wholly divine or wholly human. — Impossibility of an eclectic Christianity. — Value of the *à priori* presumption against miracles — nothing gained in point of probability by a partial rejection of the supernatural. — Christianity regarded as a Revelation must be accepted wholly or not at all. — Speculative difficulties in religion form a part of our probation — analogy between moral and intellectual temptations. — General result of an examination of the Limits of Religious Thought — Theology not a speculative science,

e

nor in the course of progressive development.— Cautions needed in the treatment of religious knowledge as regulative — this view does not solve difficulties, but only shews why they are insoluble. Instance of the neglect of this caution in Archbishop King's rule of Scripture interpretation as regards the Divine Attributes.— No explanation possible of those difficulties which arise from the universal laws of human thought — such difficulties are inherent in our mental constitution, and form part of our training and discipline during this life.— The office of Philosophy is not to give us a knowledge of the absolute nature of God, but to teach us to know ourselves and the limits of our faculties. — Conclusion.

Page 162

LECTURES.

LECTURE I.

Deuteronomy IV. 2.

" Ye shall not add unto the word which I command you, neither shall ye diminish ought from it."

Dogmatism and Rationalism are the two extremes between which religious philosophy perpetually oscillates. Each represents a system from which, when nakedly and openly announced, the well-regulated mind almost instinctively shrinks back; yet which, in some more or less specious disguise, will be found to underlie the antagonist positions of many a theological controversy. Many a man who rejects isolated portions of Christian doctrine, on the ground that they are repugnant to his reason, would hesitate to avow broadly and unconditionally that reason is the supreme arbiter of all religious truth; though at the same time he would find it hard to point out any particular in which the position of reason, in relation to the truths which he still retains, differs from that which it occupies in relation to those which he rejects. And on the other hand, there are many who, while they would by no means construct a dogmatic system on the assumption that the conclusions of reason may always be made to coincide with those of revelation, yet, for want of an accurate distinction between that which is within the province of human thought and that which is beyond it, are accustomed in practice to demand the assent of the reason to positions which it is equally incompetent to affirm or to deny. Thus they not only lessen the value of the service which it is capable of rendering within its legitimate sphere, but also indirectly countenance that very intrusion of the human intellect into sacred things, which, in some of its other aspects, they so strongly and so justly condemn.

In using the above terms, it is necessary to state at the outset the sense in which each is employed, and to emancipate them from the various and vague associations connected with their ordinary use. I do not include under the name of *Dogmatism* the mere enunciation of religious truths, as resting upon authority and not upon reasoning, nor even the formal statement or logical development of truths implicitly contained in and ultimately resting on Scriptural grounds.[a] The Dogmatist, as well as the Rationalist, is the constructor of a philosophical system; and in constructing it, however much the materials upon which he works may be given by a higher authority, yet, in connecting them together and giving them a systematic form and philosophical basis, he virtually places them on a new and merely human foundation. Indeed, whatever may be their actual antagonism in the field of religious controversy, the two terms

---

[a] This clause has been added to the sentence as it originally stood, and the next sentence slightly altered, in order to obviate a misapprehension not sufficiently guarded against in former editions. The Dogmatism above described is a very different thing from Dogmatic Theology. A theology, however systematic, which proposes its articles of faith as ultimately resting on the authority of Holy Scripture, and to be believed in obedience to that authority, differs fundamentally from the Dogmatism of the Wolfian school, which accepts the doctrines of Christianity, not because they can be proved by most certain warrants of Holy Scripture, but because they can be demonstrated from the principles of reason.

are in their proper sense so little exclusive of each other, that both were originally employed to denote the same persons;—the name *Dogmatists* or *Rationalists* being indifferently given to those medical theorists who insisted on the necessity of calling in the aid of rational principles, to support or correct the conclusions furnished by experience (1). A like signification is to be found in the later language of philosophy, when the term *Dogmatists* was used to denote those philosophers who endeavoured to explain the phenomena of experience by means of rational conceptions and demonstrations; the intelligible world being regarded as the counterpart of the sensible, and the necessary relations of the former as the principles and ground of the observed facts of the latter (2). It is in a sense analogous to this that the term may be most accurately used in reference to Theology. Scripture is to the theological Dogmatist what Experience is to the philosophical. It supplies him with the facts to which his system has to adapt itself. It contains in an unsystematic form the positive doctrines, which further inquiry has to exhibit as supported by reasonable grounds and connected into a scientific whole. Theological Dogmatism is thus an application of reason to the support and defence of pre-existing statements of Scripture (3). Rationalism, on the other hand, so far as it deals with Scripture at all, deals with it as a thing to be adapted to the independent conclusions of the natural reason, and to be rejected where that adaptation cannot conveniently be made. By *Rationalism*, without intending to limit the name to any single school or period in theological controversy, I mean generally to designate that system whose final test of truth is placed in the direct assent of the human consciousness, whether in the form of logical deduction, or moral judgment, or religious intuition; by whatever previous process those faculties may have been raised to their assumed dignity as arbitrators. The Rationalist, as such, is not bound to maintain that a divine revelation of religious truth is impossible, nor even to deny that it has actually been given. He may admit the existence of the revelation as a fact: he may acknowledge its utility as a temporary means of instruction for a ruder age: he may even accept certain portions as of universal and permanent authority (4). But he assigns to some superior tribunal the right of determining what is essential to religion and what is not: he claims for himself and his age the privilege of accepting or rejecting any given revelation, wholly or in part, according as it does or does not satisfy the conditions of some higher criterion to be supplied by the human consciousness (5).

In relation to the actual condition of religious truth, as communicated by Holy Scripture, Dogmatism and Rationalism may be considered as severally representing, the one the spirit which adds to the word of God, and the other that which diminishes from it. Whether a complete system of scientific Theology could or could not have been given by direct revelation, consistently with the existing laws of human thought and the purposes which Revelation is designed to answer, it is at least certain that such a system is not given in the Revelation which we possess, but, if it is to exist at all, must be constructed out of it by human interpretation. And it is in attempting such a construction that Dogmatism and Rationalism exhibit their most striking contrasts. The one seeks to build up a complete scheme of theological doctrine out of the unsystematic materials furnished by Scripture, partly by the more complete development of certain leading ideas; partly by extending the apparent import of the Revelation to ground which it does not avowedly occupy, and attempting by inference and analogy to solve problems which the sacred volume may indeed suggest, but which it does not directly answer; partly by endeavouring to give additional support to the scriptural statements themselves, treating them as truths, not above, but within the grasp of reason and capable of demonstration from rational premises. The other aims at the same end by opposite means. It strives to attain to unity and completeness of system, not by filling up supposed deficiencies, but by paring down supposed excrescences. Commencing with a preconceived theory of the purpose of a revelation and the form which it ought to assume, it proceeds to remove or reduce all that will not harmonize with this leading idea; sometimes explaining away in the interpretation that which it accepts as given in the letter; sometimes denying, on à *priori* grounds, the genuineness of this or that portion of the sacred text; sometimes pretending to distinguish between the several purposes of Revelation itself, and to determine what portions are intended to convey the elements of an absolute religion, valid in all countries and for all ages, and what must be regarded as relative and accidental features of the divine plan, determined by the local or temporal peculiarities of the individuals to whom it was first addressed.

The two methods thus contrasted may appear at first sight to represent the respective claims of Faith and Reason, each extended to that point at which it encroaches on the domain of the other. But in truth the contrast between Faith and Reason, if it holds good in this relation at all, does so merely by accident. It may be applicable in some instances to the disciples of the respective systems, but not to the teachers; and even as regards the former, it is but partially and occasionally true. The disciples of the Rationalist are not necessarily the disciples of reason. It is quite as possible to receive with unquestioning submission a system of religion or philosophy invented by a human teacher, as it is to believe, upon the authority of

Revelation, doctrines which no human reason is competent to discover. The so-called freethinker is as often as any other man the slave of some self-chosen master; and many who scorn the imputation of believing anything merely because it is found in the Bible would find it hard to give any better reason for their own unbelief than the *ipse dixit* of some infidel philosopher. But when we turn from the disciples to the teachers, and look to the origin of Dogmatism and Rationalism as systems, we find both alike to be the products of thought, operating in different ways upon the same materials. Faith, properly so called, is not constructive, but receptive. It cannot supply the missing portions of an incomplete system; though it may bid us remain content with the deficiency. It cannot of itself give harmony to the discordant voices of religious thought: it cannot reduce to a single focus the many-coloured rays into which the light of God's presence is refracted in its passage through the human soul; though it may bid us look forward to a time when the eyes of the blind shall be opened, and the ears of the deaf shall be unstopped; when that apparent discord shall be known but as the echo of a half-heard concert, and those diverging rays shall be blended once more in the pure white light of heaven. But Faith alone cannot suggest any actual solution of our doubts: it can offer no definite reconciliation of apparently conflicting truths; for in order to accomplish that end, the hostile elements must be examined, compared, accommodated, and joined together, one with another; and such a process is an act of thought, not of belief. Considered from this point of view, both Dogmatism and Rationalism may be regarded as emanating from the same source, and amenable to the same principles of criticism; in so far as they keep within or go beyond those limits of sound thought which the laws of man's mind or the circumstances in which he is placed, have imposed upon him.

In fact, the two systems may be considered as both aiming, though in different ways, at the same end; that end being to produce a coincidence between what we believe and what we think; to remove the boundary which separates the comprehensible from the incomprehensible. The Dogmatist employs reason to prove, almost as much as the Rationalist employs it to disprove. The one, in the character of an advocate, accepts the doctrines of revealed religion as conclusions, but appeals to the reason, enlightened, it may be, by Revelation, to find premises to support them. The other, in the character of a critic, draws his premises from reason in the first instance; and, adopting these as his standard, either distorts the revealed doctrine into conformity with them, or, if it obstinately resists this treatment, sets it aside altogether. The one strives to lift up reason to the point of view occupied by Revelation: the other strives to bring down Revelation to the level of reason. And both alike have prejudged or neglected the previous inquiry,—Are there not definite and discernible limits to the province of reason itself, whether it be exercised for advocacy or for criticism?

Thus, to select one example out of many, the revealed doctrine of Christ's Atonement for the sins of men has been alternately defended and assailed by some such arguments as these. We have been told, on the one hand, that man's redemption *could not* have been brought about by any other means (6):—that God could not, consistently with His own attributes, have suffered man to perish unredeemed, or have redeemed him by any inferior sacrifice (7):—that man, redeemed from death, must become the servant of him who redeems him; and that it was not meet that he should be the servant of any other than God (8):—that no other sacrifice could have satisfied divine justice (9):— that no other victim could have endured the burden of

God's wrath (10). These and similar arguments have been brought forward, as one of the greatest of their authors avows, to defend the teaching of the Catholic Faith on the ground of a *reasonable necessity* (11). While, on the other hand, it has been argued that the revealed doctrine itself cannot be accepted as literally true; because we cannot believe that God was angry, and needed to be propitiated (12):—because it is inconsistent with the Divine Justice that the innocent should suffer for the sins of the guilty (13):—because it is more reasonable to believe that God freely forgives the offences of His creatures (14):—because we cannot conceive how the punishment of one can do away with the guilt of another (15).

I quote these arguments only as specimens of the method in which Christian doctrines have been handled by writers on opposite sides. To examine them more in detail would detain me too long from my main purpose. I shall not therefore at present consider whether the conclusions actually arrived at, on the one side or on the other, are in themselves reasonable or unreasonable, orthodox or heretical. I am concerned only with the methods respectively employed, and the need of some rule for their employment. May reason be used without restriction in defence or refutation of religious doctrines? And if not, what are the conditions of its legitimate use? It may be that this man has defended, on reasonable grounds, none but the most essential articles of the Christian Faith: but has he pointed out any rule which can hinder the same or similar reasoning from being advanced by another in support of the most dangerous errors? It may be that that man has employed the test of reasonableness, only in the refutation of opinions concerning which the Church has pronounced no positive judgment: but has he fenced his method round with any cautions to prevent its being used for the overthrow of Christianity itself? If we can find no other ground than the arbitrary will of the man himself, why he should stop short at the particular point which he has chosen, we may not perhaps condemn the tenets of the individual, but we may fairly charge his method with the consequences to which it logically leads us.

Thus we find a late lamented writer of our own day, and at that time of our own Church, defending the doctrine of the Incarnation of Christ, on the metaphysical assumption of the real existence of an abstract humanity. "This," he tells us, "is why the existence of human nature is a thing too precious to be surrendered to the subtleties of logic, because upon its existence depends that real manhood of Christ, which renders him a co-partner with ourselves." And again: "To the reality of this work, the existence of that common nature is indispensable, whereby, as the children were partakers of flesh and blood, He himself took part of the same. Else, how would the perfect assumption of humanity have consisted with His retaining that divine personality which it was impossible that He should surrender? Since it was no new person which He took, it can only have been the substratum, in which personality has its existence (16)." In this case, our belief in the undeniable truth of the doctrine defended may dispose us to overlook the questionable character of the defence. But if we are inclined for a moment to acquiesce in this unnatural union of metaphysical premises and theological conclusions, we are recalled to ourselves by the recollection of the fearful consequence which Occam deduces from the same hypothesis of the assumption by Christ of a "substratum in which personality has its existence;"—a consequence drawn in language which we shudder to read, even as it is employed by its author, merely for the purpose of reducing to an absurdity the principles of his antagonists (17).

There is an union of Philosophy with Religion in which each contributes to the support of the other; and there is also an union which, under the appearance of support, does but undermine the foundations and prey upon the life of both. To which of these two the above argument belongs, it needs but a bare statement of its assumption to determine. It tells us that our belief in the doctrine of God manifest in the flesh indispensably depends upon our acceptance of the Realist theory of the nature of universal notions. Philosophy and Theology alike protest against such an outrage upon the claims both of Reason and of Revelation, as is implied in this association of one of the most fundamental truths of the Christian Faith with one of the most questionable speculations of mediæval metaphysics. What does Theology gain by this employment of a weapon which may at any moment be turned against her? Does it make one whit clearer to our understandings than mysterious twofold nature of one Christ, very God, and very Man? By no means. It was a truth above human comprehension before; and it remains a truth above human comprehension still. We believe that Christ is both God and Man; for this is revealed to us. We know not how He is so; for this is not revealed; and we can learn it in no other way. Theology gains nothing; but she is in danger of losing everything. Her most precious truths are cut from the anchor which held them firm, and cast upon the waters of philosophical speculation, to float hither and thither with the ever-shifting waves of thought. And what does Philosophy gain? Her just domains are narrowed, and her free limbs cramped in their onward course. The problems which she has a native right to sift to the uttermost are taken out of the field of free discussion, and fenced about with religious doctrines which it is heresy to call in question. Neither Christian truth nor philosophical inquiry can be advanced by such a system as this, which revives and sanctifies, as essential to the Catholic Faith, the forgotten follies of Scholastic Realism, and endangers the cause of religion, by seeking to explain its greatest mysteries by the lifeless forms of a worn-out controversy.

But if the tendency of Dogmatism is to endanger the interests of religious truth, by placing that which is divine and unquestionable in too close an alliance with that which is human and doubtful, Rationalism, on the other hand, tends to destroy revealed religion altogether, by obliterating the whole distinction between the human and the divine. Rationalism, if it retains any portion of revealed truth as such, does so, not in consequence of, but in defiance of, its fundamental principle. It does so by virtually declaring that it will follow reason up to a certain point, and no further; though the conclusions which lie beyond that point are guaranteed by precisely the same evidence as those which fall short of it. We may select a notable example from the writings of a great thinker, who has contributed perhaps more than any other person to give a philosophical sanction to the rationalizing theories of his countrymen, yet from whose speculative principles, rightly employed, might be extracted the best antidote to his own conclusions; even as the body of the scorpion, crushed upon the wound, is said to be the best cure for its own venom.

Kant's theory of a rational religion is based upon the assumption that the sole purpose of religion must be to give a divine sanction to man's moral duties (18). He maintains that there can be no duties towards God distinct from those which we owe towards men; but that it may be necessary, at certain times and for certain persons, to give to moral duties the authority of Divine commands (19). Let us hear then the philosopher's *rational* explanation, upon this assumption, of the duty of Prayer. It is a mere superstitious delusion, he tells us, to consider prayer as a service addressed to God, and as a means of obtaining his favour (20). The true purpose of the act is not to alter or affect in any way God's relation towards us; but only to quicken our own moral sentiments, by keeping alive within us the idea of God as a moral Lawgiver (21). He therefore neither admits the duty unconditionally, nor rejects it entirely; but leaves it optional with men to adopt that or any other means, by which, in their own particular case, this moral end may be best promoted;—as if any moral benefit could possibly accrue from the habitual exercise of an act of conscious self-deception.

The origin of such theories is, of course, to be traced to that morbid horror of what they are pleased to call Anthropomorphism, which poisons the speculations of so many modern philosophers, when they attempt to be wise above what is written, and seek for a metaphysical exposition of God's nature and attributes (22). They may not, forsooth, think of the unchangeable God as if He were their fellow man, influenced by human motives, and moved by human supplications. They want a truer, a juster idea of the Deity as He is, than that under which He has been pleased to reveal Himself; and they call on their reason to furnish it. Fools, to dream that man can escape from himself, that human reason can draw aught but a human portrait of God! They do but substitute a marred and mutilated humanity for one exalted and entire: they add nothing to their conception of God as He is, but only take away a part of their conception of man. Sympathy, and love, and fatherly kindness, and forgiving mercy, have evaporated in the crucible of their philosophy; and what is the *caput mortuum* that remains, but only the sterner features of humanity exhibited in repulsive nakedness? The God who listens to prayer, we are told, appears in the likeness of human mutability. Be it so. What is the God who does not listen, but the likeness of human obstinacy? Do we ascribe to Him a fixed purpose? our conception of a purpose is human. Do we speak of Him as continuing unchanged? our conception of continuance is human. Do we conceive Him as knowing and determining? what are knowledge and determination but modes of human consciousness? and what know we of consciousness itself, but by the contrast between successive mental states? But our rational philosopher stops short in the middle of his reasoning. He strips off from humanity just so much as suits his purpose;—"and the residue thereof he maketh a god;"—less pious in his idolatry than the carver of the graven image, in that he does not fall down unto it and pray unto it, but is content to stand afar off and reason concerning it. And why does he retain any conception of God at all, but that he retains some portions of an imperfect humanity? Man is still the residue that is left; deprived indeed of all that is amiable in humanity, but, in the darker features which remain, still man. Man in his purposes; man in his inflexibility; man in that relation to time from which no philosophy, whatever its pretensions, can wholly free itself; pursuing with indomitable resolution a preconceived design; deaf to the yearning instincts which compel his creatures to call upon him (23). Yet this, forsooth, is a philosophical conception of the Deity, more worthy of an enlightened reason than the human imagery of the Psalmist: "The eyes of the Lord are over the righteous, and His ears are open unto their prayers."[b]

Surely downright idolatry is better than this *rational* worship of a fragment of humanity. Better is the superstition which sees the image of God in the wonderful whole which God has fashioned, than the philosophy

[b] Psalm xxxiv. 15.

which would carve for itself a Deity out of the remnant which man has mutilated. Better to realise the satire of the Eleatic philosopher, to make God in the likeness of man, even as the ox or the horse might conceive gods in the form of oxen or horses, than to adore some half-hewn Hermes, the head of a man joined to a misshapen block (24). Better to fall down before that marvellous compound of human consciousness whose elements God has joined together, and no man can put asunder, than to strip reason of those cognate elements which together furnish all that we can conceive or imagine of conscious or personal existence, and to deify the emptiest of all abstractions, a something or a nothing, with just enough of its human original left to form a theme for the disputations of philosophy, but not enough to furnish a single ground of appeal to the human feelings of love, of reverence, and of fear. Unmixed idolatry is more religious than this. Undisguised atheism is more logical.

Throughout every page of holy Scripture, God reveals himself, not as a Law, but as a Person. Throughout the breadth and height and depth of human consciousness, Personality manifests itself under one condition, that of a Free Will, influenced, though not coerced, by motives. And to this consciousness God addresses Himself, when He adopts its attributes as the image under which to represent to man His own incomprehensible and ineffable nature. Doubtless in this there is much of accommodation to the weakness of man's faculties; but not more than in any other representation of any of the Divine attributes. By what right do we say that the conception of the God who hears and answers prayer [c] is an accommodation, while that of Him in whom is no variableness nor shadow of turning [d] is not so? By what right do we venture to rob the Deity of half His revealed attributes,

[c] Psalm lxv. 2; St. James v. 16.   [d] St. James i. 17.

in order to set up the other half, which rest on precisely the same evidence, as a more absolute revelation of the truth? By what right do we enthrone, in the place of the God to whom we pray, an inexorable Fate or immutable Law?—a thing with less than even the divinity of a Fetish; since *that* may be at least conceived by its worshipper as capable of being offended by his crimes and propitiated by his supplications?

Yet surely there is a principle of truth of which this philosophy is the perversion. Surely there is a sense in which we may not think of God as though He were man; as there is also a sense in which we cannot help so thinking of Him. When we read in the same narrative, and almost in two consecutive verses of Scripture, "The Strength of Israel will not lie nor repent; for He is not a man that He should repent;" and, again, "The Lord repented that He had made Saul king over Israel;"[e] we are imperfectly conscious of an appeal to two different principles of representation, involving opposite sides of the same truth: we feel that there is a true foundation for the system which denies human attributes to God; though the superstructure which has been raised upon it logically involves the denial of His very existence.

What limits then can we find to determine the legitimate provinces of these two opposite methods of religious thought, each of which, in its exclusive employment, leads to errors so fatal; yet each of which, in its utmost error, is but a truth abused? If we may not, with the Dogmatist, force Philosophy into unnatural union with Revelation, nor yet, with the Rationalist, mutilate Revelation to make it agree with Philosophy, what guide can we find to point out the safe middle course? what common element of both systems can be employed to mediate between them? It is obvious that no such element can be found by the

[e] 1 Sam. xv. 29, 35.

mere contemplation of the objects on which religious thought is exercised. We can adequately criticize that only which we know as a whole. The objects of Natural Religion are known to us in and by the ideas which we can form of them; and those ideas do not of themselves constitute a whole, apart from the remaining phenomena of consciousness. We must not examine them by themselves alone: we must look to their origin, their import, and their relation to the mind of which they are part. Revealed Religion, again, is not by itself a direct object of criticism: first, because it is but a part of a larger scheme, and that scheme one imperfectly comprehended; and, secondly, because Revelation implies an accommodation to the mental constitution of its human receiver; and we must know what that constitution is, before we can pronounce how far the accommodation extends. But if partial knowledge must not be treated as if it were complete, neither, on the other hand, may it be identified with total ignorance. The false humility which assumes that it can know nothing, is often as dangerous as the false pride which assumes that it knows everything. The provinces of Reason and Faith, the limits of our knowledge and of our ignorance, must both be clearly determined: otherwise we may find ourselves dogmatically protesting against dogmatism, and reasoning to prove the worthlessness of reason.

There is one point from which all religious systems must start, and to which all must finally return; and which may therefore furnish a common ground on which to examine the principles and pretensions of all. *The primary and proper object of criticism is not Religion, natural or revealed, but the human mind in its relation to Religion.* If the Dogmatist and the Rationalist have heretofore contended as combatants, each beating the air in his own position, without being able to reach his adversary; if they have been prevented from taking up a common ground of controversy, because each repudiates the fundamental assumptions of the other; that common ground must be sought in another quarter; namely, in those laws and processes of the human mind, by means of which both alike accept and elaborate their opposite systems. If human philosophy is not a direct guide to the attainment of religious truth (and its entire history too truly testifies that it is not), may it not serve as an indirect guide, by pointing out the limits of our faculties, and the conditions of their legitimate exercise? Witnessing, as it does, the melancholy spectacle of the household of humanity divided against itself, the reason against the feelings and the feelings against the reason, and the dim half-consciousness of the shadow of the infinite frowning down upon both, may it not seek, with the heathen Philosopher of old, to find the reconciling and regulating principle in that justice, of which the essential character is, that every member of the system shall do his own duty, and forbear to intrude into the office of his neighbour? (25).

A Criticism of the human mind, in relation to religious truth, was one of the many unrealized possibilities of philosophy, sketched out in anticipation by the far-seeing genius of Bacon. "Here therefore," he writes, "I note this deficiency, that there hath not been, to my understanding, sufficiently inquired and handled the true limits and use of reason in spiritual things, as a kind of divine dialectic: which for that it is not done, it seemeth to me a thing usual, by pretext of true conceiving that which is revealed, to search and mine into that which is not revealed; and by pretext of enucleating inferences and contradictories, to examine that which is positive: the one sort falling into the error of Nicodemus, demanding to have things made more sensible than it pleaseth God to reveal them, 'Quomodo possit homo nasci cum sit senex?' the other sort into the error of the disciples, which were scandalized at a show of contradiction, 'Quid est hoc quod dicit nobis, Modicum, et non videbitis me; et iterum, modicum, et videbitis me?'" (26).

An examination of the Limits of Religious Thought is an indispensable preliminary to all Religious Philosophy. And the limits of religious thought are but a special manifestation of the limits of thought in general. Thus the Philosophy of Religion, on its human side, must be subject to those universal conditions which are binding upon Philosophy in general. It has ever fared ill, both with Philosophy and with Religion, when this caution has been neglected. It was an evil hour for both, when Fichte made his first essay, as a disciple of the Kantian school, by an attempted Criticism of all Revelation (27). The very title of Kant's great work, and, in spite of many inconsistencies, the general spirit of its contents also, might have taught him a different lesson,—might have shewn him that Reason, and not Revelation, was the primary object of criticism. If Revelation is a communication from an infinite to a finite intelligence, the conditions of a criticism of Revelation on philosophical grounds must be identical with those which are required for constructing a Philosophy of the Infinite. For Revelation can make known the Infinite Being only in one of two ways; by *presenting* Him as He is, or by *representing* Him under symbols more or less adequate. A presentative Revelation implies faculties in man which can receive the presentation; and such faculties will also furnish the conditions of constructing a philosophical theory of the object presented. If, on the other hand, Revelation is merely representative, the accuracy of the representation can only be ascertained by a knowledge of the object represented; and this again implies the possibility of a Philosophy of the Infinite. Whatever impediments, therefore, exist to prevent the formation of such a Philosophy, the same impediments must likewise prevent the accomplishment of a complete Criticism of Revelation. Whatever difficulties or contradictions are involved in the philosophical idea of the Infinite, the same, or similar ones, must naturally be expected in the corresponding ideas which Revelation either exhibits or implies. And if an examination of the problems of Philosophy and the conditions of their solution should compel us to admit the existence of principles and modes of thought which must be accepted as true in practice, though they cannot be explained in theory; the same practical acceptance may be claimed, on philosophical grounds, in behalf of the corresponding doctrines of Revelation.

If it can be shewn that the limits of religious and philosophical thought are the same; that corresponding difficulties occur in both, and, from the nature of the case, must occur, the chief foundation of religious Rationalism is cut away from under it. The difficulties which it professes to find in Revelation are shewn to be not peculiar to Revelation, but inherent in the constitution of the human mind, and such as no system of Rationalism can avoid or overcome. The analogy, which Bishop Butler has pointed out, between Religion and the constitution and course of Nature, may be in some degree extended to the constitution and processes of the Human Mind. The representations of God which Scripture presents to us may be shewn to be adapted to the needs and accommodated to the limits of that mental constitution which He has given us; encumbered with no other difficulties than those which arise from the laws of the human mind itself; and therefore such as, notwithstanding those difficulties, may reasonably be regarded as emanating from the same Divine Author. Such an inquiry occupies indeed but a subordinate place among the direct evidences of Christianity; nor is it intended to usurp the place of those evidences. But indirectly it may have its use, in furnishing an answer to a class of objections which were very popular a few years ago, and are not yet entirely extinguished. Even if it does not contribute materially to strengthen the position occupied by the defenders of Christianity, it may serve to expose the weakness of the assailants. Human reason may, in some respects, be weak as a supporter of Religion; but it is at least strong enough to repel an attack founded on the negation of reason.

"We know in part, and we prophesy in part. But when that which is perfect is come, then that which is in part shall be done away. For now we see through a glass, darkly; but then face to face: now I know in part; but then shall I know even as also I am known."[f] Such is the Apostle's declaration of the limits of human knowledge. "The logical conception is the absolute divine conception itself; and the logical process is the immediate exhibition of God's self-determination to Being" (28). Such is the Philosopher's declaration of the extent of human knowledge. On the first of these statements is founded the entire Theology of Scripture: on the second is founded the latest and most complete exposition of the Theology of Rationalism. The one represents God, not as He is in the brightness of His own glory, dwelling in the light which no man can approach unto;[g] but as He is reflected faintly in broken and fitful rays, glancing back from the restless waters of the human soul. The other identifies the shadow with the substance, not even shrinking from the confession that, to know God as He is, man must himself be God (29). It turns from the feeble image of God in the soul of the individual man, to seek the entire manifestation of Deity in the collective conscious-

[f] 1 Cor. xiii. 9, 10, 12.   [g] 1 Tim. vi. 16.

ness of mankind. "Ye shall be as gods," was the earliest suggestion of the Tempter to the parents of the human race: "Ye are God," is the latest assurance of philosophy to the human race itself (30). Revelation represents the infinite God under finite symbols, in condescension to the finite capacity of man; indicating at the same time the existence of a further reality beyond the symbol, and bidding us look forward in faith to the promise of a more perfect knowledge hereafter. Rationalism, in the hands of these expositors, adopts an opposite view of man's powers and duties. It claims to behold God as He is *now*: it finds a common object for Religion and Philosophy in the *explanation of God* (31). It declares Religion to be *the Divine Spirit's knowledge of Himself through the mediation of the finite Spirit* (32).

"Beloved, now are we the sons of God; and it doth not yet appear what we shall be: but we know that, when He shall appear, we shall be like Him; for we shall see Him as He is. And every man that hath this hope in Him purifieth himself, even as He is pure."[h] Philosophy too confesses that like must be known by like; but, reversing the hope of the Apostle, it finds God in the forms of human thought. Its kingdom is proclaimed to be truth absolute and unveiled. It contains in itself the exhibition of God, as He is in His eternal essence, before the creation of a finite world (33). Which of these two representations contains the truer view of the capacities of human reason, it will be the purpose of the following Lectures to inquire. Such an inquiry must necessarily, during a portion at least of its course, assume a philosophical, rather than a theological aspect; yet it will not perhaps on that account be less ultimately serviceable in theological controversy. It has been acutely said, that even if Philosophy is useless, it is still useful, as the means of proving its own useless-

[h] 1 St. John iii. 2, 3.

ness (34). But it is not so much the utility as the necessity of the study, which constitutes its present claim on our attention. So long as man possesses facts of consciousness and powers of reflection, so long he will continue to exercise those powers and study those facts. So long as human consciousness contains the idea of a God and the instincts of worship, so long mental philosophy will walk on common ground with religious belief. Rightly or wrongly, men will think of these things; and a knowledge of the laws under which they think is the only security for thinking soundly. If it be thought no unworthy occupation for the Christian preacher to point out the evidences of God's Providence in the constitution of the sensible world and the mechanism of the human body; or to dwell on the analogies which may be traced between the scheme of revelation and the course of nature; it is but a part of the same argument to pursue the inquiry with regard to the structure and laws of the human mind. The path may be one which, of late years at least, has been less frequently trodden: the language indispensable to such an investigation may sound at times unwonted and uncouth; but the end is one with that of those plainer and more familiar illustrations which have taken their place among the acknowledged evidences of religion; and the lesson of the whole, if read aright, will be but to teach us that in mind, no less than in body, we are fearfully and wonderfully made[i] by Him whose praise both alike declare: that He who "laid the foundations of the earth, and shut up the sea with doors, and said, Hitherto shalt thou come, but no further," is also He who "hath put wisdom in the inward parts, and hath given understanding to the heart."[k]

---

[i] Psalm cxxxix. 14.   [k] Job xxxviii. 4, 8, 11, 36.

LECTURE II.

1 Timothy VI. 20, 21.

"Keep that which is committed to thy trust, avoiding profane and vain babblings, and oppositions of science falsely so called; which some professing have erred concerning the faith."

A PHILOSOPHY of Religion may be attempted from two opposite points of view, and by two opposite modes of development. It may be conceived either as a Philosophy of the Object of Religion; that is to say, as a scientific exposition of the nature of God; or as a Philosophy of the Subject of Religion; that is to say, as a scientific inquiry into the constitution of the human mind, so far as it receives and deals with religious ideas. The former is that branch of Metaphysics which is commonly known by the name of Rational Theology. Its general aim, in common with all metaphysical inquiries, is to disengage the real from the apparent, the true from the false: its special aim, as a Theology, is to exhibit a true representation of the Nature and Attributes of God, purified from foreign accretions, and displaying the exact features of their Divine Original. The latter is a branch of Psychology, which, at its outset at least, contents itself with investigating the phenomena presented to it, leaving their relation to further realities to be determined at a later stage of the inquiry. Its primary concern is with the operations and laws of the human mind; and its special purpose is to ascertain the nature, the origin, and the limits of the religious element in man; postponing, till after that question has been decided, the further inquiry into the absolute nature of God.

As applied to the criticism of Revelation, the first method, supposing its end to be attained, would furnish an immediate and direct criterion by which the claims of any supposed Revelation to a divine origin might be tested; while at the same time it would enable those possessed of it to dispense with the services of any Revelation at all. For on the supposition that we possess an exact idea of any attribute of the Divine Nature, we are at liberty to reject at once any portion of the supposed Revelation which contradicts that idea; and on the supposition that we possess a complete idea of that Nature as a whole, we are at liberty to reject whatever goes beyond it. And as, upon either supposition, the highest praise to which Revelation can aspire is that of coinciding, partially or wholly, with the independent conclusions of Philosophy, it follows that, so far as Philosophy extends, Revelation becomes superfluous (1). On the other hand, the second method of philosophical inquiry does not profess to furnish a direct criticism of Revelation, but only of the instruments by which Revelation is to be criticized. It looks to the human, not to the divine, and aspires to teach us no more than the limits of our own powers of thought, and the consequent distinction between what we may and what we may not seek to comprehend. And if, upon examination, it should appear that any portion of the contents of Revelation belongs to the latter class of truths, this method will enable us to reconcile with each other the conflicting claims of Reason and Faith, by shewing that Reason itself, rightly interpreted, teaches the existence of truths that are above Reason.

Whatever may be the ultimate use of the first of these methods of criticism, it is obvious that the previous question, concerning our right to use it at all, can only be satisfactorily answered by the employment of the second method. The possibility of criticism at all implies that human reason is liable to error: the possibility of a valid criticism implies that the means of distinguishing between its truth and its error may be ascertained by a previous criticism. Let it be granted, for the moment, that a religion whose contents are irreconcilable with human reason is thereby proved not to have come from God, but from man:—still the reason which judges is at least as human as the religion which is judged; and if the human representation of God is erroneous in the latter, how can we assume its infallibility in the former? If we grant for the present the fundamental position of Rationalism, namely, that man by his own reason can attain to a right conception of God, we must at any rate grant also, what every attempt at criticism implies, that he may also attain to a wrong one. We have therefore still to ask by what marks the one is to be distinguished from the other; by what method we are to seek the truth; and how we are to assure ourselves that we have found it. And to answer this question, we need a preliminary examination of the conditions and limits of human thought. Religious criticism is itself an act of thought; and its immediate instruments must, under any circumstances, be thoughts also. We are thus compelled in the first instance to inquire into the origin and value of those thoughts themselves.

A Philosophy which professes to elicit from its own conceptions all the essential portions of religious belief, is bound to justify its profession, by shewing that those conceptions themselves are above suspicion. The ideas thus exalted to the supreme criteria of truth must bear on their front unquestionable evidence that they are true and sufficient representations of the Divine Nature, such as may serve all the needs of human thought and human feeling, adequate alike for contemplation and for worship. They must manifest the clearness and distinctness which mark the strong vision of an eye gazing undazzled on the glory of Heaven, not the obscurity and confusion of one that turns away blinded from the glare, and gropes in its own darkness after the fleeting spectrum. The conviction which boasts itself to be superior to all external evidence must carry in its own inward constitution some sure indication of its truth and value.

Such a conviction may be possible in two different ways. It may be the result of a direct intuition of the Divine Nature; or it may be gained by inference from certain attributes of human nature, which, though on a smaller scale, are known to be sufficiently representative of the corresponding properties of the Deity. We may suppose the existence in man of a special faculty of knowledge, of which God is the immediate object,—a kind of religious sense or reason, by which the Divine attributes are apprehended in their own nature (2): or we may maintain that the attributes of God differ from those of man in degree only, not in kind;[a] and hence that certain mental and

---

[a] From note (3) at the end of this Lecture, it will be seen that the error of this reasoning is supposed to depend on its special application, not on its general principle. In other words, it was not the author's intention to condemn the general statement that the attributes of God differ from those of man in degree only, not in kind, but the inference, that therefore the latter are a true and adequate image of the former. The general statement may be true or not, according to the ground on which the distinction between kind and degree is made: indeed, this distinction, when applied to spiritual attributes, is too vague and arbitrary to furnish a safe criterion between truth and error. A remarkable instance of this may be seen in a note appended to Davison's *Discourses on Prophecy*, in which the author, after censuring Archbishop

moral qualities, of which we are immediately conscious in ourselves, furnish at the same time a true and adequate image of the infinite perfections of God (3). The first of these suppositions professes to convey a knowledge of God by direct apprehension, in a manner similar to the evidence of the senses: the second professes to convey the same knowledge by a logical process, similar to the demonstrations of science. The former is the method of Mysticism, and of that Rationalism which agrees with Mysticism, in referring the knowledge of divine things to an extraordinary and abnormal process of intuition or thought (4). The latter is the method of the vulgar Rationalism, which regards the reason of man, in its ordinary and normal operation, as the supreme criterion of religious truth.

On the former supposition, a system of religious philosophy or criticism may be constructed by starting from the divine and reasoning down to the human: on the latter, by starting from the human and reasoning up to the divine. The first commences with a supposed immediate knowledge of God as He is in His absolute nature, and proceeds to exhibit the process by which that nature, acting according to its own laws, will manifest itself in operation, and become known to man. The second commences with an immediate knowledge of the mental and moral attributes of man, and proceeds to exhibit the manner in which those attributes will manifest themselves, when exalted to the degree in which they form part of the nature of God. If, for example, the two systems severally undertake to give a representation of the infinite power and wisdom of God,

---

King's hypothesis of "some difference in kind, or in properties and effects, between the divine knowledge and human," or "that the actual nature of the Divine Attributes is something different from our positive notions of the human virtues," expressly admits that "the absolute *transcendency* of the divine virtue makes it of a *different species.*"

the former will profess to explain how the nature of the infinite manifests itself in the forms of power and wisdom; while the latter will attempt to shew how power and wisdom must manifest themselves when existing in an infinite degree. In their criticisms of Revelation, in like manner, the former will rather take as its standard that absolute and essential nature of God, which must remain unchanged in every manifestation; the latter will judge by reference to those intellectual and moral qualities, which must exist in all their essential features in the divine nature as well as in the human.

Thus, for example, it has been maintained by a modern philosopher, that the absolute nature of God is that of a pure Will, determining itself solely by a moral law, and subject to no affections which can operate as motives. Hence it is inferred that the same law of action must form the rule of God's manifestation to mankind as a moral Governor; and therefore that no revelation can be of divine origin, which attempts to influence men's actions by the prospect of reward or punishment (5). In this mode of reasoning, an abstract conception of the nature of God is made the criterion to determine the mode in which He must reveal Himself to man. On the other hand, we meet with an opposite style of criticism, which reasons somewhat as follows: All the excellences, it contends, of which we are conscious in the creature, must necessarily exist in the same manner, though in a higher degree, in the Creator.[b] God is indeed more wise, more just, more

---

[b] The erroneous part of this assumption lies in the words "in the same manner," not in the words "in a higher degree." The language of the text is but an echo of that in which Tertullian combats the rationalism of Marcion. "Et hæc ergo imago censenda est Dei in homine, quod eosdem motus et sensus habeat humanus animus quos et Deus, licet non tales quales Deus. Pro substantia enim et status eorum et exitus distant.

merciful than man; but for that very reason, His wisdom and justice and mercy must contain nothing that is incompatible with the corresponding attributes in their human character (6). Hence, if the certainty of man's knowledge implies the necessity of the events which he knows, the certainty of God's omniscience implies a like necessity of all things (7): if man's justice requires that he should punish the guilty alone, it is inconsistent with God's justice to inflict the chastisement of sin upon the innocent (8): if man's mercy finds its natural exercise in the free forgiveness of offences, God's mercy too must freely forgive the sins of His creatures (9). From the same premises it is consistently concluded that no act which would be wrong if performed by a man upon his own responsibility can be justified by the plea of a direct command from God (10). Abraham may not be praised for his readiness to slay his son in obedience to God's command; for the internal prohibition must always be more certain than the external precept (11). Joshua cannot be warranted in obeying the Divine injunction to exterminate the Canaanites; unless he would be equally warranted in destroying them of his own accord (12). And, as the issuing of such commands is contrary to the moral nature of God, therefore the Book which represents them as so issued is convicted of falsehood, and cannot be regarded as a Divine Revelation (13).

Denique, contrarios eorum sensus, lenitatem dico, patientiam, misericordiam, ipsamque matricem earum bonitatem, cur divina præsumitis? Nec tamen perfecte ea obtinemus, quia solus Deus perfectus. . . . . . Omnia necesse est adhibeat propter omnia; tot sensus quot et causas; et iram propter scelestos, et bilem propter ingratos, et æmulationem propter superbos, et quicquid non expedit malis. Sic et misericordiam propter errantes, et patientiam propter non resipiscentes, et præstantiam propter merentes, et quidquid bonis opus est. *Quæ omnia patitur suo more quo eum pati condecet, propter quem homo eadem patitur, æque suo more.*"— Adv. Marc. ii. 16.

In this mode of reasoning, the moral or intellectual nature of man is made the rule to determine what ought to be the revealed attributes of God, and in what manner they must be exercised.

Within certain limits both these arguments may have their value; but each is chiefly useful as a check upon the exclusive authority of the other. The philosophy which reasons downwards from the infinite is but an exaggeration of the true conviction that God's thoughts are not our thoughts, nor His ways our ways:[c] the philosophy which reasons upwards from the human bears witness, even in its perversion, to the unextinguishable consciousness, that man, however fallen, was created in the image of God.[d] But this admission tends rather to weaken than to strengthen the claims of either to be received as the supreme criterion of religious truth. The criticisms of rationalism exhibit the weakness as well as the strength of reason; for the representations which it rejects as dishonouring to God are, on its own shewing, the product of human thought, no less than the principle by which they are judged and condemned. If the human mind has passed through successive stages of religious cultivation, from the grovelling superstition of the savage to the intellectual elevation of the critic of all possible revelations, who shall assure the critic that the level on which he now stands is the last and highest that can be attained? If reason is to be the last court of appeal in religious questions, it must find some better proof of its own infallibility than is to be found in its own progressive enlightenment. Its preeminence must be shewn, not by successive approximations to the truth, but by the possession of the truth itself. Of the limits within which reason may be legitimately employed, I shall have occasion to speak hereafter. At present I am concerned only with its pretensions to such

[c] Isaiah lv. 8.   [d] Genesis i. 27.

LECT. II. IDEAS OF RATIONAL THEOLOGY.

a knowledge of the Divine Nature as can constitute the foundation of a Rational Theology as a system of scientific certainty.

There are three terms, familiar as household words in the vocabulary of Philosophy, which must be taken into account in every system of Metaphysical Theology. To conceive the Deity as He is, we must conceive Him as First Cause, as Absolute, and as Infinite. By the *First Cause* is meant that which produces all things, and is itself produced of none. By the *Absolute* is meant that which exists in and by itself, having no necessary relation to any other being (14). By the *Infinite* is meant that which is free from all possible limitation; that than which a greater is inconceivable; and which consequently can receive no additional attribute or mode of existence which it had not from all eternity.*

---

* These of course must be regarded as merely nominal definitions, intended to explain the meaning of the respective terms, prior to any consideration whether the objects denoted by those terms are conceivable or not. The meaning of a word must of course be known before we can determine whether the corresponding object is conceivable or not. A word in an unknown tongue may, for anything I know, denote something perfectly conceivable or utterly self-contradictory. The meaning of the word *infinite* is quite as intelligible as that of the word *finite*; for the two opposite terms necessarily suggest each other, and the expression "without limits" has as much meaning as "with limits." But it does not follow that the two objects are equally conceivable. The word *inconceivable* is as intelligible as *conceivable*; but it does not therefore follow that we can conceive an inconceivable object. On the process of conception proper, see above, p. xi.

The definition of the Absolute, it is now necessary to add, is intended to imply no more than the words naturally express,— namely, that the absolute does not necessarily exist in relation, not that it is incapable of so existing. The latter position, though a logical consequence of the philosophy of the absolute, and admitted as such by its most consistent teachers (see below, pp. 32, 33, 37, and notes 21, 23, 32) is not assumed in the definition.

The Infinite, as contemplated by this philosophy, cannot be regarded as consisting of a limited number of attributes, each unlimited in its kind. It cannot be conceived, for example, after the analogy of a line, infinite in length, but not in breadth; or of a surface, infinite in two dimensions of space, but bounded in the third; or of an intelligent being, possessing some one or more modes of consciousness in an infinite degree, but devoid of others. Even if it be granted, which is not the case, that such a partial infinite may without contradiction be conceived, still it will have a relative infinity only, and be altogether incompatible with the idea of the Absolute (15). The line limited in breadth is thereby necessarily related to the space that limits it: the intelligence endowed with a limited number of attributes, coexists with others which are thereby related to it, as cognate or opposite modes of consciousness (16). The metaphysical representation of the Deity, as absolute and infinite, must necessarily, as the profoundest metaphysicians have acknowledged, amount to nothing less than the sum of all reality (17). "What kind of an Absolute Being is that," says Hegel, "which does not contain in itself all that is actual, even evil included?" (18). And this language, from the bare utterance of which our religious feelings instinctively recoil, is but the logical consequence of the assumption that the so-called Philosophy of the Absolute can exhibit the real nature of God. That which is conceived as absolute and infinite must be conceived as containing within itself the sum, not only of all actual, but of all possible modes of being. For if any actual mode can be denied of it, it is related to that mode, and limited by it (19); and if any possible mode can be denied of it, it is capable of becoming more than it now is, and such a capability is a limitation. Indeed it is obvious that the entire distinction between the possible and the actual can have no existence as regards the absolutely infinite; for an unrealised possibility is necessarily a relation and a limit.ᶠ The scholastic saying, *Deus est actus purus* (20), ridiculed as it has been by modern critics, is in truth but the expression, in technical language, of the almost unanimous voice of philosophy, both in earlier and later times (21).

But these three conceptions, the Cause, the Absolute, the Infinite, all equally indispensable, do they not present a seeming contradiction to each other, when viewed in conjunction, as attributes of one and the same Being? A Cause cannot, as such, be absolute: the Absolute cannot, as such, be a cause. The cause, as such, exists only in relation to its effect: the cause is a cause of the effect; the effect is an effect of the cause. On the other hand, the conception of the Absolute implies a possible existence out of all relation (22). We attempt to escape from this apparent contradiction, by introducing the idea of succession in time. The Absolute exists first by itself, and afterwards becomes a cause. But here we are checked by the third conception, that of the Infinite. How can the Infinite become that which it was not from the first? If Causation is a possible mode of existence, that which exists without causing is not infinite; that which becomes a cause has passed beyond its former limits. Creation at any particular moment of time being thus inconceivable, the philosopher is reduced to the alternative of Pantheism, which pronounces the effect to be mere appearance, and merges all real existence in the cause (23). The validity of this alternative will be examined presently.

Meanwhile, to return for a moment to the supposition of a true causation. Supposing the Absolute to become a

---

ᶠ Not, of course, a limit of the possibility itself, but of the subject in which it resides, and which is conceived as capable of becoming more than it actually is. This is explained more fully below, in notes 21 and 23.

cause, it will follow that it operates by means of free will and consciousness. For a necessary cause cannot be conceived as absolute and infinite. If necessitated by something beyond itself, it is thereby limited by a superior power; and if necessitated by itself, it has in its own nature a necessary relation to its effect. The act of causation must therefore be voluntary; and volition is only possible in a conscious being. But consciousness again is only conceivable as a relation. There must be a conscious subject, and an object of which he is conscious. The subject is a subject to the object; the object is an object to the subject; and neither can exist by itself as the absolute. This difficulty, again, may be for the moment evaded, by distinguishing between the absolute as related to another and the absolute as related to itself. The Absolute, it may be said, may possibly be conscious, provided it is only conscious of itself (24). But this alternative is, in ultimate analysis, no less self-destructive than the other. For the object of consciousness, whether a mode of the subject's existence or not, is either created in and by the act of consciousness, or has an existence independent of it. In the former case, the object depends upon the subject, and the subject alone is the true absolute. In the latter case, the subject depends upon the object, and the object alone is the true absolute. Or if we attempt a third hypothesis, and maintain that each exists independently of the other, we have no absolute at all, but only a pair of relatives: for coexistence, whether in consciousness or not, is itself a relation (25).

The corollary from this reasoning is obvious. Not only is the Absolute, as conceived, incapable of a necessary relation to anything else; but it is also incapable of containing, by the constitution of its own nature, an essential relation within itself; as a whole, for instance, composed of parts, or as a substance consisting of attributes, or as a conscious subject in antithesis to an object (26). For if there is in the absolute any principle of unity, distinct from the mere accumulation of parts or attributes, this principle alone is the true absolute. If, on the other hand, there is no such principle, then there is no absolute at all, but only a plurality of relatives (27). The almost unanimous voice of philosophy, in pronouncing that the absolute is both one and simple, must be accepted as the voice of reason also, so far as reason has any voice in the matter (28). But this Absolute unity, as indifferent and containing no attributes, can neither be distinguished from the multiplicity of finite beings by any characteristic feature, nor be identified with them in their multiplicity (29). Thus we are landed in an inextricable dilemma. The Absolute cannot be conceived as conscious, neither can it be conceived as unconscious: it cannot be conceived as complex, neither can it be conceived as simple: it cannot be conceived by difference, neither can it be conceived by the absence of difference: it cannot be identified with the universe, neither can it be distinguished from it. The One and the Many, regarded as the beginning of existence, are thus alike incomprehensible.

The fundamental conceptions of this Rational Theology being thus self-destructive, we may naturally expect to find the same antagonism manifested in their special applications. These naturally inherit the infirmities of the principle from which they spring. If an absolute and infinite consciousness is a conception which, from a human point of view, apparently contradicts itself, we need not wonder if its several modifications seem mutually to exclude each other. A mental attribute, to be conceived as infinite, must be in actual exercise on every possible object: otherwise it is potential only with regard to those on which it is not exercised; and an unrealized potentiality is a limitation. Hence every infinite mode of consciousness must be regarded as extending over the field of every other; and their common action involves a perpetual antagonism. How, for example, can Infinite Power be able to do all things, and yet Infinite Goodness be unable to do evil?[g] How can Infinite Justice exact the utmost penalty for every sin, and yet Infinite Mercy pardon the sinner?[h] How can Infinite Wisdom know all that is to come, and yet Infinite Freedom be at liberty to do or to forbear? (30). How is the existence of Evil compatible with that of an infinitely perfect Being; for if he wills it, he is not infinitely good; and if he wills it not, his will is

[g] This difficulty is not solved by distinguishing between physical and moral ability; for the former alone can be taken into account in the consideration of power *per se*. The dilemma is concisely stated by Sir W. Hamilton, *Reid's Works*, p. 609. "If, on the one hand, we attribute to the Deity the power of moral evil, we detract from his essential goodness; and if, on the other, we deny him this power, we detract from his omnipotence."

[h] This difficulty is clearly stated by Bishop Sherlock, *Discourse I.* part iv. "Now try how far Reason can go towards discovering the means of reconcilement. Lay down first these certain and allowed principles: That it is just for God to punish sinners—That God can do nothing but what is just: and try how you can come at the other conclusion, which must be the foundation of a sinner's reconcilement to God; namely, that it is just for God not to punish sinners, and righteous in Him to receive them to favour. If reason cannot discover nor comprehend how both these propositions should be true at the same time with respect to the same persons, 'tis impossible that it should discover or comprehend the means which God makes use of to reconcile Himself to sinners: that is, it is impossible for God to make use of any means that are not mysterious, that is, above the reach and comprehension of human wisdom. This difficulty must for ever remain, as long as we attempt to scan the Divine Justice by our narrow conceptions of it. . . . . If we could see the reasons upon which the justice of God proceeds in this case, here would be no mystery. And therefore the mysteriousness of the whole proceeding arises only from hence, that our finite minds cannot comprehend the reasons and limits of the Divine Justice."

thwarted and his sphere of action limited? Here, again, the Pantheist is ready with his solution. There is in reality no such thing as evil: there is no such thing as punishment: there is no real relation between God and man at all. God is all that really exists: He does, by the necessity of His nature, all that is done: all acts are equally necessary and equally divine: all diversity is but a distorted representation of unity: all evil is but a delusive appearance of good (31). Unfortunately, the Pantheist does not tell us whence all this delusion derives its seeming existence.

Let us however suppose for an instant that these difficulties are surmounted, and the existence of the Absolute securely established on the testimony of reason. Still we have not succeeded in reconciling this idea with that of a Cause: we have done nothing towards explaining how the absolute can give rise to the relative, the infinite to the finite. If the condition of causal activity is a higher state than that of quiescence, the Absolute, whether acting voluntarily or involuntarily, has passed from a condition of comparative imperfection to one of comparative perfection; and therefore was not originally perfect. If the state of activity is an inferior state to that of quiescence, the Absolute, in becoming a cause, has lost its original perfection (32). There remains only the supposition that the two states are equal, and the act of creation one of complete indifference. But this supposition annihilates the unity of the absolute, or it annihilates itself. If the act of creation is real, and yet indifferent, we must admit the possibility of two conceptions of the absolute, the one as productive, the other as non-productive. If the act is not real, the supposition itself vanishes, and we are thrown once more on the alternative of Pantheism.

Again, how can the Relative be conceived as coming into being? If it is a distinct reality from the absolute, it must be conceived as passing from non-existence into existence. But to conceive an object as non-existent, is again a self-contradiction; for that which is conceived exists, as an object of thought, in and by that conception. We may abstain from thinking of an object at all; but, if we think of it, we cannot but think of it as existing. It is possible at one time not to think of an object at all, and at another to think of it as already in being; but to think of it in the act of becoming, in the progress from not being into being, is to think that which, in the very thought, annihilates itself. Here again the Pantheistic hypothesis seems forced upon us. We can think of creation only as a change in the condition of that which already exists; and thus the creature is conceivable only as a phenomenal mode of the being of the Creator (33).

The whole of this web of contradictions (and it might be extended, if necessary, to a far greater length) is woven from one original warp and woof;—namely, the impossibility of conceiving the coexistence of the infinite and the finite, and the cognate impossibility of conceiving a first commencement of phenomena, or the absolute giving birth to the relative. The laws of thought appear to admit of no possible escape from the meshes in which thought is entangled, save by destroying one or the other of the cords of which they are composed. Pantheism and Atheism are thus the alternatives offered to us, according as we prefer to save the infinite by the sacrifice of the finite, or to maintain the finite by denying the existence of the infinite. Pantheism thus presents itself, as to all appearance the only logical conclusion, if we believe in the possibility of a Philosophy of the Infinite. But Pantheism, if it avoids self-contradiction in the course of its reasonings, does so only by an act of suicide at the outset. It escapes from some of the minor incongruities of thought, only by the annihilation of thought and thinker alike. It is saved from the necessity of demonstrating its own falsehood, by abolishing the only conditions under which truth and falsehood can be distinguished from each other. The only conception which I can frame of substantive existence at all, as distinguished from the transient accidents which are merely modes of the being of something else, is derived from the immediate knowledge of my own personal unity, amidst the various affections which form the successive modes of my consciousness. The Pantheist tells me that this knowledge is a delusion; that I am no substance, but a mode of the absolute substance, even as my thoughts and passions are modes of me; and that in order to attain to a true philosophy of being, I must begin by denying my own being. And for what purpose is this act of self-destruction needed? In order to preserve inviolate certain philosophical conclusions, which I, the non-existent thinker, have drawn by virtue of my non-existent powers of thought. But if my personal existence, the great primary fact of all consciousness, is a delusion, what claim have the reasonings of the Pantheist himself to be considered as anything better than a part of the universal falsehood? If I am mistaken in supposing myself to have a substantial existence at all, why is that existence more true when it is presented to me under the particular form of apprehending and accepting the arguments of the pantheistic philosophy? Nay, how do I know that there is any argument at all? For if my consciousness is mistaken in testifying to the fact of my own existence, it may surely be no less mistaken in testifying to my apparent apprehension of an apparent reasoning. Nay, the very arguments which appear to prove the Pantheist's conclusion to be true, may in reality, for aught I know, prove it to be false. Or rather, no Pantheist, if he is consistent with himself, can admit the existence of a distinction between truth and falsehood at all. For if God alone exists, in whatever way that existence may be explained, He alone is the immediate cause of all that takes place. He thinks all that is thought, He does all that is done. There can be no difference between truth and falsehood; for God is the only thinker; and all thoughts are equally necessary and equally divine. There can be no difference between right and wrong; for God is the only agent; and all acts are equally necessary and equally divine (34). How error and evil, even in appearance, are possible;—how the finite and the relative can appear to exist, even as a delusion,— is a problem which no system of Pantheism has made the slightest approach towards solving (35).

Pantheism thus failing us, the last resource of Rationalism is to take refuge in that which, with reference to the highest idea of God, is speculative Atheism, and to deny that the Infinite exists at all (36). And it must be admitted that, so long as we confine ourselves to one side only of the problem, that of the inconceivability of the Infinite, this is the only position logically tenable by those who would make man's power of thought the exact measure of his duty of belief. For the infinite, as inconceivable, is necessarily shewn to be non-existent; unless we renounce the claim of reason to supreme authority in matters of faith, by admitting that it is our duty to believe what we are altogether unable to comprehend. But the logical advantage of the atheistic alternative vanishes, as soon as we view the question from the other side, and endeavour positively to represent in thought the sum total of existence as a limited quantity. A limit is itself a relation; and to conceive a limit as such, is virtually to acknowledge the existence of a correlative on the other side of it (37). By a law of thought, the significance of which has perhaps not yet been fully investigated, it is impossible to conceive a finite object of any kind, without conceiving it as one out of many,—as related to other objects, coexistent and antecedent. A first moment of time, a first unit of space, a definite sum of all existence, are thus as inconceivable as the opposite suppositions of an infinity of each (38). While it is impossible to represent in thought any object, except as finite, it is equally impossible to represent any finite object, or any aggregate of finite objects, as exhausting the universe of being. Thus the hypothesis which would annihilate the Infinite is itself shattered to pieces against the rock of the Absolute; and we are involved in the self-contradictory assumption of a limited universe, which yet can neither contain a limit in itself, nor be limited by anything beyond itself. For if it contains a limit in itself, it is both limiting and limited, both beyond the limit and within it; and if it is limited by anything else, it is not the universe (39).

To sum up briefly this portion of my argument. The conception of the Absolute and Infinite, from whatever side we view it, appears encompassed with contradictions. There is a contradiction in supposing such an object to exist, whether alone or in conjunction with others; and there is a contradiction in supposing it not to exist. There is a contradiction in conceiving it as one; and there is a contradiction in conceiving it as many. There is a contradiction in conceiving it as personal; and there is a contradiction in conceiving it as impersonal. It cannot without contradiction be represented as active; nor, without equal contradiction, be represented as inactive. It cannot be conceived as the sum of all existence; nor yet can it be conceived as a part only of that sum. A contradiction thus thoroughgoing, while it sufficiently shews the impotence of human reason as an *à priori* judge of all truth, yet is not in itself inconsistent with any form of religious belief. For it tells with equal force against all belief and all unbelief, and therefore necessitates the conclusion that belief cannot be determined solely by reason. No conclusion can be drawn from it in favour of universal scepticism; first, because universal scepticism equally destroys itself; and secondly, because the contradictions thus detected belong not to the use of reason in general, but only to its exercise on one particular object of thought. It may teach us that it is our duty, in some instances, to believe that which we cannot conceive; but it does not require us to disbelieve anything which we are capable of conceiving.

What we have hitherto been examining, be it remembered, is not the nature of the Absolute in itself, but only our own conception of that nature. The distortions of the image reflected may arise only from the inequalities of the mirror reflecting it. And this consideration leads us naturally back to the second of the two methods of religious philosophy which were mentioned at the beginning of the present Lecture. If the attempt to grasp the absolute nature of the Divine Object of religious thought thus fails us on every side, we have no resource but to recommence our inquiry by the opposite process, that of investigating the nature of the human Subject. Such an investigation will not indeed solve the contradictions which our previous attempt has elicited; but it may serve to shew us why they are insoluble. If it cannot satisfy to the full the demands of reason, it may at least enable us to lay a reasonable foundation for the rightful claims of belief. If, from an examination of the laws and limits of human consciousness, we can shew that thought is not and cannot be the measure of existence; if it can be shewn that the contradictions which arise in the attempt to conceive the infinite, have their origin, not in the nature of that which we would conceive, but in the constitution of the mind conceiving; that they are such as must necessarily accompany every form of religion, and every renunciation of religion; we may thus prepare the way for a recognition of the separate provinces of Reason and Faith. This task I shall endeavour to accomplish in my next Lecture. Meanwhile I would add but a few words, to point out the practical lesson to be drawn from our previous inquiry. It is this: that so far is human reason from being able to construct a scientific Theology, independent of and superior to Revelation, that it cannot even read the alphabet out of which that Theology must be framed. It has not been without much hesitation that I have ventured to address you in language seldom heard in this place,—to transport to the preacher's pulpit the vocabulary of metaphysical speculation. But it was only by such a course that I could hope to bring the antagonist principles of true and false religious philosophy face to face with each other. It needs but a slight acquaintance with the history of opinions, to shew how intimately, in various ages, the current forms of religious belief or unbelief have been connected with the prevailing systems of speculative philosophy. It was in no small degree because the philosophy of Kant identified religion with morality, and maintained that the supernatural and the historical were not necessary to belief (40); that Paulus explained away the miracles of Christ, as misrepresentations of natural events (41); and Wegscheider claimed for the moral reason supreme authority in the interpretation of Scripture (42); and Röhr promulgated a new Creed, from which all the facts of Christianity are rejected, to make way for ethical precepts (43). It was in like manner because the philosophy of Hegel was felt to be incompatible with the belief in a personal God, and a personal Christ, and a supernatural revelation (44); that Vatke rejected the Old Testament history, as irreconcilable with the philosophical law of religious development (45); and Strauss endeavoured by minute cavils to invalidate the

Gospel narrative, in order to make way for the theory of an ideal Christ, manifested in the whole human race (46); and Feuerbach maintained that the Supreme Being is but humanity deified, and that the belief in a superhuman God is contradictory in itself, and pernicious in its consequences (47). And if, by wandering for a little while in the tangled mazes of metaphysical speculation, we can test the worth of the substitute which this philosophy offers us in the place of the faith which it rejects; if we can shew how little such a substitute can satisfy even the intellect of man (to the heart it does not pretend to appeal), the inquiry may do some service, slight and indirect though it be, to the cause of Christian Truth, by suggesting to the wavering disciple, ere he quits the Master with whom he has hitherto walked, the pregnant question of the Apostle, "Lord, to whom shall we go?"[1] When Philosophy succeeds in exhibiting in a clear and consistent form the Infinite Being of God; when her opposing schools are agreed among themselves as to the manner in which a knowledge of the Infinite takes place, or the marks by which it is to be discerned when known; then, and not till then, may she claim to speak as one having authority in controversies of Faith. But while she speaks with stammering lips and a double tongue; while she gropes her way in darkness, and stumbles at every step; while she has nothing to offer us, but the alternative of principles which abjure consciousness or a consciousness which contradicts itself, we may well pause before we appeal to her decisions as the gauge and measure of religious truth.

In one respect, indeed, I have perhaps departed from the customary language of the pulpit, to a greater extent than was absolutely necessary;—namely, in dealing with the ideas common to Theology and Metaphysics in the

[1] St. John vi. 68.

terms of the latter, rather than in those of the former. But there is a line of argument, in which the vague generalities of the Absolute and the Infinite may be more reverently and appropriately employed than the sacred names and titles of God. For we almost instinctively shrink back from the recklessness which thrusts forward, on every occasion, the holiest names and things, to be tossed to and fro, and trampled under foot, in the excitement of controversy. We feel that the name of Him whom we worship may not lightly be held up as a riddle for prying curiosity to puzzle over: we feel that the Divine Personality of our Father in Heaven is not a thing to be pitted in the arena of disputation, against the lifeless abstractions and sophistical word-jugglings of Pantheism. We feel that, though God is indeed, in His incomprehensible Essence, absolute and infinite, it is not as the Absolute and Infinite that He appeals to the love and the fear and the reverence of His creatures. We feel that the life of religion lies in the human relations in which God reveals Himself to man, not in the Divine perfection which those relations veil and modify, though without wholly concealing. We feel that the God to whom we pray, and in whom we trust, is not so much the God eternal and infinite, without body, parts, or passions (though we acknowledge that He is all these), as the God who is "gracious and merciful, slow to anger, and of great kindness, and repenteth Him of the evil"[k] (48). Those who have observed the prevailing character of certain schools of religious thought, in that country which, more than any other, has made Religion speak the language of Metaphysics;—those who have observed how often, in modern literature, both at home and abroad, the most sacred names are played with, in familiar, almost in contemptuous intimacy, will need no other proof to convince

[k] Joel ii. 13.

them that we cannot attach too much importance to the duty of separating, as far as it can be effected, the language of prayer and praise from the definitions and distinctions of philosophy.

The metaphysical difficulties which have been exhibited in the course of this Lecture almost suggest of themselves the manner in which they should be treated. We must begin with that which is within us, not with that which is above us; with the philosophy of Man, not with that of God. Instead of asking, what are the facts and laws in the constitution of the universe, or in the Divine Nature, by virtue of which certain conceptions present certain anomalies to the human mind, we should rather ask, what are the facts and laws in the constitution of the human mind, by virtue of which it finds itself involved in contradictions, whenever it ventures on certain courses of speculation. Philosophy, as well as Scripture, rightly employed, will teach a lesson of humility to its disciple; exhibiting, as it does, the spectacle of a creature of finite intuitions, surrounded by partial indications of the Unlimited; of finite conceptions, in the midst of partial manifestations of the Incomprehensible. Questioned in this spirit, the voice of Philosophy will be but an echo of the inspired language of the Psalmist: "Thou hast beset me behind and before, and laid thine hand upon me. Such knowledge is too wonderful for me: it is high; I cannot attain unto it."[1]

[1] Psalm cxxxix. 5, 6.

LECTURE III.

Exodus XXXIII. 20, 21, 22, 23.

"AND HE SAID, THOU CANST NOT SEE MY FACE; FOR THERE SHALL NO MAN SEE ME, AND LIVE. AND THE LORD SAID, BEHOLD, THERE IS A PLACE BY ME, AND THOU SHALT STAND UPON A ROCK: AND IT SHALL COME TO PASS, WHILE MY GLORY PASSETH BY, THAT I WILL PUT THEE IN A CLIFT OF THE ROCK, AND WILL COVER THEE WITH MY HAND WHILE I PASS BY: AND I WILL TAKE AWAY MINE HAND, AND THOU SHALT SEE MY BACK PARTS; BUT MY FACE SHALL NOT BE SEEN."

My last Lecture was chiefly occupied with an examination of the ideas of the Absolute and the Infinite,—ideas which are indispensable to the foundation of a metaphysical Theology, and of which a clear and distinct consciousness must be acquired, if such a Theology is to exist at all. I attempted to shew the inadequacy of these ideas for such a purpose, by reason of the contradictions which to our apprehension they necessarily involve from every point of view. The result of that attempt may be briefly summed up as follows. We are compelled, by the constitution of our minds, to believe in the existence of an Absolute and Infinite Being,—a belief which appears forced upon us, as the complement of our consciousness of the relative and the finite. But the instant we attempt to analyse the ideas thus suggested to us, in the hope of attaining to a positive conception of the object denoted by them, we are on every side involved in inextricable confusion and contradiction. It is no matter from what point of view we commence our examination;—whether with the Theist, we admit the coexistence of the Infinite and the Finite, as distinct realities; or, with the Pantheist, deny the real existence of the Finite; or, with the Atheist, deny the real existence of the Infinite;—on each of these suppositions alike, our reason appears divided against itself, compelled to admit the truth of one hypothesis, and yet unable to overcome the apparent impossibilities of each. The philosophy of Rationalism, thus traced upwards to its highest principles, finds no legitimate resting-place, from which to commence its deduction of religious consequences.

In the present Lecture it will be my endeavour to offer some explanation of the singular phenomenon of human thought which is exhibited in these results. I propose to examine the same ideas of the Absolute and the Infinite from the opposite side, in order to see if any light can be thrown on the anomalies which they present to us, by a reference to the mental laws under which they are formed. Contradiction, whatever may be its ultimate import, is in itself not a quality of things, but a mode in which they are viewed by the mind; and the inquiry which it most immediately suggests is, not an investigation of the nature of things in themselves, but an examination of those mental conditions under which it is elicited in thought. Such an examination, if it does not enable us to extend the sphere of thought beyond a certain point, may at least serve to make us more distinctly conscious of its true boundaries.

The much-disputed question, to what class of mental phenomena the religious consciousness belongs, must be postponed to a later stage of our inquiry. At present we are concerned with a more general investigation, which the answer to that question will in nowise affect. Whether the relation of man to God be primarily presented to the human mind in the form of knowledge, or of feeling, or of practical impulse, it can be given only as a mode of consciousness, subject to those conditions under which alone consciousness is possible. Whatever knowledge is imparted, whatever impulse is communicated, whatever feeling is excited, in man's mind, must take place in a manner adapted to the constitution of its human recipient, and must exhibit such characteristics as the laws of that constitution impose upon it.. A brief examination of the conditions of human consciousness in general will thus form a proper preliminary to any inquiry concerning the religious consciousness in particular.

Now, in the first place, the very conception of Consciousness, in whatever mode it may be manifested, necessarily implies *distinction between one object and another.* To be conscious, we must be conscious of something; and that something can only be known as that which it is, by being distinguished from that which it is not (1). But distinction is necessarily limitation; for, if one object is to be distinguished from another, it must possess some form of existence which the other has not, or it must not possess some form which the other has. But it is obvious that the Infinite cannot be distinguished, as such, from the Finite, by the absence of any quality which the Finite possesses; for such absence would be a limitation. Nor yet can it be distinguished by the presence of an attribute which the Finite has not; for, as no finite part can be a constituent of an infinite whole, this differential characteristic must itself be infinite; and must at the same time have nothing in common with the finite. We are thus thrown back upon our former impossibility; for this second infinite will be distinguished from the finite by the absence of qualities which the latter possesses. A consciousness of the Infinite as such thus necessarily involves a self contradiction; for it implies the recognition, by limitation and difference, of that which can only be given as unlimited and indifferent (2).

That man can be conscious of the Infinite, is thus a supposition which, in the very terms in which it is expressed, annihilates itself. Consciousness is essentially a limitation; for it is the determination of the mind to one actual out of many possible modifications. But the Infinite, if it is to be conceived at all, must be conceived as potentially everything and actually nothing; for if there is anything in general which it cannot become, it is thereby limited; and if there is anything in particular which it actually is, it is thereby excluded from being any other thing. But again, it must also be conceived as actually everything and potentially nothing; for an unrealized potentiality is likewise a limitation (3). If the infinite can be that which it is not, it is by that very possibility marked out as incomplete, and capable of a higher perfection. If it is actually everything, it possesses no characteristic feature, by which it can be distinguished from anything else, and discerned as an object of consciousness.*

* The former assumption, which makes the absolute-infinite potentially everything and actually nothing, is, in fact, made in the philosophy of Hegel, which commences with the notion of pure being which is pure nothing, and proceeds to deduce from thence the process of becoming and all definite existence. The latter assumption, which regards the absolute-infinite as actually everything and potentially nothing, is virtually made by all those philosophers, including some orthodox theologians, as well as pantheists, who endeavour to attain to a positive conception of God as the *ens realissimum*, or sum of all true existence. See notes 17, 21, to Lecture II., and note 3 to the present Lecture. The purport of the above argument is to shew that these two contradictory conceptions spring from a violation of the laws of human thought, and that a positive conception of the absolute-infinite cannot, under those laws, be attained as a starting-point from which to deduce relative and derived existence. We must *believe that* the absolute and infinite and the relative and finite both exist; but we cannot *conceive how* they coexist, nor how the former gives existence to the latter.

This contradiction, which is utterly inexplicable on the supposition that the infinite is a positive object of human thought, is at once accounted for, when it is regarded as the mere negation of thought. If all thought is limitation;—if whatever we conceive is, by the very act of conception, regarded as finite,—*the infinite*, from a human point of view, implies with regard to its object the absence of those conditions under which thought is possible. To speak of a *Conception of the Infinite* is, therefore, at once to affirm those conditions and to deny them. The contradiction, which we discover in such a conception, is only that which we have ourselves placed there, by tacitly assuming the conceivability of the inconceivable. The condition of consciousness is distinction; and the condition of distinction is limitation. We can have no consciousness of Being in general which is not some Being in particular: a *thing*, in consciousness, is one thing out of many. In assuming the possibility of an infinite object of consciousness, I assume, therefore, that it is at the same time limited and unlimited;—actually something, without which it could not be an object of consciousness, and actually nothing, without which it could not be infinite (4).

Rationalism is thus only consistent with itself, when it refuses to attribute consciousness to God. Consciousness, in the only form in which we can conceive it, implies limitation and change,—the perception of one object out of many, and a comparison of that object with others. To be always conscious of the same object, is, humanly speaking, not to be conscious at all (5); and, beyond its human manifestation, we can have no conception of what consciousness is. Viewed on the side of the object of consciousness, the same principle will carry us further still. Existence itself, that so-called highest category of thought, is only conceivable in the form of existence modified in some particular manner. Strip off its modification, and the apparent paradox of the German philosopher becomes literally true;—pure being is pure nothing (6). We have no conception of existence which is not existence in some particular manner; and if we abstract from the manner, we have nothing left to constitute the existence. Those who, in their horror of what they call anthropomorphism, or anthropopathy, refuse to represent the Deity under symbols borrowed from the limitations of human consciousness, are bound, in consistency to deny that God exists; for the conception of existence is as human and as limited as any other. The conclusion which Fichte boldly announces, awful as it is, is but the legitimate consequence of his premises. "The moral order of the universe is itself God: we need no other, and we can comprehend no other (7)."

A second characteristic of Consciousness is, that it is only possible in the form of a *relation*. There must be a Subject, or person conscious, and an Object, or thing of which he is conscious. There can be no consciousness without the union of these two factors; and, in that union, each exists only as it is related to the other (8). The subject is a subject, only in so far as it is conscious of an object: the object is an object, only in so far as it is apprehended by a subject: and the destruction of either is the destruction of consciousness itself. It is thus manifest that a consciousness of the Absolute is equally self-contradictory with that of the Infinite. To be conscious of the Absolute as such, we must know that an object, which is given in relation to our consciousness, is identical with one which exists in its own nature, out of all relation to consciousness. But to know this identity, we must be able to compare the two together; and such a comparison is itself a contradiction. We are in fact required to compare that of which we are conscious with that of which we are not conscious; the comparison itself being an act of consciousness, and only possible through the consciousness of both its objects. It is thus manifest that, even if we could be conscious of the absolute, we could not possibly know that it *is* the absolute: and, as we can be conscious of an object as such, only by knowing it to be what it is, this is equivalent to an admission that we cannot be conscious of the absolute at all. As an object of consciousness, everything is necessarily relative; and what a thing may be out of consciousness, no mode of consciousness can tell us.

This contradiction, again, admits of the same explanation as the former. Our whole notion of existence is necessarily relative; for it is existence as conceived by us. But *Existence*, as we conceive it, is but a name for the several ways in which objects are presented to our consciousness,—a general term, embracing a variety of relations. *The Absolute*, on the other hand, is a term expressing no object of thought, but only a denial of the relation by which thought is constituted. To assume absolute existence as an object of thought is thus to suppose a relation existing when the related terms exist no longer. An object of thought exists, as such, in and through its relation to a thinker; while the Absolute, as such, is independent of all relation. The *Conception of the Absolute* thus implies at the same time the presence and the absence of the relation by which thought is constituted; and our various endeavours to represent it are only so many modified forms of the contradiction involved in our original assumption.[b] Here, too, the contradiction

---

[b] This argument is applicable, not merely to the absolute in the highest sense of the term, the Being whose existence is independent of every other being, but also to that secondary sense in which the term *absolute* is sometimes used to denote the nature of any created thing as it is in itself, as distinguished from its

is one which we ourselves have made. It does not imply that the Absolute cannot exist; but it implies, most certainly, that we cannot conceive how it exists (9).

Philosophers who are anxious to avoid this conclusion have sometimes attempted to evade it, by asserting that we may have in consciousness a partial, but not a total, knowledge of the infinite and the absolute (10). But here again the supposition refutes itself. To have a partial knowledge of an object, is to know a part of it, but not the whole. But the part of the infinite which is supposed to be known must be itself either infinite or finite. If it is infinite, it presents the same difficulties as before. If it is finite, the point in question is conceded, and our consciousness is allowed to be limited to finite objects. But in truth it is obvious, on a moment's reflection, that neither the Absolute nor the Infinite can be represented in the form of a whole composed of parts.[c] Not the Absolute; for the existence of a whole is dependent on the existence

---

appearance to human consciousness. In this latter sense, the absolute nature of created things can be *known as such* only by the Creator: they exist as He determines them to exist; and therefore their absolute nature is identical with their nature as known by Him. But when an object exists independently of the intelligence which contemplates it, we can never *know*, though we may *believe*, that its nature *per se* is identical with its nature as contemplated by us. We cannot *know* that the object as contemplated by us is in no way modified by the conditions of our own consciousness (as sensible objects are modified by the conditions of our bodily organization), because we cannot divest ourselves of those conditions, and contemplate the object apart from them. On this point I have remarked at greater length elsewhere. (*Proleg. Logica*, pp. 81-83, 2nd edit.; 73-75, 1st edit.)

[c] "On doutera cependant avec raison, si nous avons une idée d'un Tout infini, ou d'un infini composé de parties; car tout composé ne sauroit être un absolu." Leibnitz, ' *Examen des Principes de Malebranche* (*Opera*, Erdmann, p. 696). An elaborate exposition of the same principle from his own peculiar point of view is given by Schelling, *Vom Ich*, § 9.

of its parts. Not the Infinite; for if any part is infinite, it cannot be distinguished from the whole; and if each part is finite, no number of such parts can constitute the Infinite.

It would be possible, did my limits allow, to pursue the same argument at length through the various special modifications which constitute the subordinate forms of consciousness. But with reference to the present inquiry, it will be sufficient to notice two other conditions, under which all consciousness is necessarily manifested; both of which have a special bearing on the relation of philosophy to theological controversy.

All human consciousness, as being a change in our mental state, is necessarily subject to the law of *Time*, in its two manifestations of *Succession* and *Duration*. Every object, of whose existence we can be in any way conscious, is necessarily apprehended by us as succeeding in time to some former object of consciousness, and as itself occupying a certain portion of time. In the former point of view, it is manifest, from what has been said before, that whatever succeeds something else, and is distinguished from it, is necessarily apprehended as finite; for distinction is itself a limitation. In the latter point of view, it is no less manifest that whatever is conceived as having a continuous existence in time is equally apprehended as finite; for continuous existence is necessarily conceived as divisible into successive moments. One portion has already gone by; another is yet to come; each successive moment is related to something which has preceded, and to something which is to follow: and out of such relations the entire existence is made up. The acts by which such existence is manifested, being continuous in time, have, at any given moment, a further activity still to come: the object so existing must therefore always be regarded as capable of becoming something which it is not yet actually,

—as having an existence incomplete, and receiving at each instant a further completion. It is manifest, therefore, that if all objects of human thought exist in time, no such object can be regarded as exhibiting or representing the true nature of an Infinite Being.

As a necessary consequence of this limitation, it follows that an act of *Creation*, in the highest sense of the term, —that is to say, an absolutely first link in the chain of phenomena, preceded by no temporal antecedent,—is to human thought inconceivable.[d] To represent in thought the first act of the first cause of all things, I must conceive myself as placed in imagination at the point at which temporal succession commences, and as thus conscious of the relation between a phenomenon in time and a reality out of time. But the consciousness of such a relation implies a consciousness of both the related members; to realize which, the mind must be in and out of time at the same moment. Time, therefore, cannot be regarded as limited; for to conceive a first or last moment of time would be to conceive a consciousness into which time enters, preceded or followed by one from which it is

---

[d] *Inconceivable*, but not therefore *incredible*. This distinction is well stated by F. Ancillon, *Ueber Glauben und Wissen*, pp. 104, 105. "Diese Thathandlung der Freiheit, die man *vor* der bedingten Natur-Nothwendigkeit annimmt, ist die Schöpfung. Man kann weder begreifen noch erklären, wie diese Thathandlung die Nothwendigkeit hervorgebracht hat, noch dadurch die Nothwendigkeit begreiflich machen. Aber man kann nicht in der Nothwendigkeit seinen Stütz- und- Ruhe-Punct finden. Sie zwingt uns, eine Thatsache anderer Art anzunehmen. Das Geheimniss der Nothwendigkeit bietet sich nicht allein dar, es nöthigt uns, an ein anderes Geheimniss zu glauben." The whole of the discussion from which these words are taken is an excellent illustration of the distinction, constantly maintained in the present Lectures, between believing *that* a thing is, and conceiving *how* it is. "Das Wie der Schöpfung," says Ancillon, "bleibt freilich immer ein unauflösbares Räthsel."

absent. But, on the other hand, an infinite succession in time is equally inconceivable; for this succession also cannot be bounded by time, and therefore can only be apprehended by one who is himself free from the law of conceiving in time. From a human point of view, such a conception could only be formed by thrusting back the boundary for ever;—a process which itself would require an infinite time for its accomplishment (11). Clogged by these counter impossibilities of thought, two opposite speculations have in vain struggled to find articulate utterance, the one for the hypothesis of an endless duration of finite changes, the other for that of an existence prior to duration itself. It is perhaps another aspect of the same difficulty, that, among various theories of the generation of the world, the idea of a creation out of nothing seems to have been altogether foreign to ancient philosophy (12).

The limited character of all existence which can be conceived as having a continuous duration, or as made up of successive moments, is so far manifest, that it has been assumed, almost as an axiom, by philosophical theologians, that in the existence of God there is no distinction between past, present, and future. "In the changes of things," says Augustine, "there is a past and a future: in God there is a present, in which neither past nor future can be" (13). "Eternity," says Boethius, "is the perfect possession of interminable life, and of all that life at once" (14): and Aquinas, accepting the definition, adds, "Eternity has no succession, but exists all together" (15). But whether this assertion be literally true or not (and this we have no means of ascertaining), it is clear that such a mode of existence is altogether inconceivable by us, and that the words in which it is described represent not an object of thought, but one to which the conditions of human thought are inapplicable. It is impossible that man, so long as he exists in time, should contemplate an object in whose existence there is no time. For the thought by which he contemplates it must be one of his own mental states: it must have a beginning and an end: it must occupy a certain portion of duration, as a fact of human consciousness. There is therefore no manner of resemblance or community of nature between the representative thought and that which it is supposed to represent; for the one cannot exist out of time, and the other cannot exist in it (16). Nay, more: even were a mode of representation out of time possible to a man, it is utterly impossible that he should know it to be so, or make any subsequent use of the knowledge thus conveyed to him. To be conscious of a thought as *mine*, I must know it as a present condition of my consciousness: to know that it *has been mine*, I must remember it as a past condition: and past and present are alike modes of time. It is manifest, therefore, that a knowledge of the infinite, as existing out of time, even supposing it to take place at all, cannot be known to be taking place, cannot be remembered to have taken place, and cannot be made available for any purpose at any period of our temporal life (17).

The command, so often urged upon man by philosophers and theologians of various ages and schools, "In contemplating God, transcend time" (18), if meant for anything more than a figure of rhetoric, is equivalent to saying, "Be man no more; be thyself God." It amounts to the admission that, to know the infinite, the human mind must itself be infinite; because an object of consciousness which is in any way limited by the conditions of human thought, cannot be accepted as a representation of the unlimited. But two infinites cannot be conceived as existing together; and if the mind of man must become infinite to know God, it must itself be God (19). Pantheism, or self-acknowledged falsehood, are thus the only alternatives possible under this precept. If the human mind, remaining in reality finite, merely fancies itself to be infinite in its contemplation of God, the knowledge of God is itself based on a falsehood. If, on the other hand, it not merely imagines itself to be, but actually is, infinite, its personality is swallowed up in the infinity of the Deity; its human existence is a delusion: God is, literally and properly, all that exists; and the Finite, which appears to be, but is not, vanishes before the single existence of the One and All.

Subordinate to the general law of Time, to which all consciousness is subject, there are two inferior conditions, to which the two great divisions of consciousness are severally subject. Our knowledge of Body is governed by the condition of *Space;* our knowledge of Mind by that of *Personality.* I can conceive no qualities of body, save as having a definite local position; and I can conceive no qualities of mind, save as modes of a conscious self. With the former of these limitations our present argument is not concerned; but the latter, as the necessary condition of the conception of spiritual existence, must be taken into account in estimating the philosophical value of man's conception of an Infinite Mind.

The various mental attributes which we ascribe to God, Benevolence, Holiness, Justice, Wisdom, for example, can be conceived by us only as existing in a benevolent and holy and just and wise Being, who is not identical with any one of his attributes, but the common subject of them all;—in one word, in a *Person.* But Personality, as we conceive it, is essentially a limitation and a relation (20). Our own personality is presented to us as relative and limited; and it is from that presentation that all our representative notions of personality are derived. Personality is presented to us as a relation between the conscious self and the various modes of his consciousness. There is no personality in abstract thought without a thinker: there is no thinker, unless he exercises some mode of thought. Personality is also a limitation; for the thought and the thinker are distinguished from and limit each other; and the several modes of thought are distinguished each from each by limitation likewise. If I am any one of my own thoughts, I live and die with each successive moment of my consciousness. If I am not any one of my own thoughts, I am limited by that very difference, and each thought, as different from another, is limited also. This too has been clearly seen by philosophical theologians; and, accordingly, they have maintained that in God there is no distinction between the subject of consciousness and its modes, nor between one mode and another. "God," says Augustine, "is not a Spirit as regards substance, and good as regards quality; but both as regards substance. The Justice of God is one with His Goodness and with his Blessedness; and all are one with His Spirituality" (21). But this assertion, if it be literally true (and of this we have no means of judging), annihilates Personality itself in the only form in which we can conceive it. We cannot transcend our own personality, as we cannot transcend our own relation to time: and to speak of an Absolute and Infinite Person, is simply to use language which, however true it may be in a superhuman sense, denotes an object inconceivable under the conditions of human thought.

But are we therefore justified, even on philosophical grounds, in denying the Personality of God? or do we gain a higher or a truer representation of Him by asserting, with the ancient or the modern Pantheist, that God, as absolute and infinite, can have neither intelligence nor will? (22). Far from it. We dishonour God far more by identifying Him with the feeble and negative impotence of thought which we are pleased to style the Infinite, than by remaining content within those limits which He for His own good purposes has imposed upon us, and confining ourselves to a manifestation, imperfect indeed and inadequate, and acknowledged to be so, but still the highest idea that we can form, the noblest tribute that we can offer. Personality, with all its limitations, though far from exhibiting the absolute nature of God as He is, is yet truer, grander, and more elevating, more religious, than those barren, vague, meaningless abstractions in which men babble about nothing under the name of the Infinite. Personal, conscious existence, limited though it be, is yet the noblest of all existences of which man can dream; for it is that by which all existence is revealed to him: it is grander than the grandest object which man can know; for it is that which knows, not that which is known (23). "Man," says Pascal, "is but a reed, the frailest in nature; but he is a reed that thinks. It needs not that the whole universe should arm itself to crush him; —a vapour, a drop of water, will suffice to destroy him. But should the universe crush him, man would yet be nobler than that which destroys him; for he knows that he dies; while of the advantage which the universe has over him, the universe knows nothing" (24). It is by consciousness alone that we know that God exists, or that we are able to offer Him any service. It is only by conceiving Him as a Conscious Being, that we can stand in any religious relation to him at all; that we can form such a representation of Him as is demanded by our spiritual wants, insufficient though it be to satisfy our intellectual curiosity.

It is from the intense consciousness of our own real existence as Persons, that the conception of reality takes its rise in our minds: it is through that consciousness alone that we can raise ourselves to the faintest image of the supreme reality of God. What is reality, and what is appearance, is the riddle which Philosophy has put forth from the birthday of human thought; and the only approach to an answer has been a voice from the depths of the personal consciousness: "I think; therefore I am" (25). In the antithesis between the thinker and the object of his thought,—between myself and that which is related to me,—we find the type and the source of the universal contrast between the one and the many, the permanent and the changeable, the real and the apparent. That which I see, that which I hear, that which I think, that which I feel, changes and passes away with each moment of my varied existence. I, who see, and hear, and think, and feel, am the one continuous self, whose existence gives unity and connection to the whole. Personality comprises all that we know of that which exists: relation to personality comprises all that we know of that which seems to exist. And when, from the little world of man's consciousness and its objects, we would lift up our eyes to the inexhaustible universe beyond, and ask, to whom all this is related, the highest existence is still the highest personality; and the Source of all Being reveals Himself by His name, I AM[e] (26).

If there is one dream of a godless philosophy to which, beyond all others, every moment of our consciousness gives the lie, it is that which subordinates the individual to the universal, the person to the species; which deifies kinds and realizes classifications; which sees Being in generalization, and Appearance in limitation; which regards the living and conscious man as a wave on the ocean of the unconscious infinite; his life, a momentary tossing to and fro on the shifting tide; his destiny, to be swallowed up in the formless and boundless universe (27). The final conclusion of this philosophy, in direct antago-

* Exodus iii. 14.

nism to the voice of consciousness, is "I think; therefore I am not." When men look around them in bewilderment for that which lies within them; when they talk of the enduring species and the perishing individual, and would find, in the abstractions which their own minds have made, a higher and truer existence than in the mind which made them;—they seek for that which they know, and know not that for which they seek (28). They would fain lift up the curtain of their own being, to view the picture which it conceals. Like the painter of old, they know not that the curtain *is* the picture (29).

It is our duty, then, to think of God as personal; and it is our duty to believe that He is infinite. It is true that we cannot reconcile these two representations with each other; as our conception of personality involves attributes apparently contradictory to the notion of infinity. But it does not follow that this contradiction exists anywhere but in our own minds: it does not follow that it implies any impossibility in the absolute nature of God. The apparent contradiction, in this case, as in those previously noticed, is the necessary consequence of an attempt on the part of the human thinker to transcend the boundaries of his own consciousness. It proves that there are limits to man's power of thought; and it proves no more.

The preceding considerations are equally conclusive against both the methods of metaphysical theology described in my last Lecture; that which commences with the divine to reason down to the human, and that which commences with the human to reason up to the divine. For though the mere abstract expression of *the infinite*, when regarded as indicating nothing more than the negation of limitation, and therefore of conceivability, is not contradictory in itself, it becomes so the instant we attempt to apply it in reasoning to any object of thought. A thing —an object—an attribute—a person—or any other term signifying one out of many possible objects of consciousness, is by that very relation necessarily declared to be finite. An infinite thing, or object, or attribute, or person, is therefore in the same moment declared to be both finite and infinite. We cannot, therefore, start from any abstract assumption of the divine infinity, to reason downwards to any object of human thought. And on the other hand, if all human attributes are conceived under the conditions of difference, and relation, and time, and personality, we cannot represent in thought any such attribute magnified to infinity; for this again is to conceive it as finite and infinite at the same time. We can conceive such attributes, at the utmost, only *indefinitely*: that is to say, we may withdraw our thought, for the moment, from the fact of their being limited; but we cannot conceive them as *infinite*: that is to say, we cannot positively think of the absence of the limit; for, the instant we attempt to do so, the antagonistic elements of the conception exclude one another, and annihilate the whole.ᶠ

ᶠ This has been in effect remarked, with regard to ideas of quantity, by Locke, *Essay*, II., 17, 8. "Whatsoever positive ideas we have in our minds of any space, duration, or number, let them be ever so great, they are still finite; but when we suppose an inexhaustible remainder, from which we remove all bounds, and wherein we allow the mind an endless progression of thought, without ever completing the idea, there we have our idea of infinity; which, though it seems to be pretty clear when we consider nothing else in it but the negation of an end, yet, when we would frame in our minds the idea of an infinite space or duration, that idea is very obscure and confused, because it is made up of two parts, very different, if not inconsistent. For let a man frame in his mind an idea of any space or number, as great as he will: it is plain the mind rests and terminates in that idea, which is contrary to the idea of infinity, which consists in a supposed endless progression." This is in effect to say that a quantity (and from quantity Locke supposes our idea of infinity to arise) can be conceived by us as infinite only *potentially*, as capable of *indefinite progression*, not *actually*, as embracing all possible

There remains but one subterfuge to which Philosophy can have recourse, before she is driven to confess that the Absolute and the Infinite are beyond her grasp. If consciousness is against her, she must endeavour to get rid of consciousness itself. And accordingly, the most distinguished representatives of this philosophy in recent times, however widely differing upon other questions, agree in maintaining that the foundation for a knowledge of the infinite must be laid in a point beyond consciousness (30). But a system which starts from this assumption postulates its own failure at the outset. It attempts to prove that consciousness is a delusion; and consciousness itself is made the instrument of proof; for by consciousness its reasonings must be framed and apprehended. It is by reasonings, conducted in conformity to the ordinary laws of thought, that the philosopher attempts to shew that the highest manifestations of reason are above those laws. It is by representations, exhibited under the conditions of time and difference, that the philosopher endeavours to prove the existence, and deliver the results, of an intuition in which time and difference are annihilated. They thus assume, at the same moment, the truth and the falsehood of the normal consciousness; they divide the human mind against itself; and by that division prove no more than that two supposed faculties of thought mutually invalidate each other's evidence. Thus, by an act of reason, philosophy destroys reason itself: it passes at once from rationalism to mysticism, and makes

magnitude of its kind, and therefore as incapable of increase. In the latter sense of the term (as defined above, p. 31, and below, Lecture II. note 15) which is the only sense applicable to Theology. Locke's argument coincides with that in the text, in maintaining an infinite object to be inconceivable. As regards the impossibility of conceiving an actually infinite quantity, Leibnitz coincides with Locke. See his '*Examen des Principes de Malebranche*' (*Opera*, Erdmann, p. 696).

inconceivability the criterion of truth. In dealing with religious truths, the theory which repudiates with scorn the notion of believing a doctrine *although* it is incomprehensible, springs at one desperate bound clear over faith into credulity, and proclaims that its own principles must be believed *because* they are incomprehensible. The rhetorical paradox of the fervid African is adopted in cold blood as an axiom of metaphysical speculation: "It is certain, because it is impossible" (31). Such a theory is open to two fatal objections:—it cannot be communicated, and it cannot be verified. It cannot be communicated; for the communication must be made in words; and the meaning of those words must be understood; and the understanding is a state of the normal consciousness. It cannot be verified; for, to verify, we must compare the author's experience with our own; and such a comparison is again a state of consciousness. Let it be granted for a moment, though the concession refutes itself, that a man may have a cognisance of the infinite by some mode of knowledge which is above consciousness. He can never say that the idea thus acquired is like or unlike that possessed by any other man; for likeness implies comparison; and comparison is only possible as a mode of consciousness, and between objects regarded as limited and related to each other. That which is out of consciousness cannot be pronounced true; for truth is the correspondence between a conscious representation and the object which it represents. Neither can it be pronounced false; for falsehood consists in the disagreement between a similar representation and its object. Here then is the very suicide of Rationalism. To prove its own truth and the falsehood of antagonistic systems, it postulates a condition under which neither truth nor falsehood is possible.

The results to which an examination of the facts of consciousness has conducted us, may be briefly summed up as follows. Our whole consciousness manifests itself as subject to certain limits, which we are unable, in any act of thought, to transgress. That which falls within these limits, as an object of thought, is known to us as *relative* and *finite*. The existence of a limit to our powers of thought is manifested by the consciousness of *an apparent contradiction*, manifesting itself in every direction in which we strive to think, and thus implying at the same time an attempt to pass the limit, and an inability to accomplish that attempt.[g] But a limit is necessarily

[g] The text has been slightly altered, owing to the necessity of distinguishing, more carefully than had been done in former editions, between two different kinds of contradiction, the one apparent, the other real, the one compatible, the other incompatible with a belief in the existence of the corresponding object. Apparent contradictions, such as that noticed in the text, present a feature which distinguishes them from those real contradictions which are incompatible with belief. The latter are one-sided, and necessitate a belief in the opposite direction; the former are two-sided, and appear to press equally in opposite directions, from both of which together we find it impossible to exclude belief. Thus, to take an example of the unilateral kind, I find a contradiction in the conception of a circular square, and I cannot believe in its possible existence; but then, on the other hand, I am compelled to believe that every existing square is not circular. Whereas, to take an example of the bilateral kind, I find a seeming contradiction in the conception of an unlimited duration of time; but I find also a seeming contradiction in the opposite conception of an absolutely first or last moment of time; yet I find it impossible to believe that neither of these can be true, and I find it equally impossible to believe that both can be true. The reason of this distinction is obvious. The former class of contradictions exists between attributes, both of which are within the limits of positive thought, and both of which in other relations are actually conceived as existing in a certain manner in their respective objects. Thus the attributes *square* and *circular* are each conceivable in different relations; we apprehend the manner of their existence in their respective objects, and we apprehend also that the one manner of existence is incompatible with the other. Whereas the attribute of *infinity* has never

conceived as a relation between something within and something without itself; and thus the consciousness of a limit of thought implies, though it does not directly present to us, the existence of something of which we do not and cannot think. When we lift up our eyes to that blue vault of heaven, which is itself but the limit of our own power of sight, we are compelled to suppose, though we cannot perceive, the existence of space beyond, as well as within it; we regard the boundary of vision as parting the visible from the invisible. And when, in mental contemplation, we are conscious of relation and difference, as the limits of our power of thought, we regard them, in like manner, as the boundary between the conceivable and the inconceivable; though we are unable to penetrate, in thought, beyond the nether sphere, to the unrelated and unlimited which it hides from us (32). The *Absolute* and the *Infinite* are thus, like the *Inconceivable* and the *Imperceptible*, names indicating, not a possible object of thought or of consciousness, but one exempt from the conditions under which human consciousness is possible. The attempt to construct in thought an object answering to such names, necessarily results in contradiction;—a contradiction, however, which we have ourselves produced by the attempt to think;—which exists in the act of thought, but not beyond it;—which destroys the con-

been positively conceived as forming part of any complex notion. I am, therefore, compelled to believe that if so conceivable, it must be conceived by a being who is not bound by the same limits of thought and consequent conditions of combination as myself. I can thus believe in the possible conception of an infinite object by a being whose intelligence is superior to mine. To constitute a real contradiction, it is necessary that we should have a distinct conception of both the repugnant members. Where no such conception exists, the object is *above* reason, but is not *opposed* to it: we may be warranted in believing the fact of its existence, though we are unable to conceive the mode.

ception as such, but indicates nothing concerning the existence or non-existence of that which we try to conceive. It proves our own impotence, and it proves nothing more. Or rather, it indirectly leads us to believe in the existence of that Infinite which we cannot conceive; for the denial of its existence involves a contradiction, no less than the assertion of its conceivability.[h] We thus learn that the provinces of Reason and Faith are not coextensive; that it is a duty, enjoined by Reason itself, to believe in that which we are unable to comprehend.

I have now concluded that portion of my argument in which it was necessary to investigate in abstract terms the limits of human thought in general, as a preliminary to the examination of religious thought in particular. As yet we have viewed only the negative side of man's consciousness:—we have seen how it *does not* represent God,

---

[h] This argument might be carried further, according to the principle indicated in the last note. The attribute of *finiteness* is positively known to me, and the manner of its combination with other attributes in an object is known. Whatever, therefore, I am unable to conceive as finite in thought, I am equally unable to believe to be finite in existence. Now an object conceived as finite always implies the possibility of a greater object of the same kind: a finite space or velocity, *e.g.* implies a possible greater space or velocity. If such implication is inconsistent with the idea of a Supreme Being, it follows that the conception of a Deity of finite attributes is equally invalid in thought and in belief. The opposite alternative is thus forced upon us, as necessary in belief, though not comprehensible in thought. This is not a positive conception of the infinite: we know it only negatively as something different from the finite; as we know death only negatively as the opposite of life. But just as we are unable to conceive time as an absolute maximum with no time beyond it, and yet are compelled to believe that there is no conceivable duration, however great, which does not imply a greater; so, though we are unable to conceive God positively as infinite, we are yet compelled to believe that our highest positive conception falls, and must always fall, immeasurably below the reality.

and why it does not so represent Him. There remains still to be attempted the positive side of the same inquiry; namely, what does our consciousness actually tell us concerning the Divine Existence and Attributes; and how does its testimony agree with that furnished by Revelation? In prosecuting this further inquiry, I hope to be able to confine myself to topics more resembling those usually handled in this place, and to language more strictly appropriate to the treatment of Christian Theology. Yet there are advantages in the method which I have hitherto pursued, which may, I trust, be accepted as a sufficient excuse for whatever may have sounded strange and obscure in its phraseology. So long as the doubts and difficulties of philosophical speculation are familiar to us only in their religious aspect and language, so long we may be led to think that there is some peculiar defect or perplexity in the evidences of religion, by which it is placed in apparent antagonism to the more obvious and unquestionable conclusions of reason. A very brief examination of cognate questions in their metaphysical aspect will suffice to dissipate this misapprehension, and to shew that the philosophical difficulties, which rationalists profess to discover in Christian doctrines, are in fact inherent in the laws of human thought, and must accompany every attempt at religious or irreligious speculation.

There is also another consideration which may justify the Christian preacher in examining, at times, the thoughts and language of human philosophy, apart from their special application to religious truths. A religious association may sometimes serve to disguise the real character of a line of thought which, without that association, would have little power to mislead. Speculations which end in unbelief are often commenced in a believing spirit. It is painful, but at the same time instructive, to trace the gradual progress by which an unstable disciple often tears off strip by strip the wedding garment of his faith,—scarce conscious the while of his own increasing nakedness;—and to mark how the language of Christian belief may remain almost untouched, when the substance and the life have departed from it. While Philosophy speaks nothing but the language of Christianity, we may be tempted to think that the two are really one; that our own speculations are but leading us to Christ by another and a more excellent way. Many a young aspirant after a philosophical faith trusts himself to the trackless ocean of rationalism in the spirit of the too confident Apostle: "Lord, bid me come unto thee on the water."[i] And for a while he knows not how deep he sinks; till the treacherous surface on which he treads is yielding on every side, and the dark abyss of utter unbelief is yawning to swallow him up. Well is it indeed with those who, even in that last fearful hour, can yet cry, "Lord, save me," and can feel that supporting hand stretched out to grasp them, and hear that voice, so warning, yet so comforting, "O thou of little faith, wherefore didst thou doubt?"

But who that enters upon his course of mistrust shall dare to say that such will be the end of it? Far better is it to learn at the outset the nature of that unstable surface on which we would tread, without being tempted by the phantom of religious promise which shines delusively over it. He who hath ordered all things in measure and number and weight,[k] has also given to the reason of man, as to his life, its boundaries, which it cannot pass.[l] And if, in the investigation of those boundaries, we have turned for a little while to speak the language of human philosophy, the result will but be to shew that philosophy, rightly understood, teaches one lesson with the sacred volume of Revelation. With that lesson let us conclude,

[i] St. Matthew xiv. 28.　　[k] Wisdom xi. 20.
[l] Job xiv. 5.

as it is given in the words of our own judicious divine and philosopher. "Dangerous it were for the feeble brain of man to wade far into the doings of the Most High; whom although to know be life, and joy to make mention of His name; yet our soundest knowledge is to know that we know Him not as indeed He is, neither can know Him: and our safest eloquence concerning Him is our silence, when we confess without confession that His glory is inexplicable, His greatness above our capacity and reach. He is above, and we upon earth; therefore it behoveth our words to be wary and few" (33).

LECTURE IV.

Psalm LXV. 2.

"O Thou that hearest prayer, unto Thee shall all flesh come."

THAT the Finite cannot comprehend the Infinite, is a truth more frequently admitted in theory than applied in practice. It has been expressly asserted by men who, almost in the same breath, have proceeded to lay down canons of criticism, concerning the purpose of Revelation, and the truth or falsehood, importance or insignificance, of particular doctrines, on grounds which are tenable only on the supposition of a perfect and intimate knowledge of God's Nature and Counsels (1). Hence it becomes necessary to bring down the above truth from general to special statements;—to inquire more particularly wherein the limitation of man's faculties consists, and in what manner it exhibits itself in the products of thought. This task I endeavoured to accomplish in my last Lecture. To pursue the conclusion thus obtained to its legitimate consequences in relation to Theology, we must next inquire how the human mind, thus limited, is able to form the idea of a relation between man and God, and what is the nature of that conception of God which arises from the consciousness of this relation. The purpose of our inquiry is to ascertain the limits of religious thought; and for this purpose it is necessary to proceed from the limits of thought, and of human consciousness in general, to those particular forms of consciousness which, in thought or in some other mode, especially constitute the essence of Religion.

Reasonings, probable or demonstrative, in proof of the being and attributes of God, have met with a very different reception at different periods. Elevated at one time, by the injudicious zeal of their advocates, to a certainty and importance to which they have no legitimate claim, at another, by an equally extravagant reaction, they have been sacrificed in the mass to some sweeping principle of criticism, or destroyed peacemeal by minute objections in detail. While one school of theologians has endeavoured to raise the whole edifice of the Christian Faith on a basis of metaphysical proof (2); others have either expressly maintained that the understanding has nothing to do with religious belief, or have indirectly attempted to establish the same conclusion by special refutations of the particular reasonings (3).

An examination of the actual state of the human mind, as regards religious ideas, will lead us to a conclusion intermediate between these two extremes. On the one hand, it must be allowed that it is not through reasoning that men obtain the first intimation of their relation to the Deity; and that, had they been left to the guidance of their intellectual faculties alone, it is possible that no such intimation might have taken place; or at best, that it would have been but as one guess, out of many equally plausible and equally natural. Those who lay exclusive stress on the proof of the existence of God from the marks of design in the world, or from the necessity of supposing a first cause of all phenomena, overlook the fact that man learns to pray before he learns to reason,— that he feels within him the consciousness of a Supreme Being, and the instinct of worship, before he can argue from effects to causes, or estimate the traces of wisdom and benevolence scattered through the creation. But on the other hand, arguments which would be insufficient to create the notion of a Supreme Being in a mind previously

LECT. IV.   EXAMINATION OF CURRENT THEORIES.   75

destitute of it, may have great force and value in enlarging or correcting a notion already existing, and in justifying to the reason the unreasoning convictions of the heart. The belief in a God, once given, becomes the nucleus round which subsequent experiences cluster and accumulate; and evidences which would be obscure or ambiguous, if addressed to the reason only, become clear and convincing, when interpreted by the light of the religious consciousness.

We may therefore without hesitation accede to the argument of the great Critic of metaphysics, when he tells us that the speculative reason is unable to prove the existence of a Supreme Being, but can only correct our conception of such a Being, supposing it to be already obtained (4). But at the same time, it is necessary to protest against the pernicious extent to which the reaction against the use of the reason in theology has in too many instances been carried. When the same critic tells us that we cannot legitimately infer, from the order and design visible in the world, the omnipotence and omniscience of its Creator, because a degree of power and wisdom short of the very highest might possibly be sufficient to produce all the effects which we are able to discern (5); or when a later writer, following in the same track, condemns the argument from final causes, because it represents God exclusively in the aspect of an artist (6); or when a third writer, of a different school, tells us that the processes of thought have nothing to do with the soul, the organ of religion (7);—we feel that systems which condemn the use of reasoning in sacred things, may be equally one-sided and extravagant with those which assert its supreme authority. Reasoning must not be condemned for failing to accomplish what no possible mode of human consciousness ever does or can accomplish. If consciousness itself is a limitation; if every mode of consciousness is a determination of the mind in one particular manner out of many possible;—it follows indeed that the infinite is beyond the reach of man's arguments; but only as it is also beyond the reach of his feelings or his volitions. We cannot indeed reason to the existence of an infinite Cause from the presence of finite effects, nor contemplate the infinite in a finite mode of knowledge; but neither can we feel the infinite in the form of a finite affection, nor discern it as the law of a finite action. If our whole consciousness of God is partial and incomplete, composed of various attributes manifested in various relations, why should we condemn the reasoning which represents Him in a single aspect, so long as it neither asserts nor implies that that aspect is the only one in which He can be represented? If man is not a creature composed solely of intellect, or solely of feeling, or solely of will, why should any one element of his nature be excluded from participating in the pervading consciousness of Him in whom we live, and move, and have our being? A religion based solely on the reason may starve on barren abstractions, or bewilder itself with inexplicable contradictions: but a religion which repudiates thought to take refuge in feeling, abandons itself to the wild follies of fanaticism, or the diseased ecstasies of mysticism: while one which acknowledges the practical energies alone, may indeed attain to Stoicism, but will fall far short of Christianity. It is our duty indeed to pray with the spirit; but it is no less our duty to pray with the understanding also.

Taking then, as the basis of our inquiry, the admission that the whole consciousness of man, whether in thought, or in feeling, or in volition, is limited in the manner of its operation and in the objects to which it is related, let us endeavour, with regard to the religious consciousness in particular, to separate from each other the complicated threads which, in their united web, constitute the conviction of man's relation to a Supreme Being. In distinguishing, however, one portion of these as forming the origin of this conviction, and another portion as contributing rather to its further development and direction, I must not be understood to maintain or imply that the former could have existed and been recognised, prior to and independently of the cooperation of the latter. Consciousness, in its earliest discernible form, is only possible as the result of an union of the reflective with the intuitive faculties. A state of mind, to be known at all as existing, must be distinguished from other states; and, to make this distinction, we must think of it, as well as experience it. Without thought as well as sensation, there could be no consciousness of the existence of an external world: without thought as well as emotion and volition, there could be no consciousness of the moral nature of man. Sensation without thought would at most amount to no more than an indefinite sense of uneasiness or momentary irritation, without any power of discerning in what manner we are affected, or of distinguishing our successive affections from each other. To distinguish, for example, in the visible world, any one object from any other, to know the house as a house, or the tree as a tree, we must be able to refer them to distinct notions; and such reference is an act of thought. The same condition holds good of the religious consciousness also. In whatever mental affection we become conscious of our relation to a Supreme Being, we can discern that consciousness, as such, only by reflecting upon it as conceived under its proper notion. Without this, we could not know our religious consciousness to be what it is: and, as the knowledge of a fact of consciousness is identical with its existence, without this, the religious consciousness, as such, could not exist.

But notwithstanding this necessary cooperation of

thought in every manifestation of human consciousness, it is not to the reflective faculties that we must look, if we would discover the origin of religion. For to the exercise of reflection, it is necessary that there should exist an object on which to reflect; and though, in the order of time, the distinct recognition of this object is simultaneous with the act of reflecting upon it; yet, in the order of nature, the latter presupposes the former. Religious thought, if it is to exist at all, can only exist as representative of some fact of religious intuition,—of some individual state of mind, in which is presented, as an immediate fact, that relation of man to God, of which man, by reflection, may become distinctly and definitely conscious.

Two such states may be specified, as dividing between them the rude materials out of which reflection builds up the edifice of Religious Consciousness. These are the *Feeling of Dependence* and the *Conviction of Moral Obligation*. To these two facts of the inner consciousness may be traced, as to their sources, the two great outward acts by which religion in various forms has been manifested among men; *Prayer*, by which they seek to win God's blessing upon the future; and *Expiation*, by which they strive to atone for the offences of the past (8). The Feeling of Dependence is the instinct which urges us to pray. It is the feeling that our existence and welfare are in the hands of a superior Power;—not of an inexorable Fate or immutable Law; but of a Being having at least so far the attributes of Personality, that He can shew favour or severity to those dependent upon Him, and can be regarded by them with the feelings of hope, and fear, and reverence, and gratitude. It is a feeling similar in kind, though higher in degree, to that which is awakened in the mind of the child towards his parent, who is first manifested to his mind as the giver of such things as are needful, and to whom the first language he addresses is that of entreaty. It is the feeling so fully and intensely expressed in the language of the Psalmist: "Thou art He that took me out of my mother's womb: thou wast my hope, when I hanged yet upon my mother's breasts. I have been left unto thee ever since I was born: thou art my God even from my mother's womb. Be not thou far from me, O Lord: thou art my succour, haste thee to help me. I will declare thy Name unto my brethren: in the midst of the congregation will I praise thee."[a] With the first development of consciousness, there grows up, as a part of it, the innate feeling that our life, natural and spiritual, is not in our power to sustain or to prolong;—that there is One above us on whom we are dependent, whose existence we learn, and whose presence we realize, by the sure instinct of Prayer. We have thus, in the Sense of Dependence, the foundation of one great element of Religion,—the Fear of God.

But the mere consciousness of dependence does not of itself exhibit the character of the Being on whom we depend. It is as consistent with superstition as with religion;—with the belief in a malevolent, as in a benevolent Deity: it is as much called into existence by the severities, as by the mercies of God; by the suffering which we are unable to avert, as by the benefits which we did not ourselves procure (9). The Being on whom we depend is, in that single relation, manifested in the infliction of pain, as well as in the bestowal of happiness. But in order to make suffering, as well as enjoyment, contribute to the religious education of man, it is necessary that he should be conscious, not merely of *suffering*, but of *sin;*—that he should look upon pain not merely as *inflicted*, but as *deserved;* and should recognise in its Author the justice that punishes, not

[a] Psalm xxii. 9, 10, 19, 22.

merely the anger that harms. In the feeling of dependence, we are conscious of the Power of God, but not necessarily of His Goodness. This deficiency, however, is supplied by the other element of religion,—the Consciousness of Moral Obligation,—carrying with it, as it necessarily does, the Conviction of Sin. It is impossible to establish, as a great modern philosopher has attempted to do, the theory of an absolute Autonomy of the Will; that is to say, of an obligatory law, resting on no basis but that of its own imperative character (10). Considered solely in itself, with no relation to any higher authority, the consciousness of a law of obligation is a fact of our mental constitution, and it is no more. The fiction of an absolute law, binding on all rational beings, has only an apparent universality; because we can only conceive other rational beings by identifying their constitution with our own, and making human reason the measure and representative of reason in general. Why then has one part of our constitution, merely as such, an imperative authority over the remainder? What right has one portion of the human consciousness to represent itself as *duty*, and another merely as *inclination?* There is but one answer possible. The Moral Reason, or Will, or Conscience of Man, call it by what name we please, can have no authority, save as implanted in him by some higher Spiritual Being, as a *Law* emanating from a *Lawgiver*. Man can be a law unto himself, only on the supposition that he reflects in himself the Law of God;—that he shews, as the Apostle tells us, the works of that law written in his heart.[b] If he is absolutely a law unto himself, his duty and his pleasure are undistinguishable from each other; for he is subject to no one, and accountable to no one. Duty in this case becomes only a higher kind of pleasure,—a balance between the present and the future, between the larger and the smaller

[b] Romans ii. 15.

gratification. We are thus compelled, by the consciousness of moral obligation, to assume the existence of a moral Deity, and to regard the absolute standard of right and wrong as constituted by the nature of that Deity (11). The conception of this standard, in the human mind, may indeed be faint and fluctuating, and must be imperfect: it may vary with the intellectual and moral culture of the nation or the individual: and in its highest human representation, it must fall far short of the reality. But it is present to all mankind, as a basis of moral obligation and an inducement to moral progress; it is present in the universal consciousness of sin; in the conviction that we are offenders against God; in the expiatory rites by which, whether inspired by some natural instinct, or inherited from some primeval tradition, divers nations have, in their various modes, striven to atone for their transgressions, and to satisfy the wrath of their righteous Judge (12). However erroneously the particular acts of religious service may have been understood by men; yet, in the universal consciousness of innocence and guilt, of duty and disobedience, of an appeased and offended God, there is exhibited the instinctive confession of all mankind, that the moral nature of man, as subject to a law of obligation, reflects and represents, in some degree, the moral nature of a Deity by whom that obligation is imposed.

But these two elements of the religious consciousness, however real and efficient within their own limits, are subject to the same restrictions which we have before noticed as binding upon consciousness in general. Neither in the feeling of dependence, nor in that of obligation, can we be directly conscious of the Absolute or the Infinite, as such. And it is the more necessary to notice this limitation, inasmuch as an opposite theory has been maintained by one whose writings have had perhaps more influence than those of any other man, in forming the modern religious philosophy of his own country; and whose views, in all their essential features, have been ably maintained and widely diffused among ourselves. According to Schleiermacher, the essence of Religion is to be found in a feeling of absolute and entire dependence, in which the mutual action and reaction of subject and object upon each other, which constitutes the ordinary consciousness of mankind, gives way to a sense of utter, passive helplessness,—to a consciousness that our entire personal agency is annihilated in the presence of the infinite energy of the Godhead. In our intercourse with the world, he tells us, whether in relation to nature or to human society, the feeling of freedom and that of dependence are always present in mutual operation upon each other; sometimes in equilibrium; sometimes with a vast preponderance of the one or the other feeling; but never to the entire exclusion of either. But in our communion with God there is always an accompanying consciousness that the whole activity is absolutely and entirely dependent upon Him; that, whatever amount of freedom may be apparent in the individual moments of life, these are but detached and isolated portions of a passively dependent whole (13). The theory is carried still further, and expressed in more positive terms, by an English disciple, who says that, "Although man, while in the midst of finite objects, always feels himself to a certain extent independent and free; yet in the presence of that which is self-existent, infinite, and eternal, he may feel the sense of freedom utterly pass away and become absorbed in the sense of absolute dependence." "Let the relation," he continues, "of subject and object in the economy of our emotions become such that the whole independent energy of the former merges in the latter as its prime cause and present sustainer; let the subject become as nothing,—not, indeed, from its intrinsic insignificance or incapacity of moral action, but by virtue of the infinity of the object to which it stands consciously opposed: and the feeling of dependence *must* become *absolute;* for all finite power is as *nothing* in relation to the Infinite" (14).

Of this theory it may be observed, in the first place, that it contemplates God chiefly in the character of an *object of infinite magnitude.* The relations of the object to the subject, in our consciousness of the world, and in that of God, differ from each other in degree rather than in kind. The Deity is manifested with no attribute of personality: He is merely the world magnified to infinity: and the feeling of absolute dependence is in fact that of the annihilation of our personal existence in the Infinite Being of the Universe. Of this feeling, the intellectual exponent is pure Pantheism; and the infinite object is but the indefinite abstraction of Being in general, with no distinguishing characteristic to constitute a Deity. For the distinctness of an object of consciousness is in the inverse ratio to the intensity of the passive affection. As the feeling of dependence becomes more powerful, the knowledge of the character of the object on which we depend must necessarily become less and less; for the discernment of any object as such is a state of mental energy and reaction of thought upon that object. Hence the feeling of absolute dependence, supposing it possible, could convey no consciousness of God as God, but merely an indefinite impression of dependence upon something. Towards an object so vague and meaningless no real religious relation is possible (15).

In the second place, the consciousness of an absolute dependence, in which our activity is annihilated, is a contradiction in terms; for consciousness itself is an activity. We can be conscious of a state of mind as such, only by attending to it; and attention is in all cases a mode of our active energy. Thus the state of absolute dependence, supposing it to exist at all, could not be distinguished from other states; and, as all consciousness is distinction, it could not, by any mode of consciousness, be known to exist.

In the third place, the theory is inconsistent with the duty of Prayer. Prayer is essentially a state in which man is in active relation towards God; in which he is intensely conscious of his personal existence and its wants; in which he endeavours by entreaty to prevail with God. Let any one consider for a moment the strong energy of the language of the Apostle: "Now I beseech you, brethren, for the Lord Jesus Christ's sake and for the love of the Spirit, that ye strive together with me in your prayers to God for me;"[c] or the consciousness of a personal need, which pervades that Psalm in which David so emphatically declares his dependence upon God: "My God, my God, look upon me; why hast thou forsaken me, and art so far from my health, and from the words of my complaint? O my God, I cry in the day-time, but thou hearest not; and in the night season also I take no rest:"[d]—let him ponder the words of our Lord Himself: "Shall not God avenge his own elect, which cry day and night unto him?"[e] —and then let him say if such language is compatible with the theory which asserts that man's personality is annihilated in his communion with God (16).

But, lastly, there is another fatal objection to the above theory. It makes our moral and religious consciousness subversive of each other, and reduces us to the dilemma, that either our faith or our practice must be founded on a delusion. The actual relation of man to God is the same, in whatever degree man may be conscious of it. If man's dependence on God is not really destructive of his personal freedom, the religious consciousness, in denying that

[c] Romans xv. 30.   [d] Psalm xxii. 1, 2.
[e] St. Luke xviii. 7.

freedom, is a false consciousness. If, on the contrary, man is in reality passively dependent upon God, the consciousness of moral responsibility, which bears witness to his free agency, is a lying witness. Actually, in the sight of God, we are either totally dependent, or, partially at least, free. And as this condition must be always the same, whether we are conscious of it or not, it follows, that, in proportion as one of these modes of consciousness reveals to us the truth, the other must be regarded as testifying to a falsehood (17).

Nor yet is it possible to find in the consciousness of moral obligation any immediate apprehension of the Absolute and Infinite. For the free agency of man, which in the feeling of dependence is always present as a subordinate element, becomes here the centre and turning-point of the whole. The consciousness of the Infinite is necessarily excluded; first, by the mere existence of a relation between two distinct agents; and, secondly, by the conditions under which each must necessarily be conceived in its relation to the other. The moral consciousness of man, as subject to law, is, by that subjection, both limited and related; and hence it cannot in itself be regarded as a representation of the Infinite. Nor yet can such a representation be furnished by the other term of the relation,—that of the Moral Lawgiver, by whom human obligation is enacted. For, in the first place, such a Lawgiver must be conceived as a Person; and the only human conception of Personality is that of limitation. In the second place, the moral consciousness of such a Lawgiver can only be conceived under the form of a variety of attributes; and different attributes are, by that very diversity, conceived as finite. Nay, the very conception of a moral nature is in itself the conception of a limit; for morality is the compliance with a law; and a law, whether imposed from within or from without, can only be conceived to operate by limiting the range of possible actions.

Yet along with all this, though our positive religious consciousness is of the finite only, there yet runs through the whole of that consciousness the accompanying conviction that the Infinite does exist, and must exist,—though of the manner of that existence we can form no conception; and that it exists along with the Finite,—though we know not how such a coexistence is possible. We cannot be conscious of the Infinite; but we can be and are conscious of the limits of our own powers of thought; and therefore we know that the possibility or impossibility of conception is no test of the possibility or impossibility of existence. We know that, unless we admit the existence of the Infinite, the existence of the Finite is inexplicable and self-contradictory; and yet we know that the conception of the Infinite itself appears to involve contradictions no less inexplicable. In this impotence of Reason, we are compelled to take refuge in Faith, and to believe that an Infinite Being exists, though we know not how; and that He is the same with that Being who is made known in consciousness as our Sustainer and our Lawgiver. For to deny that an Infinite Being exists, because we cannot comprehend the manner of His existence, is, of two equally inconceivable alternatives, to accept the one which renders that very inconceivability itself inexplicable. If the Finite is the universe of existence, there is no reason why that universe itself should not be as conceivable as the several parts of which it is composed. Whence comes it then, that our whole consciousness is compassed about with restrictions, which we are ever striving to pass, and ever failing in the effort? Whence comes it that the Finite cannot measure the Finite? The very consciousness of our own limitations of thought bears witness to the existence of the Unlimited, who is beyond thought.

The shadow of the Infinite still broods over the consciousness of the finite; and we wake up at last from the dream of absolute wisdom, to confess, "Surely the Lord is in this place; and I knew it not."

We are thus compelled to acquiesce in at least one portion of Bacon's statement concerning the relation of human knowledge to its object: "Natura percutit intellectum radio directo; Deus autem, propter medium inæquale (creaturas scilicet), radio refracto" (18). To have sufficient grounds for believing in God is a very different thing from having sufficient grounds for reasoning about Him. The religious sentiment, which compels men to believe in and worship a Supreme Being, is an evidence of His existence, but not an exhibition of His nature. It proves *that* God is, and makes known some of His relations to us; but it does not prove *what* God is in His own Absolute Being (19). The natural senses, it may be, are diverted and coloured by the medium through which they pass to reach the intellect, and present to us, not things in themselves, but things as they appear to us. And this is manifestly the case with the religious consciousness; which can only represent the Infinite God under finite forms. But we are compelled to believe, on the evidence of our senses, that a material world exists, even while we listen to the arguments of the idealist, who reduces it to an idea or a nonentity; and we are compelled, by our religious consciousness, to believe in the existence of a personal God; though the reasonings of the Rationalist, logically followed out, may reduce us to Pantheism or Atheism. But to preserve this belief uninjured, we must acknowledge the true limits of our being: we must not claim for any fact of human consciousness the proud prerogative of revealing God as He is; for thus we throw away the only weapon which can be of avail in resisting the assaults of Scepticism. We must be content to admit, with regard to the internal consciousness of man, the same restrictions which the great philosopher just now quoted has so excellently expressed with reference to the external senses. "For as all works do show forth the power and skill of the workman, and not his image; so it is of the works of God, which do show the omnipotency and wisdom of the maker, but not his image...... Wherefore by the contemplation of nature to induce and inforce the acknowledgment of God, and to demonstrate His power, is an excellent argument;...... but on the other side, out of the contemplation of nature, or ground of human knowledge, to induce any verity or persuasion concerning the points of faith, is in my judgment not safe...... For the heathens themselves conclude as much in that excellent and divine fable of the golden chain: That men and gods were not able to draw Jupiter down to the earth; but contrariwise, Jupiter was able to draw them up to heaven" (20).

One feature deserves especial notice, as common to both of those modes of consciousness which primarily exhibit our relation towards God. In both we are compelled to regard ourselves as *Persons related to a Person*. In the feeling of dependence, however great it may be, the consciousness of *myself*, the dependent element, remains unextinguished; and, indeed, without that element there could be no consciousness of a relation at all. In the sense of moral obligation, I know *myself* as the agent on whom the law is binding: I am free to choose and to act, as a person whose principle of action is in himself. And it is important to observe that it is only through this consciousness of personality that we have any ground of belief in the existence of a God. If we admit the arguments by which this personality is annihilated, whether on the side of Materialism or on that of Pantheism, we cannot escape from the consequence to which those arguments inevitably lead,—the annihilation of God Himself. If, on the one hand, the spiritual element within me is merely dependent on the corporeal;—if *myself* is a result of my bodily organization, and may be resolved into the operation of a system of material agents,—why should I suppose it to be otherwise in the great world beyond me? If I, who deem myself a spirit distinct from and superior to matter, am but the accident and the product of that which I seem to rule, why may not all other spiritual existence, if such there be, be dependent upon the constitution of the material universe? (21). Or if, on the other hand, I am not a distinct substance, but a mode of the infinite,—a shadow passing over the face of the universe,—what is that universe which you would have me acknowledge as God? It is, says the Pantheist, the One and All (22). By no means: it is the Many, in which is neither All nor One. You have taught me that within the little world of my own consciousness there is no relation between the one and the many; but that all is transient and accidental alike. If I accept your conclusion, I must extend it to its legitimate consequence. Why should the universe itself contain a principle of unity? why should the Many imply the One? All that I see, all that I know, are isolated and unconnected phenomena; I myself being one of them. Why should the Universe of Being be otherwise? It cannot be All; for its phenomena are infinite and innumerable; and *all* implies unity and completeness. It need not be One; for you have yourself shewn me that I am deceived in the only ground which I have for believing that a plurality of modes implies an unity of substance. If there is no Person to pray; if there is no Person to be obedient;—what remains but to conclude that He to whom prayer and obedience are due,—nay, even the mock-king who usurps his name in the realms of philosophy,—is a shadow and a delusion likewise?

The result of the preceding considerations may be summed up as follows. There are two modes in which we may endeavour to contemplate the Deity: the one negative, based on a vain attempt to transcend the conditions of human thought, and to expand the religious consciousness to the infinity of its Divine Object: the other positive, which keeps within its proper limits, and views the object in a manner accommodated to the finite capacities of the human thinker. The first aspires to behold God in His absolute nature: the second is content to view Him in those relations in which he has been pleased to manifest Himself to his creatures. The first aims at a *speculative* knowledge of God as He is; but, bound by the conditions of finite thought, even in the attempt to transgress them, obtains nothing more than a tissue of ambitious self-contradictions, which indicate only what He is not (23). The second, abandoning the speculative knowledge of the infinite, as only possible to the Infinite Intelligence itself, is content with those *regulative* ideas of the Deity, which are sufficient to guide our practice, but not to satisfy our intellect (24);—which tell us, not what God is in Himself, but how He wills that we should think of Him (25). In renouncing all knowledge of the Absolute, it renounces at the same time all attempts to construct à *priori* schemes of God's Providence as it ought to be: it does not seek to reconcile this or that phenomenon, whether in nature or in revelation, with the absolute attributes of Deity; but confines itself to the actual course of that Providence, as manifested in the world; and seeks no higher internal criterion of the truth of a religion, than may be derived from its analogy to other parts of the Divine Government. Guided by this, the only true Philosophy of Religion, man is content to practise where he is unable to speculate. He acts, as one who must give an account of his conduct: he prays, believing that his prayer will be answered. He does not seek to reconcile this belief with any theory of the Infinite;

for he does not even know how the Infinite and the Finite can exist together. But he feels that his several duties rest upon the same basis: he knows that, if human action is not incompatible with Infinite Power, neither is human supplication with Infinite Wisdom and Goodness: though it is not as the Infinite that God reveals Himself in His moral government; nor is it as the Infinite that He promises to answer prayer.

"O Thou that hearest prayer, unto Thee shall all flesh come." Sacrifice, and offering, and burnt-offerings, and offering for sin, Thou requirest no more; for He whom these prefigured has offered Himself as a sacrifice once for all.ᶠ But He who fulfilled the sacrifice commanded the prayer, and Himself taught us how to pray. He tells us that we are dependent upon God for our daily bread, for forgiveness of sins, for deliverance from evil;—and how is that dependence manifested? Not in the annihilation of our personality; for we appeal to Him under the tenderest of personal relations, as the children of Our Father who is in heaven. Not as passive in contemplation, but as active in service; for we pray, "Thy will be done, as in heaven, so in earth." In this manifestation of God to man, alike in Consciousness as in Scripture, under finite forms to finite minds, as a Person to a Person, we see the root and foundation of that religious service, without which belief is a speculation, and worship a delusion; which, whatever would-be philosophical theologians may say to the contrary, is the common bond which unites all men to God. All are God's creatures, bound alike to reverence and obey their Maker. All are God's dependents, bound alike to ask for His sustaining bounties. All are God's rebels, needing daily and hourly to implore His forgiveness for their disobedience. All are God's redeemed, purchased by

ᶠ Hebrews x. 8, 10.

the blood of Christ, invited to share in the benefits of His passion and intercession. All are brought by one common channel into communion with that God to whom they are related by so many common ties. All are called upon to acknowledge their Maker, their Governor, their Sustainer, their Redeemer; and the means of their acknowledgment is Prayer.

And, apart from the fact of its having been God's good pleasure so to reveal Himself, there are manifest, even to human understanding, wise reasons why this course should have been adopted, benevolent ends to be answered by this gracious condescension. We are not called upon to live two distinct lives in this world. It is not required of us that the household of our nature should be divided against itself; that those feelings of love, and reverence, and gratitude, which move us in a lower degree towards our human relatives and friends, should be altogether thrown aside, and exchanged for some abnormal state of ecstatic contemplation, when we bring our prayers and praises and thanks before the footstool of our Father in heaven. We are none of us able to grasp in speculation the nature of the Infinite and Eternal; but we all live and move among our fellow men, at times needing their assistance, at times soliciting their favour, at times seeking to turn away their anger. We have all, as children, felt the need of the supporting care of parents and guardians: we have all, in the gradual progress of education, required instruction from the wisdom of teachers: we have all offended against our neighbours, and known the blessing of forgiveness, or the penalty of unappeased anger. We can all, therefore, taught by the inmost consciousness of our human feelings, place ourselves in communion with God, when He manifests Himself under human images. "He that loveth not his brother whom he hath seen," says the Apostle St. John, "how can he love God whom he hath not seen?"[g] Our heavenly affections must in some measure take their source and their form from our earthly ones: our love towards God, if it is to be love at all, must not be wholly unlike our love towards our neighbour; the motives and influences which prompt us, when we make known our wants and pour forth our supplications to an earthly parent, are graciously permitted by our heavenly Father to be the type and symbol of those by which our intercourse with Him is to be regulated,—with which He bids us "come boldly unto the throne of grace, that we may obtain mercy, and find grace to help in time of need."[h]

So should it be during this transitory life, in which we see through a glass, darkly;[i] in which God reveals Himself in types and shadows, under human images and attributes, to meet graciously and deal tenderly with the human sympathies of His creatures. And, although even to the sons of God, it doth not yet appear what we shall be, when we shall be like Him, and shall see Him as He is;[k] yet, if it be true that our religious duties in this life are a training and preparation for that which is to come;—if we are encouraged to look forward to and anticipate that future state, while we are still encompassed with this earthly tabernacle;—if we are taught to look, as to our great Example, to One who in love and sympathy towards His brethren was Very Man;—if we are bidden not to sorrow without hope concerning them which are asleep,[l] and are comforted by the promise that the ties of love which are broken on earth shall be united in heaven,—we may trust that not wholly alien to such feelings will be our communion with God face to face, when the redeemed

[g] 1 St. John iv. 20.   [h] Hebrews iv. 16.   [i] 1 Corinthians xiii. 12.
[k] 1 St. John iii. 2.   [l] 1 Thessalonians iv. 13.

of all flesh shall approach once more to Him that heareth prayer;—no longer in the chamber of private devotion; no longer in the temple of public worship; but in that great City where no temple is; "for the Lord God Almighty and the Lamb are the temple of it." ᵐ

ᵐ Revelation xxi. 22.

LECTURE V.

1 CORINTHIANS I. 21-24.

"FOR AFTER THAT IN THE WISDOM OF GOD THE WORLD BY WISDOM KNEW NOT GOD, IT PLEASED GOD BY THE FOOLISHNESS OF PREACHING TO SAVE THEM THAT BELIEVE. FOR THE JEWS REQUIRE A SIGN, AND THE GREEKS SEEK AFTER WISDOM: BUT WE PREACH CHRIST CRUCIFIED, UNTO THE JEWS A STUMBLING-BLOCK, AND UNTO THE GREEKS FOOLISHNESS; BUT UNTO THEM WHICH ARE CALLED, BOTH JEWS AND GREEKS, CHRIST THE POWER OF GOD, AND THE WISDOM OF GOD."

"THOUGH it were admitted," says Bishop Butler, "that this opinion of Necessity were speculatively true; yet, with regard to practice, it is as if it were false, so far as our experience reaches; that is, to the whole of our present life. For the constitution of the present world, and the condition in which we are actually placed, is as if we were free. And it may perhaps justly be concluded that, since the whole process of action, through every step of it, suspense, deliberation, inclining one way, determining, and at last doing as we determine, is as if we were free, therefore we are so. But the thing here insisted upon is, that, under the present natural government of the world, we find we are treated and dealt with as if we were free, prior to all consideration whether we are or not" (1).

That this observation has in any degree settled the speculative difficulties involved in the problem of Liberty and Necessity, will not be maintained by any one who is acquainted with the history of the controversy. Nor was it intended by its author to do so. But, like many other pregnant sentences of that great thinker, it introduces a principle capable of a much wider application than to the inquiry which originally suggested it. The vexed question of Liberty and Necessity, whose counter-arguments have become a by-word for endless and unprofitable wrangling, is but one of a large class of problems, some of which meet us at every turn of our daily life and conduct, whenever we attempt to justify in theory that which we are compelled to carry out in practice. Such problems arise inevitably, whenever we attempt to pass from the sensible to the intelligible world, from the sphere of action to that of thought, from that which appears to us to that which is in itself. In religion, in morals, in our daily business, in the care of our lives, in the exercise of our senses, the rules which guide our practice cannot be reduced to principles which satisfy our reason (2).

The very first Law of Thought, and, through Thought, of all Consciousness, by which alone we are able to discern objects as such, or to distinguish them one from another, involves in its constitution a mystery and a doubt, which no effort of Philosophy has been able to penetrate:—How can the One be many, or the Many one? (3). We are compelled to regard ourselves and our fellow men as *persons*, and the visible world around us as made up of *things*: but what is *personality*, and what is *reality*, are questions which the wisest have tried to answer, and have tried in vain. Man, as a Person, is one, yet composed of many elements;—not identical with any one of them, nor yet with the aggregate of them all; and yet not separable from them by any effort of abstraction. Man is one in his thoughts, in his actions, in his feelings, and in the responsibilities which these involve. It is I who think, I who act, I who feel; yet I am not thought, nor action, nor feeling, nor a combination of thoughts and actions and feelings heaped together. Extension, and resistance, and shape, and the various sensible qualities, make up my conception of each individual body as such; yet *the body* is not its extension, nor its shape, nor its hardness, nor its colour, nor its smell, nor its taste; nor yet is it a mere aggregate of all these with no principle of unity among them. If these several parts constitute a single whole, the unity, as well as the plurality, must depend upon some principle which that whole contains: if they do not constitute a whole, the difficulty is removed but a single step; for the same question,—what constitutes individuality?—must be asked in relation to each separate part. The actual conception of every object, as such, involves the combination of the One and the Many; and that combination is practically made every time we think at all. But at the same time no effort of reason is able to explain how such a relation is possible; or to satisfy the intellectual doubt which necessarily arises on the contemplation of it.

As it is with the first law of Thought, so it is with the first principle of Action and of Feeling. All action, whether free or constrained, and all passion, implies and rests upon another great mystery of Philosophy,—the Commerce between Mind and Matter. The properties and operations of matter are known only by the external senses; the faculties and acts of the mind are known only by the internal apprehension. The energy of the one is motion: the energy of the other is consciousness. What is the middle term which unites these two? and how can their reciprocal action, unquestionable as it is in fact, be conceived as possible in theory? (4). How can a contact between body and body produce consciousness in the immaterial soul? How can a mental self-determination produce the motion of material organs? (5). How can mind, which is neither extended nor figured nor coloured in itself, represent by its ideas the extension and figure and colour of bodies? How can the body be determined to a new position in space by an act of thought, to which space has to relation? How can thought itself be carried on by bodily instruments, and yet itself have nothing in common with bodily affections? What is the relation between the last pulsation of the material brain and the first awakening of the mental perception? How does the spoken word, a merely material vibration of the atmosphere, become echoed, as it were, in the silent voice of thought, and take its part in an operation wholly spiritual? Here again we acknowledge, in our daily practice, a fact which we are unable to represent in theory; and the various hypotheses to which Philosophy has had recourse,—the Divine Assistance, the Preestablished Harmony, the Plastic Medium, and others (6), are but so many confessions of the existence of the mystery, and of the extraordinary, yet wholly insufficient efforts made by human reason to penetrate it (7).

The very perception of our senses is subject to the same restrictions. "No priestly dogmas," says Hume, "ever shocked common sense more than the infinite divisibility of extension, with its consequences" (8). He should have added, that the antagonist assumption of a finite divisibility is equally incomprehensible; it being as impossible to conceive an ultimate unit, or least possible extension, as it is to conceive the process of division carried on to infinity. Extension is presented to the mind as a relation between parts exterior to each other, whose reality cannot consist merely in their juxtaposition. We are thus compelled to believe that extension itself is dependent upon some higher law;—that it is not an original principle of things in themselves, but a derived result of their connection with each other. But to conceive how this generation of space is possible,—how unextended objects can by their conjunction produce extension,—baffles the utmost efforts of the wildest imagination or the profoundest reflection (9). We cannot conceive how unextended matter can become extended; for of unextended matter we know nothing, either in itself or in its relations; though we are apparently compelled to postulate its existence, as implied in the appearances of which alone we are conscious. The existence of mental succession in time is as inexplicable as that of material extension in space;—a first moment and an infinite regress of moments being both equally inconceivable, no less than the corresponding theories of a first atom and an infinite division.

The difficulty which meets us in these problems may help to throw some light on the purposes for which human thought is designed, and the limits within which it may be legitimately exercised. The primary fact of consciousness, which is accepted as regulating our practice, is in itself *inexplicable*, but not *inconceivable*. There is *mystery;* but there is not yet *contradiction*. Thought is baffled, and unable to pursue the track of investigation; but it does not grapple with an idea and destroy itself in the struggle. Contradiction does not begin till we direct our thoughts, not to the fact itself, but to that which it suggests as beyond itself. This difference is precisely that which exists between following the laws of thought, and striving to transcend them;—between leaving the mystery of Knowing and Being unsolved, and making unlawful attempts to solve it. The facts,—that all objects of thought are conceived as wholes composed of parts;—that mind acts upon matter, and matter upon mind;—that bodies are extended in space, and thoughts successive in time;—do not, in their own statement, severally contain elements repulsive of each other. As mere facts, they are so far from being inconceivable, that they embody the very laws of conception itself, and are experienced at every moment as true: but though we are able, nay, compelled, to conceive them as *facts*, we find it impossible to conceive them as *ultimate facts*. They are made known to us as *relations;* and all relations are in themselves complex, and imply simpler principles;—objects to be related, and a ground by which the relation is constituted. The conception of any such relation as a fact thus involves a further inquiry concerning its existence as a consequence; and to this inquiry no satisfactory answer can be given. Thus the highest principles of thought and action, to which we can attain, are *regulative*, not *speculative*:—they do not serve to satisfy the reason, but to guide the conduct: they do not tell us what things are in themselves, but how we must conduct ourselves in relation to them.

The conclusion which this condition of human consciousness almost irresistibly forces upon us, is one which equally exhibits the strength and the weakness of the human intellect. We are compelled to admit that the mind, in its contemplation of objects, is not the mere passive recipient of the things presented to it; but has an activity and a law of its own, by virtue of which it reacts upon the materials existing without, and moulds them into that form in which consciousness is capable of apprehending them. The existence of modes of thought, which we are compelled to accept as at the same time relatively ultimate and absolutely derived,—as limits beyond which we cannot penetrate, yet which themselves proclaim that there is a further truth behind and above them,—suggests, as its obvious explanation, the hypothesis of a mind cramped by its own laws, and bewildered in the contemplation of its own forms. If the mind, in the act of consciousness, were merely blank and inert;—if the entire object of its contemplation came from without, and nothing from within;—no fact of consciousness would be inexplicable; for everything would present itself as it is. No reality would be suggested, beyond what is actually given: no question would be asked which is not already answered. For how can doubt arise, where there is no innate power in the mind to think beyond what is placed before it,—to react upon that which acts upon it? But upon the contrary supposition, all is regular, and the result such as might naturally be expected. If thought has laws of its own, it cannot by its own act go beyond them; yet the recognition of law, as a restraint, implies the existence of a sphere of liberty beyond. If the mind contributes its own element to the objects of consciousness, it must, in its first recognition of those objects, necessarily regard them as something complex, something generated partly from without and partly from within. Yet in that very recognition of the complex, as such, is implied an impossibility of attaining to the simple; for to resolve the composition is to destroy the very act of knowledge, and the relation by which consciousness is constituted. The object of which we are conscious is thus, to adopt the well-known language of the Kantian philosophy, a *phenomenon*, not a *thing in itself*;— a product, resulting from the twofold action of the thing apprehended, on the one side, and the faculties apprehending it, on the other. The perceiving subject alone, and the perceived object alone, are two unmeaning elements, which first acquire a significance in and by the act of their conjunction (10).

It is thus strictly in analogy with the method of God's Providence in the constitution of man's mental faculties, if we believe that, in Religion also, He has given us truths which are designed to be regulative, rather than speculative; intended, not to satisfy our reason, but to guide our practice; not to tell us what God is in His absolute nature, but how He wills that we should think of Him in our present finite state (11). In my last Lecture I endeavoured to shew that our knowledge of God is not a consciousness of the Infinite as such, but that of the relation of a Person to a Person ;—the conception of personality being, humanly speaking, one of *limitation*. This amounts to the admission that, in natural religion at least, our knowledge of God does not satisfy the conditions of speculative philosophy, and is incapable of reduction to an ultimate and absolute truth. And this, as we now see, is in accordance with the analogy which the character of human philosophy in other provinces would naturally lead us to expect (12). It is reasonable also that we should expect to find, as part of the same analogy, that the revealed manifestation of the Divine nature and attributes should likewise carry on its face the marks of subordination to some higher truth, of which it indicates the existence, but does not make known the substance. It is to be expected that our apprehension of the revealed Deity should involve mysteries inscrutable and doubts insoluble by our present faculties; while, at the same time, it inculcates the true spirit in which such doubts should be dealt with; by warning us, as plainly as such a warning is possible, that we see a part only, and not the whole; that we behold effects only, and not causes; that our knowledge of God, though revealed by Himself, is revealed in relation to human faculties, and subject to the limitations and imperfections inseparable from the constitution of the human mind (13). We may neglect this warning if we please: we may endeavour to supply the imperfection and thereby make it more imperfect still: we may twist and torture the divine image on the rack of human philosophy, and call its mangled relics by the high-sounding titles of the Absolute and the Infinite; but these ambitious conceptions, the instant we attempt to employ them in any act of thought, manifest at once, by their inherent absurdities, that they are not that which they pretend to be;—that, in the place of the Absolute and Infinite manifested in its own nature, we have merely the Relative and Finite contradicting itself.

We may indeed believe, and ought to believe, that the knowledge which our Creator has permitted us to attain to, whether by Revelation or by our natural faculties, is not given to us as an instrument of deception. We may believe, and ought to believe, that, intellectually as well as morally, our present life is a state of discipline and preparation for another; and that the conceptions which we are compelled to adopt, as the guides of our thoughts and actions now, may indeed, in the sight of a higher Intelligence, be but partial truth, but cannot be total falsehood. But in thus believing, we desert the evidence of Reason, to rest on that of Faith; and of the principles on which Reason itself depends, it is obviously impossible to have any other guarantee. But such a Faith, however well founded, has itself only a regulative and practical, not a speculative and theoretical application. It bids us rest content within the limits which have been assigned to us; but it cannot enable us to overleap those limits, nor exalt to a more absolute character the conclusions obtained by finite thinkers under the conditions of finite thought. But on the other hand, we must beware of the opposite extreme,—that of mistaking the inability to affirm for the ability to deny. We cannot say that our conception of the Divine Nature exactly resembles that Nature in its absolute existence; for we know not what that absolute existence is. But, for the same reason, we are equally unable to say that it does not resemble; for, if we know not the Absolute and Infinite at all, we cannot say how far it is or is not capable of likeness or unlikeness to the Relative and Finite. We must remain content with the belief that we have that knowledge of God which is best adapted to our wants and training. How far that knowledge represents God as He is, we know not, and we have no need to know.

The testimony of Scripture, like that of our natural faculties, is plain and intelligible, when we are content to accept it as a fact intended for our practical guidance: it becomes incomprehensible, only when we attempt to explain it as a theory capable of speculative analysis. We are distinctly told that there is a mutual relation between God and man, as distinct agents;—that God influences man by His grace, visits him with rewards or punishments, regards him with love or anger;—that man, within his own limited sphere, is likewise capable of "prevailing with God;"ª that his prayers may obtain an answer, his conduct call down God's favour or condemnation. There is nothing self-contradictory or even unintelligible in this, if we are content to believe *that* it is so, without striving to understand *how* it is so. But the instant we attempt to analyse the ideas of God as infinite and man as finite;— to resolve the scriptural statements into the higher principles on which their possibility apparently depends;—we are surrounded on every side by contradictions of our own raising; and, unable to comprehend how the Infinite and the Finite can exist in mutual relation, we are tempted to deny the fact of that relation altogether, and to seek a refuge, though it be but insecure and momentary, in Pantheism, which denies the existence of the Finite, or in Atheism, which rejects the Infinite. And here, again, the parallel between Religion and Philosophy holds good: the same limits of thought are discernible in relation to both. The mutual intercourse of mind and matter has been explained away by rival theories of Idealism on the one side and Materialism on the other. The unity and plurality, which are combined in every object of thought, have been assailed, on this side by the Eleatic, who maintains that all things are one, and variety a delusion (14); on that side by the Sceptic, who tells us that there is no unity, but merely a mixture of differences; that nothing is, but all things are ever becoming; that mind and body, as substances, are mere philosophical fictions, invented for the support of isolated impressions and ideas (15). The

ª Genesis xxxii. 28.

mystery of Necessity and Liberty has its philosophical as well as its theological aspect: and a parallel may be found to both in the counter-labyrinth of Continuity in Space, whose mazes are sufficiently bewildering to shew that the perception of our bodily senses, however certain as a fact, reposes, in its ultimate analysis, upon a mystery no less insoluble than that which envelopes the free agency of man in its relation to the Divine Omniscience (16).

Action, and not knowledge, is man's destiny and duty in this life; and his highest principles, both in philosophy and in religion, have reference to this end. But it does not follow, on that account, that our representations are untrue, because they are imperfect. To assert that a representation is *untrue*, because it is relative to the mind of the receiver, is to overlook the fact that truth itself is nothing more than a relation. Truth and falsehood are not properties of things in themselves, but of our conceptions, and are tested, not by the comparison of conceptions with things in themselves, but with things as they are given in some other relation. My conception of an object of sense is *true*, when it corresponds to the characteristics of the object as I perceive it; but the perception itself is equally a relation, and equally implies the cooperation of human faculties. Truth in relation to no intelligence is a contradiction in terms: our highest conception of absolute truth is that of truth in relation to all intelligences. But of the consciousness of intelligences different from our own we have no knowledge, and can make no application. Truth, therefore, in relation to man, admits of no other test than the harmonious consent of all human faculties; and, as no such faculty can take cognisance of the Absolute, it follows that correspondence with the Absolute can never be required as a test of truth (17). The utmost deficiency that can be charged against human faculties amounts only to this;—that we cannot say that we know

God as God knows Himself (18) :—that the truth of which our finite minds are susceptible may, for aught we know, be but the passing shadow of some higher reality, which exists only in the Infinite Intelligence.

That the true conception of the Divine Nature, so far as we are able to receive it, is to be found in those regulative representations which exhibit God under limitations accommodated to the constitution of man; not in the unmeaning abstractions which, aiming at a higher knowledge, distort, rather than exhibit, the Absolute and the Infinite; is thus a conclusion warranted, both deductively, from the recognition of the limits of human thought, and inductively, by what we can gather from experience and analogy concerning God's general dealings with mankind. There remains yet a third indispensable probation, to which the same conclusion must be subjected; namely, how far does it agree with the teaching of Holy Scripture?

In no respect is the Theology of the Bible, as contrasted with the mythologies of human invention, more remarkable than in the manner in which it recognises and adapts itself to that complex and self-limiting constitution of the human mind, which man's wisdom finds so difficult to acknowledge. To human reason, the personal and the infinite stand out in apparently irreconcilable antagonism; and the recognition of the one in a religious system almost inevitably involves the sacrifice of the other. The Personality of God disappears in the Pantheism of India; His Infinity is lost sight of in the Polytheism of Greece (19). In the Hebrew Scriptures, on the contrary, throughout all their variety of Books and Authors, one method of Divine teaching is constantly manifested, appealing alike to the intellect and to the feelings of man. From first to last we hear the echo of that first great Commandment: "Hear, O Israel: The Lord our God is one Lord: and thou shalt love the Lord thy God with all thine heart, and with all thy soul, and with all thy might."[b] God is plainly and uncompromisingly proclaimed as the One and the Absolute: "I am the first, and I am the last; and beside me there is no God:"[c] yet this sublime conception is never for an instant so exhibited as to furnish food for that mystical contemplation to which the Oriental mind is naturally so prone. On the contrary, in all that relates to the feelings and duties by which religion is practically to be regulated, we cannot help observing how the Almighty, in communicating with His people, condescends to place Himself on what may, humanly speaking, be called a lower level than that on which the natural reason of man would be inclined to exhibit Him. While His Personality is never suffered to sink to a merely human representation;—while it is clearly announced that His thoughts are not our thoughts, nor His ways our ways,[d] yet His Infinity is never for a moment so manifested as to destroy or weaken the vivid reality of those human attributes under which He appeals to the human sympathies of His creatures. "The Lord spake unto Moses face to face, as a man speaketh unto his friend."[e] He will listen to our supplications:[f] He will help those that cry unto Him:[g] He reserveth wrath for His enemies:[h] He is appeased by repentance:[i] He sheweth mercy to them that love Him.[k] As a King, He listens to the petitions of His subjects:[l] as a Father, He pitieth His own children.[m] It is impossible to contemplate this marvellous union of the human and the divine, so perfectly adapted to the wants of the human

---

[b] Deuteronomy vi. 4, 5. St. Mark xii. 29, 30.
[c] Isaiah xliv. 6.
[d] Isaiah lv. 8.
[e] Exodus xxxiii. 11.
[f] Psalm cxlii. 1, 2.
[g] Psalm cii. 17, 18; cxlv. 19. Isaiah lviii. 9.
[h] Nahum i. 2.
[i] 1 Kings xxi. 19. Jeremiah xviii. 8. Ezekiel xviii. 23, 30. Jonah iii. 10.
[k] Exodus xx. 6.
[l] Psalm v. 2; lxxiv. 12. Isaiah xxxiii. 22.
[m] Psalm ciii. 13.

servant of a divine Master, without feeling that it is indeed the work of Him who formed the spirit of man, and fitted him for the service of his Maker. "He sheweth His word unto Jacob, His statutes and ordinances unto Israel. He hath not dealt so with any nation; neither have the heathen knowledge of His laws."[a]

---

[a] Psalm cxlvii. 19, 20. The following excellent remarks from a recent work may be quoted in illustration and confirmation of the above statement. "Throughout the Scriptures the FIRST TRUTH in theology is conveyed *in terms of the moral system*; and very rarely in any other terms; nor ever in those of abstract thought. It might have been allowable, forty years ago, on the part of hopeful intellectualists, to imagine that a scientific theology would, at length, be educed, and set forth in propositions of a purely theoretic order. But no one can now entertain this hope who has followed the course of what is called metaphysics, throughout that period, and up to this present time. The result of the earnest endeavours of the choicest minds of Germany, France, and England, is this—to demonstrate the fact that a religious revelation of the INFINITE and ABSOLUTE BEING is not possible in any other mode than that which is employed by the inspired writers—the earlier of them, and the later.

"So much of the knowledge of God as I may be capable of admitting, I therefore look for in my Bible; and I cease to look for it from any other quarter—I mean from any conceivable future achievements of the human mind. The Scriptures, thus accepted, become to me the source of religious truths, or, as we say, doctrines and preceptive principles of all kinds. These principles and doctrines I am compelled to think and speak of *distributively*, or according to an artificial order or method; while yet doing so, I well understand that doctrines and precepts, the several articles of a creed, and the several rules of conduct, are not many items, but one Divine element, diversely uttered, to suit the limitations of reason and the changing occasions of life.

"Thus, *by necessity*, we think of the Divine Attributes, and, in doing so, stumble upon perplexities which, though they are unreal, are not to be evaded. Just at this point a knowledge of abstract science, or intellectual philosophy, may be serviceable; for it may enable me to set myself clear of *each special perplexity*, by finding that it resolves itself into the one master problem of the relation of the finite to the INFINITE. If the problem which

But if this is the lesson taught us by that earlier manifestation in which God is represented under the likeness of human attributes, what may we learn from that later and fuller revelation which tells us of One who is Himself both God and Man? The Father has revealed Himself to mankind under human types and images, that He may appeal more earnestly and effectually to man's consciousness of the human spirit within him. The Son has done more than this: He became for our sakes very Man, made in all things like unto His brethren;[o] the Mediator between God and men,[p] being both God and Man (20). Herein is our justification, if we refuse to aspire beyond those limits of human thought in which He has placed us. Herein is our answer, if any man would spoil us through philosophy and vain deceit.[q] Is it irrational to contemplate God under symbols drawn from the human consciousness? Christ is our pattern: "for in Him dwelleth all the fulness of the Godhead bodily"[r] (21). Is it unphilosophical that our thoughts of God should be subject to the law of time? It was when the fulness of the time was come, that God sent forth his Son[s] (22). Does the philosopher bid us strive to transcend the human, and to annihilate our own personality in the presence of the Infinite? The Apostle tells us to look forward to the time when we shall "all come in the unity of the faith, and of the knowledge of the Son of God, unto a perfect man, unto the measure of the stature of the fulness of

---

stands foremost in philosophic thought were solved, none of the included problems would thenceforward give us any trouble: thus, therefore, I may remove from the roadway of the religious life difficulties which belong to another path, namely, the path of ultimate abstractions."— Taylor's *Logic in Theology*, &c., pp. 301-305.

[o] Hebrews ii. 17.
[p] 1 Timothy ii. 5.
[q] Colossians ii. 8.
[r] Colossians ii. 9.
[s] Galatians iv. 4.

Christ."[t] Does human wisdom seek, by some transcendental form of intuition, to behold God as He is in His infinite nature; repeating in its own manner the request of Philip, "Lord, shew us the Father, and it sufficeth us"? Christ Himself has given the rebuke and the reply: "He that hath seen me hath seen the Father; and how sayest thou then, Shew us the Father?"[u]

The doctrine of a personal Christ, very God and very Man, has indeed been the great stumbling-block in the way of those so-called philosophical theologians who, in their contempt for the historical and temporal, would throw aside the vivid revelation of a living and acting God, to take refuge in the empty abstraction of an impersonal idea. And accordingly, they have made various elaborate attempts to substitute in its place a conception more in accordance with the supposed requirements of speculative philosophy. Let us hear on this point, and understand as we best may, the language of the great leader of the chief modern school of philosophical rationalists. "To grasp rightly and definitely in thought," says Hegel, "the nature of God as a Spirit, demands profound speculation. These propositions are first of all contained therein: God is God only in so far as He knows Himself: His own self-knowledge is moreover His self-consciousness in man, and man's knowledge *of* God, which is developed into man's self-knowledge *in* God." ... "The Form of the Absolute Spirit," he continues, "separates itself from the Substance, and in it the different phases of the conception part into separate spheres or elements, in each of which the Absolute Substance exhibits itself, first as an eternal substance, abiding in its manifestation with itself; secondly, as a distinguishing of the eternal Essence from its manifestation, which through this distinction becomes the world of appearance, into

---

[t] Ephesians iv. 13.   [u] St. John xiv. 8, 9.

which the substance of the absolute Spirit enters; thirdly, as an endless return and reconciliation of the world thus projected with the eternal Essence, by which that Essence goes back from appearance into the unity of its fulness" (23). The remainder of the passage carries out this metaphysical caricature of Christian doctrine into further details, bearing on my present argument, but with even additional obscurity;—an obscurity so great, that the effect of a literal translation would be too ludicrous for an occasion like the present. But enough has been quoted to shew that, if rationalizing philosophers have not made much progress, since the days of Job, in the ability to find out the Almighty unto perfection,[x] they have at least not gone backwards in the art of darkening counsel by words without knowledge.[y]

What is the exact meaning of this profound riddle, which the author has repeated in different forms in various parts of his writings (24);—whether he really means to assert or to deny the existence of Christ as a man;—whether he designs to represent the Incarnation and earthly life of the Son of God as a fact, or only as the vulgar representation of a philosophical idea,—is a point which has been stoutly disputed among his disciples, and which possibly the philosopher himself did not wish to see definitely settled (25). But there is another passage, in which he has spoken somewhat more plainly, and which, without being quite decisive, may be quoted as throwing some light on the tendency of his thought. "Christ," says this significant passage, "has been called by the church the God-Man. This monstrous combination[z] is to the understanding a direct contradiction;

---

[x] Job xi. 7.
[y] Job xxxviii. 2.
[z] "Diese ungeheure Zusammensetzung." The translation of *ungeheure* by *monstrous* has been censured; but I believe that it exactly expresses the author's meaning as he himself explains it; namely, "to the understanding a direct contradiction." In the

but the unity of the divine and human nature is in this respect brought into consciousness and certainty in man; in that the Diversity, or, as we may also express it, the Finiteness, Weakness, Frailty of human nature, is not incompatible with this Unity, as in the eternal Idea Diversity in no wise derogates from the Unity which is God. This is the monstrosity whose necessity we have seen. It is therein implied that the divine and human nature are not in themselves different. God in human form. The truth is, that there is but one Reason, one Spirit; that the Spirit as finite has no real existence" (26).

The dark sentences of the master have been, as might naturally be expected, variously developed by his disciples. Let us hear how the same theory is expressed in the language of one who is frequently commended as representing the orthodox theology of this school, and who has striven hard to reconcile the demands of his philosophy with the belief in a personal Christ. Marheineke assures us, that "the possibility of God becoming Man shews in itself that the divine and human nature are in themselves not separate:" that, "as the truth of the human nature is the divine, so the reality of the divine nature is the human" (27). And towards the conclusion of a statement worthy to rank with that of his master for grandiloquent obscurity, he says, "As Spirit, by renouncing Individuality, Man is in truth elevated above himself, without having abandoned the human nature: as Spirit renouncing Absoluteness,

---

same sense, Malebranche (*Entretiens sur la Métaphysique*, Entr. xiv.) says, speaking of the mystery of the Trinity, "Plus cet adorable mystère paraît *monstrueux*, souffrez cette expression des ennemis de la foi, plus il choque la raison humaine," &c., which Norris (*Reason and Faith*, p. 297) translates literally, "The more this adorable mystery appears *monstrous*, &c." The bold language of Hegel, when taken with its context, is not meant to be irreverent; however objectionable may be the philosophical theory with which it is connected.

God has lowered Himself to human nature, without having abandoned his existence as Divine Spirit. The unity of the divine and human nature is but the unity in that Spirit whose existence is the knowledge of the truth, with which the doing of good is identical. This Spirit, as God in the human nature and as Man in the divine nature, is the God-Man. The man wise in divine holiness, and holy in divine wisdom, is the God-Man. As a historical fact," he continues, "this union of God with man is manifest and real in the Person of Jesus Christ: in Him the divine manifestation has become perfectly human. The conception of the God-Man in the historical Person of Jesus Christ, contains in itself two phases in one; first, that God is manifest only through man; and in this relation Christ is as yet placed on an equality with all other men: He is the Son of Man, and therein at first represents only the possibility of God becoming Man: secondly, that in this Man, Jesus Christ, God is manifest, as in none other: this manifest Man is the manifest God; but the manifest God is the Son of God; and in this relation, Christ is God's Son; and this is the actual fufilment of the possibility or promise; it is the reality of God becoming Man" (28).

But this kind of halting between two opinions, which endeavours to combine the historical fact with the philosophical theory, was not of the nature to satisfy the bolder and more logical minds of the same school. In the theory of Strauss we find the direct antagonism between the historical and the philosophical Christ fairly acknowledged; and the former is accordingly set aside entirely, to make way for the latter. And here we have at least the advantage, that the trumpet gives no uncertain sound; —that we are no longer deluded by a phantom of Christian doctrine enveloped in a mist of metaphysical obscurity;

but the two systems stand out sharply and clearly defined, in their utter contrariety to each other. "In an individual, a God-Man," he tells us, "the properties and functions which the church ascribes to Christ contradict themselves; in the idea of the race they perfectly agree. Humanity is the union of the two natures—God become Man, the infinite manifesting itself in the finite, and the finite Spirit remembering its infinitude: it is the child of the visible Mother and the invisible Father, Nature and Spirit: it is the worker of miracles, in so far as in the course of human history the spirit more and more completely subjugates nature, both within and around man, until it lies before him as the inert matter on which he exercises his active power: it is the sinless one, for the course of its development is a blameless one; pollution cleaves to the individual only, but in the race and its history it is taken away. It is Humanity that dies, rises, and ascends to heaven; for from the negation of its natural state there ever proceeds a higher spiritual life; from the suppression of its finite character as a personal, national, and terrestrial Spirit, arises its union with the infinite Spirit of the heavens. By faith in this Christ, especially in his death and resurrection, man is justified before God: that is, by the kindling within him of the idea of Humanity, the individual man participates in the divinely human life of the species. Now the main element of that idea is, that the negation of the merely natural and sensual life, which is itself the negation of the spirit, (the negation of negation, therefore,) is the sole way to true spiritual life" (29).

These be thy gods, O Philosophy: these are the Metaphysics of Salvation (30). This is that knowledge of things divine and human, which we are called upon to substitute for the revealed doctrine of the Incarnation of the eternal Son in the fulness of time. It is for this philosophical idea, so superior to all history and fact,—this necessary process of the unconscious and impersonal Infinite,—that we are to sacrifice that blessed miracle of Divine Love and Mercy, by which the Son of God, of His own free act and will, took man's nature upon Him for man's redemption. It is for this that we are to obliterate from our faith that touching picture of the pure and holy Jesus, to which mankind for eighteen centuries has ever turned, with the devotion of man to God rendered only more heartfelt by the sympathy of love between man and man: which from generation to generation has nurtured the first seeds of religion in the opening mind of childhood, by the image of that Divine Child who was cradled in the manger of Bethlehem, and was subject to His parents at Nazareth: which has checked the fiery temptations of youth, by the thought of Him who "was in all points tempted like as we are, yet without sin:"[a] which has consoled the man struggling with poverty and sorrow, by the pathetic remembrance of Him who on earth had not where to lay His head:[b] which has blended into one brotherhood the rich and the poor, the mighty and the mean among mankind, by the example of Him who, though He was rich, yet for our sakes became poor;[c] though He was equal with God, yet took upon Him the form of a servant:[d] which has given to the highest and purest precepts of morality an additional weight and sanction, by the records of that life in which the marvellous and the familiar are so strangely yet so perfectly united;—that life so natural in its human virtue, so supernatural in its divine power: which has robbed death of its sting, and the grave of its victory, by faith in Him who "was delivered for our offences, and was raised again for our justification:"[e] which has ennobled

---

[a] Hebrews iv. 15. [b] St. Luke ix. 58. [c] 2 Corinthians viii. 9.
[d] Philippians ii. 6, 7. [e] Romans iv. 25.

and sanctified even the wants and weaknesses of our mortal nature, by the memory of Him who was an hungered in the wilderness and athirst upon the cross; who mourned over the destruction of Jerusalem, and wept at the grave of Lazarus.

Let Philosophy say what she will, the fact remains unshaken. It is the consciousness of the deep wants of our human nature that first awakens God's presence in the soul: it is by adapting His Revelation to those wants that God graciously condescends to satisfy them. The time may indeed come, though not in this life, when these various manifestations of God, "at sundry times and in divers manners,"[f] may be seen to be but different sides and partial representations of one and the same Divine Reality;—when the light which now gleams in restless flashes from the ruffled waters of the human soul, will settle into the steadfast image of God's face shining on its unbroken surface. But ere this shall be, that which is perfect must come, and that which is in part must be done away.[g] But as regards the human wisdom which would lead us to this consummation now, there is but one lesson which it can teach us; and *that* it teaches in spite of itself. It teaches the lesson which the wise king of Israel learned from his own experience: "I gave my heart to seek and search out by wisdom concerning all things that are done under heaven: I have seen all the works that are done under the sun: and, behold, all is vanity and vexation of spirit. And I gave my heart to know wisdom, and to know madness and folly: I perceived that this also is vexation of spirit."[h] And if ever the time should come to any of us, when, in the bitter conviction of that vanity and vexation, we, who would be as gods in knowledge, wake up

---

[f] Hebrews i. 1.   [g] 1 Corinthians xiii. 10.
[h] Ecclesiastes i. 13, 14, 17.

only to the consciousness of our own nakedness, happy shall we be, if then we may still hear, ringing in our ears and piercing to our hearts, an echo from that personal life of Jesus which our philosophy has striven in vain to pervert or to destroy: "Lord, to whom shall we go? thou hast the words of eternal life: and we believe and are sure that thou art that Christ, the Son of the living God."[1]

[1] St. John vi. 68, 69.

LECTURE VI.

1 Corinthians II. 11.

"For what man knoweth the things of a man, save the spirit of man which is in him? Even so the things of God knoweth no man, but the Spirit of God."

THE conclusion to be drawn from our previous inquiries is, that the doctrines of Revealed Religion, like all other objects of human thought, have a relation to the constitution of the thinker to whom they are addressed; within which relation their practical application and significance is confined. At the same time, this very relation indicates the existence of a higher form of the same truths, beyond the range of human intelligence, and therefore not capable of representation in any positive mode of thought. Religious ideas, in short, like all other objects of man's consciousness, are composed of two distinct elements,— a Matter, furnished from without, and a Form imposed from within by the laws of the mind itself. The latter element is common to all objects of thought as such: the former is the peculiar and distinguishing feature, by which the doctrines of Revelation are distinguished from other religious representations, derived from natural sources: or by which, in more remote comparison, religious ideas in general may be distinguished from those relating to other objects. Now it is indispensable, before we can rightly estimate the value of the various objections which are adduced against this or that representation of Christian doctrine, to ascertain which of these elements it is, against which the force of the objection really makes itself felt. There may be objections whose force, such as it is, tells against the revealed doctrine alone, and which are harmless when directed against any other mode of religious representation. And there may also be objections which are applicable to the form which revealed religion shares in common with other modes of human thinking, and whose force, if they have any, is in reality directed, not against Revelation in particular, but against all Religion, and indeed against all Philosophy also. Now if, upon examination, it should appear that the principal objections which are raised on the side of Rationalism properly so called,—those, namely, which turn on a supposed incompatibility between the doctrines of Scripture and the deductions of human reason,—are of the latter kind, and not of the former, Christianity is at least so far secure from any apprehension of danger from the side of rational philosophy. For the weapon with which she is assailed exhibits its own weakness in the very act of assailing. If there is error or imperfection in the essential forms of human thought, it must adhere to the thought criticizing, no less than to the thought criticized; and the result admits of but two legitimate alternatives. Either we must abandon ourselves to an absolute Scepticism, which believes nothing and disbelieves nothing, and which thereby destroys itself in believing that nothing is to be believed; or we must confess that reason, in thus criticizing, has transcended its legitimate province; that it has failed, not through its inherent weakness, but through being misdirected in its aim. We must then shift the inquiry to another field, and allow our belief to be determined, not solely by the internal character of the doctrines themselves, as reasonable or unreasonable, but, partly at least, by the evidence which can be produced in favour of their asserted origin as a fact. The reasonable believer, in short, must abstain from pronouncing judgment on the nature of the message, until he has fairly examined the credentials of the messenger.

There are two methods by which such an examination of objections may be conducted. We may commence by an analysis of thought in general, distinguishing the Form, or permanent element, from the Matter, or variable element, and then, by applying the results of that analysis to special instances, we may shew, upon deductive grounds, the formal or material character of this or that class of objections. Or we may reverse the process, commencing by an examination of the objections themselves; and, by exhibiting them in their relation to other doctrines besides those of Revelation, we may arrive at the same conclusion as to their general or special applicability. The former method is perhaps the most searching and complete, but could hardly be adequately carried out within my present limits, nor without the employment of a language more technical than would be suitable on this occasion. In selecting the latter method as the more appropriate, I must request my hearers to bear in mind the general principles which it is proposed to exhibit in one or two special instances. These are, first, that there is no rational difficulty in Christian Theology which has not its corresponding difficulty in human Philosophy; and, secondly, that therefore we may reasonably conclude that the stumbling-blocks which the rationalist professes to find in the doctrines of revealed religion arise, not from defects peculiar to revelation, but from the laws and limits of human thought in general, and are thus inherent in the method of rationalism itself, not in the objects which it pretends to criticize.

But, before applying this method to the peculiar doctrines of the Christian revelation, it will be desirable to say a few words on a preliminary condition, on which our belief in the possibility of any revelation at all is dependent. We must justify, in the first instance, the limitations which have been assigned to human reason in relation to the great foundation of all religious belief whatsoever: we must shew how far the same method warrants the assertion which has been already made on other grounds; namely, that we may and ought to believe in the existence of a God whose nature we are unable to comprehend; that we are bound to believe *that* God exists; and to acknowledge Him as our Sustainer and our Moral Governor: though we are wholly unable to declare *what* He is in His own Absolute Essence (1).

Many philosophical theologians, who are far from rejecting any of the essential doctrines of revelation, are yet unwilling to ground their acceptance of them on the duty of believing in the inconceivable. "The doctrine of the incognizability of the Divine Essence," says the learned and deep-thinking Julius Müller, "with the intention of exalting God to the highest, deprives Him of the realities, without which, as it is itself obliged to confess, we cannot really think of Him. That this negative result, just as decidedly as the assumption of an absolute knowledge of God, contradicts the Holy Scriptures, which especially teach that God becomes revealed in Christ, as it does that of the simple Christian consciousness, may be too easily shewn for it to be requisite that we should here enter upon the same: it is also of itself clear into what a strange position theology must fall by the renunciation of the knowledge of its essential object" (2). As regards the former part of this objection, I endeavoured, in my last Lecture, to shew that a full belief in God, as revealed in Christ, is not incompatible with a speculative inability to apprehend the Divine Essence. As regards the latter part, it is important to observe the exact parallel which in this respect exists between the fundamental conception of Theology and that of Philosophy. The Principle of Causality, the father, as it has been called, of metaphysical science (3), is to the philosopher what the belief in the existence of God is to the theologian. Both are principles inherent in our nature, exhibiting, whatever may be their origin, those characteristics of universality and certainty which mark them as part of the inalienable inheritance of the human mind. Neither can be reduced to a mere logical inference from the facts of a limited and contingent experience. Both are equally indispensable to their respective sciences: without Causation, there can be no Philosophy; as without God there can be no Theology. Yet to this day, while enunciating now, as ever, the fundamental axiom, that for every event there must be *a Cause*, Philosophy has never been able to determine what Causation is; to analyse the elements which the causal nexus involves; or to shew by what law she is justified in assuming the universal postulate upon which all her reasonings depend (4). The Principle of Causality has ever been, and probably ever will be, the battle-ground on which, from generation to generation, Philosophy has struggled for her very existence in the death-gripe of Scepticism; and at every pause in the contest, the answer has been still the same: "We *cannot* explain it, but we *must* believe it." Causation is not the mere invariable association of antecedent and consequent: we feel that it implies something more than this (5). Yet, beyond the little sphere of our own volitions, what more can we discover? and within that sphere, what do we discover that we can explain? (6). The unknown something, call it by what name you will,—power, effort, tendency,—still remains absolutely concealed, yet is still conceived as absolutely indispensable. Of Causality, as of Deity, we may almost say, in the emphatic language of Augustine, "Cujus nulla scientia est in anima, nisi scire quomodo eum nesciat" (7). We can speak out boldly and clearly of each, if we are asked what it is not: we are silent only when we are asked what it is. The eloquent words of the same great father are as applicable to human as to divine Philosophy: "Deus ineffabilis est: facilius dicimus quid non sit, quam quid sit. Terram cogitas; non est hoc Deus: mare cogitas; non est hoc Deus: omnia quæ sunt in terra, homines et animalia; non est hoc Deus; omnia quæ sunt in mari, quæ volant per aerem; non est hoc Deus: quidquid lucet in cœlo, stellæ, sol et luna; non est hoc Deus: ipsum cœlum; non est hoc Deus. Angelos cogita, Virtutes, Potestates, Archangelos, Thronos, Sedes, Dominationes; non est hoc Deus. Et quid est? Hoc solum potui dicere, quid non sit" (8).

From the fundamental doctrine of Religion in general, let us pass on to that of Christianity in particular. "The Catholic Faith is this: that we worship one God in Trinity, and Trinity in Unity." How, asks the objector, can the One be Many, or the Many One? or how is a distinction of Persons compatible with their perfect equality? (9). Is it not a contradiction to say, that we are compelled by the Christian Verity to acknowledge every Person by Himself to be God and Lord; and yet are forbidden by the Catholic Religion to say, There be three Gods, or three Lords? (10).

To exhibit the philosophical value of this objection, we need only make a slight change in the language of the doctrine criticized. Instead of a Plurality of Persons in the Divine Unity, we have only to speak of a Plurality of Attributes in the Divine Essence. How can there be a variety of Attributes, each infinite in its kind, and yet all together constituting but one Infinite? or how, on the other hand, can the Infinite be conceived as existing without diversity at all? We know, indeed, that various attributes exist in man, constituting in their plurality one and the same conscious self. Even here, there is a mystery which we cannot explain; but the fact is one which we are compelled, by the direct testimony of consciousness, to accept without explanation. But in admitting, as we are compelled to do, the coexistence of many attributes in one person, we can conceive those attributes only as distinct from each other, and as limiting each other. Each mental attribute is manifested as a separate and determinate mode of consciousness, marked off and limited by the very fact of its manifestation as such. Each is developed in activities and operations from which the others are excluded. But this type of conscious existence fails us altogether, when we attempt to transfer it to the region of the Infinite. That there can be but one Infinite, appears to be a necessary conclusion of reasoning; for diversity is itself a limitation: yet here we have many Infinites, each distinct from the other, yet all constituting one Infinite, which is neither identical with them nor distinguishable from them. If Reason, thus baffled, falls back on the conception of a simple Infinite Nature, composed of no attributes, her case is still more hopeless. That which has no attributes is nothing conceivable; for things are conceived by their attributes. Strip the Infinite of the Attributes by which it is distinguished as infinite, and the Finite of those by which it is distinguished as finite; and the residue is neither the Infinite as such, nor the Finite as such, nor any one being as distinguished from any other being. It is the vague and empty conception of Being in general, which is no being in particular:—a shape,

> "If Shape it might be called, that shape had none
> Distinguishable in member, joint, or limb,
> Or Substance might be called, that Shadow seemed,
> For each seemed either" (11).

The objection, "How can the One be Many, or the Many One?" is thus so far from telling with peculiar force against the Catholic doctrine of the Holy Trinity, that it has precisely the same power, or want of power, and may be urged with precisely the same effect, or want of effect, against any conception, theological or philosophical, in which we may attempt to represent the Divine Nature and Attributes as infinite, or, indeed, to exhibit the Infinite at all. The same argument applies with equal force to the conception of the Absolute. If the Divine Nature is conceived as being nothing more than the sum of the Divine Attributes, it is not Absolute; for the existence of the whole will be dependent on the existence of its several parts. If, on the other hand, it is something distinct from the Attributes, and capable of existing without them, it becomes, in its absolute essence, an absolute void,—an existence manifested by no characteristic features,—a conception constituted by nothing conceivable (12).

The same principle may be also applied to another portion of this great fundamental truth. The doctrine of the Son of God, begotten of the Father, and yet coeternal with the Father, is in no wise more or less comprehensible by human reason, than the relation between the Divine Essence and its Attributes (13). In the order of Thought, or of Nature, the substance to which attributes belong has a logical priority to the attributes which exist in relation to it. The Attributes are attributes *of a Substance.* The former are conceived as the dependent and derived; the latter as the independent and original existence. Yet in the order of Time (and to the order of Time all human thought is limited) it is as impossible to conceive the Substance existing before its Attributes, as the Attributes before the Substance (14). We cannot conceive a being originally simple, developing itself in the course of time into a complexity of attributes; for absolute simplicity cannot be conceived as containing within itself a principle of development, nor as differently related to different periods of time, so as to commence its development at any particular moment (15). Nor yet can we conceive the attributes as existing prior to the substance; for the very conception of an attribute implies relation to a substance. Yet the third hypothesis, that of their coexistence in all time, is equally incomprehensible; for this is to merge the Absolute and Infinite in an eternal relation and difference. We cannot conceive God as first existing, and then as creating His own attributes; for the creative power must then itself be created. Nor yet can we conceive the Divine Essence as constituted by the eternal coexistence of attributes; for then we have many Infinites, with no bond of unity between them. The mystery of the Many and the One, which has baffled philosophy ever since philosophy began, meets it here, as everywhere, with its eternal riddle. Reason gains nothing by repudiating Revelation; for the mystery of Revelation is the mystery of Reason also.

I should not for an instant dream of adducing this metaphysical parallel as offering the slightest approach to a *proof* of the Christian doctrine of the Trinity in Unity. What it really illustrates is, not God's Nature, but man's ignorance. Without an Absolute Knowing there can be no comprehension of Absolute Being (16). The position of human reason, with regard to the ideas of the Absolute and the Infinite, is such as equally to exclude the Dogmatism which would demonstrate Christian Doctrine from philosophical premises, and the Rationalism which rejects it on the ground of philosophical difficulties; as well as that monstrous combination of both, which distorts it in pretending to systematize it. The Infinite is known to human reason, merely as the negation of the Finite: we know what it is not; and that is all. The conviction, *that* an Infinite Being exists, seems forced upon us by the manifest incompleteness of our finite knowledge; but we have no rational means whatever of determining *what* is the nature of that Being (17). The mind is thus unable to frame for itself any speculative representation of the Divine Essence; and for that very reason, Philosophy is not entitled, on internal evidence, to accept any, or to reject any. The only question which we are reasonably at liberty to ask in this matter, relates to the evidences of the Revelation as a fact. If there is sufficient evidence, on other grounds, to shew that the Scripture, in which this doctrine is contained, is a Revelation from God, the doctrine itself must be unconditionally received, not as reasonable, nor as unreasonable, but as scriptural. If there is not such evidence, the doctrine itself will lack its proper support; but the Reason which rejects it is utterly incompetent to substitute any other representation in its place.

Let us pass on to the second great doctrine of the Catholic Faith,—that which asserts the union of two Natures in the Person of Christ. "The right faith is, that we believe and confess, that our Lord Jesus Christ, the Son of God, is God and Man: God, of the Substance of the Father, begotten before the worlds; and Man, of the Substance of His Mother, born in the world" (18).

Our former parallel was drawn from the impossibility of conceiving, in any form, a relation between the Infinite and the Infinite. Our present parallel may be found in the equal impossibility of conceiving, by the natural reason, a relation between the Infinite and the Finite;—an impossibility equally insurmountable, whether the two natures are conceived as existing in one Being, or in divers. Let us attempt, if we can, to conceive, at any moment of time, a finite world coming into existence by the fiat of an Infinite Creator. Can we conceive that the amount of existence is thereby increased,—that the Infinite and the Finite together contain more reality than formerly existed in the Infinite alone? The supposition annihilates itself; for it represents Infinite Existence as capable of becoming greater still. But, on the other hand, can we have recourse to the opposite alternative, and conceive the Creator as evolving the world out of His own Essence; the amount of Being remaining as before, yet the Infinite and the Finite both existing? This supposition also annihilates itself; for if the Infinite suffers diminution by that portion of it which becomes the Finite, it is infinite no longer; and if it suffers no diminution, the two together are but equal to the Infinite alone, and the Finite is reduced to absolute nonentity (19). In any mode whatever of human thought, the coexistence of the Infinite and the Finite is inconceivable; and yet the non-existence of either is, by the same laws of consciousness, equally inconceivable. If Reason is to be the supreme Judge of Divine Truths, it will not be sufficient to follow its guidance up to a certain point, and to stop when it is inconvenient to proceed further. There is no logical break in the chain of consequences, from Socinianism to Pantheism, and from Pantheism to Atheism, and from Atheism to Pyrrhonism; and Pyrrhonism is but the suicide of Reason itself. "Nature," says Pascal, "confounds the Pyrrhonists, and reason confounds the Dogmatists. What then becomes of man, if he seeks to discover his true condition by his natural reason? He cannot avoid one of these sects, and he cannot subsist in either" (20).

Let religion begin where it will, it must begin with that which is above Reason. What then do we gain by that parsimony of belief, which strives to deal out the Infinite in infinitesimal fragments, and to erect the largest possible superstructure of deduction upon the smallest possible foundation of faith? We gain just this: that we forsake an incomprehensible doctrine, which rests upon the word of God, for one equally incomprehensible which rests upon the word of man. Religion, to be a relation between God and man at all, must rest on a belief in the Infinite, and also on a belief in the Finite; for if we deny the first, there is no God; and if we deny the second, there is no Man. But the coexistence of the Infinite and the Finite, in any manner whatever, is inconceivable by reason; and the only ground that can be taken for accepting one representation of it, rather than another, is that one is revealed, and another is not revealed. We may seek as we will for a "Religion within the limits of the bare Reason;" and we shall not find it; simply because no such thing exists; and if we dream for a moment that it does exist, it is only because we are unable or unwilling to pursue reason to its final consequences. But if we do not, others will; and the system which we have raised on the shifting basis of our arbitrary resting-place, waits only till the wind of controversy blows against it, and the flood of unbelief descends upon it, to manifest itself as the work of the "foolish man which built his house upon the sand."

Having thus endeavoured to exhibit the limits of human reason in relation to those doctrines of Holy Scripture which reveal to us the nature of God, I shall next attempt briefly to apply the same argument to those representations which more directly declare His relation to the world.

The course of Divine Providence, in the government of the world, is represented in Scripture under the twofold aspect of *General Law* and *Special Interposition*. Not only is God the Author of the universe, and of those regular laws by which the periodical recurrence of its natural phenomena is determined;[a] but He is also exhibited as standing in a special relation to mankind; as the direct cause of events by which their temporal or spiritual welfare is affected; as accessible to the prayers

---

[a] Genesis i. 14; viii. 22; Job xxxviii. xxxix.; Psalm xix. 1-6; lxxiv. 17; civ. 5-31; cxxxv. 7; cxlviii. 6.

of His servants; as to be praised for His special mercies towards each of us in particular.[b] But this scriptural representation has been discovered by Philosophy to be irrational. God is unchangeable; and therefore He cannot be moved by man's entreaty. He is infinitely wise and good; and therefore He ought not to deviate from the perfection of His Eternal Counsels. "The religious man," says a writer of the present day, "who believes that all events, mental as well as physical, are preordered and arranged according to the decrees of infinite wisdom, and the philosopher, who knows that, by the wise and eternal laws of the universe, cause and effect are indissolubly chained together, and that one follows the other in inevitable succession,—equally feel that this ordination—this chain—cannot be changeable at the cry of man. . . . . . If the purposes of God were not wise, they would not be formed:—if wise, they cannot be changed, for then they would become unwise. . . . . . The devout philosopher, trained to the investigation of universal system,—the serene astronomer, fresh from the study of the changeless laws which govern innumerable worlds,—shrinks from the monstrous irrationality of asking the great Architect and Governor of all to work a miracle in his behalf—to interfere, for the sake of *his* convenience or *his* plans, with the sublime order conceived by the Ancient of Days in the far Eternity of the Past; for what is a special providence but an interference with established laws? and what is such interference but a miracle?" (21).

Now here, as in the objections previously noticed, the rationalist mistakes a general difficulty of all human thought for a special difficulty of Christian belief. The really insoluble problem is, how to conceive God as acting at all; not how to conceive Him as acting in this way,

[b] Psalm lxv. 2; cii. 17, 18; ciii. 1, 3; cxliii. 1, 2; cxlv. 19.

rather than in that. The creation of the world at *any* period of time;—the establishment, at *any* moment, of immutable laws for the future government of that world; —this is the real mystery which Reason is unable to fathom: this is the representation which seems to contradict our conceptions of the Divine Perfection. To that pretentious perversion of the finite which philosophy dignifies with the name of the Infinite, it is a contradiction to suppose that any change can take place at any moment;— that anything can begin to exist, which was not from all eternity. To conceive the Infinite Creator, at any moment of time, calling into existence a finite world, is, in the human point of view, to suppose an imperfection, either before the act, or after it. It is to suppose the development of a power hitherto unexercised, or the limiting to a determinate act that which was before general and indeterminate.

May we not then repeat our author's objection in another form? How can a Being of Infinite Wisdom and Goodness, without an act of self-deterioration, change the laws which have governed His own solitary existence in the far Eternity when the world was not? Or rather, may we not ask what these very phases of "changeless laws" and "far Eternity" really mean? Do they not represent God's existence as manifested under the conditions of duration and succession,—conditions which necessarily involve the conception of the imperfect and the finite? They have not emancipated the Deity from the law of Time: they have only placed Him in a different relation to it. They have merely substituted, for the revealed representation of the God who from time to time vouchsafes His aid to the needs of His creatures, the rationalizing representation of the God who, throughout all time, steadfastly refuses to do so (22).

If then the condition of Time is inseparable from all

human conceptions of the Divine Nature, what advantage do we gain, even in philosophy, by substituting the supposition of immutable order in time for that of special interposition in time? Both of these representations are doubtless *speculatively* imperfect: both depict the Infinite God under finite symbols. But for the *regulative* purposes of human conduct in this life, each is equally necessary: and who may dare, from the depths of his own ignorance, to say that each may not have its prototype in the ineffable Being of God? (23). We are sometimes told that it gives us a more elevated idea of the Divine Wisdom and Power, to regard the Creator as having finished His work once for all, and then abandoned it to its own unerring laws, than to represent Him as interfering, from time to time, by the way of direct personal superintendence :—just as it implies higher mechanical skill to make an engine which shall go on perpetually by its own motion, than one which requires to be continually regulated by the hand of its maker (24). This ingenious simile fails only in the important particular, that both its terms are utterly unlike the objects which they profess to represent. The world is not a machine; and God is not a mechanic. The world is not a machine; for it consists, not merely of wheels of brass, and springs of steel, and the fixed properties of inanimate matter; but of living and intelligent and free-acting persons, capable of personal relations to a living and intelligent and free-acting Ruler. And God is not a mechanic; for the mechanic is separated from his machine by the whole diameter of being; as mind, giving birth to material results; as the conscious workman, who meets with no reciprocal consciousness in his work. It may be a higher evidence of mechanical skill to abandon brute matter once for all to its own laws; but to take this as the analogy of God's dealings with His living creatures—as well tell us that the highest image of parental love and forethought is that of the ostrich, "which leaveth her eggs in the earth, and warmeth them in dust"[c] (25).

But if such conclusions are not justified by our à priori knowledge of the Divine nature, are they borne out empirically by the actual constitution of the world? Is there any truth in the assertion, so often put forth as an undeniable discovery of modern science, "that cause and effect are indissolubly chained together, and that one follows the other in inevitable succession"? There is just that amount of half-truth which makes an error dangerous; and there is no more. Experience is of two kinds, and Philosophy is of two kinds;—that of the world of matter, and that of the world of mind,—that of physical succession, and that of moral action. In the material world, if it be true that the researches of science *tend towards* (though who can say that they will ever reach?) the establishment of a system of fixed and orderly recurrence; in the mental world, we are no less confronted, at every instant, by the presence of contingency and free will (26). In the one we are conscious of a chain of phenomenal effects: in the other of *self*, as an acting and originating cause. Nay, the very conception of the immutability of the law of cause and effect is not so much derived from the positive evidence of the former, as from the negative evidence of the latter. We believe the succession to be necessary, because nothing but mind can be conceived as interfering with the successions of matter; and, where mind is excluded, we are unable to imagine contingence (27). But what right has this so-called philosophy to build a theory of the universe on material principles alone, and to neglect what experience daily and hourly forces upon our notice,—the perpetual interchange of the relations of matter and mind? In passing from the material to the moral world, we pass at once from the

[c] Job xxxix. 14.

phenomenal to the real; from the successive to the continuous; from the many to the one; from an endless chain of mutual dependence to an originating and self-determining source of power. That mysterious, yet unquestionable presence of *Will*:—that agent, uncompelled, yet not uninfluenced, whose continuous existence and productive energy are summed up in the word *Myself*:—that perpetual struggle of good with evil:—those warnings and promptings of a Spirit, striving with our spirit, commanding, yet not compelling; acting upon us, yet leaving us free to act for ourselves:—that twofold consciousness of infirmity and strength in the hour of temptation:—that grand ideal of what we ought to be, so little, alas! to be gathered from the observation of what we are:—that overwhelming conviction of Sin in the sight of One higher and holier than we:—that irresistible impulse to Prayer, which bids us pour out our sorrows and make our wants known to One who hears and will answer us:—that indefinable yet inextinguishable consciousness of a direct intercourse and communion of man with God, of God's influence upon man, yea, and (with reverence be it spoken) of man's influence upon God:—these are facts of experience, to the full as real and as certain as the laws of planetary motions and chemical affinities;—facts which Philosophy is bound to take into account, or to stand convicted as shallow and one-sided;—facts which can deceive us, only if our whole Consciousness is a liar, and the boasted voice of Reason itself but an echo of the universal lie.

Even within the domain of Physical Science, however much analogy may lead us to conjecture the universal prevalence of law and orderly sequence, it has been acutely remarked that the phenomena which are most immediately important to the life and welfare of man are precisely those which he never has been, and probably never will be, able to reduce to a scientific calculation

(28). The astronomer, who can predict the exact position of a planet in the heavens a thousand years hence, knows not what may be his own state of health to-morrow, nor how the wind which blows upon him will vary from day to day.[d] May we not be permitted to conclude, with a distinguished Christian philosopher of the present day, that there is a Divine Purpose in this arrangement of nature; that while enough is displayed to stimulate the intellectual and practical energies of man, enough is still concealed to make him feel his dependence upon God? (29).

For man's training in this life, the conceptions of General Law and of Special Providence are both equally necessary: the one, that he may labour for God's blessings; and the other, that he may pray for them. He sows, and reaps, and gathers in his produce, to meet the different seasons, as they roll their unchanging course: he acknow-

[d] This argument admits of a further development, in which it may be applied to meet some of the recent objections urged, on supposed scientific grounds against the efficacy of prayer, as employed in times of natural calamity, such as pestilence or famine. The celestial phenomena, recurring at regular intervals, and calculable to a second, are by no means a type of the manner in which the whole course of nature is subject to law. On the contrary, there are other classes of natural phenomena, with respect to which matter is to some extent directly subject to the influence of mind; man being capable, by his own free action, not indeed of changing or suspending the laws of nature, but of producing, in accordance with those laws, a different succession of phenomena from that which would have taken place without his interposition. Franklin sends up his electric kite, and diverts the fluid with which the thunder-cloud is charged to a course different from that which it otherwise would have taken; and the same thing is now done by every man who erects a lightning-conductor. Subject to these influences, the material world must be regarded, not as a rigid system of preordained antecedents and consequents, but as an elastic system, which is undoubtedly capable of being influenced by the will of man, and which may therefore, without violation of any scientific principle, be supposed to be also under the influence of the will of God.

ledges also that "neither is he that planteth anything, neither he that watereth; but God that giveth the increase."ᵉ He labours in the moral training of himself and others, in obedience to the general laws of means and ends, of motives and influences; while he asks, at the same time, for wisdom from above to guide his course aright, and for grace to enable him to follow that guidance. Necessary alike during this our state of trial, it may be that both conceptions alike are but shadows of some higher truth, in which their apparent oppositions are merged in one harmonious whole. But when we attempt, from our limited point of view, to destroy the one, in order to establish the other more surely, we overlook the fact that our conception of General Law is to the full as human as that of Special Interposition;—that we are not really thereby acquiring a truer knowledge of the hidden things of God, but are measuring Him by a standard derived from the limited representations of man (30).

Subordinate to the conception of Special Providence, and subject to the same laws of thought in its application, is that of *Miraculous Agency*. I am not now going to waste an additional argument in answer to that shallowest and crudest of all the assumptions of unbelief, which dictatorially pronounces that Miracles are impossible;—an assumption which is repudiated by the more philosophical among the leaders of Rationalism itself (31); and which implies that he who maintains it has such a perfect and intimate acquaintance with the Divine Nature and Purposes, as to warrant him in asserting that God cannot or will not depart from the ordinary course of His Providence on any occasion whatever. If, as I have endeavoured to shew, the doctrine of Divine Interposition is not in itself more opposed to reason than that of General Law; and if the asserted immutability of the laws of nature is, at the utmost,

ᵉ 1 Corinthians iii. 7.

tenable only on the supposition that material nature alone is spoken of,—we are not warranted, on any ground, whether of deduction from principles or of induction from experience, in denying the possible suspension of the Laws of Matter by the will of the Divine Mind. But the question on which it may still be desirable to say a few words, before concluding this portion of my argument, is one which is disputed, not necessarily between the believer and the unbeliever, but often between believers equally sincere and equally pious, differing only in their modes of representing to their own minds the facts and doctrines which both accept. Granting, that is to say, that variations from the established sequence of physical phenomena may take place, and have taken place, as Scripture bears witness;— are such variations to be represented as departures from or suspensions of natural law; or rather, as themselves the result of some higher law to us unknown, and as miraculous only from the point of view of our present ignorance? (32).

Which of these representations, or whether either of them, is the true one, when such occurrences are considered in their relation to the Absolute Nature of God, our ignorance of that nature forbids us to determine. Speculatively, to human understanding, it appears as little consistent with the nature of the Absolute and Infinite to be subject to universal law, as it is to act at particular moments. But as a regulative truth, adapted to the religious wants of man's constitution, the more natural representation, that of a departure from the general law, seems to be also the more accurate. We are liable, in considering this question, to confound together two distinct notions under the equivocal name of *Law*. The first is a positive notion, derived from the observation of facts, and founded, with various modifications, upon the general idea of the *periodical recurrence of phenomena*. The other is a merely negative notion, deduced from a supposed apprehension of the Divine Nature, and professing to be based on the idea of the eternal Purposes of God. Of the former, the ideas of *succession* and *repetition* form an essential part. To the latter, the idea of Time, in any form, has no legitimate application; and it is thus placed beyond the sphere of human thought. Now, when we speak of a Miracle as the possible result of some higher law, do we employ the term *law* in the former sense, or in the latter? do we mean a law which actually exists in the knowledge of God; or one which, in the progress of science, may come to the knowledge of man?—one which might be discovered by a better acquaintance with the Divine Counsels; or one which might be inferred from a larger experience of natural phenomena? If we mean the former, we do not know that a more perfect acquaintance with the Divine Counsels, implying, as it does, the elevation of our faculties to a superhuman level, might not abolish the conception of Law altogether. If we mean the latter, we assume that which no experience warrants us in assuming; we endanger the religious significance and value of the miracle, only for the sake of removing God a few degrees further back from that chain of phenomena which is admitted ultimately to depend upon Him. A miracle, in one sense, need not be necessarily a violation of the laws of nature. God may make use of natural instruments, acting after their kind; as man himself, within his own sphere, does in the production of artificial combinations. The great question, however, still remains: Has God ever, for religious purposes, exhibited phenomena in certain relations, which the observed course of nature and the artistic skill of man are unable to bring about, or to account for?

I have thus far endeavoured to apply the principle of the Limits of Religious Thought to some of those representations which are usually objected to by the Rationalist, as in apparent opposition to the Speculative Reason of man. In my next Lecture I shall attempt to pursue the same argument in relation to those doctrines which are sometimes regarded as repugnant to man's Moral Reason. The lesson to be derived from our present inquiry may be given in the pregnant sentence of a great philosopher, but recently taken from us: "No difficulty emerges in Theology which had not previously emerged in Philosophy" (33). The intellectual stumbling-blocks which men find in the doctrines of Revelation are not the consequence of any improbability or error peculiar to the things revealed; but are such as the thinker brings with him to the examination of the question;—such as meet him on every side, whether he thinks with or against the testimony of Scripture; being inherent in the constitution and laws of the Human Mind itself. But must we therefore acquiesce in the melancholy conclusion, that self-contradiction is the law of our intellectual being;—that the light of Reason, which is God's gift, no less than Revelation, is a delusive light, which we follow to our own deception? Far from it: the examination of the Limits of Thought leads to a conclusion the very opposite of this. Reason does not deceive us if we will only read her witness aright; and Reason herself gives us warning when we are in danger of reading it wrong. The light that is within us is not darkness; only it cannot illuminate that which is beyond the sphere of its rays. The self-contradictions into which we inevitably fall when we attempt certain courses of speculation, are the beacons placed by the hand of God in the mind of man, to warn us that we are deviating from the track that He designs us to pursue; that we are striving to pass the barriers which He has planted around us. The flaming sword turns every way against those who strive, in the strength of their own reason, to force their passage to the tree of life. Within her own province, and among her own objects, let Reason go forth, conquering and to conquer.

The finite objects, which she can clearly and distinctly conceive, are her lawful empire and her true glory. The countless phenomena of the visible world; the unseen things which lie in the depths of the human soul;—these are given into her hand; and over them she may reign in unquestioned dominion. But when she strives to approach too near to the hidden mysteries of the Infinite;—when, not content with beholding afar off the partial and relative manifestations of God's presence, she would "turn aside and see this great sight," and know why God hath revealed Himself thus;—the voice of the Lord Himself is heard, as it were, speaking in warning from the midst: "Draw not nigh hither: put off thy shoes from off thy feet; for the place whereon thou standest is holy ground."[f]

[f] Exodus iii. 5.

LECTURE VII.

Ezekiel XVIII. 25.

" YET YE SAY, THE WAY OF THE LORD IS NOT EQUAL. HEAR NOW, O HOUSE OF ISRAEL; IS NOT MY WAY EQUAL? ARE NOT YOUR WAYS UNEQUAL?"

"IF I build again the things which I destroyed, I make myself a transgressor."[a] This text might be appropriately prefixed to an examination of that system of moral and religious criticism which, at the close of the last century, succeeded for a time in giving a philosophical connection to the hitherto loose and floating theological rationalism of its age and country (1). It was indeed a marvellous attempt to send forth from the same fountain sweet waters and bitter, to pull down and to build up by the same act and method. The result of the Critical Philosophy, as applied to the speculative side of human Reason, was to prove beyond all question the existence of certain necessary forms and laws of intuition and thought, which impart a corresponding character to all the objects of which Consciousness, intuitive or reflective, can take cognisance. Consciousness was thus exhibited as a Relation between the human mind and its object; and this conclusion, once established, is fatal to the very conception of a Philosophy of the Absolute. But by an inconsistency scarcely to be paralleled in the history of philosophy, the author of this comprehensive criticism attempted to deduce a partial conclusion from universal premises, and to exempt the

[a] Galatians ii. 18.

speculations of moral and religious thought from the relative character with which, upon his own principles, all the products of human consciousness were necessarily invested. The Moral Law, and the ideas which it carries with it, are, according to this theory, not merely facts of human consciousness, conceived under the laws of human thought, but absolute, transcendental realities, implied in the conception of all Reasonable Beings as such, and therefore independent of the law of Time, and binding, not on man as man, but on all possible intelligent beings, created or uncreated (2). The Moral Reason is thus a source of absolute and unchangeable realities; while the Speculative Reason is concerned only with phenomena, or things modified by the constitution of the human mind (3). As a corollary to this theory, it follows that the law of human morality must be regarded as the measure and adequate representative of the moral nature of God;—in fact, that our knowledge of the Divine Being is identical with that of our own moral duties;—for God is made known to us, as existing at all, only in and by the moral reason : we do not look upon actions as binding because they are commanded by God; but we know them to be divine commands because we are bound by them (4). Applying these principles to the criticism of Revealed Religion, the philosopher maintains that no code of laws claiming divine authority can have any religious value, except as approved by the moral reason (5); that there can be no duties of faith or practice towards God, distinct from the moral obligations which reason enjoins (6) ; and that, consequently, every doctrine to which this test is inapplicable is either no part of revelation at all, or at best can only be given for local and temporary purposes, of which the enlightened reason need no longer take any account (7).

Amid much that is true and noble in this teaching when confined within its proper limits, its fundamental weakness as an absolute criterion of religious truth is so manifest as hardly to need exposure. The fiction of a moral law binding in a particular form upon all possible intelligences, acquires this seeming universality, only because human intelligence is made the representative of all. I can conceive moral attributes only as I know them in consciousness: I can imagine other minds only by first assuming their likeness to my own. To construct a theory, whether of practical or of speculative reason, which shall be valid for other than human intelligences, it is necessary that the author should himself be emancipated from the conditions of human thought. Till this is done, the so-called Absolute is but the Relative under another name: the universal consciousness is but the human mind striving to transcend itself.

The very characteristics of Universality and Necessity, with which our moral obligations are invested, point to an origin the very reverse of that which the above theory supposes. For these characteristics are in all cases due to the presence of the formal and personal element in the phenomena of consciousness, and appear most evidently in those conceptions in which the matter as well as the manner of thinking is drawn from the laws or formal conditions of experience. Of these conditions, I have in a former Lecture enumerated three, Time, Space, and Personality: the first as the condition of human consciousness in general; the second and third as the conditions of the same consciousness in relation to the phenomena of matter and of mind respectively (8). From these are derived three corresponding systems of *necessary truths* in the highest human sense of the term: the science of Numbers being connected with the condition of Time; that of Magnitudes with Space; and that of Morals with Personality. These three sciences rest on similar bases, and are confined within the same limits: all being equally necessary and valid within the legitimate bounds of human intelligence; and all equally negative and self-contradictory, when we attempt to pass beyond those bounds. The contradictions involved in the conceptions of Infinite Number and Infinite Magnitude find their parallel when we attempt to conceive the attributes of an Infinite Morality: the necessity which is manifested in the finite relations of the two former is the counterpart of that which accompanies those of the latter (9). That Moral Obligation, conceived as a law binding upon man, must be regarded as immutable so long as man's nature remains unchanged, is manifest from the character of the conception itself, and follows naturally from a knowledge of its origin. An act of Duty is presented to my consciousness as enjoined by a Law whose obligation upon myself is directly and intuitively discerned. It thus differs essentially from the phenomena of external nature, whose laws are not immediately perceived, but inferred from the observed recurrence of facts. The immediate consciousness of Law unavoidably carries with it the conviction of necessity and immutability in relation to the agent who is subject to it. For to suppose that a moral law can be reversed or suspended in relation to *myself*;—to suppose a conviction of *right* unaccompanied by an obligation to act, or a conviction of *wrong* unaccompanied by an obligation to forbear—is to suppose a reversal of the conditions of my personal existence;—a supposition which annihilates itself; since those conditions are implied in the attempt to conceive my personal existence at all. The Moral Sense is thus, like the intuitions of Time and Space, an *à priori* law of the human mind, not determined by experience as it is, but determining beforehand what experience ought to be. But it is not thereby elevated above the conditions of human intelligence; and the attempt so to elevate it is especially inadmissible in that philosophy which resolves Time and

Space into forms of the human consciousness, and limits their operation to the field of the phenomenal and the relative.

That there is an Absolute Morality, based upon, or rather identical with, the Eternal Nature of God, is indeed a conviction forced upon us by the same evidence as that on which we believe that God exists at all. But *what* that Absolute Morality is, we are as unable to fix in any human conception, as we are to define the other attributes of the same Divine Nature. To human conception it seems impossible that absolute morality should be manifested in the form of a *law of obligation;* for such a law implies relation and subjection to the authority of a lawgiver. And, as all human morality is manifested in this form, the conclusion seems unavoidable, that human morality, even in its highest elevation, is not identical with, nor adequate to measure, the Absolute Morality of God (10).

A like conclusion is forced upon us by a closer examination of human morality itself. To maintain the immutability of moral principles in the abstract is a very different thing from maintaining the immutability of the particular acts by which those principles are manifested in practice. The parallel between the mathematical and the moral sciences, as systems of necessary truth, holds good in this respect also. As principles in the abstract, the laws of morality are as unchangeable as the axioms of geometry. That duty ought in all cases to be followed in preference to inclination, is as certain a truth as that two straight lines cannot enclose a space. In their concrete application both principles are equally liable to error:—we may err in supposing a particular visible line to be perfectly straight; as we may err in supposing a particular act to be one of duty (11). But the two errors, though equally possible, are by no means equally important. For mathematical science, as such, is complete in its merely theoretical aspect; while moral science is valuable chiefly in its application to practice. It is in their concrete form that moral principles are adopted as guides of conduct and canons of judgment; and in this form they admit of various degrees of uncertainty or of positive error. But the difference between the highest and the lowest conception of moral duty is one of degree, not of kind; the interval between them is occupied by intermediate stages, separated from each other by minute and scarcely appreciable differences, and the very conception of a gradual progress in moral enlightenment implies the possibility of a further advance, of a more exalted intellect, and a more enlightened conscience. While we repudiate, as subversive of all morality, the theory which maintains that each man is the measure of his own moral acts; we must repudiate also, as subversive of all religion, the opposite theory, which virtually maintains that man may become the measure of the absolute Nature of God.

God did not *create* Absolute Morality: it is coeternal with Himself; and it were blasphemy to say that there ever was a time when God was and Goodness was not. But God did create the human manifestation of morality, when He created the moral constitution of man, and placed him in those circumstances by which the eternal principles of right and wrong take a special form in relation to this present life (12). For it is manifest, to take the simplest instances, that the Sixth Commandment of the Decalogue, in its literal obligation, is relative to that state of things in which men are subject to death; and the seventh, to that in which there is marrying and giving in marriage; and the eighth, to that in which men possess temporal goods. It is manifest, to take a more general ground, that the very conception of moral obligation implies a superior authority, and an ability to transgress what that authority commands; that it implies a complex, and therefore a limited nature in the moral agent; the intellect, which apprehends the duty, being distinct from the will, which obeys or disobeys. That there is a higher and unchangeable principle embodied in these forms, we have abundant reason to believe; and yet we cannot, from our present point of view, examine the same duties apart from their human element, and separate that which is relative and peculiar to man in this life from that which is absolute and common to all moral beings. In this respect again, our moral conceptions offer a remarkable analogy to the cognate phenomena on which other systems of necessary truth are based. Take, for example, the idea of Time, the foundation of the science of Number. We find no difficulty in believing that this present world was created at some definite point of time; but we are unable to regard the same moment as the creation of Time itself. On the contrary, we are compelled to believe that there was a time before as well as after the creation of the world: that the being of God reaches back in boundless duration beyond the moment when He said, Let there be light, and there was light. But when we attempt to unite this conviction with another, necessary to the completion of the thought; —when we try to conceive God as an Infinite Being, existing in continuous duration,—the contradictions, which beset us on every side, admonish us that we have transcended the boundary within which alone human thought is possible. And so too, while we are compelled to believe that the creation of man's moral nature was not identical with the creation of morality itself;—that the great principles of all that is holy and righteous existed in God, before they assumed their finite form in the heart of man;—we still find ourselves baffled in every attempt to conceive an infinite moral nature, or its condition, an infinite personality: we find ourselves compelled to walk by faith, and not by sight;—to admit that we have knowledge enough to guide us in our moral training here; but not enough to unveil the hidden things of God (13).

In so far, then, as Morality, in its human character, depends upon conditions not coeternal with God, but created along with man, in so far we are not justified in regarding the occasional suspension of human duties, by the same authority which enacted them, as a violation of the immutable principles of morality itself. That there are limits indeed, within which alone this rule can be safely applied;—that there are doctrines and practices which carry on their front convincing proof that they cannot have been revealed or commanded by God;—that there are systems of religion which by this criterion may be shewn to have sprung, not from divine appointment, but from human corruption,—is not for an instant denied. In my concluding Lecture I shall endeavour to point out some of the conditions under which this kind of evidence is admissible. For the present, my argument is concerned, not with special and occasional commands, but with universal and perpetual doctrines; not with isolated facts recorded in sacred history, but with revealed truths, forming an integral portion of religious belief. In this point of view, I propose to apply the principle hitherto maintained, of the Limits of Religious Thought, to the examination of those doctrines of the Christian Faith which are sometimes regarded as containing something repugnant to the Moral Reason of man.

The Atoning Sacrifice of Christ has been the mark assailed by various attacks of this kind; some of them not very consistent with each other; but all founded on some supposed incongruity between this doctrine and the moral attributes of the Divine Nature. By one critic, the doctrine is rejected because it is more consistent with the infinite mercy of God to pardon sin freely, without any atonement whatsoever (14). By another, because, from the unchangeable nature of God's laws, it is impossible that sin can be pardoned at all (15). A third maintains that it is unjust that the innocent should suffer for the sins of the guilty (16). A fourth is indignant at the supposition that God can be angry (17); while a fifth cannot see by what moral fitness the shedding of blood can do away with sin or its punishment (18). The principle which governs these and similar objections is, that we have a right to assume that there is, if not a perfect identity, at least an exact resemblance between the moral nature of man and that of God; that the laws and principles of infinite justice and mercy are but magnified images of those which are manifested on a finite scale;—that nothing can be compatible with the boundless goodness of God, which appears incompatible with the little goodness of which man may be conscious in himself.

The value of this principle, as an absolute criterion of religious truth, may be tested by the simple experiment of applying the same reasoning to an imaginary revelation constructed on the rational principles of some one of the objectors. Let us suppose then, that, instead of the Christian doctrine of the Atonement, the Scriptures had told us of an absolute and unconditional pardon of sin, following upon the mere repentance of the sinner. It is easy to imagine how ready our reasoning theologians would be with their philosophical criticisms, speculative or moral. Does it not, they might say, represent man as influencing God;—the Finite as controlling, by the act of repentance, the unchangeable self-determinations of the Infinite? Does it not depict the Deity as acting in time, as influenced by motives and occasions, as subject to human feelings? Does it not tend to weaken our impression of the hatefulness of sin, and to encourage carelessness in the sinner, by the easy terms on which he is promised forgiveness? (19). If it is unworthy of God to represent Him as angry and needing to be propitiated, how can philosophy tolerate the conception that He is placable, and to be softened by repentance? And what moral fitness has repentance to do away with the guilt or punishment of a past transgression? Whatever moral fitness there exists between righteousness and God's favour, the same must exist between sin and God's anger: in whatever degree that which deserves punishment is not punished, in that degree God's justice is limited in its operation. A strictly moral theory requires, therefore, not free forgiveness, but an exactly graduated proportion between guilt and suffering, virtue and happiness (20). If, on the other hand, we maintain that there is no moral fitness in either case, we virtually deny the existence of a moral Deity at all: we make God indifferent to good or evil as such: we represent Him as rewarding and punishing arbitrarily and with respect of persons. The moral objection, in truth, so far as it has any weight at all, has no special application to the Christian doctrine: it lies against the entire supposition of the remission of sins on any terms and by any means: and if it has been more strongly urged by Rationalists against the Christian representation than against others, this is merely because the former has had the misfortune to provoke hostility by being found in the Bible.

It is obvious indeed, on a moment's reflection, that the duty of man to forgive the trespasses of his neighbour, rests precisely upon those features of human nature which cannot by any analogy be regarded as representing an image of God (21). Man is not the author of moral law: he is not, as man, the moral governor of his fellows: he has no authority, merely as man, to punish moral transgressions as such. It is not as sin, but as injury, that vice is a transgression against man: it is not that his holiness is outraged, but that his rights or his interests are impaired. The duty of forgiveness is imposed as a check, not upon the justice, but upon the selfishness of man: it is not designed to extinguish his indignation against vice, but to restrain his tendency to exaggerate his own personal injuries (22). The reasoner who maintains, "it is a duty in man to forgive sins, therefore it must be morally fitting for God to forgive them also," overlooks the fact that this duty is binding upon man on account of the weakness and ignorance and sinfulness of his nature; that he is bound to forgive, as one who himself needs forgiveness; as one whose weakness renders him liable to suffering; as one whose self-love is ever ready to arouse his passions and pervert his judgment.

Nor yet would the advocates of the Moral Reason gain anything in Theology by the substitution of a rigid system of reward and punishment, in which nothing is forgiven, but every act meets with its appropriate recompense. We have only to suppose that this were the doctrine of Revelation, to imagine the outcry with which it would be assailed. "It is moral," the objector might urge, "only in the harsher and less amiable features of human morality: it gives us a God whom we may fear, but whom we cannot love; who has given us affections with which He has no sympathy, and passions for whose consequences He allows no redress; who created man liable to fall, and placed him in a world of temptations, knowing that he would fall, and purposing to take advantage of his frailty to the utmost." Criticisms of this kind may be imagined without number;— nay, they are actually found in more than one modern work, the writers of which have erroneously imagined that they were assailing the real teaching of Scripture (23). Verily, this vaunted Moral Reason is a "Lesbian rule" (24). It may be applied with equal facility to the criticism of every possible scheme of Divine Providence; and therefore we may be permitted to suspect that it is not entitled to implicit confidence against any (25).

The endless controversy concerning Predestination and Free Will, whether viewed in its speculative or in its moral aspect, is but another example of the hardihood of human ignorance. The question, as I have observed before, has its philosophical as well as its theological aspect: it has no difficulties peculiar to itself: it is but a special form of the fundamental mystery of the coexistence of the Infinite and the Finite. Yet, with this mystery meeting and baffling human reason at every turn, theologians have not scrupled to trace in their petty channels the exact flow and course of Infinite wisdom; one school boldly maintaining that even Omniscience itself has no knowledge of contingent events; another asserting, with equal confidence, that God's knowledge must be a restraint on man's freedom (26). If philosophy offers for the moment an apparent escape from the dilemma, by suggesting that God's knowledge is not properly *foreknowledge*, as having no relation to time (27); the suggestion itself is one which can neither be verified as a truth nor even distinctly conceived as a thought; and the Rationalist evades the solution by shifting the ground of attack, and retorts that Prophecy at least is anterior to the event which it foretells; and that a prediction of human actions is irreconcilable with human freedom (28). But the whole meaning of the difficulty vanishes as soon as we acknowledge that the Infinite is not an object of human thought at all. There can be no consciousness of a relation, whether of agreement or of opposition, where there is not a consciousness of both the objects related. That a man, by his own power, should be able with certainty to foretell the future, implies that the laws of that future are fixed and unchangeable; for man can only foresee particular occurrences through a knowledge of the general law on which they depend.

But is this relation of cause to effect, of law to its consequences, really a knowledge or an ignorance? Is the causal relation itself a law of things, or only a human mode of representing phenomena? Supposing it were possible for man, in some other state of intelligence, to foresee a future event without forseeing it as the result of a law, —would that knowledge be a higher or a lower one than he at present possesses?—would it be the removal of some reality which he now sees, or only of some limitation under which he now sees it? (29). Man can only foresee what is certain; and from his point of view, the foreknowledge depends upon the certainty. But, apart from the human conditions of thought, in relation to a more perfect intelligence, can we venture to say, even as regards temporal succession, whether necessity is the condition of foreknowledge, or foreknowledge of necessity, or whether indeed necessity itself has any existence at all? (30). May not the whole scheme of Law and Determinism indicate a weakness, rather than a power of the human mind; and are there not facts of consciousness which give some support to this conjecture? (31). Can anything be *necessary* to an intellect whose thought creates its own objects? Can any necessity of things determine the cognitions of the Absolute Mind, even if those cognitions take place in succession to each other? These questions admit of no certain answer; but the very inability to answer them proves that dogmatic decisions on either side are the decisions of ignorance, not of knowledge.

But the problem, be its difficulties and their origin what they may, is not peculiar to Theology, and receives no additional complication from its position in Holy Writ. The very same question may be discussed in a purely metaphysical form, by merely substituting the universal law of causation for the universal knowledge of God. What is the meaning and value of that law of the human mind which apparently compels us to think that every event whatever has its determining cause? And how is that conviction reconcilable with a liberty in the human will to choose between two alternatives? The answer is substantially the same as before. The freedom of the will is a positive fact of our consciousness :—as for the principle of causality, we know not whence it is, nor what it is. We know not whether it is a law of things, or a mode of human representation; whether it denotes an impotence or a power; whether it is innate or acquired. We know not in what the causal relation itself consists; nor by what authority we are warranted in extending its significance beyond the temporal sequence which suggests it and the material phenomena in which that sequence is undisturbed.

And is not the same conviction of the ignorance of man, and of his rashness in the midst of ignorance, forced upon us by the spectacle of the arbitrary and summary decisions of human reason on the most mysterious as well as the most awful of God's revealed judgments against sin,—the sentence of Eternal Punishment? We know not what is the relation of Sin to Infinite Justice. We know not under what conditions, consistently with the freedom of man, the final spiritual restoration of the impenitent sinner is possible; nor how, without such a restoration, guilt and misery can ever cease. We know not whether the future punishment of sin will be inflicted by way of natural consequence or of supernatural visitation; whether it will be produced from within or inflicted from without. We know not how man can be rescued from sin and suffering without the co-operation of his own will; nor what means can cooperate with that will, beyond those which are offered to all of us during our state of trial (32). It becomes us to speak cautiously and reverently on a matter of which God has revealed so little, and that little of such awful moment;

but if we may be permitted to criticize the arguments of the opponents of this doctrine with the same freedom with which they have criticized the ways of God, we may remark that the whole apparent force of the moral objection rests upon two purely gratuitous assumptions. It is assumed, in the first place, that God's punishment of sin in the world to come is so far analogous to man's administration of punishment in this world, that it will take place as a special infliction, not as a natural consequence. And it is assumed, in the second place, that punishment will be inflicted solely with reference to the sins committed during the earthly life;—that the guilt will continue finite, while the misery is prolonged to infinity (33). Are we then so sure, it may be asked, that there can be no sin beyond the grave? Can an immortal soul incur God's wrath and condemnation, only so long as it is united to a mortal body? With as much reason might we assert that the angels are incapable of obedience to God, that the devils are incapable of rebellion. What if the sin perpetuate itself,—if the prolonged misery be the offspring of the prolonged guilt? (34).

Against this it is urged that sin cannot for ever be triumphant against God (35). As if the whole mystery of iniquity were contained in the words *for ever!* The real riddle of existence,—the problem which confounds all philosophy,—aye, and all religion too, so far as religion is a thing of man's reason,—is the fact that evil exists *at all;* not that it exists for a longer or a shorter duration. Is not God infinitely wise and holy and powerful *now?* and does not sin exist along with that infinite holiness and wisdom and power? Is God to become more holy, more wise, more powerful hereafter; and must evil be annihilated to make room for His perfections to expand? Does the infinity of His eternal nature ebb and flow with every increase or diminution in the sum of human guilt and misery? Against this immovable barrier of the existence of evil, the waves of philosophy have dashed themselves unceasingly since the birthday of human thought, and have retired broken and powerless, without displacing the minutest fragment of the stubborn rock, without softening one feature of its dark and rugged surface (36). We may be told that evil is a privation, or a negation, or a partial aspect of the universal good, or some other equally unmeaning abstraction; whilst all the while our own hearts bear testimony to its fearful reality, to its direct antagonism to every possible form of good (37). But this mystery, vast and inscrutable as it is, is but one aspect of a more general problem; it is but the moral form of the ever-recurring secret of the Infinite. How the Infinite and the Finite in any form of antagonism or other relation, can exist together;—how infinite power can coexist with finite activity: how infinite wisdom can coexist with finite contingency: how infinite goodness can coexist with finite evil:—how the Infinite can exist in any manner without exhausting the universe of reality:—this is the riddle which Infinite Wisdom alone can solve, the problem whose very conception belongs only to that Universal Knowing which fills and embraces the Universe of Being. When Philosophy can answer this question;—when she can even state intelligibly the notions which its terms involve,—then, and not till then, she may be entitled to demand a solution of the far smaller difficulties which she finds in revealed religion:—or rather, she will have solved them already; for from this they all proceed, and to this they all ultimately return.

The reflections which this great and terrible mystery of Divine Judgment has suggested, receive perhaps some further support when we contemplate it in another aspect, and one more legitimately within the province of human reason:—that is to say, in its analogy to the actual constitution and course of nature. "The Divine moral government which religion teaches us," says Bishop Butler, " implies that the consequence of vice shall be misery, in some future state, by the righteous judgment of God. That such consequent punishment shall take effect by His appointment, is necessarily implied. But as it is not in any sort to be supposed that we are made acquainted with all the ends or reasons for which it is fit future punishment should be inflicted, or why God has appointed such and such consequent misery should follow vice; and as we are altogether in the dark, how or in what manner it shall follow, by what immediate occasions, or by the instrumentality of what means; there is no absurdity in supposing it may follow in a way analogous to that in which many miseries follow such and such courses of action at present; poverty, sickness, infamy, untimely death from diseases, death from the hands of civil justice. There is no absurdity in supposing future punishment may follow wickedness of course, as we speak, or in the way of natural consequence, from God's original constitution of the world; from the nature He has given us, and from the condition in which He places us; or in a like manner as a person rashly trifling upon a precipice, in the way of natural consequence, falls down; in the way of natural consequence, breaks his limbs, suppose; in the way of natural consequence of this, without help perishes" (38).

And if we may be permitted to extend the same analogy from the constitution of external nature to that of the human mind; may we not trace something not wholly unlike the irrevocable sentence of the future, in that dark and fearful, yet too certain law of our nature, by which sin and misery ever tend to perpetuate themselves; by which evil habits gather strength with every fresh indulgence, till it is no longer, humanly speaking, in the power of the sinner to shake off the burden which his own deeds have laid upon him? In that mysterious condition of the depraved will, compelled, and yet free,—the slave of sinful habit, yet responsible for every act of sin, and gathering deeper condemnation as the power of amendment grows less and less;—may we not see some possible foreshadowing of the yet deeper guilt and the yet more hopeless misery of the worm that dieth not, and the fire that is not quenched? The fact, awful as it is, is one to which our every day's experience bears witness: and who shall say that the invisible things of God may not, in this as in other instances, be shadowed forth to us in the things that are seen?

The same argument from analogy is indeed applicable to every one of the difficulties which Rationalism professes to discover in the revealed ways of God's dealings with man. The Fall of Adam, and the inherited corruption of his posterity, find their parallel in the liability to sin which remains unextinguished throughout man's moral progress; and in that mysterious, though certain, dispensation of Providence, which ordains that not only bodily taints and infirmities, but even moral dispositions and tendencies, should, in many instances, descend from father to son; and which permits the child of sinful parents to be depraved by evil example, before he knows how, by his own reason, clearly to discern between right and wrong; before he has strength of his own will, to refuse the evil and choose the good (39). There is a parallel too in that strange, yet too familiar fact, of vice persisted in, with the clearest and strongest conviction of its viciousness and wretchedness: and the scepticism which denies that man, if created sinless, could so easily have fallen from innocence, finds its philosophical counterpart in the paradox of the ancient moralist, who maintained that conscious sin is impossible, because nothing can be stronger than knowledge (40). Justification by faith through the merits of Christ is at least in harmony with that course of things established by

Divine providence in this world; in which so many benefits, which we cannot procure for ourselves or deserve by any merit of our own, are obtained for us by the instrumentality of others; and in which we are so often compelled, as an indispensable condition of obtaining the benefit, to trust in the power and good will of those whom we have never tried, and to believe in the efficacy of means whose manner of working we know not (41). The operations of Divine Grace, influencing, yet not necessitating, the movements of the human soul, find their corresponding fact and their corresponding mystery in the determinations of the Will;—in that Freedom to do or leave undone, so certain in fact, so inexplicable in theory, which consists neither in absolute indifference nor in absolute subjection; which is acted upon and influenced by motives, yet in its turn acts upon and controls their influences, prevented by them, and yet working with them (42). But it is unnecessary to pursue further an argument which, in all its essential features, has already been fully exhibited by a philosopher whose profound and searching wisdom has answered by anticipation nearly every cavil of the latest form of Rationalism, no less than those of his own day. We may add here and there a detail of application, as the exigencies of controversy may suggest; but the principle of the whole, and its most important consequences, have been established and worked out more than a century ago, in the unanswerable argument of Butler.

The warning which his great work contains against "that idle and not very innocent employment of forming imaginary models of a world, and schemes of governing it" (43), is as necessary now as then, as applicable to moral as to speculative theories. Neither with regard to the physical nor to the moral world, is man capable of constructing a Cosmogony; and those Babels of Reason, which Philosophy has built for itself, under the names of

Rational Theories of Religion, and Criticisms of every Revelation, are but the successors of those elder children of chaos and night, which with no greater knowledge, but with less presumption, sought to describe the generation of the visible universe. It is no disparagement of the value and authority of the Moral Reason in its regulative capacity, within its proper sphere of human action, if we refuse to exalt it to the measure and standard of the Absolute and Infinite Goodness of God. The very Philosopher whose writings have most contributed to establish the supreme authority of Conscience in man, is also the one who has pointed out most clearly the existence of analogous moral difficulties in nature and in religion, and the true answer to both,—the admission that God's Government, natural as well as spiritual, is a scheme imperfectly comprehended.

In His Moral Attributes, no less than in the rest of His Infinite Being, God's Judgments are unsearchable, and His ways past finding out.[b] While He manifests Himself clearly as a Moral Governor and Legislator, by the witness of the Moral Law which He has established in the hearts of men, we cannot help feeling, at the same time, that that Law, grand as it is, is no measure of His Grandeur, that He Himself is beyond it, though not opposed to it, distinct, though not alien from it. We feel that He who planted in man's conscience that stern unyielding Imperative of Duty, must Himself be true and righteous altogether; that He from whom all holy desires, all good counsels, and all just works do proceed, must Himself be more holy, more good, more just than these. But when we try to realize in thought this sure conviction of our faith, we find that here, as everywhere, the Finite cannot fathom the Infinite, that, while in our hearts we believe, yet our thoughts at times are sore troubled. It is consonant to the whole analogy of our earthly state of trial, that, in this as in other features

[b] Romans xi. 33.

of God's Providence, we should meet with things impossible to understand and difficult to believe; by which reason is baffled and faith tried;—acts whose purpose we see not; dispensations whose wisdom is above us; thoughts which are not our thoughts, and ways which are not our ways. In these things we hear, as it were, the same loving voice which spoke to the wondering disciple of old: "What I do, thou knowest not now; but thou shalt know hereafter."[c] The luminary by whose influence the ebb and flow of man's moral being is regulated, moves around and along with man's little world, in a regular and bounded orbit: one side, and one side only, looks downwards upon its earthly centre; the other, which we see not, is ever turned upwards to the all-surrounding Infinite. And those tides have their seasons of rise and fall, their places of strength and weakness; and that light waxes and wanes with the growth or decay of man's mental and moral and religious culture; and its borrowed rays seem at times to shine as with their own lustre, in rivalry, even in opposition, to the source from which they emanate. Yet is that light still but a faint and partial reflection of the hidden glories of the Sun of Righteousness, waiting but the brighter illumination of His presence, to fade and be swallowed up in the full blaze of the heaven kindling around it;—not cast down indeed from its orbit, nor shorn of its true brightness and influence, but still felt and acknowledged in its real existence and power, in the memory of the past discipline, in the product of the present perfectness,—though now distinct no more, but vanishing from sight, to be made one with the Glory that beams from the "Father of lights, with whom is no variableness, neither shadow of turning."[d]

[c] St. John xiii. 7.   [d] St. James i. 17.

LECTURE VIII.

St. John V. 36.

"THE WORKS WHICH THE FATHER HATH GIVEN ME TO FINISH, THE SAME WORKS THAT I DO, BEAR WITNESS OF ME, THAT THE FATHER HATH SENT ME."

To construct a complete Criticism of any Revelation, it is necessary that the Critic should be in possession of a perfect Philosophy of the Infinite. For, except on the supposition that we possess an exact knowledge of the whole Nature of God, such as only that Philosophy can furnish, we cannot know for certain what are the purposes which God intends to accomplish by means of Revelation, and what are the instruments by which those purposes may be best carried out. If then it can be shewn, as I have attempted to shew in the previous Lectures, that the attainment of a Philosophy of the Infinite is utterly impossible under the existing laws of human thought, it follows that it is not by means of philosophical criticism that the claims of a supposed Revelation can be adequately tested. We are thus compelled to seek another field for the right use of Reason in religious questions; and what that field is, it will not be difficult to determine. To Reason, rightly employed, within its proper limits and on its proper objects, our Lord Himself and His Apostles openly appealed in proof of their divine mission; and the same proof has been unhesitatingly claimed by the defenders of Christianity in all subsequent ages. In other words, the legitimate object of a rational criticism of revealed religion, is not to be found in the *contents* of that religion, but in its *evidences*.

At first sight it may appear as if this distinction involved no real difference; for the contents of a revelation, it might be objected, are included among its evidences. In one sense, no doubt they are; but that very inclusion gives them a totally different significance and weight from that to which they lay claim when considered as the basis of a philosophical criticism. In the one case they are judged by their conformity to the supposed nature and purposes of God: in the other, by their adaptation to the actual circumstances and wants of man. In the one case they are regarded as furnishing a single and a certain criterion; for, on the supposition that our reason is competent to determine, from our knowledge of the Divine Nature, what the characteristics of a true Revelation ought to be, we are entitled, by virtue of that criterion alone, to reject without hesitation whatever does not satisfy its requirements. In the other case they are regarded as furnishing only one probable presumption out of many;—a presumption which may confirm and be confirmed by coinciding testimony from other sources, or, on the contrary, may be outweighed, when we come to balance probabilities, by conflicting evidence on the other side.

The practical conclusion, which may be deduced from the whole previous survey of the Limits of Religious Thought, is this: that if no one faculty of the human mind is competent to convey a direct knowledge of the Absolute and the Infinite, no one faculty is entitled to claim pre-eminence over the rest, as furnishing especially *the criterion* of the truth or falsehood of a supposed Revelation. There are presumptions to be drawn from the internal character of the doctrines which the revelation contains: there are presumptions to be drawn from the facts connected with its first promulgation: there are presumptions to be drawn from its subsequent history and the effects which it has produced among mankind. But the true evidence, for or against the religion, is not to be found in any one of these taken singly and exclusively; but in the resultant of all, fairly examined and compared together; the apparently conflicting evidences being balanced against each other, and the apparently concurring evidences estimated by their united efficacy.

A truth so obvious as this may perhaps be thought hardly worth announcing as the result of an elaborate inquiry. But the whole history of religious controversy bears witness that, however evident in theory, there is no truth more liable to be neglected in practice. The defenders of Christianity are not altogether free from the charge of insisting exclusively or preeminently upon some one alone of its evidences: the assailants, under the influence of a still more exclusive reaction, have assumed that a method which fails to accomplish everything has succeeded in accomplishing nothing; and, flying at once to the opposite extreme, have in their turn appealed to some one infallible criterion, as constituting a royal road to philosophical unbelief.

In the present day we are feeling the pernicious effects of a reaction of this kind. Because the writings of Paley and his followers in the last generation laid a principal stress on the direct historical evidences of Christianity, we meet now with an antagonist school of writers, who perpetually assure us that history has nothing whatever to do with religion (1); that an external revelation of religious truth is impossible (2); that we may learn all that is essential to the Gospel by inward and spiritual evidence only (3). In the spirit of the Pharisees of old, who said, "This man is not of God, because he keepeth not the sabbath day,"[a] we are now told that the doctrine must in all cases prove the miracles, and not the miracles the doctrine (4); that the external evidence of miracles is

[a] St. John ix. 16.

entirely useless for the support of the religious philosophy of Christ (5); that man no more needs a miraculous revelation of things pertaining to religion than of things pertaining to agriculture or manufactures (6). And, as is usually the case in such reactions, the last state has become worse than the first:—a slight comparative neglect of the internal evidence on the one side has been replaced by an utter repudiation of all external evidence on the other: a trifling disproportion in the edifice of the Christian Faith has been remedied by the entire removal of some of its main pillars of support. The crying evil of the present day in religious controversy is the neglect or contempt of the external evidences of Christianity: the first step towards the establishment of a sound religious philosophy must consist in the restoration of those evidences to their true place in the Theological system.

The evidence derived from the internal character of a religion, whatever may be its value within its proper limits, is, as regards the divine origin of the religion, purely negative. It may prove in certain cases (though even here the argument requires much caution in its employment) that a religion *has not* come from God; but it is in no case sufficient to prove that it *has* come from Him (7). For the doctrines revealed must either be such as are within the power of man's natural reason to verify, or such as are beyond it. In the former case, the reason which is competent to verify may also be competent to discover: the doctrine is tested by its conformity to the conclusions of human philosophy: and the wisdom which sits in judgment on the truth of a doctrine must itself be presumed to have an equal power of discerning the truth. In the latter case, where the doctrine is beyond the power of human reason to discover, it can be accepted only as resting on the authority of the teacher who proclaims it; and that authority itself must then be guaranteed by the external evidence of a superhuman mission. To advance a step beyond the merely negative argument, it is necessary that the evidence contained in the character of the doctrine itself should be combined with that derived from the exterior history. When, for example, the Divine Origin of Christianity is maintained, on the ground of its vast moral superiority to all Heathen systems of Ethics; or on that of the improbability that such a system could have been conceived by a Galilean peasant among the influences of the contemporary Judaism; the argument is legitimate and powerful; but its positive force depends not merely on the internal character of the doctrine, but principally on its relation to certain external facts (8).

And even the negative argument, which concludes from the character of the contents of a religion that it *cannot* have come from God, however legitimate within its proper limits, is one which requires considerable caution in the application. The lesson to be learnt from an examination of the Limits of Religious Thought is not that man's judgments are *worthless* in relation to divine things; but that they are *fallible:* and the probability of error in any particular case can never be fairly estimated without giving their full weight to all collateral considerations. We are indeed bound to believe that a Revelation given by God can never contain anything that is really unwise or unrighteous; but we are not always capable of estimating exactly the wisdom or righteousness of particular doctrines or precepts.[b] And we are bound to bear in mind that

[b] "From these things it is easy to see distinctly how our ignorance, as it is the common, is really a satisfactory answer to all objections against the justice and goodness of Providence. If a man, contemplating any one providential dispensation, which had no relation to any others, should object, that he discerned in it a disregard to justice, or a deficiency of goodness; nothing would be less an answer to such objection than our ignorance in other parts of Providence, or in the possibilities of things, no way

exactly in proportion to the strength of the remaining evidence for the divine origin of a religion, is the probability that we may be mistaken in supposing this or that portion of its contents to be unworthy of God. Taken in conjunction, the two arguments may confirm or correct each other: taken singly and absolutely, each may vitiate the result which should follow from their joint application. We do not certainly know the exact nature and operation of the moral attributes of God: we can but infer and conjecture from what we know of the moral attributes of man: and the analogy between the Finite and the Infinite can never be so perfect as to preclude all possibility of error in the process. But the possibility becomes almost a certainty, when any one human faculty is elevated by itself into an authoritative criterion of religious truth, without regard to those collateral evidences by which its decisions may be modified and corrected.

"The human mind," says a writer of the present day, "is competent to sit in *moral* and *spiritual* judgment on a professed revelation; and to decide, if the case seem to require it, in the following tone: This doctrine attributes to God, that which we should all call harsh, cruel, or unjust in man: it is therefore intrinsically inadmissible." .... "In fact," he continues, "all Christian apostles and missionaries, like the Hebrew prophets, have always refuted Paganism by direct attacks on its immoral and unspiritual doctrines; and have appealed to the consciences of heathens, as competent to decide in the controversy" (9). Now an

related to what he was contemplating. But when we know not but the parts objected against may be relative to other parts unknown to us; and when we are unacquainted with what is, in the nature of the thing, practicable in the case before us; then our ignorance is a satisfactory answer; because some unknown relation, or some unknown impossibility, may render what is objected against just and good; nay, good in the highest practicable degree."—Butler, *Analogy*, Part i. ch. 7.

appeal of this kind may be legitimate or not, according to the purpose for which it is made, and the manner in which it is applied. The primary and proper employment of man's moral sense, as of his other faculties, is not *speculative*, but *regulative*. It is not designed to tell us what are the absolute and immutable principles of Right, as existing in the eternal nature of God; but to discern those relative and temporary manifestations of them, which are necessary for human training in this present life. But if morality, in its human manifestation, contains a relative and temporary, as well as an absolute and eternal element, an occasional suspension of the human Law is by no means to be confounded with a violation of the divine Principle. We can only partially judge of the moral government of God, on the assumption that there is an analogy between the divine nature and the human: and in proportion as the analogy recedes from perfect likeness, the decisions of the human reason necessarily become more and more doubtful. The primary and direct inquiry, which human reason is entitled to make concerning a professed revelation, is,—how far does it tend to promote or to hinder the moral discipline of man? It is but a secondary and indirect question, and one very liable to mislead, to ask how far it is compatible with the Infinite Goodness of God.

Thus, for example, it is one thing to condemn a religion on account of the habitual observance of licentious or inhuman rites of worship, and another to pronounce judgment on isolated facts, historically recorded as having been done by divine command, but not perpetuated in precepts for the imitation of posterity. The former are condemned for their regulative character, as contributing to the perpetual corruption of mankind; the latter are condemned on speculative grounds, as inconsistent with our preconceived notions of the character of God. "There are some particular precepts in Scripture," says Bishop Butler, "given to particular persons, requiring actions which would be immoral and vicious, were it not for such precepts. But it is easy to see, that all these are of such a kind, as that the precept changes the whole nature of the case and of the action; and both constitutes and shews that not to be unjust or immoral, which, prior to the precept, must have appeared, and really have been so: which may well be, since none of these precepts are contrary to immutable morality. If it were commanded to cultivate the principles and act from the spirit of treachery, ingratitude, cruelty; the command would not alter the nature of the case or of the action in any of these instances. But it is quite otherwise in precepts which require only the doing an external action; for instance, taking away the property or life of any. For men have no right to either life or property, but what arises solely from the grant of God: when this grant is revoked, they cease to have any right at all in either: and when this revocation is made known, as surely it is possible it may be, it must cease to be unjust to deprive them of either. And though a course of external acts, which without command would be immoral, must make an immoral habit: yet a few detached commands have no such natural tendency. . . . . There seems no difficulty at all in these precepts, but what arises from their being offences: *i. e.* from their being liable to be perverted, as indeed they are, by wicked designing men to serve the most horrid purposes; and, perhaps, to mislead the weak and enthusiastic. And objections from this head are not objections against revelation; but against the whole notion of religion, as a trial; and against the general constitution of nature" (10).

There is indeed an obvious analogy between these temporary suspensions of the laws of moral obligation and that corresponding suspension of the laws of natural phenomena which constitutes our ordinary conception of a Miracle. So much so, indeed, that the former might without impropriety be designated as *Moral Miracles*.[c] In both, the Almighty is regarded as suspending, for special

[c] This expression, which has been employed, though not quite from the same point of view, by Skelton (*Deism Revealed*, p. 103, ed. 1824), is to be interpreted strictly according to the analogy between acts so called and physical miracles, and implies no consequences with regard to the former which are not also true of the latter. The ground of the analogy is simply this: that just as a man may be enabled by divine power, supernaturally given, to perform an act which would not be possible to his natural powers, so a man may be justified by divine authority, supernaturally given, in doing an act which he would not be justified in doing of his own natural will. The same analogy must, of course, be observed in the details of the comparison: *e. g.* 1°, The divine interposition is supposed in both cases to be equally real. If any man misrepresents or mistakes his own designs or delusions for divine commands, his acts no more come under the above head than similar cases of imposture or self-deception with regard to natural phenomena can be classed as real physical miracles. 2°, As a physical miracle is not a breach of natural law, neither is a moral miracle a breach of moral law. In neither case is it supposed that the same antecedent is followed at different times by different consequents; but in both a new antecedent, the divine interposition, is introduced, which takes the case out of the class to which the law relates. 3°, As the physical miracle is not a departure from God's eternal purposes, but is as much a part of His divine plan as any natural event, so a moral miracle is not a departure from the plan of God's moral government, but a part of it; though neither is included under the ordinary laws discoverable by human science. An argument identical in principle with that in the text is employed by Waterland, in reply to the objection of Tindal, cited above, Lecture II. note 10. "Here," he says, "was no *dispensing* with any *law of nature*; but the circumstance of a *Divine* command (a very material circumstance indeed) altered the whole *case*, changed the quality of the act, and made it no breach of the law of nature. For what law of nature forbids a man the executing of God's will, where the Divine right to what he would have executed is clear and indisputable?"—*Scripture Vindicated*, on Numb. xxi. 2, 3.

purposes, not the eternal laws which constitute His own absolute Nature, but the created laws, which He imposed at a certain time upon a particular portion of His creatures. Both are isolated and rare in their occurrence; and apparently, from the nature of the case, must be so, in order to unite harmoniously with the normal manifestations of God's government of the world. A perpetual series of physical miracles would destroy that confidence in the regularity of the course of nature, which is indispensable to the cultivation of man's intellectual and productive energies: a permanent suspension of practical duties would be similarly prejudicial to the cultivation of his moral character. But the isolated character of both classes of phenomena removes the objection which might otherwise be brought against them on this account: and this objection is the only one which can legitimately be urged, on philosophical grounds, against the *conception* of such cases as *possible;* as distinguished from the historical evidence, which may be adduced for or against their *actual occurrence*.

Even within its own legitimate province, an argument of this kind may have more or less weight, varying from the lowest presumption to the highest moral certainty, according to the nature of the offence which we believe ourselves to have detected, and the means which we possess of estimating its character or consequences. It is certain that we are not competent judges of the Absolute Nature of God: it is not certain that we are competent judges, in all cases, of what is best fitted for the moral discipline of man. But granting to the above argument its full value in this relation; it is still important to remember that we are dealing, not with demonstrative but with probable evidence, not with a single line of reasoning, but with a common focus, to which many and various rays converge; that we have not solved the entire problem, but only obtained one of the elements contributing to its solution. And the combined result of all these elements is by no means identical with the sum of their separate effects. The image, hitherto employed; of a balance of probabilities, is, in one respect at least, very inadequate to express the character of Christian evidence. It may be used with some propriety to express the provisional stage of the inquiry, while we are still uncertain to which side the evidence inclines; but it becomes inapplicable as soon as our decision is made. For the objections urged against a religion are not like the weights in a scale, which retain their full value, even when outweighed on the other side: —on the contrary, they become absolutely worthless, as soon as we are convinced that there is superior evidence to prove that the religion is true. We may not say, for example, that certain parts of the Christian scheme are unwise or unrighteous, though outweighed by greater acts of righteousness and wisdom :—we are bound to believe that we were mistaken from the first in supposing them to be unwise or unrighteous at all. In a matter of which we are so ignorant and so liable to be deceived, the objection which fails to prove everything proves nothing: from him that hath not, is taken away even that which he seemeth to have. And on the other hand, an objection which really proves anything proves everything. If the teaching of Christ is in any one thing not the teaching of God, it is in all things the teaching of man : its doctrines are subject to all the imperfections inseparable from man's sinfulness and ignorance: its effects must be such as can fully be accounted for as the results of man's wisdom, with all its weakness and all its error.

Here then is the issue, which the wavering disciple is bound seriously to consider. Taking into account the various questions whose answers, on the one side or the other, form the sum total of Evidences for or against the claims of the Christian Faith;—the genuineness and authenticity of the documents; the judgment and good faith of the writers; the testimony to the actual occurrence of prophecies and miracles, and their relation to the religious teaching with which they are connected; the character of the Teacher Himself, that one portrait, which, in its perfect purity and holiness and beauty, stands alone and unapproached in human history or human fiction; those rites and ceremonies of the elder Law, so significant as typical of Christ, so strange and meaningless without Him; those predictions of the promised Messiah, whose obvious meaning is rendered still more manifest by the futile ingenuity which strives to pervert them (11); the history of the rise and progress of Christianity, and its comparison with that of other religions; the ability or inability of human means to bring about the results which it actually accomplished; its antagonism to the current ideas of the age and country of its origin; its effects as a system on the moral and social condition of subsequent generations of mankind; its fitness to satisfy the wants and console the sufferings of human nature; the character of those by whom it was first promulgated and received; the sufferings which attested the sincerity of their convictions; the comparative trustworthiness of ancient testimony and modern conjecture; the mutual contradictions of conflicting theories of unbelief, and the inadequacy of all of them to explain the facts for which they are bound to account;—taking all these and similar questions into full consideration, are you prepared to affirm, as the result of the whole inquiry, that Jesus of Nazareth was an impostor, or an enthusiast, or a mythical figment; and his disciples crafty and designing, or well-meaning but deluded men? For be assured, that nothing short of this is the conclusion which you must maintain, if you reject one jot or one tittle of the whole doctrine of Christ. Either He was what He proclaimed Himself to be—the Incarnate Son of God, the Divine Saviour of a fallen world,—and if so, we may not divide God's Revelation, and dare to put asunder what He has joined together, —or the civilized world for eighteen centuries has been deluded by a cunningly devised fable; and He from whom that fable came has turned that world from darkness to light, from Satan to God, with a lie in His right hand.

Many who would shrink with horror from the idea of rejecting Christ altogether, will yet speak and act as if they were at liberty to set up for themselves an eclectic Christianity; separating the essential from the superfluous portions of Christ's teaching; deciding for themselves how much is permanent and necessary for all men, and how much is temporary and designed only for a particular age and people (12). Yet if Christ is indeed God manifest in the flesh, it is surely scarcely less impious to attempt to improve His teaching, than to reject it altogether. Nay, in one respect it is more so; for it is to acknowledge a doctrine as the revelation of God, and at the same time to proclaim that it is inferior to the wisdom of man. That it may indeed come, and has come, within the purposes of God's Providence, to give to mankind a Revelation partly at least designed for a temporary purpose and for a limited portion of mankind;—a Law in which something was permitted to the hardness of men's hearts,[d] and much was designed but as a shadow of good things to come;[e]—this we know, to whom a more perfect Revelation has been given. But to admit that God may make His own Revelation more perfect from time to time, is very different from admitting that human reason, by its own knowledge, is competent to separate the perfect from the imperfect, and to construct for itself an absolute religion out of the fragments of an incomplete Revelation. The experiment has been tried under the elder and less perfect

[d] St. Matthew xix. 8.   [e] Hebrews x. 1.

dispensation; but the result can hardly be considered so successful as to encourage a repetition of the attempt. The philosophical improvement of the Hebrew Scriptures produced, not the Sermon on the Mount, but the Creed of the Sadducee. The ripened intelligence of the Jewish people, instructed, as modern critics would assure us, by the enlightening influence of time, and by intercourse with foreign nations, bore fruit in a conclusion singularly coinciding with that of modern rationalism: "The Sadducees say that there is no resurrection, neither angel, nor spirit"[f] (13). And doubtless there were many then, as now, to applaud this wonderful discovery, as a proof that "religious truth is necessarily progressive, because our powers are progressive" (14); and to find a mythical or critical theory, to explain or to set aside those passages of Scripture which appeared to inculcate a contrary doctrine. Unfortunately for human wisdom, Prometheus himself needs a Prometheus. The lapse of time, as all history bears witness, is at least as fruitful in corruption as in enlightenment; and reason, when it has done its best, still needs a higher reason to decide between its conflicting theories, and to tell us which is the advanced, which the retrograde Theology (15).

In one respect indeed, this semi-rationalism, which admits the authority of Revelation up to a certain point and no further, rests on a far less reasonable basis than the firm belief which accepts the whole, or the complete unbelief which accepts nothing. For whatever may be the antecedent improbability which attaches to a miraculous narrative, as compared with one of ordinary events, it can affect only the narrative taken as a whole, and the entire series of miracles from the greatest to the least. If a single miracle is once admitted as supported by competent evidence, the entire history is at once removed from the

[f] Acts xxiii. 8.

ordinary calculations of more or less probability. One miracle is sufficient to shew that the series of events with which it is connected is one which the Almighty has seen fit to mark by exceptions to the ordinary course of His Providence: and this being once granted, we have no *à priori* grounds to warrant us in asserting that the number of such exceptions ought to be larger or smaller. If any one miracle recorded in the Gospels,—the Resurrection of Christ, for example,—be once admitted as true; the remainder cease to have any antecedent improbability at all, and require no greater evidence to prove them than is needed for the most ordinary events of any other history. For the improbability, such as it is, reaches no further than to shew that it is unlikely that God should work miracles at all; not that it is unlikely that He should work more than a certain number.

Our right to criticize at all depends upon this one question: "What think ye of Christ? whose Son is He?"[g] What is it that constitutes our need of Christ? Is it a conviction of guilt and wretchedness, or a taste for Philosophy? Do we want a Redeemer to save us from our sins, or a moral Teacher to give us a plausible theory of human duties? Christ can be our Redeemer only if He is what He proclaims Himself to be, the Son of God, sent into the world, that the world through Him might be saved.[h] If He is not this, His moral teaching began with falsehood, and was propagated by delusion. And if He is this, what but contempt and insult can be found in that half allegiance which criticizes while it bows; which sifts and selects while it submits; which approves or rejects as its reason or its feelings or its nervous sensibilities may dictate; which condescends to acknowledge Him as the teacher of a dark age and an ignorant people; bowing the knee before Him, half in reverence, half in mockery, and crying "Hail, King of the Jews"? If

[g] St. Matthew xxii. 42. [h] St. John iii. 17.

Christ is a mere human teacher, we of this nineteenth century can no more be Christians than we can be Platonists or Aristotelians. He belongs to that past which cannot repeat itself: His modes of thought are not ours: His difficulties are not ours: His needs are not ours. He may be our Teacher, but not our Master; for no man is master over the free thoughts of his fellow-men: we may learn from Him, but we sit in judgment while we learn: we modify His teaching by the wisdom of later ages: we refuse the evil and choose the good. But remember that we can do this, only if Christ is a mere human teacher, or if we of these latter days have received a newer and a better revelation. If now, as of old, He speaks as never man spake;[i]—if God, who at sundry times and in divers manners spake in time past unto the fathers by the prophets, hath in these last days spoken unto us by His Son,[k]—what remains for us to do, but to cast down imaginations, and every high thing that exalteth itself against the knowledge of God, and to bring into captivity every thought to the obedience of Christ?[l] The witness which Christ offers of Himself either proves everything, or it proves nothing. No man has a right to say, "I will accept Christ as I like, and reject Him as I like: I will follow the holy Example; I will turn away from the atoning Sacrifice: I will listen to His teaching; I will have nothing to do with His mediation: I will believe Him when He tells me that He came from the Father, because I feel that His doctrine has a divine beauty and fitness; but I will not believe Him when He tells me that He is one with the Father, because I cannot conceive how this unity is possible." This is not philosophy, which thus mutilates man: this is not Christianity, which thus divides Christ (16). If Christ is no more than one of us, let us honestly renounce the shadow of allegiance to an usurped authority, and boldly proclaim that every man

---

[i] St. John vii. 46. [k] Hebrews i. 1, 2. [l] 2 Corinthians x. 5.

is his own Redeemer. If Christ is God, no less than man, let us beware, lest haply we be found even to fight against God.[m]

Beyond question, every doubt which our reason may suggest in matters of religion is entitled to its due place in the examination of the evidences of religion; if we will treat it as a part only and not the whole; if we will not insist on a positive solution of that which, it may be, is given us for another purpose than to be solved. It is reasonable to believe that, in matters of belief as well as of practice, God has not thought fit to annihilate the free will of man; but has permitted speculative difficulties to exist as the trial and the discipline of sharp and subtle intellects, as He has permitted moral temptations to form the trial and the discipline of strong and eager passions (17). Our passions are not annihilated when we resist the temptation to sin: why should we expect that our doubts must be annihilated if we are to resist the temptation to unbelief? This correspondence of difficulties is so far from throwing doubt on the divine origin of Revelation, that it rather strengthens the proof that it has emanated from that Giver whose other gifts are subject to like conditions. We do not doubt that the conditions of our moral trial tend towards good and not towards evil: that human nature, even in its fallen state, bears traces of the image of its Maker, and is fitted to be an instrument in His moral government. And we believe this, notwithstanding the existence of passions and appetites which, isolated and uncontrolled, appear to lead in an opposite direction. Is it then more reasonable to deny that a system of revealed religion, whose unquestionable tendency as a whole is to promote the glory of God and the welfare of mankind, can have proceeded from the same Author, merely because we may be unable to detect the same character in

[m] Acts v. 39.

some of its minuter features, viewed apart from the system to which they belong?

It would of course be impossible now to enter upon any detailed examination of the positive Evidences of Christianity. The purpose of the foregoing Lectures will have been answered, if they can only succeed in clearing the way for a candid and impartial inquiry; by shewing what are the limits within which it must be confined, and what kind of reasoning is inadmissible, as transgressing those limits. The conclusion, which an examination of the conditions of human thought unavoidably forces upon us, is this: There can be no such thing as a positive science of Speculative Theology; for such a science must necessarily be based on an apprehension of the Infinite; and the Infinite, though we are compelled to believe in its existence, cannot be positively apprehended in any mode of the human Consciousness. The same impediment which prevents the *formation* of Theology as a science, is also manifestly fatal to the theory which asserts its *progressive development*. We can test the progress of knowledge, only by comparing its successive representations with the objects which they profess to represent: and as the object in this case is inaccessible to human faculties, we have no criterion by which to distinguish between progress and mere fluctuation. The so-called progress in Theology is in truth only an advance in those conceptions of man's moral and religious duties which form the basis of natural religion;—an advance which is regulative and not speculative; which is primarily and properly a knowledge, not of God's nature, but of man's obligations; and which is the result, not of an immediate intuition of the Nature of the Infinite, but of a closer study of the Laws of the Finite. A progress of this kind can obviously have no place in relation to those truths, if such there be, which human reason is incapable of discovering for itself: and to assert its applicability to the criticism of Revealed Religion, is to beg the entire question in dispute, by assuming, without the slightest authority, that Revelation *cannot be* anything more than a republication of Natural Religion (18).

But, on the other hand, there is an opposite caution no less needed, in making use of the counter-theory, which regards the doctrines of Revelation as truths accommodated to the finite capacities of man; as serving for regulative, not for speculative knowledge; and as not amenable to any criticism based on human representations of the Infinite. This theory is useful, not as explaining the difficulties involved in religious thought, but as shewing why we must leave them unexplained; not as removing the mysteries of revelation, but as shewing why such mysteries must exist. This caution has not always been sufficiently observed, even by those theologians who have shewn the most just appreciation of the limits of man's faculties in the comprehension of divine things. Thus, to mention an example of an ancient method of interpretation which has been revived with considerable ability and effect in modern times,—the rule, that the Attributes ascribed to God in Scripture must be understood as denoting correspondence in Effects, but not similarity of Causes, is one which is liable to considerable misapplication: it contains indeed a portion of the truth, but a portion which is sometimes treated as if it were the whole. "Ira et hujusmodi," says Aquinas, "attribuuntur Deo secundum similitudinem effectus" (19): and the same language has been employed by a distinguished Prelate of our own Church, in a passage probably familiar to many of us. "The meaning," says Archbishop King, "confessedly is, that He will as certainly punish the wicked as if He were inflamed with the passion of anger against them; that He will as infallibly reward the good, as we will those for whom we have a particular and affectionate love; that when men turn from their wickedness, and do what is agreeable to the divine command, He will as surely change His dispensations towards them, as if He really repented, and had changed His mind" (20).

This is no doubt a portion of the meaning; but is it the whole? Does Scripture intend *merely* to assert a resemblance in the effects, and none at all in the causes? If so, it is difficult to see why the natural rule of accommodation should have been reversed; why a plain and intelligible statement concerning the Divine Acts should have been veiled under an obscure and mysterious image of the Divine Attributes. If God's Anger means no more than His infliction of punishments; if His Love means no more than His bestowal of rewards; it would surely have been sufficient to have told us that God punishes sin and rewards obedience, without the interposition of a fictitious feeling as the basis of the relation. The conception of a God who acts is at least as human as that of a God who feels; and though both are but imperfect representations of the Infinite under finite images, yet, while both rest upon the same authority of Scripture, it is surely going beyond the limits of a just reserve in speaking of divine mysteries, to assume that the one is merely the symbol, and the other the interpretation. It is surely more reasonable, as well as more reverent, to believe that these partial representations of the Divine Consciousness, though, as finite, they are unable speculatively to represent the Absolute Nature of God, have yet each of them a regulative purpose to fulfil in the training of the mind of man: that there is a religious influence to be imparted to us by the thought of God's Anger, no less than by that of His Punishments; by the thought of His Love, no less than by that of His Benefits: that both, inadequate and human as they are, yet dimly indicate some corresponding reality in the Divine Nature:[n] and that to merge one in the other is not to gain a purer representation of God as He is, but

[n] In confirmation of this view I am happy to be able to quote the following remarks from a very able and excellent work written since the first publication of these Lectures. "What is the treatment which I should give to these symbols? Am I at liberty to say—These are figures, they are metaphors, in the oriental style, and as such, if I am in search of their exact import, they must be shorn of much of their apparent value? The very contrary of this should, as I think, be the rule of interpretation in the case. Oriental writers do indeed indulge themselves in the use of extravagant similes when they are framing adulations for the ear of potentates; but this is not the style of the Biblical writers; and when they are teaching theology in terms and phrases proper to the finite mind, which are the only terms available, or, indeed, *possible*, they accumulate such figurative terms as *substitutes* for *terms of the Infinite*. Thus, in teaching what they teach concerning the Divine Power—they say of the Most High such things as these: That HE taketh up the isles as a very little thing; that with HIM the mountains are only as the small dust of the balance; that HE stays the raging of the sea, and says to its proud waves—Thus far shall ye go, and no further. They say of God—that HE spreadeth forth the heavens as a tent to dwell in; and that as a garment, some time hence, HE shall roll them together. .... These metaphors are cumulative terms of the finite, employed for teaching me truths concerning the INFINITE, which could neither be taught nor learned in any other manner, whether by me or by the loftiest and largest of human minds. .... The abstractions of the finite reason become delusive fictions when they are put forward as applicable to the INFINITE: whereas the figures and (as they might be called) the fictions of a symbolic style are lights on the highway of eternal truth, when we take them for what they are— our *only* guides on that road."—Taylor's *Logic in Theology, &c.*, pp. 321-323.

The same thing had been said in substance, several years before, by one who was then the chief representative of a very different school of English theology. "Let then the Catholic dogmas, as such, be freely admitted to convey no true idea of Almighty God, but only an earthly one, gained from earthly figures. .... Still there may be a certain correspondence between the idea, though earthly, and its heavenly archetype, such that the idea belongs to the arche-

only to mutilate that under which He has been pleased to reveal Himself (21).

It is obvious, indeed, that the theory of an adaptation of divine truths to human faculties entirely changes its significance, as soon as we attempt to give a further adaptation to the adapted symbol itself;—to modify into a still lower truth that which is itself a modification of a higher. The instant we undertake to say that this or that speculative or practical interpretation is the *only real meaning* of that which Scripture represents to us under a different image, we abandon at once the supposition of an accommodation to the necessary limits of human thought, and virtually admit that the ulterior significance of the representation falls as much within those limits as the representation itself (22). Thus interpreted, the principle no longer offers the slightest safeguard against Rationalism:—nay, it becomes identified with the fundamental vice of Rationalism itself;—that of explaining away what we are unable to comprehend.

The adaptation for which I contend is one which admits of no such explanation. It is not an adaptation to the ignorance of one man, to be seen through by the superior knowledge of another; but one which exists in relation to the whole human race, as men, bound by the laws of man's thought; as creatures of time, instructed in the things of eternity; as finite beings, placed in relation to and communication with the Infinite. I believe that Scripture teaches, to each and all of us, the lesson which it was designed to teach, so long as we are men upon earth, and not as the angels in heaven (23). I believe that, " now we see through a glass darkly,"—in an enigma;—but that *now* is one which encompasses the whole race of mankind,

type, in a sense in which no other earthly idea belongs to it, as being the nearest approach to it which our present state allows."—Newman's *University Sermons*, pp. 341, 342.

from the cradle to the grave, from the creation to the day of judgment: that dark enigma is one which no human wisdom can solve; which Reason is unable to penetrate; and which Faith can only rest content with here, in hope of a clearer vision to be granted hereafter. If there be any who think that the Laws of Thought themselves may change with the changing knowledge of man; that the limitations of Subject and Object, of Duration and Succession, of Space and Time, belong to the vulgar only, and not to the philosopher:—if there be any who believe that they can think without the consciousness of themselves as thinking, or of anything about which they think; that they can be in such or such a mental state, and yet for no period of duration; that they can remember this state and make subsequent use of it, without conceiving it as antecedent, or as standing in any order of time to their present consciousness; that they can reflect upon God without their reflections following each other, without their succeeding to any earlier or being succeeded by any later state of mind:—if there be any who maintain that they can conceive Justice and Mercy and Wisdom, as neither existing in a just and merciful and wise Being, nor in any way distinguishable from each other:—if there be any who imagine that they can be conscious without variety, or discern without differences;—these and these alone may aspire to correct Revelation by the aid of Philosophy; for such alone are the conditions under which Philosophy can attain to a scientific knowledge of the Infinite God.

The intellectual difficulties which Rationalism discovers in the contents of Revelation (I do not now speak of those which belong to its external evidences) are such as no system of Rational Theology can hope to remove; for they are inherent in the constitution of Reason itself. Our mental laws, like our moral passions, are designed to serve the purposes of our earthly culture and discipline; both have their part to perform in moulding the intellect and the will of man through the slow stages of that training here whose completion is to be looked for hereafter. Without the possibility of temptation, where would be the merit of obedience? Without room for doubt, where would be the righteousness of faith? (24). But there is no temptation which taketh us, as Christians, but such as is common to man; and there is no doubt that taketh us, but such as is common to man also. It is the province of Philosophy to teach us this; and it is the province of Religion to turn the lesson to account. The proud definition of ancient sages, which bade the philosopher, as a lover of wisdom, strive after the knowledge of things divine and human, would speak more soberly and more truly by enjoining a Knowledge of things human, as subservient and auxiliary to Faith in things divine (25). Of the Nature and Attributes of God in His Infinite Being, Philosophy can tell us nothing: of man's inability to apprehend that Nature, and why he is thus unable, she tells us all that we can know, and all that we need to know. "Know thyself," was the precept inscribed in the Delphic Temple, as the best lesson of Heathen wisdom (26). "Know thyself," was the exhortation of the Christian Teacher to his disciple, adding, "if any man know himself, he will also know God" (27). He will at least be content to know so much of God's nature as God Himself has been pleased to reveal; and, where Revelation is silent, to worship without seeking to know more.

Know thyself in the various elements of thy intellectual and moral being; all alike will point reverently upward to the throne of the Invisible; but none will scale that throne itself, or pierce through the glory which conceals Him that sitteth thereon. Know thyself in thy powers of Thought, which, cramped and confined on every side, yet bear witness, in their very limits, to the Illimitable beyond.

Know thyself in the energies of thy Will, which, free and yet bound, the master at once and the servant of Law, bows itself under the imperfect consciousness of a higher Lawgiver, and asserts its freedom but by the permission of the Almighty. Know thyself in the yearnings of thy Affections, which, marvellously adapted as they are to their several finite ends, yet testify in their restlessness to the deep need of something better (28). Know thyself in that fearful and wonderful system of Human Nature as a whole, which is composed of all these, and yet not one with any nor with all of them; that system to whose inmost centre and utmost circumference the whole system of Christian Faith so strangely yet so fully adapts itself. It is to the whole Man that Christianity appeals: it is as a Whole and in relation to the whole Man that it must be judged (29). It is not an object for the thought alone, nor for the will alone, nor for the feelings alone. It may not be judged by reference to this petty cavil or that minute scruple: it may not be cut down to the dimensions and wants of any single ruling principle or passion. We have no right to say that we will be Christians as far as pleases us, and no further; that we will accept or reject, according as our understanding is satisfied or perplexed (30). The tree is not then most flourishing, when its branches are lopped, and its trunk peeled, and its whole body cut down to one hard unyielding mass; but when one principle of life pervades it throughout; when the trunk and the branches claim brotherhood and fellowship with the leaf that quivers, and the twig that bends to the breeze, and the bark that is delicate and easily wounded, and the root that lies lowly and unnoticed in the earth. And man is never so weak as when he seems to be strongest, standing alone in the confidence of an isolated and self-sufficing Intellect: he is never so strong as when he seems to be weakest, with every thought and resolve, and passion, and affection, from the highest to the lowest, bound together in one by the common tie of a frail and feeble Humanity. He is never so weak as when he casts off his burdens, and stands upright and unencumbered in the strength of his own will: he is never so strong as when, bowed down in his feebleness, and tottering under the whole load that God has laid upon him, he comes humbly before the throne of grace, to cast his care upon the God who careth for him. The life of man is one, and the system of Christian Faith is one: each part supplying something that another lacks; each element making good some missing link in the evidence furnished by the rest. But we may avail ourselves of that which satisfies our own peculiar needs, only by accepting it as part and parcel of the one indivisible Whole. Thus only shall we grow in our Christian Life in just proportion of every part; the intellect instructed, the will controlled, the affections purified, "till we all come, in the unity of the faith and of the knowledge of the Son of God, unto a perfect man, unto the measure of the stature of the fulness of Christ: that we henceforth be no more children, tossed to and fro, and carried about with every wind of doctrine, by the sleight of men, and cunning craftiness, whereby they lie in wait to deceive; but speaking the truth in love, may grow up into Him in all things, which is the Head, even Christ; from whom the whole body, fitly joined together and compacted by that which every joint supplieth, according to the effectual working in the measure of every part, maketh increase of the body unto the edifying of itself in love."[o]

[o] Ephesians iv. 13-16.

NOTES.

LECTURE I.

Note I. p. 3.

SEE Galen, *De Sectis*, c. 1. In this sense, the *Dogmatists* or *Rationalists* were distinguished from the *Empirics*. For the corresponding philosophical sense of the term, see Sextus Empiricus, *Pyrrh. Hyp.* I. § 1-3.

Note II. p. 3.

" Der Dogmatismus hat seinen Namen davon, dass er das Verhältniss zwischen den Dingen an sich und den Erscheinungen als einen Causalzusammenhang zu demonstriren, d. h. dogmatisch festzusetzen, sich anmasst; und behauptet dass die Dinge an sich den Grund von allem enthalten, was wir an dem Menschen und in der Naturwelt wahrnehmen."—Poelitz, *Kant's Vorlesungen über die Metaphysik.* Einleitung, p. xxi.

Note III. p. 3.

Of the theological method of Wolf, the leader of philosophical dogmatism in the eighteenth century, Mr. Rose observes, "He maintained that philosophy was indispensable to theology, and that, together with biblical proofs, a mathematical or strictly demonstrative dogmatical system, according to the principles of reason, was absolutely necessary. His own works carried this theory into practice, and after the first clamours against them had subsided, his opinions gained more attention, and it was not long before he had a school of vehement admirers who far outstripped him in the use of his own principles. We find some of them not content with applying demonstration to the truth of the system, but endeavouring to establish each separate dogma, the Trinity, the nature of the Redeemer, the Incarnation, the eternity of punishment, on philosophical, and, strange as it may appear, some of these truths on mathematical grounds."[a]

The language of Wolf himself may be quoted as expressing exactly the relation between Scripture and human reason mentioned

[a] *State of Protestantism in Germany*, p. 54. Second edition.

in the text. "*Scriptura sacra Theologiæ naturali adjumento est. Etenim in Scriptura sacra ea quoque de Deo docentur, quæ ex principiis rationis de eodem demonstrari possunt: id quod nemo negat, qui in lectione Scripturæ sacræ fuerit versatus. Suppeditat igitur Theologiæ naturali propositiones, quæ in ea demonstrari debent, consequenter philosophus eas non demum invenire, sed tantummodo demonstrare tenetur.*"[b]

The writings of Canz, a disciple of the Wolfian philosophy, are mentioned by Mr. Rose, and by Dr. Pusey (*Historical Inquiry*, p. 116), as exemplifying the manner in which this philosophy was applied to doctrinal theology. The following extracts from his attempted demonstration of the doctrine of the Trinity may be interesting to the reader, not only on account of the extreme rarity of the work from which they are taken, but also as furnishing a specimen of the dogmatic method, and shewing the abuse to which it is liable in injudicious hands.

"*Cum character omnis substantiæ in vi quadam agendi positus sit, Deus erit judicandus ex infinita agendi vi, idque generatim. Ea vis agendi, quoniam infinita est, complectitur omnes perfectiones, ideoque non ponitur in nuda facultate, quæ ab exercitio agendi nonnunquam cessat, quod imperfectionis foret; non collocatur in viribus hoc aut istud solum agendi; quod similiter cancellos proderet; sed in perdurante actu, eodemque purissimo, omnia operandi, quæcunque perfectissime, ideoque et sapientissime, una agi licet. Est igitur substantia plane singularis.*

"*Cum Deus porro actus purissimus sit, qui omnia in omnibus operatur, sequitur res finitas, quæ esse possunt et non possunt, rationem suæ existentiæ in se ipsis non invenire, sed in eo qui omnia operatur, i. e. Deo. Est igitur in Deo, quod primo loco intelligimus, Vis infinita Creandi.*

"*Sed quoniam, quæ creata sunt, omnia, ut media et fines, se mutuo respiciunt, ipsa autem, ultimo scopo, referuntur ad gloriam Dei, perspicuum est, esse in Deo infinitam Sapientiæ Vim, seu, ut Scriptura loquitur,* λόγον, *qui, cum veritas in harmonia rerum sufficienti ratione coordinatarum et sibi succedentium ponatur, omnem omnino possibilem veritatem perspicacia sua comprehendat.*

"*Quemadmodum denique infinita in rebus creatis bona sunt, et vero Deus omnia operans et hæc bona præstitisse judicetur; ita non est intellectu difficile, esse in Deo summam Amandi Vim. Ille enim amat, qui, quoties potest, aliorum felicitatem variis bonis auget.*

* * * * * * *

[b] *Theologia Naturalis, Pars Prior*, § 2.

"Subsistere dicitur quod existit, si complemento suo potitum est, nec procedit ultra. Fit enim progressus a possibili ad agendi vim, ab agendi vi, ad actum operandi, eumque talem quem determinavi. Tum subsistitur, nec proceditur quasi ultra.

"Quidquid hoc modo in existendo ultra non procedit, id ὑφιστάμενον vocant Metaphysici, cui si donum intelligentiæ seu ratio accesserit, tum existit Persona.

"His præmissis videamus an in Dei natura quidquam sit, quod trium Personarum titulo dignum. Est utique in Deo immensa vis agendi, ideoque Substantiæ singularissimæ indicium. Invenire etiam licet triplicem actum, qui illam vim, omnia operando, in omni triplici rerum genere, complet.

"Triplex illa operandi actus non solum existit quia praestruit vim agendi; sed et subsistit quilibet, quia nec pars est, nec pars socia alterius, nec denique operatio unius alterius est.

"Atqui cadit in hunc triplicem immensum, qua divina vis completur, actum, sui conscientia, et præteritorum pariter ac futurorum sensus. Est igitur quisque intelligens, ideoque Persona.

"Cum tres ejusmodi actus sint in Deo seu in Divina Natura, quæ immensa vis agendi est, sequitur in eadem Tres esse Personas, quæ unam illam infinitam vim immensa operatione triplici compleant et exerceant.

"Quoniam in omni quodcunque creatum et intelligendi facultate præditum est, vis operandi, intelligendi, amandi, non nisi Una operatione totali, seu Uno Actu compleri potest; sequitur in omni finito non esse posse nisi unicam personam.

"Ternio igitur Personarum in Deo a Natura Infinita qua tali proficiscitur. Quod erat demonstrationis propositum." c

Leibnitz, the great master of Wolf and his disciples, in the *Discours de la Conformité de la Foi avec la Raison*, prefixed to his *Théodicée*, § 59, decidedly condemns all attempts to render the mysteries of religion comprehensible by demonstration.

Note IV. p. 4.

Kant defines Rationalism, as distinguished from Naturalism and Supernaturalism, in the following terms. "Der, welcher blos die natürliche Religion für moralischnothwendig, d. i. für Pflicht erklärt,

---

c *Philosophiæ Wolfianæ Consensus cum Theologia*, Francofurti et Lipsiæ, 1737. This volume forms the third part of the *Philosophiæ Leibnitianæ et Wolfianæ usus in Theologia*, of which the first part was published in 1728, and the second in 1732. The third part is extremely rare. The two former parts were reprinted in 1749.

kann auch der *Rationalist* (in Glaubenssachen) genannt werden. Wenn dieser die Wirklichkeit aller übernatürlichen göttlichen Offenbarung verneint, so heisst er *Naturalist;* lässt er nun diese zwar zu, behauptet aber dass sie zu kennen und für wirklich anzunehmen, zur Religion nicht nothwendig erfordert wird, so würde er ein *reiner Rationalist* genannt werden können; hält er aber den Glauben an dieselbe zur allgemeinen Religion für nothwendig, so würde er der reine *Supernaturalist* in Glaubenssachen heissen können."[d] In the text, the term is used in a somewhat wider extent than that of the above definition. It is not necessary to limit the name of *Rationalist* to those who maintain that Revelation as a whole is unnecessary to religion; nor to those whose system is based solely on moral principles. There may be a partial as well as a total rationalism: it is possible to acknowledge in general terms the authority of Scripture, and yet to exercise considerable license in rejecting particular portions as speculatively incomprehensible or morally unnecessary. The term is sometimes specially applied to the Kantian school of theologians, of whom Paulus and Wegscheider are representatives. In this sense Hegel declares his antagonism to the Rationalism of his day;[e] and Strauss, in his controversies with the naturalist critics of the Gospels, frequently speaks of their method as "Rationalism." In the sense in which the term is employed in the text, Hegel and Strauss are themselves as thoroughly rationalists as their opponents. Even Schleiermacher, though a decided antagonist of the naturalist school, is himself a partial Rationalist of another kind; for with him the Christian Consciousness, *i. e.* the internal experience resulting to the individual from his connexion with the Christian community, is made a test of religious truth almost as arbitrary as the Moral Reason of Kant. On the strength of this self-chosen criterion, Schleiermacher sets aside, among other doctrines, as unessential to Christian belief, the supernatural conception of Jesus, the facts of His resurrection, ascension, and the prediction of His future judgment of the world; asserting that it is impossible to see how such facts can be connected with the redeeming power of Christ.[f] Indeed in some of

[d] *Religion innerhalb der Grenzen der blossen Vernunft* (*Werke*, ed. Rosenkranz, x. p. 185). For different senses in which the term *Rationalist* has been used, see Wegscheider, *Instit. Theol.* § 10; Rose, *State of Protestantism in Germany*, Introd. p. xvii.

second edition; Kahnis, *Internal History of German Protestantism*, p. 169, Meyer's translation.

[e] *Geschichte der Philosophie* (*Werke*, XIII. p. 96).

[f] *Der Christliche Glaube*, § 97, 99.

the details of his system he falls into pure Rationalism; as in his speculations on the existence of Angels, good and evil, on the Fall of Man, on eternal Punishment, on the two Natures of Christ, and on the equality of the Persons in the Holy Trinity.

The so-called Spiritualism of the present day is again only Rationalism disguised; for feeling or intuition is but an arbitrary standard, resting solely on the personal consciousness, and moreover must be translated into distinct thought, before it can be available for the purposes of religious criticism.

Note V. p. 4.

Thus Wegscheider represents the claim of the Rationalists. "Sanæ rationi facultatem vindicant religionis doctrinam qualemcunque a revelatione opinata supernaturali derivatam dijudicandi, ejusque argumentum non nisi ad leges cogitandi agendique rationi insitas exactum probandi."—*Inst. Theol.* § 10. See also Röhr, *Briefe über den Rationalismus*, p. 31.

Note VI. p. 7.

"Quapropter si non decet Deum aliquid injuste aut inordinate facere, non pertinet ad ejus libertatem, aut benignitatem, aut voluntatem, peccantem qui non solvit Deo, quod abstulit, impunitum dimittere."—Anselm, *Cur Deus Homo*, i. 12. "Ipsa namque perversitatis spontanea satisfactio, vel a non satisfaciente pœnæ exactio (excepto hoc quod Deus de malis multimodis bona facit) in eadem universitate locum tenent suum et ordinis pulchritudinem. Quas si divina sapientia, ubi perversitas rectum ordinem perturbare nititur, non adderet, fieret in ipsa universitate, quam Deus debet ordinare, quædam ex violata ordinis pulchritudine deformitas et Deus in sua dispositione videretur deficere. Quæ duo quoniam sicut sunt inconvenientia, ita sunt impossibilia, necesse est ut omne peccatum satisfactio aut pœna sequatur."—*Ibid.* i. 15. "Si ergo sicut constat, necesse est ut de hominibus perficiatur illa superna civitas; nec hoc esse valet, nisi fiat prædicta satisfactio, quam nec potest facere, nisi Deus, nec debet nisi homo; necesse est ut eam faciat Deus homo."—*Ibid.* ii. 6. Compare Alex. ab Ales. *Summa Theologiæ*, P. III. Memb. 7, where the same argument is concisely stated.

Note VII. p. 7.

Anselm, *Cur Deus Homo*, l. II. c. 16.

Note VIII. p. 7.

Anselm, *Cur Deus Homo*, l. I. c. 5.

Note IX. p. 7.

"Deus ita misericors est, ut sit etiam simul justus; misericordia non excludit in eo æternam justitiæ regulam, sed summum et admirabile est in eo misericordiæ et justitiæ temperamentum; ergo non potuit peccatum salva divina justitia absque æquivalente pretio in Dei judicio homini remitti. Nullum ergo aliud supererat remedium, quam ut ipse Dei Filius humanam naturam assumeret, ac in ea et per eam satisfaceret. Deus non debebat; homo non poterat."—J. Gerhard, *Loci Theologici, De Persona et Officio Christi*, c. viii.

Note X. p. 8.

"Quia nuda creatura non potuisset sustinere immensum onus iræ Dei, totius mundi peccatis debitæ."—Chemnitz, *De Duabus Naturis in Christo*, c. xi.

Note XI. p. 8.

Such is the demand of Anselm's interlocutor, which he himself undertakes to satisfy: "Ut rationabili necessitate intelligam esse oportere omnia illa quæ nobis Fides Catholica de Christo credere præcipit."—*Cur Deus Homo*, l. I. c. 25. To arguments founded on this principle the judicious remarks of Bishop Butler may be applied: "It may be needful to mention that several questions, which have been brought into the subject before us, and determined, are not in the least entered into here: questions which have been, I fear, rashly determined, and perhaps with equal rashness contrary ways. For instance, whether God could have saved the world by other means than the death of Christ, consistently with the general laws of His government." [g]

Note XII. p. 8.

"In what did this satisfaction consist? Was it that God was angry, and needed to be propitiated like some heathen deity of old? Such a thought refutes itself by the very indignation which it calls up in the human bosom."—Jowett, *Epistles of St. Paul*, vol. ii. p. 472.[h] "Neither *can* there be any such thing as vicarious atonement

---

[g] *Analogy*, Part II. Ch. 5.
[h] In this and other quotations from | Professor Jowett's work, I have retained the language of his first edition, which

or punishment, which, again, is a relic of heathen conceptions of an angered Deity, to be propitiated by offerings and sacrifices."—Greg, *Creed of Christendom*, p. 265. "The religion of types and notions can travel only in a circle from whence there is no escape. It is but an elaborate process of self-confutation. After much verbiage it demolishes what it created, and having begun by assuming God to be angry, ends, not by admitting its own gross mistake, but by asserting *Him* to be changed and reconciled."—Mackay, *Progress of the Intellect*, vol. ii. p. 504. Compare Wegscheider, *Inst. Theol.* § 141.

Note XIII. p. 8.

"Quid enim iniquius, quam insontem pro sontibus puniri, præsertim cum ipsi sontes adsunt, qui ipsi puniri possunt."—F. Socinus, *Prælect. Theol.* c. xviii. "That each should have his exact due is *just*—is the best for himself. That the consequence of his guilt should be transferred from him to one who is innocent (although that innocent one be himself willing to accept it) whatever else it be, is not *justice*."—Froude, *Nemesis of Faith*, p. 70. Compare F. W. Newman, *Phases of Faith*, p. 92; Greg, *Creed of Christendom*, p. 265. A similar objection is introduced, and apparently approved, by Mr. Maurice, *Theological Essays*, p. 139.

Note XIV. p. 8.

"Nemo est qui injurias sibi allatas, debitaque secum contracta, summo jure condonare et remittere non queat, nulla vera pro ipsis satisfactione accepta. Igitur, nisi velimus Deo minus concedere quam hominibus ipsis concedatur, confitendum omnino est, Deum jure potuisse nobis peccata nostra ignoscere, nulla pro ipsis vera satisfactione accepta."—F. Socinus, *Prælect. Theol.* c. xvi. "Now it is certainly required of us, that if our brother only *repent*, we should forgive him, even though he should repeat his offence seven times a day. On the same generous maxim, therefore, we cannot but conclude that the Divine Being acts towards us."—Priestley, *History of Corruptions*, vol. i. p. 151. "Every good man has learned to forgive, and when the offender is penitent, to forgive freely—without punishment or retribution: whence the conclusion is in-

in most instances is necessary to explain the allusions to it in my own text. But it is only justice to the distinguished author to state that in his second edition, while retaining the substance of his original teaching, he has considerably modified the language in which it is expressed and the arguments by which it is supported.

evitable, that God also forgives, as soon as the sin is repented of."—
F. W. Newman, *The Soul*, pp. 99, 100. "Was it that there was a
debt due to Him, which must be paid ere its consequences could be
done away? But even 'a man's' debt may be freely forgiven."
—Jowett, *Epistles of St. Paul*, vol. ii. p. 472. Compare also Maurice, *Theol. Essays*, p. 138; and Garve, quoted by Röhr, *Briefe über
den Rationalismus*, p. 442.

Note XV. p. 8.

"Pecuniariæ pœnæ ideo pro altero pendi possunt, quia unius
pecunia alterius effici potest; ut cum quis pecuniam pœnæ nomine
pro alio quopiam solvit, tunc is, pro quo solvitur, tacite reipsa prius
ea pecunia donatur, ipseque eam solvisse censetur. At mors unius
corporisve ulla vexatio, alterius fieri non potest."—F. Socinus, *Prælect. Theol.* c. xviii. "Est siquidem pecunia, ut jurisconsulti loquuntur,
reale quiddam, et idcirco ab alio in alium transferri potest. Pœnæ
vero, et quæ peccatis hominum ex lege Dei debentur, sunt quiddam
personale, et propterea ejusmodi, quæ illi ipsi, qui eas dat, perpetuo
adhæreant, nec in alium queant transferri."—F. Socinus, *Christianæ
Religionis Institutio* (*Opera*, 1656, vol. i. p. 665). "Diese ursprüngliche, oder überhaupt vor jedem Guten, das er immer thun mag,
vorhergehende Schuld, die auch dasjenige ist, das, und nichts mehr,
wir unter dem *radicalen* Bösen verstanden, kann aber auch, so viel
wir nach unserem Vernunftrecht einsehen, nicht von einem andern
getilgt werden, denn sie ist keine *transmissibile* Verbindlichkeit, die
etwa, wie eine Geldschuld (bei der es dem Gläubiger einerlei ist, ob
der Schuldner selbst oder ein Anderer für ihn bezahlt) auf einen
Andern übertragen werden kann, sondern die Allerpersönlichste,
nämlich die Sündenschuld, die nur der Strafbare, nicht der Unschuldige, er mag auch noch so grossmüthig seyn sie für jenen übernehmen zu wollen, tragen kann."—Kant, *Religion innerhalb der
Grenzen der blossen Vernunft*, p. 84, ed. Rosenkranz. Compare
Coleridge, *Aids to Reflection*, p. 249, ed. 1839. His argument is
chiefly an expansion of Kant's. An able answer to this class of
objections will be found in Mr. Macdonnell's *Donnellan Lectures*,
p. 167.

Note XVI. p. 9.

Wilberforce, *Doctrine of the Incarnation*, pp. 44, 45, 4th edition.
The germ of this theory may perhaps be found in Damascenus, *De
Fide Orthod.*, lib. iii. c. 6. See Dorner, *Lehre von der Person Christi*,
p. 115. It also partially appears, in a form more adapted to the

realistic controversy, in Anselm, particularly in his treatise *De Fide Trinitatis et de Incarnatione Verbi*, written to refute the theological errors of the nominalist Roscelin. In modern times, a similar theory has found favour with those philosophers of the Hegelian school, who, in opposition to the development represented by Strauss, have undertaken the difficult task of reconciling the philosophy of their master with historical Christianity. In this point of view it has been adopted by Schaller in his 'Der historische Christus und die Philosophie,' and by Göschel in his 'Beiträge zur Speculativen Philosophie von Gott und dem Menschen und von den Gottmenschen.' For an account of these theories, see Dorner, p. 462, 477. A similar view is maintained by Marheineke, *Grundlehren der Christlichen Dogmatik*, § 338, and by Dorner himself, *Lehre von der Person Christi*, p. 527.

Note XVII. p. 9.

"Item sequitur quod aliquid de essentia Christi erit miserum et damnatum, quia illa natura communis existens realiter in Christo et in damnato erit damnatum, quia in Juda." Occam, *Logica*, p. I. c. 15.

Note XVIII. p. 11.

"Religion ist (subjectiv betrachtet) das Erkenntniss aller unserer Pflichten als göttlicher Gebote."—Kant, *Religion innerhalb der Grenzen der blossen Vernunft*, p. 184, ed. Rosenkranz. In the same spirit, Fichte says, "Da alle Religion Gott nur als moralischen Gesetzgeber darstellt, so ist alles, was nicht Gebot des Moralgesetztes in uns ist, auch nicht das seinige, und es ist kein Mittel ihm zu gefallen, als durch Beobachtung desselben."—*Versuch einer Kritik aller Offenbarung* (*Werke*, v. p. 127). This is exactly the theory of Religion which is refuted in anticipation by Bishop Butler (*Analogy*, p. II. c. i.) as the only opinion of those who hold that the "only design" of Revelation "must be to establish a belief of the moral system of nature, and to enforce the practice of natural piety and virtue."

Note XIX. p. 11.

Ibid., pp. 184, 186.

Note XX. p. 12.

"Das Beten, als ein innerer *förmlicher* Gottesdienst, und darum als Gnadensmittel gedacht, ist ein abergläubischer Wahn."—*Ibid.*, p. 235.

Note XXI. p. 12.

"Ein herzlicher Wunsch, Gott in allem unserm Thun und Lassen wohlgefällig zu seyn, d. i. die alle unsere Handlungen begleitende Gesinnung, sie als ob sie im Dienste Gottes geschehen, zu betreiben, ist der *Geist des Gebets*, der ohne Unterlass in uns stattfinden kann und soll. Diesen Wunsch aber (es sey auch nur innerlich) in Worte und Formeln einzukleiden, kann höchstens nur den Werth eines Mittels zu wiederholter Belebung jener Gesinnung in uns selbst bei sich führen, unmittelbar aber keine Beziehung aufs göttliche Wohlgefallen haben, eben darum auch nicht für Jedermann Pflicht seyn, weil ein Mittel nur dem vorgeschrieben werden kann, der es zu gewissen Zwecken bedarf." . . . . "In jenem Wunsche, als dem Geiste des Gebets, sucht der Mensch nur auf sich selbst (zu Belebung seiner Gesinnungen vermittelst der *Idee von Gott*), in diesem aber, da er sich durch Worte, mithin äusserlich erklärt *auf* Gott zu wirken."—Kant *Religion, u. s. w.* p. 235. Cf. Fichte, *Kritik aller Offenbarung,* p. 127. For an account of a similar view advocated in Scotland in the last century, by Dr. Leechman and others, see Combe's *Constitution of Man*, ch. ix. Subsequent writers have repeated the above theory in various forms, and in various spirits, but all urging the same objection, from the supposed unchangeable nature of God. See Schleiermacher, *Der Christliche Glaube*, § 147, and his sermon 'Die Kraft des Gebetes,' *Predigten*, I. p. 24; Strauss, *Glaubenslehre*, II. p. 387; Foxton, *Popular Christianity*, p. 113; Parker, *Theism, Atheism, and Popular Theology*, p. 65; Emerson, *Essay on Self-Reliance*; and a remarkable passage from Greg's *Creed of Christendom*, quoted in Lecture VI. p. 130. Some valuable remarks on the other side will be found in two writers, usually opposed to each other, but for once united in vindicating the religious instincts of mankind from the perversions of a false philosophy. See F. W. Newman, *The Soul*, p. 118, and 'Correspondence of R. E. H. Greyson, Esq.,' vol. i. p. 278. Kant's theory is ably criticized by Drobisch, *Grundlehren der Religionsphilosophie*, p. 267. Some excellent remarks on the same subject will be found in Dr. Hannah's *Discourses on the Fall and its Results*, p. 260.

Note XXII. p. 12.

Thus Fichte lays it down, as one of the tests of a true Revelation, that it must not countenance an *objective Anthropomorphism* of God. In illustration of this canon he says, "Können wir Gott wirklich durch unsere Empfindungen bestimmen, ihn zum Mitleiden, zum Erbarmen, zur Freude bewegen, so ist er nicht der Unveränderliche, der Alleingenugsame, der Alleinselige, so ist er noch durch etwas anderes, als durch das Moralgesetz bestimmbar; so können wir auch wohl hoffen, ihn durch Winseln und Zerknirschung zu bewegen, dass er anders mit uns verfahre, als der Grad unserer Moralität es verdient hätte. Alle diese sinnlichen Darstellungen göttlicher Eigenschaften müssen also nicht als objectiv gültig angekündigt werden: es muss nicht zweideutig gelassen werden, ob Gott *an sich* so beschaffen sey, oder ob er uns nur zum Behuf unseres sinnlichen Bedürfnisses erlauben wolle, ihn so zu denken."[1] On this principle, he considers the notions of a Resurrection and a Day of Judgment as having a merely subjective validity.[j] In another passage, he speaks of the representation of God under conditions of time as "eine grobe Anthropomorphose;"[k] apparently not seeing that the notion of unchangeableness is at least as much one of time, and therefore of Anthropomorphism, as that of compassion or joy. In a similar spirit, a later writer observes, "Bei dem grossen Gewicht, das man so oft auf die Persönlichkeit Gottes legt, mischt sich gar zu leicht das Interesse des Anthropopathismus und Anthropomorphismus ein."[l] In another passage, Fichte says, "Wer da sagt: du sollst dir keinen Begriff von Gott machen, sagt mit anderen Worten: du sollst dir keinen Götzen machen'; und sein Gebot bedeutet geistig dasselbe was das uralte Mosaische sinnlich: Du sollst dir kein Bildniss machen."[m] These words may perhaps have suggested the cognate remarks of Professor Jowett: "It would be little better than idolatry to fill the mind with an idea of God which represented him in fashion as a man. And in using a figure of speech, we are bound to explain to all who are capable of understanding, that we speak in a figure only, and to remind them that logical categories may give as false and imperfect a conception of the Divine nature in our own age, as graven images in the days of the patriarchs.[n] If by *logical categories* are meant analogical representations formed from the facts of human consciousness, this passage may be so interpreted as to imply either an important truth, or a dangerous error. If interpreted to

---

[1] *Versuch einer Kritik aller Offenbarung* (*Werke*, v. p. 135).
[j] *Ibid.* p. 136, 137.
[k] *Ibid.* p. 109.
[l] Baur, *Christliche Gnosis*, p. 705.
[m] *Gerichtliche Verantwortung* (*Werke*, v. p. 267). In like manner, Herder says, "Also wenn wir von Gott reden, lieber keine Bilder! Auch in der Philosophie ist dies unser erstes Gebot, wie im Gesetz Moses." *Gott. Einige Gespräche über Spinoza's System.* (*Werke*, viii. p. 228.)
[n] *Epistles of St. Paul*, vol. ii. p. 404.

mean that such representations of God cannot be regarded as adequate expressions of His absolute and infinite nature, it states a truth, the importance of which can hardly be over-estimated; but if it be meant, as Fichte undoubtedly meant, to signify that mental no less than bodily images, are, regarded from a human point of view, false and idolatrous, the author would do well to tell us what we can substitute in their place. "We may confidently challenge all natural Theology," says Kant, "to name a single distinctive attribute of the Deity, whether denoting intelligence or will, which, apart from Anthropomorphism, is anything more than a mere word, to which not the slightest notion can be attached, which can serve to extend our theoretical knowledge."[o] Kant, however, attempts to avoid the conclusion to which this admission necessarily leads;— namely, that Anthropomorphism, in this sense of the term, is the indispensable condition of all human theology. As regards the charge of Idolatry, it is best answered in the words of Storr: "Hanc Dei imaginem non *nosmet ipsi nobis fecimus, sed Deus proposuit.*"[p] The very commandment which forbids the representation of God by a bodily likeness, does so by means of two other human representations, that of a mental state, and that of a consequent course of action: "Thou shalt not make to thyself any graven image; for I the Lord thy God am a jealous God, and visit the sins of the fathers upon the children." The Satire of Xenophanes has been repeated by modern critics in a manner which deprives it entirely of its original point. Thus Mr. Theodore Parker says, "A Beaver or a Reindeer, if possessed of religious faculties, would also conceive of the Deity with the limitations of its own personality, as a Beaver or a Reindeer."[q] The satire loses its entire force, when transferred from bodily forms to mental attributes. In imagining a Beaver or a Reindeer with a personal consciousness, we so far imagine him as resembling man, notwithstanding the difference of bodily form. The sarcasm therefore amounts to no more than this; that human consciousness in another body would be subject to the same limits of religious thought as in its present one. One of the latest specimens of

[o] *Kritik der praktischen Vernunft*, p. 282, ed. Rosenkranz. Compare the remarkable words of Jacobi (*Von den göttlichen Dingen, Werke*, iii. p. 418, 422). "Den Menschen erschaffend theomorphisirte Gott. Nothwendig anthropomorphisirt darum der Mensch. ... Wir bekennen uns demnach zu einem von der Ueberzeugung: dass der Mensch Gottes Ebenbild in sich trage— unzertrennlichen Anthropomorphismus, und behaupten, ausser diesem Anthropomorphismus, der von jeher Theismus genannt wurde, ist nur Gottesläugnung oder Fetichismus."

[p] *Annotationes quædam Theologicæ*, p. 10.

[q] *Discourse of Matters pertaining to Religion*, p. 100.

this kind of philosophy is furnished by Professor Baden Powell, in his 'Christianity without Judaism,' p. 108. "It is not one of the least remarkable of these Anthropomorphisms," he says, "that (as in former instances) the disclosure of the Divine purpose is made under the figure of Jehovah entering into a *covenant* with his people —an idea specially adapted to a nation of the lowest moral capacity." It is curious to contrast this supercilious language of the modern critic with the very different spirit in which St. Paul, whom even modern criticism will hardly regard as an example " of the lowest moral capacity," treats the same figure of a covenant between God and man.

Note XXIII. p. 13.

This remark may seem at first sight not so appropriate in relation to Kant as to some other advocates of a similar theory, such, for instance, as Mr. Greg, whose remarks on prayer are quoted in Lecture VI. p. 130. For Kant, in language at least, expressly denies that any temporal consecution can be included in the conception of God.ʳ But, in truth, this denial is and must be merely verbal. For the moral law, in Kant's own theory, is regarded as a divine command because it is conceived as a perpetual obligation, binding upon all human acts; and the perpetuity of the obligation, in relation to successive acts, necessarily implies the idea of Time. Thus God in relation to man, as a moral Governor, is necessarily manifested under the condition of time; and this manifestation is the only philosophical representation of God which the Kantian philosophy recognises as valid. Indeed, if Time be, as Kant maintains, a necessary form of human consciousness, the conception of a Being existing out of time can have no place in the consciousness of any human thinker.

Note XXIV. p. 14.

Xenophanes, apud Clem. Alex. *Strom.* v. p. 601 :

'Αλλ' εἴτοι χεῖρας γ' εἶχον βόες ἠὲ λέοντες,
Ἢ γράψαι χείρεσσι καὶ ἔργα τελεῖν ἅπερ ἄνδρες,
Ἵπποι μέν θ' ἵπποισι, βόες δέ τε βουσὶν ὁμοῖοι [ὁμοίας]
Καί κε θεῶν ἰδέας ἔγραφον καὶ σώματ' ἐποίουν
Τοιαῦθ' οἷόν περ καὐτοὶ δέμας εἶχον ὁμοῖον.

Note XXV. p. 17.

Plato, *Republic*, iv. p. 433.

ʳ *Religion innerhalb der Grenzen der blossen Vernunft*, p. 57, ed. Rosenkranz.

Note XXVI. p. 18.

Advancement of Learning. (*Works*, ed. Montagu, vol. ii. p. 303.)

Note XXVII. p. 18.

Versuch einer Kritik aller Offenbarung, Königsberg, 1792; 2nd ed. 1793. (Fichte's *Werke*, v. p. 9.) A few specimens of the criticisms hazarded in this work will be sufficient to show the arbitrary character of the method on which it proceeds. The author assumes that God is determined entirely and solely by the moral law as conceived by man; and that Religion, therefore, must consist solely in moral duties.^s Hence he lays down, among others, the following criteria, without satisfying which, no Revelation can be accepted as of divine origin.

There must have been a moral necessity for it at the time of its publication (p. 113).

It must not draw men to obedience by any other motive than reverence for God's holiness. Hence it must not contain any prospect of future reward or punishment (p. 115).

It must not communicate any knowledge unattainable by the natural reason (p. 122).

It must contain only such moral rules as may be deduced from the principle of the practical reason (p. 124).

It must not promise any supernatural aids to men in the performance of their duty (p. 129).

Kant's own work, *Religion innerhalb der Grenzen der blossen Vernunft*, Königsberg, 1793, is based on a similar principle; and many of his conclusions are identical with those of Fichte. He agrees with his disciple in maintaining that no doctrine can be received on the authority of Revelation, without the concurrent testimony of Reason;^t and that a moral life is the only duty which God can require of man.^u Hence he defines Religion as "the acknowledgment of all our duties as divine commands;" and asserts that there can be no special duties towards God distinct from our moral obligations to our fellow-men.^x In accordance with these principles, he advocates, and in some instances applies, a method of Scripture interpretation, which consists in forcing every available doctrine and precept into a so-called moral significance, and rejecting as unessential whatever will not bear this treatment.^y Thus in the

^s *Werke*, v. pp. 42, 55. ^t *Werke*, x. p. 228. ^u *Ibid.* p. 122.
  ^x *Ibid.* p. 184. ^y *Ibid.* pp. 98, 130.

59th Psalm, the enemies of David are interpreted to mean the evil passions which he wished to overcome.

The narrowness of Kant's fundamental assumption, even as regards the human side of religion only, is pointed out by Willm, *Histoire de la Philosophie Allemande*, vol. ii. p. 47: "A force de voir dans la religion surtout un moyen de moralisation, Kant en a trop borné la divine mission; il a oublié que la religion doit être de plus une source de consolation et d'espérance au milieu des misères de la vie présente, et que par de puissants motifs et de hautes méditations elle-doit venir au secours de la fragilité humaine, nous servir d'appui dans la double lutte que nous avons à soutenir contre la tentation au mal et contre la souffrance." See also Drobisch, *Grundlehren der Religionsphilosophie*, p. 264, who adopts a similar ground of criticism.

NOTE XXVIII. p. 20.

"Bei der Exposition des reinen Begriffes ist noch weiter angedeutet worden, dass derselbe der absolute göttliche Begriff selbst ist, so dass in Wahrheit nicht das Verhältniss einer *Anwendung* stattfinden würde, sondern jener logische Verlauf die unmittelbare Darstellung des Selbstbestimmung Gottes zum Seyn wäre."—Hegel, *Logik* (*Werke*, v. p. 170). In like manner his disciple Marheineke says, "Nur in diese Idee aufgenommen und in ihr aufgehoben ist der menschliche Geist fähig, Gott zu erkennen. Sein wahres Sicherheben zu Gott durchs Denken ist aber stets zugleich ein Erhobenseyn, das Eingerücktseyn des menschlichen Denkens Gottes in das göttliche Denken Gottes."[1] Such passages are instructive as shewing the only conditions under which, according to the admission of its ablest advocates, a Philosophy of the Absolute is attainable by human thought. In reference to these lofty pretensions, Sir William Hamilton justly speaks of "the scheme of pantheistic omniscience, so prevalent among the sequacious thinkers of the day."[2]

NOTE XXIX. p. 20.

"Es ist, ausser Gott, gar nichts wahrhaftig und in der eigentlichen Bedeutung des Wortes da, denn—das *Wissen*: und dieses Wissen

[1] *Grundlehren der Christlichen Dogmatik*, § 21. In another passage of the same work (§ 84) he says, "Wie Gott in der Erkenntniss seiner selbst sich nicht ausser sich hat, noch als der sich erkennende ein anderes ist, als der erkannte, der Geist vielmehr beider Einheit und Wesen, so ist die Idee des Absoluten selber die absolute, und als solche der Standpunct des Wissens und der Wissenschaft."

[2] *Discussions*, p. 787.

ist das göttliche Daseyn selber, schlechthin und unmittelbar, und inwiefern wir das Wissen sind, sind wir selber in unserer tiefsten Wurzel das göttliche Daseyn."—Fichte, *Anweisungen zum seligen Leben* (*Werke*, v. p. 448). "Der Mensch, das Vernunftwesen überhaupt, ist hingestellt, eine Ergänzung der Welterscheinung zu seyn: aus ihm, aus seiner Thätigkeit soll sich entwickeln, was zur Totalität der Offenbarung Gottes fehlt, da die Natur zwar das ganze göttliche Wesen, aber nur in Realen empfängt; das Vernunftwesen soll das Bild derselben göttlichen Natur, wie sie an sich selbst ist, demnach im Idealen ausdrücken."—Schelling, *Vorlesungen über die Methode des Academischen Studium*, p. 18. "Gott ist unendlich, Ich endlich, dies sind falsche, schlechte Ausdrücke, Formen die dem nicht angemessen sind, was die Idee ist, was die Natur der Sache ist. Das Endliche ist nicht das Seyende, eben so ist das Unendliche nicht fest; diese Bestimmungen sind nur *Momente des Processes*. Gott ist ebenso auch als Endliches, und das Ich ebenso als Unendliches . . . . Gott ist die Bewegung zum Endlichen und dadurch als Aufhebung desselben zu sich selbst; im Ich, als dem sich als endlich aufhebenden, kehrt Gott zu sich zurück, und ist nur Gott als diese Rückkehr. Ohne Welt ist Gott nicht Gott."—Hegel, *Vorlesungen über die Philosophie der Religion* (*Werke*, xi. p. 194). "Dass der Mensch von Gott weiss, ist nach der Wesentlichen Gemeinschaft ein gemeinschaftliches Wissen—d. i. der Mensch weiss nur von Gott, insofern Gott im Menschen von sich selbst weiss, diess Wissen ist Selbstbewusstseyn Gottes, aber ebenso ein Wissen desselben von Menschen, und diess Wissen Gottes vom Menschen ist Wissen des Menschen von Gott. Der Geist des Menschen, von Gott zu wissen, ist nur der Geist Gottes selbst."—*Ibid.* xii. p. 496. "Das vernünftige Wissen der Wahrheit ist zunächst als ein Wissen von Gott das Wissen durch Gott, das Wissen in seinem Geiste und durch ihn. Von dem endlichen, relativen Denken kann Gott, der nichts endliches und relatives ist, nicht gedacht und gewusst werden. In diesem Wissen hingegen ist das Ich über sich und die Subjectivität des isolirten Bewusstseyns seiner selbst hinaus, es ist in Gott und Gott in ihm. In dem menschlichen Geiste ist Gott sich nicht durch diesen, sondern durch sich selbst offenbar, und so auch dem menschlichen Geiste offenbar."—Marheineke, *Grundlehren der Christlichen Dogmatik*, § 115.

Rationalism here takes up a common ground with Mysticism, and the logical process of the Hegelians becomes identical with the ecstatic intuition of the Neo-Platonists. Compare the language of Plotinus, Enn. VI. L. ix. c. 9. Ὁρᾶν δή ἐστιν ἐνταῦθα κἀκεῖνον καὶ ἑαυτὸν, ὡς ὁρᾷν θέμις ἑαυτὸν μὲν ἠγλαϊσμένον, φωτὸς πλήρη νοητοῦ, μᾶλλον δὲ φῶς αὐτὸ καθαρὸν, ἀβαρῆ, κοῦφον, θεὸν γενόμενον, μᾶλλον δὲ ὄντα. In the same strain sings the "Cherubic Wanderer" Angelus Silesius:

> "In Gott wird nichts erkannt; er ist ein einig Ein;
> Was man in ihm erkennt, das muss man selber sein." [b]

For an exactly similar doctrine, asserted in the Hindu Vedas, see Dr. Mill's *Observations on the application of pantheistic principles to the criticism of the Gospel*, p. 159.

NOTE XXX., p. 21.

Hegel, in his Lectures on the Philosophy of Religion, thus interprets the history of Christ. "In dieser ganzen Geschichte ist den Menschen zum Bewusstseyn gekommen, und das ist die Wahrheit, zu der sie gelangt sind: dass die Idee Gottes für sie Gewissheit hat, dass das Menschliche unmittelbarer, präsenter Gott ist und zwar so, dass in dieser Geschichte, wie sie der Geist auffast, selbst die Darstellung des Processes ist dessen, was der Mensch, der Geist ist." [c] The view here obscurely intimated is more explicitly stated by his disciple, Strauss, whose theory is little more than the legitimate development of his master's. In his *Christliche Glaubenslehre*, § 33, he sums up the results of the speculations of modern philosophy concerning the personality of God, in the following words: "Weil Gott an sich die ewige Persönlichkeit selbst ist, so hat er ewig das Andere seiner, die Natur, aus sich hervorgehen lassen, um ewig als selbstbewusster Geist in sich zurückzukehren. Oder, die Persönlichkeit Gottes muss nicht als Einzelpersönlichkeit, sondern als Allpersönlichkeit gedacht werden; statt unsrerseits das Absolute zu personificiren, müssen wir es als das in's Unendliche sich selbst personificirende begreifen lernen." This view is still more plainly stated in a fearful passage of his *Leben Jesu*, § 151, which the reader will find quoted at length in Lecture V., p. 114. The critic of Strauss, Bruno Bauer, in his *Kritik der evangelischen Geschichte der Synoptiker*, § 91, adopts the same view, observing, "Ueberhaupt das religiöse Bewusstseyn der sich selbst entfremdete Geist ist:" and to this origin he ascribes the doctrine of Christ's Divinity: "Der historische Christus ist der Mensch, den das religiöse Bewusstseyn in den Himmel erhoben hat." Feuerbach, in his *Wesen des Chris-*

---

[b] *Cherubinischer Wandersmann*, I. 285. Quoted by Strauss, *Christliche Glaubenslehre*, 1. p. 531.   [c] *Werke*, XII. p. 307.

tenthums,[d] from a different point of view, arrives at a similar conclusion, maintaining that God is but the personification of the general notion of humanity. Emerson gives us occasional glimpses of the same philosophy. Thus in his "Christian Teacher" he explains the Divinity of Christ: "He saw that God incarnates himself in man, and evermore goes forth anew to take possession of his world. He said in this jubilee of sublime emotion: 'I am divine. Through me, God acts; through me, speaks. Would you see God, see me; or see thee, when thou also thinkest as I now think.'"[e] And, in the "Over-Soul," in still more daring language, he says: "In all conversation between two persons, tacit reference is made as to a third party, to a common nature. That third party or common nature is not social; it is impersonal, is God."[f]

Another form of this deification of humanity is that of M. Comte, who agrees with Strauss and Feuerbach, in finding God only in the human race. This discovery is announced as the grand consummation of the Positive Philosophy. "Cette appréciation finale condense l'ensemble des conceptions positives dans la seule notion d'un être immense et éternel, l'Humanité, dont les destinées sociologiques se développent toujours sous la prépondérance nécessaire des fatalités biologiques et cosmologiques. Autour de ce vrai Grand-Etre, moteur immédiat de chaque existence individuelle ou collective, nos affections se concentrent aussi spontanément que nos pensées et nos actions."[g] From this grand ideal of humanity, unworthy individuals of the race are excluded; but, "si ces producteurs de fumier ne font vraiment point partie de l'Humanité, une juste compensation vous prescrit de joindre au nouvel Etre-Suprême tous ses dignes auxiliaires animaux."[h] Such is the brilliant discovery which entitles its author, in his own modest estimate, to be considered as uniting in his own person the characters of St. Paul and Aristotle, as the founder at once of true religion and sound philosophy.[i]

[d] See Ewerbeck, *Qu'est ce que la Religion d'après la nouvelle Philosophie Allemande*, pp. 271, 390, 413.
[e] *Essays* (Orr's Edition, 1851), p. 511.
[f] *Ibid.* p. 125.
[g] *Catéchisme Positiviste*, p. 19.
[h] *Catéchisme Positiviste*, p. 31. Thus, under the auspices of the positive philosophy, we return once more to the worship of the ibis, the ichneumon, and the cat. The Egyptians had the same reverence for their "dignes auxiliaires animaux." "Nullam beluam, nisi ob aliquam utilitatem, quam ex ea caperent, consecraverunt." (Cicero, *De Natura Deorum*, I. 36.)
[i] This exquisite passage must be quoted in the original to be properly appreciated. "En appliquant aussitôt ce principe évident, je devais spontanément choisir l'angélique interlocutrice, qui après une seule année d'influence objective, se trouve, depuis plus de six ans, subjectivement associée à toutes mes pensées comme à tous mes senti-

"O worthy thou of Egypt's wise abodes,
A decent priest, where monkeys were the gods!"

Note XXXI., p. 21.

"Die Gegenstand der Religion wie der Philosophie ist *die ewige Wahrheit* in ihrer Objectivität selbst, Gott und Nichts als Gott und die Explication Gottes." Hegel, *Philosophie der Religion*. (*Werke*, XI. p. 21.)

Note XXXII., p. 21.

"So ist die Religion Wissen des göttlichen Geistes von sich *durch Vermittlung des endlichen Geistes.*"—Hegel, *Werke*, XI. p. 200. "Wir haben die Religion näher bestimmt als Selbstbewusstseyn Gottes." —*Ibid.*, XII. p. 191. Compare Marheineke, *Grundlehren der Christlichen Dogmatik*, § 420. "Die Religion ist demnach gar nichts anders, als das Daseyn des göttlichen Geistes im menschlichen, aber ein Daseyn, welches Leben, ein Leben, welches Bewusstseyn, ein Bewusstseyn, welches in seiner Wahrheit das Wissen ist. Dieses Wissen des Menschen ist wesentlich göttlich; denn es ist zunächst das Wissen des göttlichen Geistes selbst, und die Religion an und für sich."

Note XXXIII., p. 21.

"Die Logik ist sonach als das System der reinen Vernunft, als das Reich des reinen Gedankens zu fassen. *Dieses Reich ist die Wahrheit, wie sie ohne Hülle an und für sich selbst ist.* Mann kann sich deswegen ausdrücken, dass dieser Inhalt die *Darstellung Gottes* ist, *wie er in seinem ewigen Wesen vor der Erschaffung der Natur und eines endlichen Geistes ist.*"—Hegel, *Logik* (*Werke*, III. p. 33).

Note XXXIV., p. 22.

Clemens Alex. *Strom.*, i. 2. Πρῶτον μὲν, εἰ καὶ ἄχρηστος εἴη φιλοσοφία, εἰ εὔχρηστος ἡ τῆς ἀχρηστίας βεβαίωσις, εὔχρηστος.

ments. C'est par elle que je suis enfin devenu, pour l'Humanité, un organe vraiment double, comme quiconque a dignement subi l'ascendant féminin. Sans elle, je n'aurais jamais pu faire activement succéder la carrière de Saint Paul à celle d'Aristote, en fondant la religion universelle sur la saine philosophie, après avoir tiré celle-ci de la science réelle."—*Preface*, p. xxii.

LECTURE II.

Note I., p. 24.

"UNLESS we have independent means of knowing that *God knows the truth, and is disposed to tell it to us*, his word (if we be ever so certain that it is really his word) might as well not have been spoken. But if we know, independently of the Bible, that God knows the truth, and is disposed to tell it to us, obviously we know a great deal more also. We know not only the existence of God, but much concerning his character. For, only by discerning that he has Virtues similar in kind to human Virtues, do we know of his truthfulness and his goodness. Without this *à priori* belief, a book-revelation is a useless impertinence."—F. W. Newman, *The Soul*, p. 58. With this *à priori* belief, it is obvious that a book-revelation is, as far as our independent knowledge extends, still more impertinent; for it merely tells us what we knew before. See an able criticism of this theory in the *Eclipse of Faith*, p. 73 sqq.

Note II., p. 26.

"Da uns ferner das, was ein grosser Theil der Philosophen vor uns für die Vernunft ausgegeben haben, noch unter die Sphäre des Verstandes fällt, so werden wir für die höchste Erkenntnissart eine von jenen unerreichte Stelle haben, und sie als diejenige bestimmen, durch welche Endliches und Unendliches im Ewigen, nicht aber das Ewige im Endlichen oder Unendlichen erblickt wird."—Schelling, *Bruno*, p. 163 (compare p. 69). "Es giebt aber noch andere Sphären, die beobachtet werden können, nicht bloss diese, deren Inhalt nur Endliches gegen Endliches ist, sondern solche, wo das Göttliche als an und für sich seyendes im Bewusstseyn ist."—Hegel, *Philosophie der Religion* (*Werke*, XI. p. 196). In like manner, Mr. Newman speaks of the Soul as "the organ of specific information to us" respecting things spiritual;[a] and Mr. Parker says, "that there is a connection between God and the soul, as between light and the eye, sound and the ear, food and the palate, &c."[b]

---

[a] *The Soul*, p. 3.
[b] *Discourse of Matters pertaining to Religion*, p. 130.

Note III., p. 27.

"Cette substance simple primitive doit renfermer éminemment les *perfections* contenues dans les substances dérivatives qui en sont les effets; ainsi elle aura la *puissance*, la *connoissance*, et la *volonté* parfaites, c'est-à-dire, elle aura une toute-puissance, une omniscience, et une bonté souveraines. Et comme la *justice*, prise généralement, n'est autre chose que la bonté conforme à la sagesse, il faut bien qu'il y ait aussi une justice souveraine en Dieu."—Leibnitz, *Principes de la Nature et de la Grace*, § 9. "Being conscious that I have personally a little Love, and a little Goodness, I ask concerning it, as concerning Intelligence,—where did I pick it up? and I feel an invincible persuasion, that if I have some moral goodness, the great Author of my being has infinitely more. He did not merely make rocks and seas and stars and brutes, but the human Soul also; and *therefore* I am assured, he possesses all the powers and excellencies of that soul in an infinitely higher degree."—F. W. Newman, *Reply to the Eclipse of Faith*, p. 26. This argument, however true in its general principle, is liable to considerable error in its special applications. The remarks of Bishop Browne are worth consideration, as furnishing a caution on the other side. "To say that God is infinite in perfection, means nothing *real* and *positive* in him, unless we say, in a *kind* of perfection altogether inconceivable to us as it is in itself. For the multiplying or magnifying the greatest perfections whereof we have any direct conception or idea, and then adding our gross notion only of *indefinite* to them, is no other than heaping up together a number of *imperfections* to form a chimera of our imagination."—*Divine Analogy*, p. 271.

Note IV., p. 27.

Compare Wegscheider's definition of Mysticism, *Instit. Theol.* § 5 "Ad superstitionem propius accedit vel ejus species est *mysticismus* ille, seu persuasio de singulari animæ, sensibus quidem acrioribus imbutæ et phantasiæ ludibriis deditæ, facultate ad *immediatum* cum numine ipso aut naturis cœlestibus commercium jam in hac vita perveniendi, quo mens *immediate* cognitione rerum divinarum ac beatitudine perfruatur."

Note V., p. 28.

Fichte, *Versuch einer Kritik aller Offenbarung.* (*Werke*, V. pp. 40, 115.) The following remarks of Mr. Parker are another application of the same principle, substituting however, as if on purpose to shew the contradictory conclusions to which such a method of reasoning may lead, the conception of perfect love and future compensation, for that of a moral nature with no affections and no future promises. "This we know, that the Infinite God must be a perfect Creator, the sole and undisturbed author of all that is in Nature. . . . . Now a perfect Motive for Creation,—what will that be? It must be absolute Love, producing a desire to bless everything which He creates. . . . . If God be infinite, then He must make and administer the world from perfect motives, for a perfect purpose, and as a perfect means,—all tending to the ultimate and absolute blessedness of each thing He directly or mediately creates; the world must be administered so as to achieve that purpose for each thing. Else God has made some things from a motive and for a purpose not benevolent, or as a means not adequate to the benevolent purpose. These suppositions are at variance with the nature of the Infinite God. I do not see how this benevolent purpose can be accomplished unless all animals are immortal, and find retribution in another life."—*Theism, Atheism and the Popular Theology,* pp. 108, 109, 198.

Note VI., p. 29.

" The nature of the case implies, that the human mind is competent to sit in *moral* and *spiritual* judgment on a professed revelation, and to decide (if the case seem to require it) in the following tone : ' This doctrine attributes to God that which we should all call harsh, cruel, or unjust in man : it is therefore intrinsically inadmissible.' "—Newman, *The Soul,* p. 58. For an able refutation of this reasoning, see the *Defence of the Eclipse of Faith,* p. 38.

Note VII., p. 29.

" To suppose the future volitions of moral agents not to be necessary events; or, which is the same thing, events which it is not impossible but that they may not come to pass : and yet to suppose that God certainly foreknows them, and knows all things; is to suppose God's Knowledge to be inconsistent with itself."—Edwards, *On the Freedom of the Will,* part II., sect. 12.

Note VIII., p. 29.

" Let us suppose a great prince governing a wicked and rebellious people. He has it in his power to punish, he thinks fit to pardon them. But he orders his only and well-beloved son to be put to death, to expiate their sins, and to satisfy his royal vengeance. Would this proceeding appear to the eye of reason, and in the unprejudiced light of nature, wise, or just, or good?"—Bolingbroke, *Fragments or Minutes of Essays* (*Works*, vol. v. p. 289, ed. 1754). Compare Newman, *Phases of Faith*, p. 92. See also above, Lecture I., note 13.

NOTE IX., p. 29.

"*Intellectually*, we of necessity hold that the highest human perfection is the best type of the divine. . . . . Every good man has learnt to forgive, and when the offender is penitent, to forgive freely—without punishment or retribution: whence the conclusion is inevitable, that God also forgives, as soon as sin is repented of."—Newman, *The Soul*, p. 99. "It may be collected from the principles of *Natural Religion*, that God, on the sincere repentance of offenders, will receive them again into favour, and render them capable of those rewards *naturally* attendant on right behaviour."—Warburton, *Divine Legation*, b. ix. ch. 2. Compare, on the other side, Magee on the Atonement, notes iv. and xxiv. See also above, Lecture I., note 14.

NOTE X., p. 29.

"A divine command is pleaded in vain, except it can be shewn that the thing supposed to be commanded is not inconsistent with the law of nature; which if God can dispense with in any one case, he may in all."—Tindal, *Christianity as old as the Creation*, p. 272, quoted and answered by Waterland, *Scripture Vindicated*, on Numbers xxi. 2, 3.

NOTE XI., p. 29.

Kant, *Streit der Facultäten*, p. 321. ed. Rosenkranz. Newman, *Phases of Faith*, p. 150. Parker, *Discourse of Matters pertaining to Religion*, p. 84.

NOTE XII., p. 29.

Tindal, apud Waterland, *l. c.* Newman, *Phases of Faith*, p. 151.

NOTE XIII., p. 29.

Newman, *The Soul*, p. 60. Greg, *Creed of Christendom*, p. 8.

Note XIV., p. 31.

"The Absolute is that which is free from all *necessary* relation, that is, which is free from every relation *as a condition of existence;* but it may exist in relation, provided that relation be not a necessary condition of its existence; that is, provided the relation may be removed without affecting its existence." .... "The Infinite expresses the entire absence of all limitation, and is applicable to the one Infinite Being in all his attributes."—Calderwood, *Philosophy of the Infinite*, pp. 36, 37. The definitions may be accepted, though they lead to conclusions the very opposite of those which the ingenious author has attempted to establish. The Absolute, as above defined, is taken in the first of the two senses distinguished by Sir W. Hamilton, *Discussions*, p. 14; and in this sense it is the necessary complement of the idea of the Infinite. The other sense, in which the Absolute is contradictory of the Infinite, is irrelevant to the present argument.

Note XV., p. 32.

"That only is absolutely and properly *infinite*, which is infinite, not according to our conceipt or kind of infinity, but that which is *infinite* in *Being.* This was that *infinity* which the ancients well defined when they said, *Infinitum est extra quod nihil est:* Infinity is that without which nothing is or can be. For as infinity in longitude includes all length conceivable, and infinity in solid magnitudes all dimensions imaginable, so must *infinite being* include all Being possible; and it is impossible for any being to be without or besides that wherein all *being* possible is contained."—Jackson, *On the Divine Essence and Attributes*, p. 29, ed. 1628.

"*Infinitum absolute sic dictum* est, quod continet omnem rem, sive omnem perfectionem quæ aut esse aut concipi potest: id vos *infinitum perfectione* vocare soletis. *Infinitum secundum quid*, verbi causa, *extensionem*, est, quod omnem extensionem complectitur, quæ esse potest et intelligi."—Werenfels, *De Finibus Mundi Dialogus* (*Dissertationes*, 1716, vol. ii. p. 192). In the latter sense, Clarke speaks of the error of "imagining all Infinites to be equal, when in things disparate they manifestly are not so; an *infinite Line* being not only *not equal* to, but *infinitely less* than an *infinite Surface*, and an *infinite Surface* than *Space infinite in all Dimensions.*"[c] This

---

[c] *Demonstration of the Being and Attributes of God*, Prop. 1.

remark assumes that an infinite extension is a possible object of conception at all; whereas, in fact, the attempt to conceive it involves the same fundamental contradictions which accompany the notion of the Infinite in every other aspect. This is ingeniously shewn by Werenfels, in the above Dialogue, p. 218. "D. Sed tune existimas igitur, lineam infinitam omnino sine repugnantia concipi non posse? Ph. Ita sane; et ab hac sententia abduci nequeo, nisi solide quis vestrum ad hanc demonstrationem respondeat; eam autem, nisi vestra audiendi patientia deficit, breviter hic denuo proponam. Videtis hanc lineam $b \quad a \quad c$. Constituamus eam esse infinitam, et ultra terminos b et c in infinitum protendi. Dividatur hæc linea in puncto a. Manifestum est has partes inter se esse æquales; quia utraque incipit in puncto a, et protenditur in infinitum. Nunc te, Dædale, rogo; hæ duæ partes suntne finitæ an infinitæ? D. Finitæ. Ph. Ita ex duobus finitis componeretur infinitum; quod repugnat. D. Fateor errorem. Infinitæ sunt. Ph. Jam in Scyllam incidis: ita partes essent æquales toti; infinitum enim infinito æquale est. Præterea vides, utramque partem in puncto a terminari; non igitur finibus et terminis caret. Quid tu, Polymathes, ad hæc? Po. Habeo quod respondeam. Utraque harum partium ab una parte finita est, nempe in puncto a, ab altera infinita, quia ultra puncta b et c in infinitum extenditur. Ph. Callide, acute, nihil supra. At ego quæro, an numerus partium talium, qualis linea ab et ac, in utravis sectione lineæ infinitæ sit infinitus? Po. Aio. Ph. Sed num ille numerus cui æqualis potest addi, et cujus duplum non modo concipio, sed est revera in rerum natura, infinitus est? Quod si etiam hoc ais, numerus infinitus non omnes habet unitates, sed præter eum concipi possunt totidem unitates, quibus ille careat, eique possunt addi. Hoc autem si non repugnat, quid tandem erit quod repugnet? Po. Sed quid, si finito partium numero hujus magnitudinis qualis linea ab constare dico utramvis sectionem datæ lineæ? Ph. Linea igitur data est finita; quia duo numeri finiti inter se additi efficiunt numerum finitum: id quod erat demonstrandum." To the same effect Bacon (*Nov. Org.* Pars I., Aph. 48) says, " Neque rursus cogitari potest quomodo æternitas defluxerit ad hunc diem; cum distinctio illa quæ recipi consuevit, quod sit *infinitum a parte ante et a parte post*, nullo modo constare possit; quia inde sequeretur, quod sit unum infinitum alio infinito majus, atque ut consumatur infinitum, et vergat ad finitum."

The contradictions thus involved in the notion of infinite magnitudes in space, are not solved by maintaining, with Spinoza and

Clarke, that infinite quantity is not composed of parts:[d] for space with no parts is as inconceivable as space composed of an infinite number of parts. These contradictions sufficiently shew that relative infinity, no less than absolute, regarded as an actual magnitude, is not a positive object of thought at all. The above reasoning is not refuted, nor the conclusion deduced from it affected, by the admission of what is called *infinity* in mathematical reasonings; for the mathematician uses the term *infinite* in a different sense from the metaphysician, answering to what the latter calls *indefinite*.[e] Thus Dr. Whewell (*Philosophy of Discovery*, p. 324) endeavours to refute the above reasoning of Werenfels, by saying, " the definition of an infinite number is not that it contains all possible unities; but this—that the progress of numeration, being begun according to a certain law, goes on without limit."[f] Now this definition is pre-

[d] See Spinoza, *Epist*. XXIX. *Ethica*, P. I. Prop. xv.; and Clarke, *Demonstration*, Prop. i. A curious psychological discrepancy may be observed in relation to this controversy. Spinoza maintains that quantity as represented in the imagination is finite, but that as conceived by the intellect it is infinite. Werenfels, on the contrary, asserts that the imagined quantity is infinite, the conceived finite. The truth is, that in relation to Space, which is not a general notion containing individuals under it, conception and imagination are identical; and the notions of an ultimate limit of extension and of an unlimited extension, are both equally self-contradictory from every point of view.

[e] Three notions must be carefully distinguished from each other: 1°. That of a magnitude actually infinite, *i.e.* so great that a greater is inconceivable. (see the definitions of Jackson and Werenfels at the beginning of this note, and that of Spinoza, below, note 10). In this sense, it is manifest that all infinites of the same kind are equal; for if one line, *e.g.*, is greater than another, the second, by definition, is not infinite. 2°. That of a magnitude potentially infinite, *i.e.* capable of increase, according to a certain law, without limit, and thus greater than any assignable finite magnitude (see Dr. Whewell's definition cited above). 3°. That of a magnitude greater than a given finite magnitude, but with no actual limit assigned to it (See Peacock's *Algebra*, Art. 935, ed. 1845). Of these, the first is called by metaphysicians *infinite*, and the second *indefinite*; while by mathematicians the second is called *infinite*, and the third *indefinite*. Hence any reasoning based on the mathematical use of the term *infinite* is irrelevant as regards the metaphysical. The first is the only sense in which the term can be applied to the Divine Attributes.

[f] Dr. Whewell pursues the argument as follows: "It is easy to conceive how one infinite number may be larger than another infinite number, in any proportion. If, for instance, we take the progression of the natural numbers 1, 2, 3, 4, &c., and the progression of the square numbers 1, 4, 9, 16, &c., any term of the latter series will be greater than the corresponding term of the other series, in a ratio constantly increasing; and the infinite term of the one, infinitely greater than the corresponding infinite term of the other." But this argument assumes that there can be an infinite term in such series; whereas, if the series goes on increasing for ever, the infinite term is never reached. It is, in fact, saying that the series goes on without end, and yet that it has an end or actual term in which infinity is attained.

cisely that which Descartes, speaking as a metaphysician, gives, not of the *infinite*, but of the *indefinite*: "Nos autem illa omnia, in quibus sub aliqua consideratione nullum finem poterimus invenire, non quidem affirmabimus esse infinita, sed ut indefinita spectabimus. Ita quia non possumus imaginari extensionem tam magnam, quin intelligamus adhuc majorem esse posse, dicemus magnitudinem rerum possibilium esse indefinitam. Et quia non potest dividi aliquod corpus in tot partes, quin singulæ adhuc ex his partibus divisibiles intelligantur, putabimus quantitatem esse indefinite divisibilem."—(Principia I., 26). So, too, Cudworth: "There appeareth no sufficient ground for this positive infinity of space; we being certain of no more than this, that be the world, or any figurative body, never so great, it is not impossible but that it might be still greater and greater without end. Which *indefinite increasableness* of body and space seems to be mistaken for a *positive infinity* thereof. . . . To conclude therefore: by space without the finite world is to be understood nothing but the possibility of body, further and further, without end, yet so as never to reach to infinity; and such a space as this was there also, before this world was created, a possibility of so much body to be produced. But space and actual distance, as really mensurable by yards and poles, though it may be greater and greater without end, yet can it not be *positively infinite*, so as that there could be no more added to it." —(*Works*, ed. Harrison, vol. III. p. 131, cf. vol. II. p. 527.) And Locke, while using the term *infinity* in its mathematical sense, for a "supposed endless progression" (the potentially infinite), yet distinguishes this from the other sense of the term (the actually infinite). "Whether any one," he says, "has or can have a positive idea of an actual infinite number, I leave him to consider, till his infinite number be so great that he himself can add no more to it; and as long as he can increase it, I doubt he himself will think the idea he hath of it a little too scanty for positive infinity."—(*Essay* II., 17, 16.) Leibnitz, in his criticism of Locke, says, "le vrai infini à la rigueur n'est que dans *l'absolu*, qui est antérieur à toute composition et n'est point formé par l'addition des parties."—(*Nouv. Essais*, II. 17.) And in another place he adds, "Accurate loquendo, loco numeri infiniti dicendum est plura adesse quam numero ullo exprimi possint; aut loco lineæ rectæ infinitæ, productam esse rectam ultra quamvis magnitudinem quæ assignari potest, ita ut semper major recta adsit. . . . Ego philosophice loquendo non magis statuo magnitudines infinite parvas quam infinite magnas, seu non magis infinitesimas quam infinituplas. Utrasque enim per modum loquendi compendiosum pro mentis fictionibus habeo, ad calculum aptis, quales sunt radices imaginariæ in Algebrâ. Interim demonstravi magnum has expressiones usum habere ad compendium cogitandi adeoque ad inventionem; et in errorem ducere non posse, cum pro *infinite parvo* substituere sufficiat *tam parvum quam quis volet*, ut error sit minor dato, unde consequitur errorem dari non posse."ᵍ —(*Opera*, ed. Erdmann, p. 436. See also *Théodicée, Discours*, § 70, *Examen des Principes de Malebranche*, p. 696, Erdmann.) Pascal, again, speaks of indefinitely increasable magnitudes, not as *infinite*, but as infinitely removed from infinity proper. " C'est-à-dire, en un mot, que quelque mouvement, quelque nombre, quelque espace, quelque temps que ce soit, il y en a toujours un plus grand et un moindre; de sorte qu'ils se soutiennent tous entre le néant et l'infini, étant toujours infiniment éloignés de ces extrêmes."—(*De l'Esprit Géométrique, Pensées*, p. 451, ed. Havet.) The view of all the above philosophers is substantially the same as that maintained long before by Aristotle, that magnitudes can only be conceived as infinite *potentially*, not *actually*.—(*Phys. Ausc.*, III. 6.) The language of two eminent modern mathematicians, speaking as such, may be cited to the same effect. " The mind," says Dean Peacock, "is as incapable of conceiving the relation of different orders of infinities as it is of conceiving infinity itself, and it is only when the relation between them is the necessary result of symbolical language, and of those several laws of their combination which the rules of Algebra impose upon them, that they can become the proper object of our reasonings."—(*Algebra*, Art. 939.) And Mr. Todhunter says, "We can form no distinct conception of an infinite magnitude, and the word can only be used in mathematics as an abbreviation, in the manner of the examples here given" (*e. g.* when we say, " the tangent of an angle of 90° is infinity" it is an abbreviation of " as we increase an angle gradually up to 90°, the tangent of the angle increases; and by taking the angle near enough to 90° we may make the tangent as great as we please "). The ambiguity of language might be avoided by distinguishing the *indefinite*, that which is capable of perpetual addition, from the *infinite*, that which is so great as to admit of no addition in

---

ᵍ M. Vera, in his *Introduction à la Philosophie de Hegel*, p. 158, says, " Au fond, l'infiniment petit des mathématiciens c'est l'indéfini, non seulement dans ses applications, mais dans sa notion. Et c'est ce que comprit Leibnitz, qui à l'expression qu'il avait adoptée d'abord d'*infiniment petit*, voulut substituer celle d'*indéfiniment petit*." I am not sure whether the above quotation from Leibnitz is the passage to which M. Vera refers, but it expresses the same doctrine in substance, if not in the very words.

thought. Concerning these two, Sir W. Hamilton well says, "We cannot conceive the infinite regress of time. . . . If we dream of effecting this, we only deceive ourselves by substituting the *indefinite* for the *infinite*, than which no two notions can be more opposed" (*Discussions*, p. 29).

Note XVI., p. 32.

"Per *Deum* intelligo ens absolute infinitum, hoc est, substantiam constantem infinitis attributis, quorum unumquodque æternam et infinitam essentiam exprimit. *Dico absolute infinitum, non autem in suo genere. Quicquid enim in suo genere tantum infinitum est, infinita de eo attributa negare possumus ; quod autem absolute infinitum est, ad ejus essentiam pertinet quicquid essentiam exprimit et negationem nullam involvit.*"—Spinoza, *Ethica*, P. I. Def. VI.

Note XVII., p. 32.

See Spinoza, *l. c.*; Malebranche, *Recherche de la Vérité*, L. IV. Ch. XI; Wolf, *Theologia Naturalis*, P. II. § 15; Kant, *Kritik der reinen Vernunft*, p. 450, ed. Rosenkranz; *Vorlesungen über die Metaphysik*, ed. Poelitz, p. 276; Schelling, *Vom Ich*, § 10. The conclusion follows so inevitably from the assumption that the philosophical definition of the absolute-infinite represents a real and positive conception, that it has been admitted in express terms by orthodox theologians, who would have rejected with horror the pantheistic consequences which it logically involves. Thus Jackson (*On the Divine Essence and Attributes*, p. 38, ed. 1628) says, "From the former definition of absolute infinity (*infinitum est extra quod nihil est*) we may conclude that unless all power, unless all wisdom, unless all goodness, unless all that truly is, or can possibly be supposed to have true being, be identically contained in God's Essence, he could not be absolutely infinite or illimited in being." The assumption, however, ultimately annihilates itself; for if any object of conception exhausts the universe of reality, it follows that the mind which conceives it has no existence. The older form of this representation is criticized by Hegel, *Encyklopädie*, § 36. His own conception of God, however, virtually amounts to the same thing. A similar view is implied in his criticism of Aristotle, whom he censures for regarding God as one object out of many. See *Geschichte der Philosophie*, *Werke*, XIV. p. 283.

Note XVIII., p. 32.

Geschichte der Philosophie, Werke, XV. p. 275. See also, *Philosophie der Religion, Werke,* XI. p. 24. *Encyklopädie,* § 19, 20, 21. Compare Schelling, *Philosophie und Religion,* p. 35, quoted by Willm, *Histoire de la Philosophie Allemande,* vol. iii. p. 301. Schleiermacher (*Der Christliche Glaube,* § 80) is compelled in like manner to assert that God must be in some manner the author of evil; an opinion which is also maintained by Mr. Parker, *Theism, Atheism, and the Popular Theology,* p. 119.

Note XIX., p. 32.

"Ea res dicitur *in suo genere finita,* quæ alia ejusdem naturæ terminari potest. Ex. gr. corpus dicitur finitum, quia aliud semper majus concipimus. Sic cogitatio alia cogitatione terminatur." Spinoza, *Ethica,* P. I. Def. II.

Note XX., p. 33.

See Aquinas, *Summa,* P. I. Qu. II. Art. 3, Qu. IX. Art. 1. "Actus simplicissimus," says Hobbes contemptuously, "signifieth nothing."[h] And Clarke in like manner observes, "Either the words signify nothing, or else they express only the perfection of his power."[i]

Note XXI., p. 33.

See Plato, *Republic,* II. p. 381; Aristotle, *Metaph.* VIII. 8, 15; Augustine, *Enarratio in Ps.* ix. 11, *De Trinitate,* xv. c. 15; Hooker, *E. P.* b. i. c. 5; Descartes, *Meditatio Tertia,* p. 22, ed. 1685; Spinoza, *Ethica,* P. I. Prop. xvii. Schol.; Hartley, *Observations on Man,* Prop. cxv.; Herder, *Gott, Werke,* viii. p. 180; Schleiermacher, *Der Christliche Glaube,* § 54; Hegel, *Werke,* xiv. p. 290; Marheineke, *Grundlehren der Christlichen Dogmatik,* § 195. The conclusion, that God actually does all that he can do; and, consequently, that there is no possibility of free action in any finite being, can only be avoided by the admission, which is ultimately forced upon us, that our human conception of the infinite is not the true one. Müller (*Christliche Lehre von der Sünde,* ii. p. 251, third edit.) endeavours to meet this conclusion by a counter-argument. He shews that it is equally a

---

[h] *Questions concerning Liberty, Necessity, and Chance,* Animadversions, No. XXIV. See, on the other side, Bramhall, *Works,* vol. iv. p. 524.

[i] *Demonstration,* Prop. IV. See, on the other side, Hegel, *Geschichte der Philosophie, Werke,* XIV. p. 290.

limitation of the Divine Nature to suppose that God is compelled of necessity to realize in act everything which he has the power to accomplish. This argument completes the dilemma, and brings into full view the counter-impotencies of human thought in relation to the infinite. We cannot conceive an Infinite Being as capable of becoming that which he is not; nor, on the other hand, can we conceive him as actually being all that he can be.

In reference to the remarks in the text, it may perhaps be necessary, as the meaning of the passage has been mistaken by some of its reviewers, to explain that, in speaking of an unrealized possibility as a limit, it is not meant that it is a limit of the possibility itself, but of the subject in which it resides, and which is conceived as being capable of becoming more than it actually is. This unrealized possibility or *potentiality* must not be confounded with *power* (see Lecture III. note 3); though in certain relations the two may be correlative terms. *Power* in such relations has reference to a definite act to be done : *potentiality* has reference to the state of the subject in which the unexerted power resides. Power as such is not conceived as a limitation : the fact that a portion of power remains unexerted carries with it the idea of expansion rather than of restriction. But potentiality is essentially a limit, not of the power as power, but of the subject in which it resides. The conception of potentiality is incompatible with that of infinity, because it involves the possibility of two distinct conceptions of the infinite, the one as acting, the other as only capable of acting.

Note XXII., p. 33.

"Now it is sufficiently manifest, that a thing *existing absolutely* (*i.e.* not under relation), and a thing *existing absolutely as a cause*, are contradictory. The former is the absolute negation of all relation; the latter is the absolute affirmation of a particular relation. A cause is a *relative*, and what exists absolutely as a cause, exists absolutely under relation."—Sir W. Hamilton, *Discussions*, p. 34.

Note XXIII., p. 33.

That a belief in Creation is incompatible with a philosophy of the Absolute, was clearly seen by Fichte, who consistently denounces it, as a Jewish and Heathenish notion and the fundamental error of all false Metaphysics. He even goes so far as to maintain that St. John, the only teacher of true Christianity, did not believe in the

Creation, and that the beginning of his Gospel was designed to contradict the Mosaic narrative. See his *Anweisung zum seligen Leben* (*Werke*, v. p. 479). Compare Schelling, *Bruno*, p. 60, who regards the finite as necessarily coeternal with the infinite. So also Rothe, *Theologische Ethik*, § 40, asserts that the doctrine of a creation in time is inconsistent with the essential nature of God, as unchangeable and necessarily creative. Spinoza's attempted demonstration that one substance cannot be produced from another,[k] though in itself a mere juggle of equivocal terms, yet testifies in like manner to his conviction, that to deny the possibility of creation is an indispensable step to a philosophy of the Absolute. Cognate to these theories are the speculations of Hermogenes, mentioned by Tertullian, *Adv. Herm.* c. 2; and of Origen, *De Princ.* i. 2, 10. Of the latter, Neander well observes: "Here, therefore, there occurred to him those reasons against a beginning of creation generally, which must ever suggest themselves to the reflecting mind, which cannot rest satisfied with simple faith in that which to itself is incomprehensible. Supposing that to create is agreeable to the divine essence, how is it conceivable that what is thus conformable to God's nature should at any time have been wanting? Why should not those attributes which belong to the very essence of the Deity, His almighty power and goodness, be always active? A transition from the state of not-creating to the act of creation is inconceivable without a change, which is incompatible with the being of God."[1] The same considerations have led to the theories of M. Cousin (*Introduction à l'Histoire de la Philosophie*, 5ème leçon, and of M. Saisset, *Essai de Philosophie Religieuse*, p. 418, ed. 1859), who regard creative activity as an essential attribute of God, and therefore as realized from all eternity. Against this theory, which excludes the possibility of a creation in time, see Sir W. Hamilton, *Discussions*, p. 35.

Note XXIV., p. 34.

Arist. *Metaph.* XI. 9. Εἴτε γὰρ μηθὲν νοεῖ, τί ἂν εἴη τὸ σεμνόν; ἀλλ ἔχει ὥσπερ ἂν εἰ ὁ καθεύδων. εἴτε νοεῖ, τούτου δ᾽ ἄλλο κύριον (οὐ γάρ ἐστι τοῦτο ὅ ἐστιν αὐτοῦ ἡ οὐσία νόησις, ἀλλὰ δύναμις), οὐκ ἂν ἡ ἀρίστη οὐσία εἴη. διὰ γὰρ τοῦ νοεῖν τὸ τίμιον αὐτῷ ὑπάρχει. . . . Αὐτὸν ἄρα νοεῖ, εἴπερ ἐστὶ τὸ κράτιστον, καὶ ἔστιν ἡ νόησις νοήσεως νόησις. Plotinus, on the other hand, shews that even self-consciousness, as

---

[k] *Ethica*, P. I. Prop. vi.
[1] *Church History*, English translation, Vol. II. p. 281, Bohn's edition.

involving a logical distinction between subject and object, is incompatible with the notion of the Absolute.—See *Enn.* V. 1. VI. c. 2.

NOTE XXV., p. 34.

Plotinus, *Enn.* III. 1. IX. c. 3. Διπλοῦν δὲ τὸ νοοῦν, καὶ αὐτὸ νοεῖ, καὶ ἐλλειπὲς, ὅτι ἐν τῷ νοεῖν ἔχει τὸ εὖ, οὐκ ἐν τῇ ὑποστάσει. *Enn.* V. 1. VI. c. 2. Πρῶτόν τε οὐκ ἔσται δύο ὄν, ὅ τε νοῦς ὁ τὸ νοητὸν ἔχων οὐκ ἂν συσταίη μὴ οὔσης οὐσίας καθαρῶς νοητοῦ, ὃ πρὸς μὲν τον νοῦν νοητὸν ἔσται, καθ' ἑαυτὸ δὲ οὔτε νοοῦν οὔτε νοητὸν κυρίως ἔσται· τό τε γὰρ νοητὸν, ἑτέρῳ· ὅ τε νοῦς το ἐπιβάλλον τῇ νοήσει κενὸν ἔχει, ἄνευ τοῦ λαβεῖν καὶ ἑλεῖν τὸ νοητὸν ὃ νοεῖ. *Enn.* V. 1. VI. c. 6. Ἔπειτα οὐδ' ἡ νόησις νοεῖ, ἀλλὰ τὸ ἔχον τὴν νόησιν. Δύο οὖν πάλιν αὖ ἐν τῷ νοοῦντι γίγνεται· τοῦτο δὲ οὐδαμῇ δύο. Cf. Porphyr. *Sent.* XV. Εἰ δὲ πολλὰ καὶ τὰ νοητά· πολλὰ γὰρ ὁ νοῦς νοεῖ, καὶ οὐχ ἕν· πολλὰ ἂν εἴη ἐξ ἀνάγκης καὶ αὐτός. κεῖται δὲ πρὸ τῶν πολλῶν τὸ ἕν, ὥστε ἀνάγκη πρὸ τοῦ νοῦ εἶναι τὸ ἕν. " The Absolute, as absolutely universal, is absolutely *one*; absolute unity is convertible with the absolute negation of plurality and difference; *the Absolute,* and the *Knowledge of the Absolute,* are therefore *identical.* But knowledge, or intelligence, supposes a plurality of terms—the plurality of subject and object. Intelligence, whose essence is plurality, cannot therefore be identified with the Absolute, whose essence is unity; and if known, the Absolute, *as known,* must be different from the Absolute, *as existing;* that is, there must be two Absolutes—an Absolute in knowledge, and an Absolute in existence: which is contradictory."—Sir W. Hamilton, *Discussions,* p. 33.

NOTE XXVI., p. 35.

Clem. Alex. *Strom.* V. 12. p. 587. Οὐκ ἂν δὲ ὅλον εἴποι τις αὐτὸν ὀρθῶς· ἐπὶ μεγέθει γὰρ τάττεται τὸ ὅλον, καί ἐστι τῶν ὅλων πατήρ. οὐδὲ μὴν μέρη τινὰ αὐτοῦ λεκτέον· ἀδιαίρετον γὰρ τὸ ἕν. Plotinus, *Enn.* V. 1. VI. c. 5. Ὅ δ' ἐστι πάντῃ ἕν, ποῦ χωρήσεται πρὸς αὐτό; ποῦ δ' ἂν δέοιτο συναισθήσεως; On this point the earlier and later forms of Pantheism are divided against each other. Spinoza (*Eth.* P. I. Def. 6) defines the Deity as composed of an infinite number of attributes. "Per *Deum* intelligo ens absolute infinitum, hoc est, substantiam constantem infinitis attributis, quorum unumquodque æternam et infinitam essentiam exprimit." Hegel, on the contrary, in his Lectures on the proofs of the existence of God, regards a plurality of attributes as incompatible with the idea of the Infinite. " Hier zeigt sich die Verschiedenheit, die Trennung, Mehrheit der Prädicate, die nur in der Einheit das Subject verknüpft, an ihnen selbst aber in Unterschiedenheit, womit sie selbst in Gegensatz und damit in Widerstreit kämen, wären, somit aufs entschiedenste als etwas Unwahres, und die Mehrheit von Bestimmungen als ungehörige Kategorie."[m] The lesson to be learnt from both is the same. No human form of thought can represent the Infinite:—a truth which Spinoza attempts to evade by multiplying such forms to infinity, and Hegel by renouncing human thought altogether.

Note XXVII., p. 35.

That the Absolute cannot be conceived as composed of a plurality of attributes, but only as the one substance conceived apart from all plurality, is shewn by Plotinus, *Enn.* V. 1. VI. c. 3. Εἰ δὲ πολλὰ τὸ αὐτὸ οὐδὲν κωλύειν φήσουσιν, ἐν τούτοις ὑποκείμενον ἔσται· οὐ δύναται γὰρ πολλὰ, μὴ ἑνὸς ὄντος, ἀφ' οὗ, ἢ ἐν ᾧ, ἢ ὅλως ἑνός, καὶ τούτου πρώτου τῶν ἄλλων ἀριθμουμένου, ὃ αὐτὸ ἐφ' ἑαυτοῦ δεῖ λαβεῖν μόνον. Εἰ δὲ ὁμοῦ εἴη μετὰ τῶν ἄλλων, δεῖ τοῦτο συλλαβόντα αὐτὸ μετὰ τῶν ἄλλων, ὅμως δὲ ἕτερον τῶν ἄλλων ὄν, ἐᾶν ὡς μετ' ἄλλων, ζητεῖν δὲ τοῦτο τὸ ὑποκείμενον τοῖς ἄλλοις, μηκέτι μετὰ τῶν ἄλλων, ἀλλ' αὐτὸ καθ' ἑαυτό. Compare Proclus, *Inst. Theol.* c. 1. Πᾶν πλῆθος μετέχει πῃ τοῦ ἑνός· εἰ γὰρ μηδαμῇ μετέχοι, οὔτε τὸ ὅλον ἓν ἔσται, οὔθ' ἕκαστον τῶν πολλῶν, ἐξ ὧν τὸ πλῆθος, ἀλλ' ἔσται καὶ ἕκ τινων ἕκαστον πλῆθος, καὶ τοῦτο εἰς ἄπειρον, καὶ τῶν ἀπείρων τούτων ἕκαστον ἔσται πάλιν πλῆθος ἄπειρον. To the same effect is the reasoning of Augustine, *De Trinitate*, vi. c. 6, 7. "In unoquoque corpore aliud est magnitudo, aliud color, aliud figura. Potest enim et diminuta magnitudine manere idem color et eadem figura, et colore mutato manere eadem figura et eadem magnitudo, et figura eadem non manente tam magnum esse et eodem modo coloratum: et quæcunque alia simul dicuntur de corpore, possunt et simul et plura sine cæteris commutari. Ac per hoc multiplex esse convincitur natura corporis, simplex autem nullo modo ... Sed tamen etiam in anima cum aliud sit artificiosum esse, aliud inertem, aliud acutum, aliud memorem, aliud cupiditas, aliud timor, aliud lætitia, aliud tristitia, possintque et alia sine aliis, et alia magis, alia minus, innumerabilia et innumerabiliter in animæ natura inveniri; manifestum est non simplicem sed multiplicem esse naturam. Nihil enim simplex mutabile est; omnis autem creatura mutabilis. Deus vero multipliciter quidem dicitur magnus,

---

[m] *Werke*, XII. p. 419. See also *Encyklopädie*, § 28 (*Werke*, VI. p. 62).

bonus, sapiens, beatus, verus, et quidquid aliud non indigne dici videtur: sed eadem magnitudo ejus est, quæ sapientia; non enim mole magnus est, sed virtute: et eadem bonitas quæ sapientia et magnitudo, et eadem veritas quæ illa omnia: et non est ibi aliud beatum esse, et aliud magnum, aut sapientem, aut verum aut bonum esse, aut omnino ipsum esse." A similar argument, but based on the idea of the Infinite, is used by Jackson, *On the Divine Essence and Attributes*, p. 37 :—" He that assumes any of these attributes to be what another is not, or Divine Essence not to be identically what all these are, must grant as well the Attributes as the Essence to be finite and limited. If *power* in God have a being distinct from *wisdom*, and wisdom another being distinct from *goodness*, one must needs want so much of infinite being as another hath of proper being distinct from it, and at best they can but be infinite *secundum quid*, or in their rank. Again, if any of them be what Essence identically is not, Essence cannot be infinite, because *wisdom, power,* and *being [goodness?]* have their several beings distinct from it." *Ibid.*, p. 38 :—" Wheresoever it can be truly said, *this* is one, and *that* another, or *this* is not *that*, each hath distinct limits. But seeing our imagination or phantasy is divisible, and our purest intellectual conceipts of infinity but finite, we cannot think of God as *infinite* in *power, infinite* in *wisdom*, and in *essence*; but we must frame a conceit of power distinct from our conceit of essence, and a conceit of wisdom distinct from both. And this plurality of conceipts in us usually brings forth a conceit of plurality betwixt his Essence and his Attributes; unless our understandings be vigilant and attentive to correct our phantasies by this following, and the like known philosophical truth." See also Aquinas, *Summa*, P. I. Qu. III. Art. 5, 6, 7. Schleiermacher, *Der Christliche Glaube*, § 50; Schelling, *Vom Ich*, § 9.

Note XXVIII., p. 35.

See Plato, *Republic*, II. p. 380, VI. p. 511, VII. p. 517; *Timæus*, p. 31. Aristotle, *Metaph*. XI. 8, 18: 10, 14; *Eth. Nic.* VII. 14, 8. Cicero, *Tusc. Quæst.* I. 29; *De Nat. Deor.* II. 11. Plotinus, *Enn.* II. 9, 1; III. 9, 3; V. 4, 1; VI. 5, 1; 9, 6. Proclus, *Inst. Theol.* c. i. xxii. lix. cxxxiii. Clemens Alex., *Strom.* V. p. 587. Origen, *De Princ.* I. 1, 6. Augustine, *De Civ. Dei*, VIII. 6: *De Trinitate*, VI. 6; VII. 1; XV. 5, 13. Aquinas, *Summa*, P. I. Qu. III. Art. 7; Qu. VII. Art. 2; Qu. XI. Art. 3. Leibnitz, *Monadologie*, § 39, 40, 47. Clarke, *Demon-*

stration, Prop. vi. vii.   Schelling, *Vom Ich,* § 9;   *Bruno,* p. 185. Rothe, *Theol. Ethik,* § 8.

NOTE XXIX., p. 35.

"Hinc ergo clare patet, nullam rem unam aut unicam nominari, nisi postquam alia res concepta fuit, quæ (ut dictum est) cum ea convenit. Quoniam vero Dei existentia ipsius sit essentia, deque ejus essentia universalem non possimus formare ideam, certum est, eum qui Deum unum vel unicum nuncupat, nullam de Deo habere ideam, vel improprie de eo loqui."—Spinoza, *Epist.* L. Compare Schleiermacher, *Der Christliche Glaube,* § 56. Schelling, *Vom Ich,* § 9.

NOTE XXX., p. 36.

"Quod enim dicebat *si possibile est,* non ad potentiam Dei referebat solum, sed etiam ad justitiam ejus; quoniam in quantum ad potentiam quidem Dei, omnia possibilia sunt, sive justa sive injusta; quantum autem ad justitiam ejus, qui non solum potens est, sed etiam justus, non sunt omnia possibilia, sed ea solum quæ justa sunt."—Origen *in S. Matt.* xxvi. 42; compare *c. Celsum,* III. 70. Origen speaks still more strongly in a remarkable fragment of the *De Principiis,* which has been preserved in the original: Ἐν τῇ ἐπινοουμένῃ ἀρχῇ τοσοῦτον ἀριθμὸν τῷ βουλεύματι αὐτοῦ ὑποστῆσαι τὸν Θεὸν νοερῶν οὐσιῶν ὅσον ἠδύνατο διαρκέσαι· πεπερασμένην γὰρ εἶναι καὶ τὴν δύναμιν τοῦ Θεοῦ λεκτέον, καὶ μὴ προφάσει εὐφημίας τὴν περιγραφὴν αὐτῆς περιαιρετέον· ἐὰν γὰρ ᾖ ἄπειρος ἡ θεία δύναμις, ἀνάγκη αὐτὴν μηδὲ ἑαυτὴν νοεῖν. The language of Hooker (*E. P.* b. I. ch. 2, § 3) is more cautious and reverent, but contains the same acknowledgment of what, from a human point of view, is limitation. "If therefore it be demanded why, God having power and ability infinite, the effects notwithstanding of that power are all so limited as we see they are; the reason hereof is the end which he hath proposed, and the law whereby his wisdom hath stinted the effects of his power in such sort, that it doth not work infinitely, but correspondently unto that end for which it worketh." A similar argument from a writer of a different school will be found in Tucker's *Light of Nature Pursued,* Vol. III. Ch. 16, § 7, ed. 1805. Some excellent remarks on the limitation of man's faculties with regard to the Divine Attributes, will be found in Mr. Meyrick's sermon, *God's Revelation and Man's Moral Sense considered in reference to the Sacrifice of the Cross,*

p. 14. See the Collection of Sermons on *Christian Faith and the Atonement*, Oxford, 1856.

NOTE XXXI., p. 37.

Thus Spinoza (*Ethica*, P. I. Prop. 26) says, "Res quae ad aliquid operandum determinata est, a Deo necessario sic fuit determinata;" and, carrying the same theory to its inevitable consequence, he consistently maintains (P. IV. Prop. 64) that the notion of evil only exists in consequence of the inadequacy of our ideas. Hegel in like manner (*Encykl.* § 35) reduces evil to a mere negation, which may be identified with good in the absolute. See also above, note xviii., p. 218.

NOTE XXXII., p. 37.

Plato, *Rep.* II. p. 381. Πότερον οὖν ἐπὶ τὸ βέλτιόν τε καὶ κάλλιον μεταβάλλει ἑαυτόν, ἢ ἐπὶ τὸ χεῖρον καὶ τὸ αἴσχιον ἑαυτοῦ; Ἀνάγκη, ἔφη, ἐπὶ τὸ χεῖρον, εἴπερ ἀλλοιοῦται· οὐ γάρ που ἐνδεᾶ γε φήσομεν τὸν Θεὸν κάλλους ἢ ἀρετῆς εἶναι. Ὀρθότατα, ἦν δ' ἐγώ, λέγεις. καὶ οὕτως ἔχοντος δοκεῖ ἄν τίς σοι, ὦ Ἀδείμαντε, ἑκὼν αὑτὸν χείρω ποιεῖν ὁπῃοῦν ἢ θεῶν ἢ ἀνθρώπων; Ἀδύνατον, ἔφη. Compare Augustine, *In Joannis Evangelium*, Tract. XXIII. 9. "Non invenis in Deo aliquid mutabilitatis, non aliquid quod aliter nunc sit, aliter paulo ante fuerit. Nam ubi invenis aliter et aliter, facta est ibi quaedam mors: mors enim est, non esse quod fuit . . . . Quidquid ergo et a meliore in deterius, et a deteriore in melius moritur, non est hoc Deus." To the same effect, Bishop Beveridge, *On the Thirty-nine Articles*, p. 30, ed. 1845, says, "And further, if God should be moved or changed, it must be either from better to worse, from worse to better, or from equal to equal. From better to worse he cannot be changed, for then he would be corrupted, and want some perfection after his change, which he had before, and so cease to be the chiefest good, and by consequence God. From worse to better if he should change, before his change he was not God, because he wanted some perfection or degree of goodness, which he hath after: after his change he would not be God, because he had a beginning, and so not eternal. From equal to equal also he cannot change, for then too he would not be God absolutely perfect, wanting some perfection before his change, which he had after, and some perfection after his change, which he had before." And so Jacobi (*Von den göttlichen Dingen*, *Werke*, III. p. 391) says of the system of Schelling: "Man erwäge, dass der allein *wahre* und lebendige Gott (die Natur) sich.

weder vermehren noch vermindern, weder erhöhen noch erniedern kann; sondern dass dieser Gott, *æqual* Natur oder Universum, von Ewigkeit zu Ewigkeit, sowohl der Qualität als der Quantität nach, immer einer und derselbe bleibt. Es würde darum auch absolut unmöglich seyn, dass er irgend einen Wechsel in sich verursachte, sich als *Veränderungskraft* darthäte, wenn er nicht die Veränderlichkeit, die *Zeitlichkeit*, der Wechsel selbst wäre. Diese Veränderlichkeit selbst ist aber, sagt man uns, in ihrer *Wurzel* ein *Unveränderliches*, nämlich die heilige ewig schaffende Urkraft der Welt; in ihrer *Frucht* hingegen, in der expliciten wirklichen Welt, *ein absolut Veränderliches*, so dass in jedem einzelnen bestimmten Moment, das All der Wesen nichts ist. Demnach ist unwidersprechlich das Schöpferwort des naturalistischen Gottes, welches er von Ewigkeit zu Ewigkeit ausspricht: *Es werde Nichts!* Er ruft hervor *aus dem Seyn das Nichtseyn*; wie der Gott des Theismus *aus dem Nichtseyn hervorruft das Seyn*." Compare Sir W. Hamilton's criticism of Cousin, *Discussions*, p. 36; and see also above, note xxiii. p. 220.

Note XXXIII., p. 38.

"What," says Sir W. Hamilton, "is our thought of creation? It is not a thought of the mere springing of nothing into something. On the contrary, creation is conceived, and is by us conceivable, only as the evolution of existence from possibility into actuality, by the fiat of the Deity . . . And what is true of our concept of creation, holds of our concept of annihilation. We can think no real annihilation,—no absolute sinking of something into nothing. But as creation is cogitable by us, only as a putting forth of Divine power, so is annihilation by us only conceivable, as a withdrawal of that same power. All that is now *actually* existent in the universe, this we think and must think, as having, prior to creation, *virtually* existed in the Creator; and in imagining the universe to be annihilated, we can only conceive this, as the retractation by the Deity of an overt energy into latent power. In short, it is impossible for the human mind to think what it thinks existent, lapsing into absolute non-existence, either in time past or in time future."[a]

[a] *Discussions*, p. 620. Compare a remarkable passage in Herder's *Gott* (*Werke*, VIII. p. 241), where the author maintains a similar view of the impossibility of conceiving creation from or reduction to nothing. But Herder is speaking as a professed defender of Spinoza. Sir W. Hamilton's system is in all its essential features the direct antagonist of Spinoza; and even in the present passage the apparently pantheistic hypothesis is represented as the result not of thought, but of an inability to think. Still it is to be

With all deference to this great philosopher, I cannot help thinking that a different representation would have been more in harmony with the main principles of his own system. We cannot conceive creation at all, neither as a springing of nothing into something, nor as an evolution of the relative from the absolute; for the simple reason, that the first terms of both hypotheses, nothing and the absolute, are equally beyond the reach of human conception. But while creation as a *process in the act of being accomplished*, is equally inconceivable on every hypothesis, creation as a *result already completed*, presents no insurmountable difficulty to human thought, if we consent to abandon the attempt to apprehend the absolute. There is no difficulty in conceiving that the amount of existence in the universe may at one time be represented by A, and at another by $A+B$; though we are equally unable to conceive how B can come out of nothing, and how A or any part of A can become B while A remains undiminished. But the result, no less than the process, becomes self-contradictory when we attempt to conceive A as absolute and infinite; for in that case $A+B$ must be something greater than infinity. A more detailed examination of this theory of creation and of causation in general has been attempted in the second edition of the author's *Prolegomena Logica*, note C.

NOTE XXXIV., p. 40.

"Der Pantheismus lehrt dass alles gut sei, denn alles sei nur eines, und jeder Anschein von dem, was wir Unrecht oder Schlecht nennen, nur eine leere Täuschung. Daher der zerstörende Einfluss desselben auf das Leben, in dem, man mag sich nun in den Ausdrücken auch drehen, und an den durch die Stimme des Gewissens überall hervortretenden Glauben anschliessen wie man will, im Grunde doch, wenn man dem verderblichen Principe nur getreu bleibt, die Handlungen des Menschen für gleichgültig, und der ewige Unterschied zwischen Gut und Böse, zwischen Recht und Unrecht, ganz aufgehoben, und für nichtig erklärt werden muss."— F. Schlegel, *Ueber die Sprache und Weisheit der Indier*, b. III. c. 2 (Werke VIII. p. 324). "Si c'est Dieu qui pense en moi, ma pensée est absolue; non seulement je ne puis penser autrement que je ne pense, ... mais je ne puis choisir parmi mes conceptions, approuver ou rechercher les unes, rejeter et fuir les autres, toutes étant néces-

---

regretted that the distinguished author should have used language liable to be misunderstood in this respect, especially as it scarcely accords with the general principles of his own system.

saires et parfaites, toutes divines; je deviens enfin une machine à penser, une machine intelligente, mais irresponsable."—Bartholmèss, *Histoire des Doctrines Religieuses de la Philosophie Moderne*, Introduction, p. xxxvii. These necessary consequences of Pantheism are fully exhibited by Spinoza, *Ethica*, P. I. Prop. 26; P. II. Props. 32, 33, 34, 35; P. IV. Prop. 64. Hegel (*Werke* XI. pp. 95, 203, 390) endeavours, not very successfully, to defend his own philosophy from the charge of Pantheism and its consequences. His defence amounts to no more than the assertion that God cannot be identified with the universe of finite objects, in a system in which finite objects have no real existence. Thus explained, the system is identical with Pantheism in the strictest sense of the term. All that is proved is, that it cannot with equal propriety be called Pantatheism.

NOTE XXXV., p. 40.

" The dialectic intellect, by the exertion of its own powers exclusively, can lead us to a general affirmation of the supreme reality, of an absolute being. But here it stops. It is utterly incapable of communicating insight or conviction concerning the existence or possibility of the world, as different from Deity. It finds itself constrained to identify, more truly to confound, the Creator with the aggregate of his creatures, and, cutting the knot which it cannot untwist, to deny altogether the reality of all finite existence, and then to shelter itself from its own dissatisfaction, its own importunate queries, in the wretched evasion, that of nothings, no solution can be required: till pain haply, and anguish, and remorse, with bitter scoff and moody laughter inquire;—Are we then indeed nothings?—till through every organ of sense nature herself asks;— How and whence did this sterile and pertinacious nothing acquire its plural number?—*Unde, quæso hæc nihili in nihila tam portentosa transnihilatio?*—and lastly;—What is that inward mirror, in and for which these nothings have at least relative existence?"—Coleridge, *The Friend*, vol. III. p. 213.

NOTE XXXVI., p. 40.

The limitation, *speculative* Atheism, is necessary; for the denial of the Infinite does not in every case constitute practical Atheism. For it is not under the form of the Infinite that the idea of God is distinctly presented in worship; and it is possible to adore a superior Being, without positively asking how far that superiority extends. In fact, the inquiry into the nature of the Absolute and Infinite was actually prosecuted by Heathen philosophers as a purely metaphysical study, without any necessary connection with their religious belief. It is only when we are able to investigate the problem of the relation between the infinite and the finite, and to perceive that the latter cannot be regarded as expressing the true idea of the Deity, that the denial of the infinite becomes Atheism in speculation. On the alternative between Christianity and Atheism, some excellent remarks will be found in the *Restoration of Belief*, p. 248.

NOTE XXXVII., p. 40.

"Es pflegt viel auf die Schranken des Denkens gehalten zu werden, und es wird behauptet, es könne über die Schranke nicht hinausgegangen werden. In dieser Behauptung liegt die Bewusstlosigkeit, dass darin selbst, dass etwas als Schranke bestimmt ist, darüber bereits hinausgegangen ist. Denn eine Bestimmtheit, Grenze, ist als Schranke nur bestimmt, in Gegensatz gegen sein Anderes überhaupt, als gegen sein *Unbeschränktes*; das Andere einer Schranke ist eben das *Hinaus* über dieselbe."—Hegel, *Logik* (*Werke*, III. p. 136). Compare *Encyklopädie*, § 60 (*Werke*, VI. p. 121). In maintaining that a limit as such always implies something beyond, and, consequently, that the notion of a limited universe is self-contradictory, Hegel is unquestionably right; but he is wrong in attempting to infer from thence the non-limitation of thought. For that which is limited is not necessarily limited by something of the same kind;—nay the very conception of *kinds* is itself a limitation. Hence the consciousness that thought is limited by something beyond itself, by no means implies that thought itself transcends that limit. A prisoner chained up feels that his motion is limited, by his inability to *move* into the space which he *sees* or *imagines* beyond the length of his chain. On Hegel's principles, he ought to know his inability by actually moving into it.

NOTE XXXVIII., p. 41.

These opposite limitations fall under the general Law of the Conditioned enunciated by Sir W. Hamilton. "The mind is astricted to think in certain forms; and, under these, thought is possible only in the conditioned interval between two unconditioned contradictory extremes or poles, each of which is altogether inconceivable, but of which, on the principle of Excluded Middle, the one or the other is necessarily true."° The lamented author has left us only a few fragmentary specimens of the application of this canon to the vexed questions of metaphysical speculation, and the principal one of these, in some of its details, may be open to objections; but the truth of the principle itself is unquestionable; and its value, rightly applied, in confining the inquiries of philosophy within their legitimate boundaries, can hardly be estimated too highly.

NOTE XXXIX., p. 41.

"Alles Endliche ist, vermöge seines Begriffes, begrenzt durch sein Entgegengesetztes: und absolute Endlichkeit ist ein sich selbst widersprechender Begriff."—Fichte, *Grundlage der gesammten Wissenschaftslehre* (*Werke*, I. p. 185).

NOTE XL., p. 43.

Religion innerhalb der Grenzen der blossen Vernunft, p. 98, 122, 137. For the influence of Kant on the rationalist theology, see Rosenkranz, *Geschichte der Kant'schen Philosophie*, b. III. cap. 2. Amand Saintes, *Histoire du Rationalisme en Allemagne*, l. II. ch. 11. Kahnis, *History of German Protestantism*, translated by Meyer, p. 167.

NOTE XLI., p. 43.

Paulus, in the preface to his *Leben Jesu*, expressly adopts, though without naming the author, Kant's theory, that miracles are indifferent to religion, and that the whole essence of Christianity consists in morality. Consistently with these principles, he maintains (§ 2) that the historical inquirer can admit no event as credible which cannot be explained by natural causes. The entire details of the evangelical narrative are explained by this method. The miracles of healing were performed by medical skill, which Christ imparted to his disciples, and thus was enabled to heal, not by a word, but by deputy. Thus he coolly translates the words of the centurion, Matt. viii. 8, "Wenn auch Er nur einen Befehl an einen der Seinigen geben wolle, um in seinem Namen für die Heilung zu sorgen." The feeding of the five thousand consisted merely in persuading the richer travellers to share their provisions with the poorer. The stilling of the tempest was effected by steering round a point which cut off the wind. Lazarus and the widow's son of

° *Discussions*, p. 618.

Nain were both cases of premature interment. Our Lord's own death was merely a swoon, from which he was restored by the warmth of the sepulchre and the stimulating effect of the spices. Such are a few specimens of *historical inquiry*. The various explanations of Paulus are examined in detail and completely refuted by Strauss. The natural hypothesis had to be annihilated, to make way for the mythical.

NOTE XLII., p. 43.

Wegscheider, though he expressly rejects Kant's allegorizing interpretations of Scripture (*see Institutiones Theologiæ*, § 25), agrees with him in maintaining the supreme authority of reason in all religious questions, and in accommodating all religious doctrines to Ethical precepts.—(*Præf.* p. viii. ix.) Accordingly, in the place of the allegory, he adopts the convenient theory of adaptation to the prejudices of the age; by which a critic is enabled at once to set aside all doctrines which do not harmonize with his own views. Among the doctrines thus rejected, as powerless for the true end of religion, and useless or even prejudicial to piety, are those of the Trinity, the Atonement, the Corruption of human nature, Justification, and the Resurrection of the body. See § 51.

NOTE XLIII., p. 43.

See his *Grund- und Glaubens-Sätze der Evangelisch-Protestantischen Kirche*, p. 70 (2nd edition). This work of Röhr was principally directed against the Lutheran symbolical books; but the Catholic Creeds are also included in his sweeping condemnations. Of the Apostles' Creed he observes: "Our age needs a more logically correct, and a more comprehensive survey of the pure evangelical faith than is afforded by the so-called Apostles' Creed, which is good for its immediate and ordinary purpose, but too short, too aphoristic, and too historical for that which is here proposed" (p. 49). Of the Nicene and Athanasian Creeds he remarks in a note: "The Niceno-Constantinopolitan and the pseudo-Athanasian Creeds, with their decidedly antiscriptural dogmas, are here altogether out of the question, however much they were admitted by the reformers, in all honesty and faith, as truly scriptural." Röhr agrees with Kant in separating the historical facts of Christianity from the religion itself (p. 157), and in maintaining that morality is the only mode of honouring God (p. 56). His proposed creed, from which everything "historical" is studiously excluded, runs as follows:—

"There is one true God, proclaimed to us by his only-begotten Son, Jesus Christ. To this God, as the most perfect of all Beings, as the Creator, Sustainer, and Governor of the world, and as the Father and Instructor of men and of all rational spirits, the deepest veneration is due. This veneration is best rendered by active striving after virtue and righteousness, by zealous control of the inclinations and passions of our sensual and evilly-disposed nature, and by honest entire fulfilment of our duty, according to the exalted example of Jesus, whereby we may assure ourselves of the aid of his divine Spirit. In the consciousness of the filial relation into which we thereby enter with him, we may, in earthly need, reckon with confidence on his fatherly help, in the feeling of our moral weakness and unworthiness, upon his grace and mercy assured to us through Christ, and in the moment of death be assured that we shall continue to exist immortally and receive a recompense in a better life."

The celebrated *Briefe über den Rationalismus*, by the same author, have at least the merit of being an honest and logical exposition of Rationalist principles and their consequences, without disguise or compromise. The commendation, however, to which in this respect the work is partly entitled, cannot be extended to the concluding letter, in which the author endeavours to establish, for himself and his fellow rationalists, the right to discharge the spiritual functions, and subscribe to the confessions, of a church whose doctrines they disbelieve; and even to make use of their position to unsettle the faith of the young committed to their instruction.

Note XLIV., p. 43.

The character of Hegel's philosophy in this respect is sufficiently shewn by Strauss, *Streitschriften*, Heft III. p. 57 sqq.

Note XLV., p. 43.

Vatke's *Religion des Alten Testamentes*, forms the first part of his *Biblische Theologie wissenschaftlich dargestellt*; Berlin, 1835. In the Introduction (§ 7, 12, 13), the author lays down a law of the development of religion as a process of the infinite Spirit in self-revelation, according to the principles of the Hegelian philosophy. As a consequence of this law, he maintains that it is impossible for an individual to raise himself, even by the aid of divine revelation, above the spiritual position of his age, or for a nation to rise or fall from its normal stage of religious cultivation (pp. 87, 181). By this canon the entire narrative of Scripture is made to stand or fall. The account of a primitive revelation and subsequent alienation from God, must be rejected, because the human consciousness must attain to perfection through a succession of progressive stages (p. 102). The book of Genesis has no historical value; and we cannot decide whether the patriarchs before Moses had any knowledge of the one true God (pp. 1£0, 184). Moses himself, as represented in the scriptural account, is altogether inconceivable; for he appears at a period when, according to the laws of historical development, the time was not yet ripe for him (p. 183). Much of the history of Moses must be regarded as a mythus, invented by the priests at a later period (p. 186). The political institutions attributed to him could not possibly have been founded by him (p. 211). The ceremonial laws are such as could neither have been discovered by an individual *nor made known by divine revelation* (p. 218). The Passover was originally a feast of the sun, in celebration of his entering into the sign Aries, which fully accounts for the offering of a male lamb (p. 492). As regards the decalogue, the second commandment must be considered as an interpolation of a later date; for it implies a higher degree of abstraction than could have been reached in the Mosaic age (p. 234). The lapses into idolatry recorded in the book of Judges are highly improbable; for a whole people cannot fall back from a higher to a lower state of religious culture (p. 181). The books of Samuel betray their legendary origin by the occurrence of round numbers, and by the significant names of the first three kings (p. 289). The wisdom attributed to Solomon is irreconcilable with his subsequent idolatry; and the account must therefore be regarded as legendary (309). Such are a few of the results of the so-called philosophy of history exercised on the narrative of Scripture. The book is valuable in one respect, and in one only. It shews the reckless manner in which rationalism finds it necessary to deal with the sacred text, before it can be accommodated to the antisupernatural hypothesis. To those who believe that a record of facts as they are is more trustworthy than a theory of facts as they ought to be on philosophical principles, the very features which the critic is compelled to reject become additional evidence of the truth of the scripture narrative.

Note XLVI. p. 44.

The Hegelian element of Strauss's *Leben Jesu* is briefly exhibited at the end of the book (§ 150). The body of the work is mainly occupied with various cavils, some of them of the very minutest philosophy, designed to invalidate the historical character of the Gospel narratives. Among these precious morsels of criticism, we meet with such objections as the following. That the name of the angel Gabriel is of Hebrew origin (§ 17). That the angel, instead of inflicting dumbness on Zacharias, ought to have merely reprimanded him (*ibid.*). That a real angel would not have proclaimed the advent of the Messiah in language so strictly Jewish (§ 25). That the appearance of the star to the magi would have strengthened the popular belief in the false science of astrology (§ 34). That John the Baptist, being an ascetic, and therefore necessarily prejudiced and narrow-minded, could not have considered himself inferior to one who did not practise similar mortifications (§ 46). That Jesus could not have submitted to the rite of baptism, because that rite symbolised a future Messiah (§ 49). That if there is a personal devil, he cannot take a visible form (§ 54). That it is improbable that Jesus, when he read in the synagogue at Nazareth, should have lighted on an apposite passage of the prophet Isaiah (§ 58). That Jesus could not have known that the woman of Samaria had had five husbands, because it is not probable that each of them had left a distinct image in her mind, and because a minute knowledge of the history of individuals is degrading to the prophetic dignity (§ 69). That it is impossible to understand "how he, whose vocation had reference to the depths of the human heart, should be tempted to occupy himself with the fish-frequented depths of the waters" (§ 71). That Jesus could not have ridden into Jerusalem on an ass whereon never man sat, because unbroken asses are difficult to manage (§ 110). That the resurrection of the dead is impossible, because the inferior principles, whose work is corruption, will not be inclined to surrender back the dominion of the body to its former master, the soul (§ 140). That the ascension of Christ is impossible, because a body which has flesh and bones cannot be qualified for a heavenly abode; because it cannot liberate itself from the laws of gravity; and because it is childish to regard heaven as a definite locality (§ 142).—It is not creditable to the boasted enlightenment of the age, that a work which can seriously urge such petty quibbles as these should have obtained so much reputation and influence. In studying the philosophy which has given birth to such consequences, we see a new verification of the significant remark of Clemens Alexandrinus: 'Η γὰρ κατὰ τὴν θείαν παράδοσιν φιλοσοφία ἵστησι τὴν πρόνοιαν καὶ βεβαιοῖ· ἧς ἀναιρεθείσης, μῦθος ἡ περὶ τὸν Σωτῆρα οἰκονομία φαίνεται.ᵖ "Strauss, the Hegelian theologian," says Sir W. Hamilton, " sees in Christianity only a *mythus*. Naturally: for his Hegelian 'Idea,' itself a myth, and confessedly finding itself in everything, of course finds in anything a myth."ᑫ As the labours of Strauss on the Gospel narratives have been sometimes compared to those of Niebuhr on the history of Rome, it may be instructive to peruse the opinion of the great historian on the cognate theories of a few years' earlier date. "In my opinion," writes Niebuhr in 1818, "he is not a Protestant Christian, who does not receive the historical facts of Christ's early life, in their literal acceptation, with all their miracles, as equally authentic with any event recorded in history, and whose belief in them is not as firm and tranquil as his belief in the latter; who has not the most absolute faith in the articles of the Apostles' Creed, taken in their grammatical sense; who does not consider every doctrine and every precept of the New Testament as undoubted divine revelation, in the sense of the Christians of the first century, who knew nothing of a Theopneustia. Moreover a Christianity after the fashion of the modern philosophers and pantheists, without a personal God, without immortality, without human individuality, without historical faith, is no Christianity at all to me; though it may be a very intellectual, very ingenious philosophy. I have often said that I do not know what to do with a metaphysical God, and that I will have none but the God of the Bible, who is heart to heart with us."ʳ

Niebuhr did not live to witness the publication of the *Leben Jesu*; but the above passage is as appropriate as if it had been part of an actual review of that work.

Note XLVII. p. 44.

With Feuerbach's *Wesen des Christenthums* I am only acquainted through the French translation by M. Ewerbeck, which forms the principal portion of the volume entitled, *Qu'est-ce que la Religion d'après la nouvelle Philosophie Allemande.* The following extracts will sufficiently show the character of the work. "Le grand mystère, ou plutôt le grand secret, de la religion, le voici: l'homme objective son être, et après l'avoir objectivé il se rend lui-même objet de ce nouveau sujet" (p. 129). "Dieu est la notion, l'idée personnifiée de la personnalité, il est l'apothéose de la personne humaine, le moi sans le toi, la fière subjectivité séparée d'avec l'univers, l'égoïté qui

---

ᵖ *Stromata*, I. 11. p. 296.
ᑫ *Discussions*, p. 787.

ʳ *Life and Letters of B. G. Niebuhr*, vol. II. p. 123.

se suffit à elle-même" (p. 219). "Dieu est la notion du genre, mais cette notion personnifiée et individualisée à son tour ; il est la notion du genre ou son essence, et cette essence comme entité universelle, comme renfermant toutes les perfections possibles, comme possédant toutes les qualités humaines débarrassées de leurs limites" (p. 271). "Là, où la religion exprime le rapport entre l'homme et l'essence humaine, elle est bonne et humanitaire. Là, où la religion exprime le rapport entre l'homme et l'essence humaine *changée en un être surnaturel*, elle est illogique, menteuse, et porte dans ses flancs le germe de toutes les horreurs qui désolent la société depuis soixante siècles" (p. 340). "L'athéisme est le fruit de la contradiction dans l'existence de Dieu. . . . . On nous dit que Dieu existe réellement et non réellement à la fois, nous avons donc parfaitement le droit de couper court à cette existence absurde et de dire : il n'y a pas de Dieu" (p. 350). '"Nous inférons de ce qui précède que la personnalité divine, dont l'homme se sert pour attribuer ses propres idées et ses propres qualités à un être surhumain, n'est rien autre chose que la personnalité humaine mise en dehors du moi. C'est cet acte psychologique qui est devenu la base de la doctrine spéculative de Hegel, qui enseigne que la conscience que l'homme a de Dieu est la conscience que Dieu a de lui-même" (p. 390). The occasional notes which the translator has added to this work are, if possible, still more detestable than the text. So much disregard of truth and decency as is shewn in some of his remarks on Christianity, has probably seldom been compressed into the same compass.

NOTE XLVIII. p. 45.

"Christ, who taught his disciples, and us in them how to pray, propounded not the knowledge of God, though without that he could not hear us; neither represented he his power, though without that he cannot help us; but comprehended all in this relation, *When ye pray, say, Our Father."*—Pearson on the Creed, article I.

LECTURE III.

Note I. p. 49.

"Alles, was für uns *Etwas* ist, ist es nur, inwiefern es etwas anderes auch *nicht* ist; alle Position ist nur möglich durch Negation; wie denn das Wort *bestimmen* selbst nichts anderes bedeutet, als *beschränken.*"—Fichte, *Gerichtliche Verantwortung* (*Werke*, V. p. 265). "Das Endliche besteht in Beziehung auf sein Anderes, welches seine Negation ist und sich als dessen Gränze darstellt."—Hegel, *Encykl.* § 28 (*Werke*, VI. p. 63). Compare Plotinus, *Enn.* V. l. iii. c. 12. Τὸ δέ ἐστιν, ἄνευ τοῦ τι, ἕν. εἰ γάρ τι ἕν, οὐκ ἂν αὐτὸ ἕν· τὸ γὰρ αὐτὸ πρὸ τοῦ τι.—*Enn.* VI. l. vii. c. 39. Δεῖ γὰρ τὸν νοῦν ἀεὶ ἑτερότητα καὶ ταυτότητα λαμβάνειν, εἴπερ νοήσει. Ἑαυτόν τε γὰρ οὐ διακρινεῖ ἀπὸ τοῦ νοητοῦ τῇ πρὸς αὐτὸ ἑτέρου σχέσει, τά τε πάντα οὐ θεωρήσει μηδεμίας ἑτερότητος γενομένης, εἰς τὸ πάντα εἶναι.—Spinoza, *Epist.* 50. "Hæc ergo determinatio ad rem juxta suum esse non pertinet; sed e contra est ejus non-esse." The canon, undeniable from a human point of view, that all consciousness is limitation, seems to have had some influence on modern philosophical theories concerning the Divine Nature. Thus Hegel maintains that God must become limited to be conscious of himself,[a] and defines Religion as the Divine Spirit's knowledge of himself, by means of the finite Spirit.[b]

Note II. p. 49.

"Ita nullis unquam fatigabimur disputationibus de infinito. Nam sane quum simus finiti, absurdum esset nos aliquid de ipso determinare, atque sic illud quasi finire ac comprehendere conari." Descartes, *Principia*, I. 26. "The second reason of our short and imperfect notions of the Deity is, *the Infinity* of it. For this we must observe, That we can perfectly know and comprehend nothing, but as it is represented to us under some certain Bounds and Limitations. . . . . Upon which account, what a loss must we needs be at, in

---

[a] *Werke*, XI. p. 193.   [b] *Ibid.* p. 200.

understanding or knowing the Divine Nature, when the very way of our knowing seems to carry in it something opposite to the thing known. For the way of knowing it is by defining, limiting, and determining; and the thing known is that of which there neither are nor can be any Bounds, Limits, Definitions, or Determinations." South, *Animadversions upon Sherlock*, ch. II. p. 55. ed. 1693. " Alles unser Denken ist ein Beschränken; und eben in dieser Rücksicht heisst es *begreifen*; zusammengreifen etwas aus einer Masse von *bestimmbaren*; so dass immer ausserhalb der gezogenen Grenze noch etwas bleibe, das nicht mit hineinbegriffen ist, und also dem Begriffenen nicht zukommt."—Fichte, *Gerichtliche Verantwortung* (*Werke*, V. p. 265). " Was ich begreife, wird durch mein blosses Begreifen zum Endlichen, und dieses lässt auch durch unendliche Steigerung und Erhöhung sich nie ins Unendliche umwandeln." Fichte, *Bestimmung des Menschen* (*Werke*, II. p. 304). " Das *Subject ohne Prädicat* ist, was in der Erscheinung das *Ding ohne Eigenschaften* das *Ding-an-sich* ist, ein leerer unbestimmter Grund; es ist so der *Begriff in sich selbst*, welcher erst am Prädicate eine Unterscheidung und Bestimmtheit erhält."—Hegel, *Logik*, Th. II. (*Werke*, V. p. 70). Compare *Philosophie der Religion* (*Werke*, XI. p. 30). *Encyklopädie*, § 28, 29 *Werke*, VI. p. 65). " Es ist eine vollkommen sichere Thatsache des Bewusstseyns, dass wir uns ein *schlechthin* Unbestimmtes überhaupt gar nicht zu denken vermögen, d. h. dass ein solches schlechthin nicht Inhalt unsers Bewusstseyns seyn kann. Daraus folgt, dass Alles und Jedes eben damit, dass es Inhalt unsers Bewusstseyns wird, zugleich eine wenn auch relative Bestimmtheit für dasselbe erhalten muss."—Ulrici, *Glauben und Wissen*, p. 47.

NOTE III. p. 50.

The opposite sides of this contradiction are indicated in the following passages. Aristotle, *Phys.* III. 6, 13: Ἔστι γὰρ τὸ ἄπειρον τῆς τοῦ μεγέθους τελειότητος ὕλη καὶ τὸ δυνάμει ὅλον, ἐντελεχείᾳ δ' οὔ . . . . Διὸ καὶ ἄγνωστον ᾗ ἄπειρον. εἶδος γὰρ οὐκ ἔχει ἡ ὕλη. Compare *Metaph.* viii. 8, 16: Τὸ ἄρα δυνατὸν εἶναι ἐνδέχεται καὶ εἶναι καὶ μὴ εἶναι· τὸ αὐτὸ ἄρα δυνατὸν καὶ εἶναι καὶ μὴ εἶναι. Τὸ δὲ δυνατὸν μὴ εἶναι ἐνδέχεται μὴ εἶναι· τὸ δ' ἐνδεχόμενον μὴ εἶναι, φθαρτόν. . . . Οὐθὲν ἄρα τῶν ἀφθάρτων ἁπλῶς δυνάμει ἐστὶν ὂν ἁπλῶς. For a full discussion of the distinction between *potentiality* and *actuality* (the δύναμις and ἐντελέχεια or ἐνέργεια of Aristotle), see Trendelenburg on Arist. *De Anima*, p. 295. Compare Arist. *Metaph.* viii. 6. 2:

"Ἔστι δ' ἡ ἐνέργεια τὸ ὑπάρχειν τὸ πρᾶγμα, μὴ οὕτως ὥσπερ λέγομεν δυνάμει. Λέγομεν δὲ δυνάμει οἷον ἐν τῷ ξύλῳ Ἑρμῆν καὶ ἐν τῇ ὅλῃ τὴν ἡμίσειαν, ὅτι ἀφαιρεθείη ἄν, καὶ ἐπιστήμονα καὶ τὸν μὴ θεωροῦντα ἂν δυνατὸς ᾖ θεωρῆσαι· τὸ δ' ἐνεργείᾳ. This distinction plays a part in the controversy between Bramhall and Hobbes, the former of whom says, "The nearer that anything comes to the essence of God, the more remote it is from our apprehension. But shall we therefore make potentialities, and successive duration, and former and latter, or a part without a part (as they say), to be in God? Because we are not able to understand clearly the Divine perfection, we must not therefore attribute any imperfection to Him."[c] To this Hobbes replies, "Nor do I understand what derogation it can be to the divine perfection, to attribute to it potentiality, that is, in English, power."[d] "By *potentiality*," retorts Bramhall, "he understandeth 'power' or might; others understand possibility or indetermination. Is not he likely to confute the Schoolmen to good purpose?" Hobbes concludes by saying, "There is no such word as potentiality in the Scriptures, nor in any author of the Latin tongue. It is found only in School divinity, as a word of art, or rather as a word of craft, to amaze and puzzle the laity."[f] This charge may be answered in the words of Trendelenburg. "In explicandis his notionibus, ex ipso philosophiæ secessu depromtis, Latinæ linguæ in philosophicis et laxa remissio et læva inopia in angustias quasdam nos rediget, ut perspicuitatis gratia ad scholasticos terminos confugiendum sit."[g]

But to go from the word to the thing. The contradiction thus involved in the notion of the Infinite has given rise to two opposite representations of it: the one, as the affirmation of all reality; the other, as the negation of all reality. The older metaphysicians endeavoured to exhaust the infinite by an endless addition of predicates; hence arose the favourite representation of God, as the *Ens perfectissimum*, or sum of all realities, which prevailed in the Wolfian Philosophy, and was accepted by Kant.[h] On the other hand, the post-Kantian metaphysicians perceived clearly that all predication is necessarily limitation, and that to multiply attributes is merely to represent the infinite under a variety of finite determinations.

[c] *Works*, vol. IV. p. 158.
[d] *Works*, ed. Molesworth, vol. V. p. 342.
[e] *Works*, vol. IV. p. 425.
[f] *Works*, ed. Molesworth, vol. IV. p. 299.
[g] *In Arist. de Anima*, p. 295.
[h] See Wolf, *Theologia Naturalis*, Pars II. § 6, 14; Kant, *Kritik der reinen Vernunft*, p. 450, ed. Rosenkranz.

The consummation of this point of view was attained in the principle of Hegel, that pure being is pure nothing, and that all determinate being (Daseyn) is necessarily limited.[1] Hence his constant assertion that God cannot be represented by predicates.[k] Both schools of philosophy are right in what they deny, and wrong in what they affirm. The earlier metaphysicians were right in assuming that thought is only possible by means of definite conceptions; but they were wrong in supposing that any multiplication of such conceptions can amount to a representation of the infinite. The later metaphysicians were right in opposing this error; but they fell into the opposite extreme of imagining that by the removal of determinations the act of thought and its object could become infinite. In truth, a thought about nothing is no thought at all; and the rejection of determinations is simply the refusal to think. The conclusion to be drawn from the entire controversy is, that the infinite, as such, is not an object of human thought.

Note IV. p. 51.

"The adding infinity to any idea or conception necessarily finite, makes up no other than a curious contradiction for a divine attribute. . . . . You make up an attribute of knowledge or wisdom *infinitely finite;* which is as chimerical and gigantic an idea as an infinite human body."—Bp. Browne, *Divine Analogy*, p. 77. "Bedingungen des Unbedingten entdecken, dem absolut *Nothwendigen* eine Möglichkeit *erfinden*, und es *construiren* zu wollen, um es *begreifen* zu können, scheint als ein ungereimtes Unternehmen sogleich einleuchten zu müssen."—Jacobi, *Ueber die Lehre des Spinoza (Werke*, IV. Abth. II. p. 153). "Du bist von Endlichen nicht dem Grade, sondern der Art nach verschieden. Sie machen dich durch jene Steigerung nur zu einem grösseren Menschen, und immer zu einem grösseren; nie aber zum Gotte, zum Unendlichen, der keines Maasses fähig ist."—Fichte, *Bestimmung des Menschen (Werke*, II. p. 304.

Note V. p. 51.

" Si supponeremus esse hominem, oculis quidem claris cæterisque videndi organis recte se habentibus compositum, nullo autem alio sensu præditum, eumque ad eandem rem eodem semper colore et

---

[1] See *Werke*, III. p. 73; IV. p. 26, 27; V. p. 70; VI. p. 63.
[k] See *Werke*, VI. p. 65; XI. p. 31, 153; XII. p. 220, 418.

specie sine ulla vel minima varietate apparentem obversum esse, mihi certe, quicquid dicant alii, non magis videre videretur, quam ego videor mihi per tactus organa sentire lacertorum meorum ossa. Ea tamen perpetuo et undiquaque sensibilissima membrana continguntur. Attonitum esse et fortasse aspectare eum, sed stupentem dicerem, videre non dicerem; adeo sentire semper idem, et non sentire, ad idem recidunt."—Hobbes, *Elementa Philosophiæ*, Sect. I. P. IV. c. 25, 5.

NOTE VI. p. 52.

The paradox of Hegel, if applied, where alone we have any data for applying it, to the necessary limits of human thought, becomes no paradox at all, but an obvious truth, almost a truism. Our conceptions are limited to the finite and the determinate; and a thought which is not of any definite object, is but the negation of all thinking. Hegel's error consists in mistaking an impotence of thought for a condition of existence. That pure being is in itself pure nothing, is more than we can be warranted in assuming; for we have no conception of pure being at all, and no means of judging of the possibility of its existence. The absurdity becomes still more glaring, when this pure nothing is represented as containing in itself a process of self-development,—when being and non-being, which are absolutely one and the same, are regarded at the same time as two opposite elements, which by their union constitute *becoming*, and thus give rise to finite existence. But this absurdity is unavoidable in a system which starts with the assumption that thought and being are identical, and thus abolishes at the outset the possibility of distinguishing between the impotence of thought and its activity.

NOTE VII. p. 52.

Ueber den Grund unseres Glaubens an eine göttliche Weltregierung (*Werke*, V. p. 186). In a subsequent work written in defence of this opinion, Fichte explains himself as meaning that existence, as a conception of sensible origin, cannot be ascribed to God.[1] That the conception of existence is, like all other human representations, incompetent to express the nature of the Absolute, has been frequently admitted by philosophers and theologians. Thus Plato

[1] *Appellation an das Publicum gegen die Anklage des Atheismus* (*Werke*, V. p. 220).

describes the supreme good, οὐκ οὐσίας ὄντος τοῦ ἀγαθοῦ, ἀλλ' ἔτι ἐπέκεινα τῆς οὐσίας πρεσβείᾳ καὶ δυνάμει ὑπερέχοντος,[m] and his language is borrowed by Athanasius to express the absolute nature of God;[n] Plotinus in like manner says that the One is above being;[o] and Schelling, the Plotinus of Germany, asserts that the Absolute in its essence is neither ideal nor real, neither thought nor being.[p] This position is perfectly tenable so long as it is confessed that the Absolute is not the object of theological or philosophical speculation, and, consequently, that the provinces of thought and existence are not coextensive. But without this safeguard, there is no middle course between an illogical theology and an atheistical logic. The more pious minds will take refuge in mysticism, and seek to reach the absolute by a superhuman process; the more consistent reasoners will rush into the opposite extreme, and boldly conclude that that which is inconceivable is also non-existent.

NOTE VIII. p. 52.

Sextus Empiricus, *Adv. Math.* VII. 311. Ὅλου δ' ὄντος τοῦ καταλαμβάνοντος οὐδὲν ἔτι ἔσται τὸ καταλαμβανόμενον· τῶν δὲ ἀλογωτάτων ἐστὶ τὸ εἶναι μὲν τὸν καταλαμβάνοντα, μὴ εἶναι δὲ τὸ οὗ ἐστὶν ἡ κατάληψις. Plotinus, *Enn.* V. III. 10. Δεῖ τοίνυν τὸ νοοῦν, ὅταν νοῇ, ἐν δυσὶν εἶναι, καὶ ἢ ἔξω θάτερον, ἢ ἐν τῷ αὐτῷ ἄμφω, καὶ ἀεὶ ἐν ἑτερότητι τὴν νόησιν εἶναι. Compare Hegel, *Philosophie der Religion* (*Werke*, XI. p. 167). "Im Bewusstseyn, insofern ich von einem Gegenstande weiss und ich in mich gegen denselben reflectirt bin, weiss ich *den Gegenstand* als das *Andere meiner*, mich daher durch ihn *beschränkt* und *endlich*."—Marheineke, *Grundlehren*, § 84. "Dieses aber geschieht so, dass in der absoluten Idee, in der die Wissenschaft ihren Standpunct nimmt, das Subject nicht ein Anderes, als das Object, sondern, wie sie die Idee des Absoluten ist, als des Objects, es so auch in ihr, als der absoluten Idee, Subject, und also die absolute Idee nicht von Gott selbst verschieden ist."

---

[m] *Republic*, VI. p. 509.

[n] *Oratio c. Gentes*, c. 2. ὁ ὑπερέκεινα πάσης οὐσίας καὶ ἀνθρωπίνης ἐπινοίας ὑπάρχων, ἅτε δὴ ἀγαθὸς καὶ ὑπερκαλὸς ὤν. Compare Damascenus, *De Fide Orthod.* I. 4. οὐδὲν γὰρ τῶν ὄντων ἐστίν· οὐχ ὡς μὴ ὤν, ἀλλ' ὡς ὡς ὑπὲρ πάντα τὰ ὄντα, καὶ ὑπὲρ αὐτὸ τὸ εἶναι ὤν·

[o] *Enn.* V. i. 10. τὸ ἐπέκεινα ὄντος τὸ ἕν. Compare Proclus, *Inst. Theol.* c. 115. δῆλον δὴ ὅτι πάντων ἐστὶν ἐπέκεινα τῶν εἰρημένων ἅπας θεός, οὐσίας, καὶ ζωῆς, καὶ νοῦ.

[p] *Bruno*, p. 57. "Das Absolute nun haben wir bestimmt als, dem Wesen nach, weder ideal noch real, weder als Denken, noch als Seyn."

Note IX. p. 54.

In exhibiting the two universal conditions of human consciousness, that of *difference between objects*, and that of *relation between object and subject*, I have considered each with reference to its more immediate and obvious application; the former being viewed in connection with the Infinite, and the latter with the Absolute. But at the same time it is obvious that the two conditions are so intimately connected together, and the ideas to which they relate so mutually involved in each other, that either argument might be employed with equal force in the other direction. For difference is a relation, as well as a limit; that which is one out of many being related to the objects from which it is distinguished. And the subject and object of consciousness, in like manner, are not only related to, but distinguished from, each other; and thus each is a limit to the other: while, if either of them could be destroyed, a conception of the infinite by the finite would be still impossible; for either there would be no infinite to be conceived, or there would be no finite to conceive it.

The three Laws of Thought commonly acknowledged by logicians, those of Identity, Contradiction, and Excluded Middle, are but the above two conditions viewed in relation to a given notion. For in the first place every definite notion, as such, is discerned in the two relations of identity and difference, as being that which it is, and as distinguished from that which it is not. These two relations are expressed by the Laws of Identity and Contradiction. And in the second place, a notion is distinguished from all that it is not (A from not-A), by means of the mutual relation of both objects to a common subject, the universe of whose consciousness is constituted by this distinction. This mutual relation is expressed by the Law of Excluded Middle.

Note X. p. 54.

"Though we cannot fully comprehend the Deity, nor exhaust the infiniteness of its perfection, yet may we have an idea or conception of a Being absolutely perfect; such a one as is nostro modulo conformis, 'agreeable and proportionate to our measure and scantling;' as we may approach near to a mountain, and touch it with our hands, though we cannot encompass it all round, and enclasp it within our arms."—Cudworth, *Intellectual System*, ch. 5 (vol. ii. p. 518, ed. Harrison). "We grant that the mind is limited, but does it thence follow that the object of thought must be limited? We think not.

We grant that the mind cannot *embrace* the Infinite, but we nevertheless consider that the mind may have a notion of the Infinite. No more do we believe that the mind, as finite, can only recognise finite objects, than we believe that the eye, because limited in its power can only recognise those objects whose entire extension comes within the range of vision. As well tell us that because a mountain is too large for the eye of a mole, therefore the mole can recognise no mountain: as well tell us that because the world is too large for the eye of a man, therefore man can recognise no world,—as tell us that because the Infinite cannot be embraced by the finite mind, therefore the mind can recognise no Infinite."—Calderwood, *Philosophy of the Infinite*, p. 12. The illustrations employed by both authors are unfortunate. The part of the mountain, touched by the hand of the man, or seen by the eye of the mole, is, *ex hypothesi*, as a part of a larger object, imperfect, relative, and finite. And the world, which is confessedly too large for the eye of a man, must, in its unseen portion, be apprehended, not by sight, but by some other faculty. If therefore the Infinite is too large for the mind of man, it can only be recognised by some other mind, or by some faculty in man which is not mind. But no such faculty is or can be assumed. In admitting that we do not recognise the Infinite in its entire extension, it is admitted that we do not recognise it *as infinite*. The attempted distinction is sufficiently refuted in the words of Bishop Browne. "If it is said that we may then *apprehend* God directly, though not *comprehend* him; that we may have a direct and immediate knowledge *partly*, and in some *degree*; and though not of his *Essence*, yet of the *Perfections* flowing from it: I answer, that all the Attributes and Perfections of God are in their real Nature as infinite as his very Essence; so that there can be no such thing as having a direct view of him in part; for whatever is in God is equally Infinite. If God is to be apprehended at all by any direct and immediate idea, he must be apprehended *as Infinite*; and in that very act of the mind, he would be *comprehended*; and there is no medium between apprehending an Infinite Being *directly* and *analogically*."[q]

NOTE XI. p. 57.

The brevity with which this argument is necessarily expressed in the text, may render a few words of explanation desirable. Of

---

[q] *Divine Analogy*, p. 37. The author is speaking of our knowledge in a future state; but his arguments are more properly applicable to our present condition.

course, it is not meant that no period of time can be conceived, except in a time equally long; for this would make a thousand years as inconceivable as an eternity. But though there is nothing inconceivable in the notion of a thousand years, or any other large amount of time, such a notion is conceivable only under the form of a *portion of time*, having other time before and after it. An infinite duration, on the other hand, can only be conceived as having no time before or after it, and hence as having no relation or resemblance to any amount of finite time, however great. The mere conception of an indefinite duration, bounding every conceivable portion of time, is thus wholly distinct from that of infinite duration; for infinity can neither bound nor be bounded by any duration beyond itself.

This distinction has perhaps not been sufficiently observed by an able and excellent writer of the present day, in a work, the principal portions of which are worthy of the highest commendation. Dr. M'Cosh argues in behalf of a positive conception, as the foundation of our belief in the infinite,[r] in opposition to the theory of Sir W. Hamilton, in the following manner:—" To whatever point we go out in imagination, we are sure that we are not at the limits of existence; nay, we believe that, to whatever farther point we might go, there would be something still farther on." " Such," he continues, " seems to us to be the true psychological nature of the mind's conviction in regard to the infinite. It is not, as Sir W. Hamilton represents it, a mere impotence to conceive that existence, that time or space should cease, but a positive affirmation that they do not cease."[s]

[r] In the former editions, I wrote, "argues in behalf of a positive conception of infinity." This expression Dr. M'Cosh, in the last edition of his work, points out as a misrepresentation, adding, " it is not an adequate conception of infinity, but still the belief is positive, and there is the positive mental conception or apprehension of an object believed in. I gladly accept the correction, and have altered the language of my remarks accordingly; though it seems to me that this explanation reduces the theory of the Author almost if not quite to an identity with that of Sir W. Hamilton, which he is professedly opposing. For this " positive conception of an object believed in," if it is not a positive conception of the infinite as such, can only be a conception of the finite or of the indefinite. That such a conception, positive as regards the finite or indefinite, but negative as regards the infinite, may give rise to a positive belief in the latter, is not, as far as I am aware, opposed to any principle of the philosophy of the conditioned. But, whatever shade of difference more acute minds may detect between the two doctrines, I am glad to find my apparent line of separation from so able and reverent a thinker as Dr. M'Cosh, reduced to even smaller dimensions than I had originally supposed.

[s] *Method of the Divine Government*, p. 534, 6th edition.

This theory, as explained by the author in his last edition, differs from that of Sir W. Hamilton rather in language than in substance. Indeed the discrepancy is so small that it would hardly be necessary to notice it, had not the excellent author, by his mode of stating his view, given it the appearance of an antagonism greater than on examination will be found to exist. A "positive affirmation" is not in itself opposed to an "impotence to conceive:" we may be, by the constitution of our minds, compelled to believe in the one rather than the other of two contradictory alternatives, neither of which can be comprehended in the form of a positive conception. That this is the case in the present instance;—that the affirmation, however positive, cannot, as Dr. M'Cosh himself admits, be referred to a positive conception of the Infinite as affirmed, may be shewn, among other grounds, by the following considerations.

In the first place, this "something still farther on" is not itself primarily an object of conception, but merely the boundary of conception. It is a condition unavoidable by all finite thought, that whatever we conceive must be related to something else which we do not conceive. I think of a thousand years as bounded by a further duration beyond it. But if, secondarily, we turn our attention to this boundary itself, it is not then actually conceived as either limited or unlimited on its remoter side: we do not positively think of it as having no boundary; but we are unable to think of it as having a boundary. It is thus presented to us as *indefinite*, but not as *infinite*. And the result will be the same, if to our conception of a thousand years we add cycle upon cycle, till we are wearied with the effort. An idea which we tend towards, but never reach, is indefinite, but not infinite; for at whatever point we rest, there are conditions beyond, which remain unexhausted.

In the second place, even if we could positively conceive this further duration as going on for ever, we should still be far removed from the conception of infinity. For such a duration is given us as bounding and bounded by our original conception of a thousand years: it is limited at its nearer extremity, though unlimited at the other. If this be regarded as infinite, we are reduced to the self-contradictory notion of infinity related to a time beyond itself. Is a thousand years, *plus* its infinite boundary, greater than that boundary alone, or not? If it is, we have the absurdity of a greater than the infinite. If it is not, the original conception of a thousand years, from relation to which that of infinity is supposed to arise, is itself reduced to a non-entity, and cannot be related to anything.

This contradiction may be avoided if we admit that our conception of time, as bounded, implies an apprehension of the indefinite, but not of the infinite.

The difference between Dr. M'Cosh's view and that of Sir W. Hamilton is at any rate so slight, that the subsequent remarks of the former might be fully accepted by the most uncompromising adherent of the latter. "The mind seeks in vain to embrace the infinite in a positive image, but is constrained to believe, when its efforts fail, that there is a something to which no limits can be put." All that need practically be contended for by the supporters of the negative theory, is, first that this inability to assign limits indicates directly only an indefiniteness in our manner of thinking, but not necessarily an infinity in the object about which we think; and, secondly, that our indirect *belief* in the infinite, whether referred to an impotence or to a power of mind, is not of such a character that we can deduce from it any logical consequences available in philosophy or in theology. The sober and reverent tone of religious thought which characterises Dr. M'Cosh's writings warrants the belief that he would not himself repudiate these conclusions.

NOTE XII. p. 57.

For the antagonist theories of a beginning of time itself, and of an eternal succession in time, see Plato, *Timæus*, pp. 37, 38, and Aristotle, *Phys.* VIII. 1. The two theories are ably contrasted in Professor Butler's *Lectures on the History of Ancient Philosophy*, vol. ii. p. 185, sqq. Plato does not appear to regard the beginning of time as the beginning of material existence, but only of the sensible phenomena of matter. The insensible substratum of the phenomena seems to have been regarded by him as coeternal with the Deity.[t] It has been conjectured, indeed, that to this matter was attributed a perpetual existence in successive duration, as distinguished from the existence of the Deity, in a manner devoid of all succession.[u] This hypothesis perhaps relieves the theory from the apparent paradox of an existence *before* time (*before* being itself a temporal

---

[t] See *Timæus*, p. 49-53. Plato's opinion however has been variously represented. For some account of the controversies on this point, see Mosheim's Dissertation, *De Creatione ex Nihilo*, translated in Harrison's edition of Cudworth, vol. III. p. 140; Brucker, *Historia Philosophiæ*, vol. I. p. 676.

Compare also Professor Thompson's note, in Butler's *Lectures on the History of Ancient Philosophy*, vol. II. p. 189, and the Introduction to the French translation of Aristotle's *Metaphysics*, by MM. Pierron and Zévort, p. xci.

[u] See Mosheim's note in Harrison's Cudworth, vol. II. p. 551.

relation), but it cannot be easily reconciled with the language of Plato; and moreover, it only avoids one paradox by the introduction of another,—that of a state of existence out of time *contemporaneous* with one in time.

NOTE XIII. p. 57.

In Joann. Evang. Tract XXXVIII. 10. "Discute rerum mutationes, invenies Fuit et Erit: cogita Deum, invenies Est, ubi Fuit et Erit esse non possit."—Compare *Confess.* XI. c. 11; *Enarr.* in Ps. II. 7; *De Civ. Dei*, XI. 21. See also Cudworth, vol. II. p. 529, ed. Harrison; Herder, *Gott, Werke*, VIII. p. 139. Various other passages from St. Augustine to the same effect are cited in a note to Bp. Beveridge's *Discourse on the Thirty-nine Articles*, p. 18, ed. 1846. To these may be added the remarkable words of Beveridge himself: "And therefore, though I cannot apprehend His mercy to Abel, in the beginning of the world, and His mercy to me now, but as two distinct expressions of His mercy, yet as they are in God, they are but one and the same act; as they are in God, I say, who is not measured by time as our apprehensions of Him are, but is Himself eternity: a centre without a circumference, eternity without time. Indeed, when we speak of eternity, time is but as a parenthesis clasped in of both sides with it: neither is the eternity before time before that eternity that is after time; for there is but one eternity: and these words, *before* and *after*, *past* and *to come*, are solecisms in eternity, being only fitted to express the several successions of time by."

NOTE XIV. p. 57.

De Consol. Philos. L. V. Pr. 6. "Eternitas igitur est interminabilis vitæ tota simul et perfecta possessio."

NOTE XV. p. 57.

Summa, P. I. Qu. X. Art. I. "Sic ergo ex duobus notificatur æternitas. Primo ex hoc, quod id quod est in æternitate est interminabile, id est, principio et fine carens; ut terminus ad utrumque referatur. Secundo per hoc, quod ipsa æternitas successione caret, tota simul existens."—Compare Plotinus, *Enn.* II. 1. vii. c. 2. Πάντα ταῦτα ἰδὼν αἰῶνα εἶδεν, ἰδὼν ζωὴν μένουσαν ἐν τῷ αὐτῷ, ἀεὶ παρὸν τὸ πᾶν ἔχουσαν, ἀλλ' οὐ νῦν μὲν τόδε, αὖθις δ' ἕτερον, ἀλλ' ἅμα τὰ πάντα.— Proclus, *Theol.* c. 52. Πᾶν τὸ αἰώνιον ὅλον ἅμα ἐστίν. Several historical notices relating to this theory are given by Petavius, *Theologica Dogmata*, De Deo, l. III. c. 4.

NOTE XVI. 58.

"Nec tamen fieri potest, ut recordemur nos ante corpus exstitisse, quandoquidem nec in corpore ulla ejus vestigia dari, nec æternitas tempore definiri, nec ullam ad tempus relationem habere potest."—Spinoza, *Ethica*, P. V. Prop. 23. "Ewigkeit im reinen Sinne des Worts kann durch keine Zeitdauer erklärt werden, gesetzt, dass man diese auch endlos (*indefinite*) annähme. Dauer ist eine unbestimmte Fortsetzung des Daseyns, die schon in jedem Moment ein Mass der Vergänglichkeit, des Zukünftigen wie des Vorgangenen, mit sich führet. Dem Unvergänglichen, durch sich Unveränderlichen kann sie so wenig zugeschrieben werden, dass vielmehr, sein reiner *Begriff* mit dieser zu gemischten *Fantasie* verschwindet."—Herder, *Gott* (*Werke*, VIII. p. 140). "Insofern das Ich ewig ist, hat es gar keine *Dauer*. Denn Dauer ist nur in Bezug auf Objekte denkbar. Man spricht von einer Ewigkeit der Dauer (æviternitas), d. i. von einem Daseyn in *aller* Zeit, aber Ewigkeit im reinen Sinne des Worts (æternitas) ist Seyn in *keiner* Zeit."—Schelling, *Vom Ich*, § 15. Cognate to, or rather identical with, these speculations, is the theory advocated by Mr. Maurice (*Theological Essays*, p. 422, sqq.), "that eternity is not a lengthening out or continuation of time; that they are generically different."

NOTE XVII. p. 58.

In the acute and decisive criticism of Schelling by Sir W. Hamilton, this objection is urged with great effect. "We cannot, at the same moment, be in the intellectual intuition and in common consciousness; we must therefore be able to connect them by an act of memory—of recollection. But how can there be a *remembrance* of the Absolute and its Intuition? As out of time, and space, and relation, and difference, it is admitted that the Absolute cannot be construed to the understanding. But as remembrance is only possible under the conditions of the understanding, it is consequently impossible to remember anything anterior to the moment when we awaken into consciousness; and the *clairvoyance* of the Absolute, even granting its reality, is thus, after the crisis, as if it had never been."—*Discussions*, p. 23.

NOTE XVIII. p. 58.

See Augustine, *In Joann. Evang.* Tract XXXVIII. 10. "Cogita Deum, invenies Est, ubi Fuit et Erit esse non possit. Ut ergo et tu sis, transcende tempus. Sed quis transcendet viribus suis? Levet illuc ille qui Patri dixit, *Volo ut ubi ego sum, et ipsi sint mecum.*" This precept has found great favour with mystical theologians. Thus Eckart, in a sermon published among those of Tauler, says, "Nothing hinders the soul so much in its knowledge of God as time and place. Time and place are parts, and God is one; therefore, if our soul is to know God, it must know Him above time and place."[v] And the author of the *Theologia Germanica*, c. 7 : " If the soul shall see with the right eye into eternity, then the left eye must close itself and refrain from working, and be as though it were dead. For if the left eye be fulfilling its office toward outward things; that is, holding converse with time and the creatures; then must the right eye be hindered in its working; that is, in its contemplation."[w] So too Swedenborg, in his *Angelic Wisdom concerning Divine Providence*, § 48 : " That what is infinite in itself and eternal in itself is divine, can be seen, and yet cannot be seen by men: it can be seen by those who think of infinite not from space, and of eternal not from time; but cannot be seen by those who think of infinite and eternal from space and time."[x] In the same spirit sings Angelus Silesius :

"Mensch, wo du deinen Geist schwingst über Ort und Zeit,
So kannst du jeden Blick sein in der Ewigkeit."[y]

The modern German mysticism is in this respect nowise behind the earlier. Schelling says of his Intuition of the Absolute, "Das reine Selbstbewusstseyn ist ein Act, der ausserhalb aller Zeit liegt und alle Zeit erst constituirt."[z] And again, "Da aber im Absoluten das Denken mit dem Anschauen schlechthin Eins, so werden auch die Dinge nicht bloss durch ihre Begriffe als unendlich, sondern durch ihre Ideen als ewig, mithin ohne alle Beziehung, selbst die der Entgegensetzung, auf Zeit, und mit absoluter Einheit der Möglichkeit und Wirklichkeit, in ihm, als der höchsten Einheit des Denkens und Anschauens, ausgedrückt seyn."[a] Schleiermacher (*Der Christliche*

[v] *Life and Sermons of Dr. John Tauler*, translated by Susanna Winkworth, p. 190.

[w] *Theologia Germanica*, translated by Susanna Winkworth, p. 20.

[x] English translation, p. 27.

[y] *Cherubinischer Wandersmann*, I. 12. Quoted by Strauss, *Glaubenslehre*, II. p. 738.

[z] *System des Transcendentalen Idealismus*, p. 59. (*Werke*, III. p. 375.)

[a] *Bruno*, p. 58.

Glaube, § 52) endeavours to find something analogous to the Divine Eternity, in the timeless existence of the personal self, as the permanent subject of successive modes of consciousness. The analogy, however, fails in two respects; first, because the permanent self cannot be contemplated apart from its successive modes, but is discerned only in relation to them; and, secondly, because, though not itself subject to the condition of *succession,* it is still in time under that of *duration.* Kant truly remarks on all such mystical efforts to transcend time: " Alles lediglich darum, damit die Menschen sich endlich doch einer *ewigen Ruhe* zu erfreuen haben möchten, welche denn ihr vermeintes seliges Ende aller Dinge ausmacht; eigentlich ein Begriff, mit dem ihnen zugleich der Verstand ausgeht und alles Denken selbst ein Ende hat." [b]

NOTE XIX. p. 58.

This is directly admitted by Fichte, who says, in his earliest work, " Wie der unendliche Verstand sein Daseyn und seine Eigenschaften anschauen möge, können wir, ohne selbst der unendliche Verstand zu seyn, nicht wissen." [c] But of the two alternatives which this important admission offers, Fichte himself, in his subsequent writings, as well as his successors in philosophy, chose the wrong one. See above, Lecture I. note 29.

NOTE XX. p. 59.

" Ueber den Sprachgebrauch der Worte *Person, Persönlichkeit,* u. f. schlage man Wörterbücher auf . . . . alle sagen in ihren gesammelten Stellen, dass diese Worte ein *Eigenthümliches oder Besondres unter einer gewissen Apparenz* bezeichnen; welcher Nebenbegriff dem Unendlichen im Gegensatz der Welt gar nicht zukommt."—Herder, *Gott* (*Werke,* VIII. p. 199). " Was nennt ihr denn nun Persönlichkeit und Bewusstseyn? doch wohl dasjenige, was ihr in euch selbst gefunden, an euch selbst kennen gelernt, und mit diesem Namen bezeichnet habt? Dass ihr aber dieses ohne Beschränkung und Endlichkeit schlechterdings nicht denkt, noch denken könnt, kann euch die geringste Aufmerksamkeit auf eure Construction dieses Begriffs lehren."—Fichte, *Ueber göttliche Weltregierung* (*Werke,* V. p. 187). Schleiermacher, in like manner, in his second Discourse on Religion, offers a half apology for Pantheism, on the ground of the

---

[b] *Das Ende aller Dinge* (*Werke,* VII. p. 422).
[c] *Versuch einer Kritik aller Offenbarung* (*Werke,* V. p. 42).

limitation implied in the notions of personality and consciousness.[d] And Strauss remarks: "Als Personen fühlen und wissen wir uns nur im Unterschiede von andern gleichartigen Personen ausser uns, von denen wir uns unterscheiden, mithin als endliche; in diesem Gebiete der Endlichkeit und für dasselbe gebildet, scheint folglich der Begriff der Persönlichkeit ausserhalb desselben jeden Sinn zu verlieren, und ein Wesen, welches kein Anderes seinesgleichen ausser sich hat, auch keine Person sein zu können."— *Christliche Glaubenslehre*, I. p. 504.

Note XXI. p. 60.

De Trinitate, XV. c. 5. "Proinde si dicamus, Æternus, immortalis, incorruptibilis, vivus, sapiens, potens, speciosus, justus, bonus, beatus, spiritus; horum omnium novissimum quod posui quasi tantummodo videtur significare substantiam, cætera vero hujus substantiæ qualitates: sed non ita est in illa ineffabili simplicique natura. Quidquid enim secundum qualitates illic dici videtur, secundum substantiam vel essentiam est intelligendum. Absit enim ut spiritus secundum substantiam dicatur Deus, et bonus secundum qualitatem: sed utrumque secundum substantiam . . . . quamvis in Deo idem sit justum esse quod bonum, quod beatum, idemque spiritum esse quod justum et bonum et beatum esse."—*Ibid.* VI. c. 4. "Deo autem hoc est esse quod est fortem esse, aut justum esse, aut sapientem esse, et si quid de illa simplici multiplicitate, vel multiplici simplicitate dixeris, quo substantia ejus significetur." Other passages to the same effect are cited in a note to Bishop Beveridge's *Discourse on the Articles*, p. 14, ed. 1846. Compare Aquinas, *Summa*, P. I. Qu. XI. Art. 1: "Considerandum tamen est, quod propter divinam simplicitatem consideratur duplex identitas realis in divinis, eorum quæ differunt in rebus creatis. Quia enim divina simplicitas excludit compositionem formæ et materiæ, sequitur, quod in divinis idem est abstractum et concretum, ut Deitas ut Deus. Quia vero divina simplicitas excludit compositionem subjecti et accidentis, sequitur, quod quicquid attribuitur Deo, est ejus essentia: et propter hoc, sapientia et virtus idem sunt in Deo, quia ambo sunt in divina essentia." See also above, Lecture II. note 27.

Note XXII. p. 60.

Plotinus, *Enn.* VI. l. ix. c. 6. Πᾶν δ' ὃ ἂν λέγηται ἐνδεές, τοῦ εὖ καὶ τοῦ σώζοντός ἐστιν ἐνδεές· ὥστε τῷ ἑνὶ οὐδὲν ἀγαθόν ἐστιν, οὐδὲ

---

[d] *Werke*, I. pp. 259, 280.

βούλησις τοίνυν οὐδενός· ἀλλ' ἔστιν ὑπεράγαθον, καὶ αὐτὸ οὐχ ἑαυτῷ, τοῖς δ' ἄλλοις ἀγαθὸν, εἴ τι αὐτοῦ δύναται μεταλαμβάνειν· οὐδὲ νόησις, ἵνα μὴ ἑτερότης, οὐδὲ κίνησις· πρὸ γὰρ κινήσεως καὶ πρὸ νοήσεως. Τί γὰρ καὶ νοήσει; ἑαυτόν. Πρὸ νοήσεως τοίνυν ἀγνοῶν ἔσται, καὶ νοήσεως δεήσεται, ἵνα γνῷ ἑαυτὸν ὁ αὐτάρκης ἑαυτῷ.—Spinoza, *Eth.* P. I. Prop. 17. Schol. "Si intellectus ad divinam naturam pertinet, non poterit, uti noster intellectus, posterior (ut plerisque placet) vel simul natura esse cum rebus intellectis, quandoquidem Deus omnibus rebus prior est causalitate: sed contra veritas et formalis rerum essentia ideo talis est, quia talis in Dei intellectu existit objective. . . . . Quum itaque Dei intellectus sit unica rerum causa, videlicet (ut ostendimus) tam earum essentiæ, quam earum existentiæ, debet ipse necessario ab iisdem differre tam ratione essentiæ, quam ratione existentiæ. Nam causatum differt a sua causa præcise in eo, quod a causa habet. . . . Atqui Dei intellectus est et essentiæ et existentiæ, nostri intellectus causa: ergo Dei intellectus, quatenus divinam essentiam constituere concipitur, a nostro intellectu tam ratione essentiæ, quam ratione existentiæ differt, nec in ulla re, præterquam in nomine, cum eo convenire potest, ut volebamus. Circa voluntatem eodem modo proceditur, ut facile unusquisque videre potest."—Compare P. I. Prop. 32. Cor. 1, 2, and P. II. Prop. II. Cor., where Spinoza maintains that God is not conscious in so far as he is infinite, but becomes conscious in man;—a conclusion identical with that of the extreme Hegelian school; and indeed substantially the same with that of Hegel himself.—See above, Lecture I. notes 29, 32.

NOTE XXIII. p. 61.

Anselm. *Monolog.* c. 66. "Cum igitur pateat quia nihil de hac natura possit percipi per suam proprietatem, sed per aliud, certum est quia per illud magis ad ejus cognitionem acceditur, quod illi magis per similitudinem propinquat. Quicquid enim inter creata constat illi esse similius, id necesse est esse sua natura præstantius. . . . . Proculdubio itaque tanto altius creatrix essentia cognoscitur, quanto per propinquiorem sibi creaturam indagatur . . . . Patet itaque quia sicut sola est mens rationalis inter omnes creaturas, quæ ad ejus investigationem assurgere valeat; ita nihilominus eadem sola est, per quam maxime ipsamet ad ejusdem inventionem proficere queat."—Compare Aquinas, *Summa*, P. I. Qu. XXIX. Art. 3. "Persona significat id quod est perfectissimum in tota natura, sive subsistens in rationali natura. Unde, cum omne illud quod est perfectionis, Deo sit attribuendum, eo quod ejus essentia continet in se omnem perfectionem, conveniens est ut hoc nomen, persona, de Deo dicatur, non tamen eodem modo quo dicitur de creaturis; sed excellentiori modo: sicut et alia nomina quæ creaturis a nobis imposita Deo attribuuntur." And Jacobi, at the conclusion of an eloquent denunciation of the Pantheism of his own day, truly observes, " Ein Seyn ohne Selbstseyn ist durchaus und allgemein unmöglich. Ein Selbstseyn aber ohne Bewusstseyn, und wieder ein Bewusstseyn ohne Selbstbewusstseyn, ohne Substanzialität und wenigstens angelegte Persönlichkeit, vollkommen eben so unmöglich; eines wie das andre nur gedankenloser Wortschall. Also Gott ist nicht, ist das Nichseyende im höchsten Sinne, wenn er nicht ein *Geist* ist; und er ist kein Geist, wenn ihm die Grundeigenschaft des Geistes, das Selbstbewusstseyn, Substanzialität und Persönlichkeit, mangelt."[e] In the same spirit, and with a just recognition of the limits of human thought, M. Bartholmèss says, " Celui qui répugne à emprunter quelques traits de ressemblance à la partie morale de la création, sera forcé d'en tirer de la partie physique, de la partie mathématique, de la partie logique; il fera Dieu à l'image du monde corporel, à l'image d'une grandeur géométrique ou arithmétique, à l'image d'une abstraction dialectique; toujours, en s'élançant au Créateur, il s'appuiera sur un endroit quelconque de la création."[f] To the same effect a distinguished living writer of our own country observes, " The worshipper carried through the long avenues of columns and statues, and the splendid halls of the ancient temple of Egyptian Thebes, was not conducted at last to a more miserable termination, when in the inner shrine he found one of the lower animals, than the follower of a modern philosopher, when conducted through processes, laws, and developments, to a divinity who has less of separate sensation, consciousness, and life, than the very brutes which Egypt declared to be its gods."[g]

NOTE XXIV. p. 61.

Pensées, P. I. Art. IV. § 6. In like manner, in another passage, Pascal says, " Tous les corps, le firmament, les étoiles, la terre, et les royaumes, ne valent pas le moindre des esprits; car il connaît tout cela, et soi-même; et le corps, rien."[h]

The following spirited translation of Jacobi[i] is from the pen of

[e] *Ueber eine Weissagung Lichtenberg's* (*Werke*, III. p. 240). Compare also the Preface to Vol. IV. p. xlv.

[f] *Histoire des Doctrines religieuses de la Philosophie Moderne*, Introduction, p. xli.

[g] M'Cosh, *Method of the Divine Government*, p. 461 (4th edition).

[h] *Pensées*, P. II. Art. X. § 1.

[i] *Von den göttlichen Dingen* (*Werke*, III. p. 425).

Sir W. Hamilton, and occurs in the second of his *Lectures on Metaphysics*, p. 40. The entire Lecture from which it is taken constitutes a forcible and admirably illustrated argument to the same effect. " *Nature conceals God :* for through her whole domain Nature reveals only fate, only an indissoluble chain of mere efficient causes without beginning and without end, excluding, with equal necessity, both providence and chance. An independent agency, a free original commencement, within her sphere and proceeding from her powers, is absolutely impossible. Working without will, she takes counsel neither of the good nor of the beautiful; creating nothing, she casts off from her dark abyss only eternal transformations of herself, unconsciously and without an end; furthering with the same ceaseless industry decline and increase, death and life,—never producing what alone is of God and what supposes liberty,—the virtuous, the immortal. *Man reveals God :* for Man by his intelligence rises above nature, and in virtue of this intelligence is conscious of himself, as a power not only independent of, but opposed to, nature, and capable of resisting, conquering, and controlling her. As man has a living faith in this power, superior to nature, which dwells in him, so has he a belief in God, a feeling, an experience of his existence. As he does not believe in this power, so does he not believe in God : he sees, he experiences naught in existence but nature,—necessity,—fate."

NOTE XXV. p. 62.

Descartes, *Discours de la Méthode*, P. IV., *Principia*, P. I. § 7. That the Cartesian *cogito, ergo sum*, is not intended as a syllogism, in which thought and existence are two distinct attributes, but as a statement of the fact, that personal existence consists in consciousness, has been sufficiently shewn by M. Cousin, in his Essay, 'Sur le vrai sens du *cogito, ergo sum*.' The same view has been well stated by Mr. Veitch, in the introduction to his translation of the *Discours de la Méthode*, p. xxii. M. Bartholmèss (*Histoire des Doctrines religeuses*, I. p. 23) happily renders *ergo* by *c'est-à-dire*. It must be remembered, however, that the *cogito* of Descartes is not designed to express the phenomena of reflection alone, but is coextensive with the entire consciousness. This is expressly affirmed in the *Principia*, P. I. § 9. " Cogitationis nomine intelligo illa omnia, quæ nobis consciis in nobis fiunt, quatenus eorum in nobis conscientia est. Atque ita non modo intelligere, velle, imaginari, sed etiam sentire, idem est hic quod cogitare." The dictum, thus extended, may perhaps be advantageously modified by disengaging the essential from the accidental features of consciousness; but its main principle remains unshaken; namely, that our conception of real existence, as distinguished from appearance, is derived from, and depends upon, the distinction between the one conscious subject and the several objects of which he is conscious. The rejection of consciousness, as the primary constituent of substantive existence, constitutes Spinoza's point of departure from the principles of Descartes, and at the same time, the fundamental error of his system. Spinoza in fact transfers the notion of *substance*, which is originally derived from the consciousness of personality, and has no positive significance out of that consciousness, to the absolute, which exists and is conceived by itself,—an object to whose existence consciousness bears no direct testimony, and whose conception involves a self-contradiction.

Note XXVI. p. 62.

" *Ich bin, der ich bin*. Dieser Machtspruch begründet alles. Sein Echo in der menschlichen Seele ist die Offenbarung Gottes in ihr . . . Was den Menschen zum Menschen, d. i. zum *Ebenbilde Gottes* macht, heisset *Vernunft*. Diese beginnet mit dem—Ich bin . . . Vernunft ohne Persönlichkeit ist Unding, das gleiche Unding mit jener *Grundmaterie* oder jenem *Urgrunde*, welcher Alles und nicht Eines, oder Eines und Keines, die Vollkommenheit des Unvollkommenen, des absolut Unbestimmte ist, und *Gott* genannt wird von denen, die nicht wissen wollen von dem wahren Gott, aber dennoch sich scheuen ihn zu läugnen—mit den Lippen." Jacobi, *Von den göttlichen Dingen* (*Werke*, III. p. 418).

Note XXVII. p. 62.

For notices of Schelling's philosophy in this respect, see Bartholmèss, *Histoire des Doctrines religieuses*, II. p. 116, and Willm, *Histoire de la Philosophie Allemande*, III. p. 318. "L'école de Schelling," says Madame de Stael, "suppose que l'individu périt en nous, mais que les qualités intimes que nous possédons rentrent dans le grand tout de la création éternelle. Cette immortalité-là ressemble terriblement à la mort."[k] Schelling's views on this point are more completely developed by his disciple Blasche, in his *Philosophische Unsterblichkeitlehre*, especially §§ 18, 55, 56, 72. The tendency of Hegel's teaching is in the same direction; the

[k] *De l'Allemagne*, Partie III. ch. 7.

individual being with him only an imperfect and insignificant phase of the universal:[1] and a personal immortality, though not openly denied, seems excluded by inference; an inference which his successors have not hesitated to make.[m] Schleiermacher concludes his Second Discourse on Religion with these remarkable words: "Eben so ist das Ziel und der Charakter eines religiösen Lebens nicht die Unsterblichkeit, wie viele sie wünschen und an sie glauben, oder auch nur zu glauben vorgeben . . . nicht jene Unsterblichkeit ausser der Zeit und hinter der Zeit, oder vielmehr nur nach dieser Zeit aber doch in der Zeit, sondern die Unsterblichkeit, die wir schon in diesem zeitlichen Leben unmittelbar haben können, und die eine Aufgabe ist, in deren Lösung wir immerfort begriffen sind. Mitten in der Endlichkeit Eins werden mit dem unendlichen und ewig sein in jedem Augenblick, das ist die Unsterblichkeit der Religion." And later, in *Der Christliche Glaube*, § 158, while admitting that the belief in a personal immortality follows naturally from the doctrine of the twofold nature of Christ, he notwithstanding thinks it necessary to apologise for those who reject this belief on pantheistic principles: "Denn von hier aus lässt sich auf gleiche Weise behaupten, einerseits dass das Gottesbewusstseyn das Wesen jedes im höheren Sinne selbstbewussten oder vernünftigen Lebens constituire, auf der andern Seite aber auch, dass wenn der Geist in dieser Productivität wesentlich unsterblich ist, doch die einzelne Seele nur eine vorübergehende

[1] *Phänomenologie des Geistes*, Vorrede (*Werke*, II. p. 22).
[m] See Michelet, *Geschichte der letzten Systeme der Philosophie*, II. p. 638. Strauss, in his *Christliche Glaubenslehre*, § 106-110, gives an instructive account of some of the speculations of recent German writers on this question: his own commentary being not the least significant portion. "Damit," he says, "legt ja das Ich den Willen an den Tag, nicht blos seine Subjectivität überhaupt, sondern auch deren particuläre Bestimmungen und Verhältnisse, in alle Ewigkeit fortzuführen, d. h. aus seiner Endlichkeit keinen Schritt herauszugehen." And again: "Nur die Anlage der Gattung ist unendlich und unerschöpflich: . . die des Einzelwesens, als Momentes der Gattung, kann nur eine endliche sein." His inquiry concludes with the well-known words, "Das Jenseits ist zwar in allen die Eine, in seiner Gestalt als zukünftiges aber der letzte Feind, welchen die speculative Kritik zu bekämpfen und wo möglich zu überwinden hat." And Feuerbach, another 'advanced' disciple of the Hegelian school, has written an Essay on Death and Immortality, for the purpose of shewing that a belief in personal annihilation is indispensable to sound morality and true religion; that the opposite belief is connected with all that is "satanic" and "bestial;" and that temporal death is but an image of God, the "great objective negation:" and has indicated significantly, in another work, the philosophical basis of his theory, by an aphorism the direct contradictory to that of Descartes, "Cogitans nemo sum. Cogito, ergo omnes sum homines."

Action dieser Productivität sei, mithin eben so wesentlich vergänglich . . . Mit einer solchen Entsagung auf die Fortdauer der Persönlichkeit würde sich eine Herrschaft des Gottesbewusstseyns vollkommen vertragen, welche auch die reinste Sittlichkeit und die höchste Geistigkeit des Lebens verlangte." Mr. Atkinson, from the side of materialism, arrives at a similar conclusion: "What more noble and glorious than a calm and joyful indifference about self and the future, in merging the individual in the general good,— the general good in universal nature."[n] And M. Comte comes forward with his substitute of "subjective immortality," i. e. being remembered by other people, as a far nobler and truer conception of a future life than that held by theologians.[o] But the most systematic and thoroughgoing exponent of this philosophy is Schopenhauer. With him, the species is the exhibition in time of the idea or real being, of which the individual is but the finite and transient expression.[p] In the same sense in which the individual was generated from nothing, he returns to nothing by death.[q] To desire a personal immortality is to desire to perpetuate an error to infinity; for individual existence is the error from which it should be the aim of life to extricate ourselves.[r] Judaism, which teaches a creation out of nothing, consistently asserts that death is annihilation; while Christianity has borrowed its belief in immortality from India, and inconsistently engraved it on a Jewish stem.[s] The true doctrine however is not to be found in these, but in the Indian Vedas, whose superior wisdom can only be ascribed to the fact, that their authors, living nearer in point of time to the origin of the human race, comprehended more clearly and profoundly the true nature of things.[t] As a relief from this desolating pantheism, it is refreshing to turn to the opposite language of Neander. "Man could not become conscious of God as his God, if he were not a personal spirit, divinely allied, and destined for eternity, an eternal object (as an individual) of God; and thereby far above all natural and perishable beings, whose perpetuity is that of the species, not the individual."[u]

[n] *Letters on the Laws of Man's Nature and Development*, p. 189.
[o] *Catéchisme Positiviste*, p. 169.
[p] *Die Welt als Wille und Vorstellung*, II. p. 484, 487, 511.
[q] *Ibid.* p. 482, 498.
[r] *Ibid.* p. 494.
[s] *Ibid.* p. 489, 617.
[t] *Ibid.* p. 487.
[u] *Life of Jesus Christ*, p. 309, (Bohn's edition).

Note XXVIII. p. 63.

"On a grande raison de se récrier sur la manière étrange des hommes, qui se tourmentent en agitant des questions mal-conçues. Ils cherchent ce qu'ils savent, et ne savent pas ce qu'ils cherchent." Leibnitz, *Nouveaux Essais*, L. II. Ch. 21 § 14.

Note XXIX. p. 63.

See the acute criticism of the Kantian distinction between *things* and *phenomena*, by M. Willm, in his *Histoire de la Philosophie Allemande*, vol. I. p. 177. "Il n'est pas nécessaire d'admettre que ce qui s'interpose entre les objets et la raison, altère et fausse pour ainsi dire la vue des objets, et il se peut que les lois de l'esprit soient en même temps les lois des choses telles qu'elles sont. Hegel a dit justement qu'il se pourrait fort bien, qu'après avoir pénétré derrière la scène qui est ouverte devant nous, nous n'y trouvassions rien; ajoutons qu'il se pourrait que ce prétendu voile qui semble couvrir le tableau et que nous cherchons à lever fût le tableau lui-même." Kant unquestionably went too far, in asserting that things in themselves *are not* as they appear to our faculties:[x] the utmost that his premises could warrant him in asserting is, that we cannot tell whether they are so or not. And even this degree of scepticism, though tenable as far as external objects are concerned, cannot legitimately be extended to the personal self. I exist as I am conscious of existing; and this conscious self is itself the *Ding an sich*, the standard by which all representations of personality must be judged, and from which our notion of reality, as distinguished from appearance, is originally derived. To this extent Jacobi's criticism of Kant is just and decisive. "Alles unser Philosophiren ist ein Bestreben, hinter die Gestalt der Sache, d. i. zur Sache selbst, zu kommen; aber wie könnten wir dies, da wir alsdann hinter

---

[x] A critic in the *National Review* (No. xv. p. 219) "cannot persuade himself" that Kant ever said any such thing; adding, that if he did so, "he fell into variance with the whole spirit of his philosophy." Kant's own words are sufficiently explicit on this point. "Wir haben also sagen wollen: dass alle unsere Anschauung nichts als die Vorstellung von Erscheinung sey: dass die Dinge, die wir anschauen, nicht das an sich selbst sind, wofür wir sie anschauen, noch ihre Verhältnisse so an sich selbst beschaffen sind, als sie uns erscheinen." *Kritik der r. V.* p. 49, ed. Rosenkranz. This assertion, originally made in the first edition of the *Kritik*, stands unaltered in the subsequent impressions. It will be found at p. 59 of the fifth edition, published in 1799. Indeed it is so far from being at variance with the whole spirit of Kant's philosophy, that it follows naturally from his theory of the mere subjectivity of space and time.

uns selbst, ja hinter die gesammte Natur der Dinge, hinter ihren Ursprung kommen müssten?"[1]

NOTE XXX. p. 65.

The Intellectual Intuition of Schelling has been noticed above. See notes 16, 17, 18, pp. 249 sqq. The method of Hegel, in its aim identical with that of Schelling, differs from it chiefly in making thought, instead of intuition, the instrument of reaching the Absolute. As Schelling assumes the possibility of an intuition superior to time and difference, so Hegel postulates the existence of a logical process emancipated from the laws of identity and contradiction. The Understanding and the Reason are placed in sharp antagonism to each other. The one is a faculty of finite thinking, subject to the ordinary laws of thought: the other is a faculty of infinite thinking, to which those laws are inapplicable. Hence the principles of Identity, of Contradiction, and of Excluded Middle are declared to be valid merely for the abstract understanding, from which reason is distinguished by the principle of the Identity of Contradictories.[2] But this assertion, indispensable as it is to Hegel's system, involves more consequences than the author himself would be willing to admit. The important admission, that an infinite object of thought can only be apprehended by an infinite act of thinking, involves the conclusion, that the understanding and the reason have no common ground on which either can make itself intelligible to the other; for the very principles which to the one are a criterion of truth, are to the other an evidence of falsehood. Moreover, the philosophy which regards the union of contradictories as essential to the conceptions of the reason is bound in consistency to extend the same condition to its judgments and deductions; for whatever is one-sided and partial in the analysis of a notion, must be equally so in those more complex forms of thought into which notions enter. The logic of the understanding must be banished entirely, or not at all. Hence the philosopher may neither defend his own system, nor refute his adversary, by arguments reducible to

---

[1] *Ueber das Unternehmen des Kriticismus* (*Werke*, III. p. 176).

[2] See *Logik*, B. II. c. 2; *Encyklopädie*, § 28, 115, 119, *Geschichte der Philosophie*, *Werke*, XV. p. 598. See also his attempt to rescue speculative philosophy from the assaults of scepticism, *Werke*, XIV. p. 511, 512. He charges the sceptic with first making reason finite, in order to overthrow it by the principles of finite thought. The defence amounts to no more than this: "The laws of thought are against me; but I refuse to be bound by their authority."

the ordinary logical forms; for these forms rest on the very laws of thought which the higher philosophy is supposed to repudiate. Hegel's own polemic is thus self-condemned; and his attempted refutation of the older metaphysicians is a virtual acknowledgment of the validity of their fundamental principles. If the so-called infinite thinking is a process of thought at all, it must be a process entirely *sui generis*, isolated and unapproachable, as incapable as the intuition of Schelling of being expressed in ordinary language, or compared, even in antagonism, with the processes of ordinary reasoning. The very attempt to expound it thus necessarily postulates its own failure.

But this great thinker has rendered one invaluable service to philosophy. He has shewn clearly what are the only conditions under which a philosophy of the Absolute could be realized; and his attempt has done much to facilitate the conclusion, to which philosophy must finally come, that the Absolute is beyond the reach of human thought. If such a philosophy were possible at all, it would be in the form of the philosophy of Hegel. And Hegel's failure points to one inevitable moral. All the above inconsistency and division of the human mind against itself might be avoided by acknowledging the supreme authority of the laws of thought over all human speculation; and by recognising the consequent distinction between positive and negative thinking,—between the lawful exercise of the reason within its own province, and its abortive efforts to pass beyond it. But such an acknowledgment amounts to a confession that thought and being are not identical, and that reason itself requires us to believe in truths that are beyond reason. And to this conclusion speculative philosophy itself leads us, if in no other way, at least by the wholesome warning of its own pretensions and failures.

NOTE XXXI., p. 66.

Tertullian, *De Carne Christi*, c. 5. "Natus est Dei Filius; non pudet, quia pudendum est: et mortuus est Dei Filius; prorsus credibile est, quia ineptum est: et sepultus, resurrexit; certum est, quia impossibile."

NOTE XXXII., p. 68.

See above, Lecture II., note 37.

Note XXXIII., p. 72.

Hooker, *E. P.* b. I. ch. ii. § 2. Very similar to the language of Hooker is that of Walter Charleton. "For whoever shall duly consider how impossible it must be for *humanity*, dull, gross, and narrow humanity, to behold *Invisibility*, derive *Independency*, calculate *Eternity*, circumscribe *Incircumscription*, limit *Omnipotence*, understand *Omniscience*, &c., and how dangerous a phrensy that brain must be disordered withal, that attempts to describe what it doth not, cannot know, will soon be satisfied that *amazement* and pious *silence* is the best lecture that can be read on that immense subject, of which when we have said all we can, we have said nothing, if we look forward upon that inexhaustible abyss of excellencies, which must remain unspoken of, and indeed uncomprehended; that a professed *Nescience* in this particular is the complement or zenith of all other *Science* which the mind of man is capable of in this life."—*The Darkness of Atheism dispelled by the Light of Nature* (1652), p. 2. Compare also the words of Jacobi, *An Fichte* (*Werke*, III. p. 7). "Ein Gott, der *gewusst* werden könnte, wäre gar kein Gott,"—words which are in fact little more than a translation of those of St. Augustine, Serm. cxvii. "De Deo loquimur; quid mirum si non comprehendis? Si enim comprehendis, non est Deus."

LECTURE IV.

Note I. p. 73.

Thus Wegscheider, after expressly admitting (*Instit. Theol.* § 52) that the infinite cannot be comprehended by the finite, and that its idea can only be represented by analogy and symbol, proceeds to assert, with the utmost confidence, that the attributes of omnipotence and omniscience do not truly represent the internal nature of God (§ 69); that a plurality of persons in the Godhead is manifestly repugnant to reason, and that the infinite God cannot assume the nature of finite man (§ 92); that the fall of man is inconsistent with the divine attributes (§ 117); that repentance is the only mode of expiating sin reconcilable with the moral nature of God (§ 138); that the doctrine of Christ's intercession is repugnant to the divine nature (§ 143).

By a somewhat similar inconsistency, Mr. Newman, while fully acknowledging that we cannot have any perfect knowledge of an infinite mind, and that infinity itself is but a negative idea, yet thinks it necessary to regard the soul as a separate organ of specific information, by which we are in contact with the infinite; and dogmatizes concerning the similarity of divine and human attributes, in a manner which nothing short of absolute knowledge can justify (See *The Soul*, pp. 1, 3, 34, 54, 58). He compares the infinite to the "illimitable haziness" which bounds the sphere of distinct vision. The analogy would be serviceable to his argument, if we possessed two sets of eyes, one for clearness and one for haziness; one to be limited, and the other to discern the limitation. The hypothesis of a separate faculty of consciousness, whether called soul, reason, or intellectual intuition, to take cognisance of the infinite, is only needed for those philosophers who undertake to develope a complete philosophy of the infinite as such. But the success of the various attempts in this province has not been such as to give any trustworthy evidence of the existence of such a faculty.

Note II. p. 74.

See above, Lecture I. note 3.

Note III. p. 74.

See Mr. Rose's remarks on the reaction against the Wolfian demonstrative method. *State of Protestantism in Germany*, p. 206 (second edition).

Note IV. p. 75.

See Kant, *Kritik der reinen Vernunft*, p. 497, ed. Rosenkranz. This admission, rightly understood, need not be considered as detracting from the value of the speculative arguments as auxiliaries. All that is contended for is, that the foundation must be laid elsewhere, before their assistance, valuable as it is, can be made available. Thus understood, this view coincides with that expressed by Sir W. Hamilton, in the second of his *Lectures on Metaphysics*, p. 26: "that the phenomena of matter, taken by themselves (you will observe the qualification, taken by themselves,) so far from warranting any inference to the existence of a God, would, on the contrary, ground even an argument to his negation,—that the study of the external world, taken with, and in subordination to, that of the internal, not only loses its atheistic tendency, but, under such subservience, may be rendered conducive to the great conclusion, from which, if left to itself, it would dissuade us." The atheistic tendency is perhaps too strongly stated; as the same phenomena may be surveyed, by different individuals, in different spirits and with different results: but the main position, that the belief in God is primarily based on mental, and not on material phenomena, accords with the view taken in the text.

Note V. p. 75.

Kant, *Kritik der rein. Vern.* p. 488. *Kritik der prakt. Vern.* p. 284. Compare Hume, *Dialogues concerning Natural Religion*, Part V. Kant's argument is approved by Hegel, *Philosophie der Religion* (*Werke*, XII., p. 37). The objection which it urges is of no value, unless we admit that man possesses an adequate notion of the infinite as such. Otherwise the notion of power indefinitely great, which the phenomena certainly suggest, is, both theoretically and practically, undistinguishable from the infinite itself. This has been well remarked by a recent writer. See *Selections from the Correspondence of R. E. H. Greyson*, Vol. II. p. 329.

NOTE VI. p. 75.

Jowett, *Epistles of St. Paul*, Vol. II. p. 406. Professor Jowett considers the comparison between the works of nature and those of art as not merely inadequate, but positively erroneous. He says, " As certainly as the man who found a watch or piece of mechanism on the sea-shore would conclude, ' here are marks of design, indications of an intelligent artist,' so certainly, if he came across the meanest or the highest of the works of nature, would he infer, ' this was not made by man, nor by any human art and skill.' He sees at first sight that the sea-weed beneath his feet is something different in kind from the productions of man."ᵃ But surely the force of teleological argument does not turn upon the *similarity* of the objects, but on their *analogy*. The point of comparison is, that in the works of nature, as well as in those of art, there is an adaptation of means to ends, which indicates an intelligent author. And such an adaptation may exist in an organized body, no less than in a machine, notwithstanding numerous differences in the details of their structure. The evidence of this general analogy is in nowise weakened by Professor Jowett's special exceptions.

NOTE VII. p. 75.

" When the spiritual man (as such) cannot judge, the question is removed into a totally different court from that of the Soul, the court of the critical understanding. . . . The processes of thought have nothing to quicken the conscience or affect the soul."—F. W. Newman, *The Soul*, p. 245 (second edition). Yet he allows in another place, (not quite consistently,) that " pure intellectual error, depending on causes wholly unmoral, *may* and *does* perpetuate moral illusions, which are of the deepest injury to spiritual life." p. 169. Similar in principle, though not pushed to the same extreme consequences, is the theory of Mr. Morell, who says, " Reason up to a God, and the best you can do is to hypostatize and deify the final product of your own faculties; but admit the reality of an intellectual intuition, (as the mass of mankind virtually do,) and the absolute stands before us in all its living reality."ᵇ This distinc-

---

ᵃ This argument is substantially the same with that of Hume, *Dialogues concerning Natural Religion*, Part II. " If we see a house, we conclude, with the greatest certainty, that it had an architect or builder. . . . But surely you will not affirm that the universe bears such a resemblance to a house, that we can with the same certainty infer a similar cause."

ᵇ *Philosophy of Religion*, p. 39.

tion he carries so far as to assert that "to speak of logic, as such, being inspired, is a sheer absurdity;" because "the process either of defining or of reasoning requires simply the employment of the formal laws of thought, the accuracy of which can be in no way affected by any amount of inspiration whatever:"[o] and in another passage he maintains, to the same effect, that "the *essential* elements of religion in general, as of Christianity in particular, appertain strictly to the intuitional portion of our nature, and may be realized in all their varied influence without the cooperation of any purely reflective processes."[d] Here he apparently overlooks the fact that the intuitive and reflective faculties invariably act in conjunction; that both are equally necessary to the existence of consciousness as such; and that logical forms are never called into operation, except in conjunction with the matter on which they are exercised.

Note VIII. p. 78.

In acknowledging Expiation as well as prayer to be prompted by the natural feelings of men, I have no intention of controverting the opinion, so ably maintained by Archbishop Magee and Mr. Faber, of the divine origin of the actual rite of sacrifice. That the religious instincts of men should indicate the need of supplication and expiation, is perfectly consistent with the belief that the particular mode of both may have been first taught by a primitive revelation. That religion, in both its constituent elements, was communicated to the parents of the human race by positive revelation, seems the most natural inference from the Mosaic narrative.[e] Yet we may admit that the positive institution must from the first have been adapted to some corresponding instinct of human nature; without which it would be scarcely possible to account for its continuance and universal diffusion, as well as for its various corruptions. We may thus combine the view of Archbishop Magee with that exhibited by Archbishop Thompson, *Bampton Lectures*, pp. 30, 48.

Note IX. p. 79.

That the mere feeling of dependence by itself is not necessarily religious, is shown by Hegel, *Philosophie der Religion* (*Werke*, XII. p.

---

[o] *Philosophy of Religion*, p. 173, 174.
[d] *Ibid.*, p. 193.
[e] Even Mr. Davison, who contends for the human origin of the patriarchal sacrifices, which he regards as merely eucharistic and penitentiary, expressly admits the divine appointment of expiatory offerings. See his *Inquiry into the Origin of Primitive Sacrifice* (*Remains*, p. 121).

173). Speaking of the Roman worship of evil influences, Angerona, Fames, Robigo, &c., he rightly remarks that in such representations all conception of Deity is lost, though the feeling of fear and dependence remains. To the same effect is his sarcastic remark, that according to Schleiermacher's theory, the dog is the best Christian.[f] Mr. Parker (*Discourse of Religion*, Ch. 1) agrees with Schleiermacher in resolving the religious sentiment into a mere sense of dependence; though he admits that this sentiment does not, itself, disclose the character of the object on which it depends. Referred to this principle alone, it is impossible to regard religious worship as a moral duty. Some good remarks on this subject will be found in Dr. Alliott's *Psychology and Theology*, p. 45.

NOTE X. p. 80.

See Kant, *Metaphysik der Sitten*, Abschn. II. (pp. 61, 71, ed. Rosenkranz.) His theory has been ably combated by Julius Müller, *Christliche Lehre von der Sünde*, B. I. c. 2. Compare also Hooker, *E. P.* I. ix. 2. Some excellent remarks to the same effect will be found in M'Cosh's *Method of the Divine Government*, p. 298, (fourth edition,) and in Bartholmèss, *Histoire des Doctrines religieuses de la Philosophie moderne*, vol. i. p. 405. Selden, *Table Talk*, p. 84, ed. 1856, disposes of the whole question in a few words: " How should I know I ought not to steal. I ought not to commit adultery? . . . 'Tis not because I think I ought not to do them, nor because you think I ought not: if so, our minds might change: whence then comes the restraint? From a higher Power: nothing else can bind. I cannot bind myself; for I may untie myself again; nor an equal cannot bind me; for we may untie one another: it must be a superior power, even God Almighty."

NOTE XI. p. 81.

The theory which regards absolute morality as based on the immutable *nature* of God, must not be confounded with that which places it in his arbitrary *will*. The latter view, which was maintained by Scotus, Occam, and others among the schoolmen, is severely criticized by Sir James Mackintosh, *Dissertation on the Progress of Ethical Philosophy*, section III., and by Müller, *Christliche Lehre von der Sünde*, B. I. c. 3. The former principle is adopted by

---

[f] See Rosenkranz, *Hegel's Leben*, p. 346.

Cudworth, as the basis of his treatise on Eternal and Immutable Morality. See B. I. c. 3., B. IV. c. 4.

NOTE XII. p. 81.

On the universality of expiatory rites, see Magee on the Atonement, note V. On their origin, see the same work, notes XLI., XLVI. to LI., LIV. to LVIII., and Mr. Faber's *Treatise on the Origin of Expiatory Sacrifice*.

NOTE XIII. p. 82.

Schleiermacher, *Der Christliche Glaube*, § 4.

NOTE XIV. p. 83.

Morell, *Philosophy of Religion*, p. 75. Mr. Morell here goes beyond the theory of his master, Schleiermacher. The latter (*Der Christliche Glaube*, § 4) admits that this supposed feeling of absolute dependence can never be completely attained in any single act of consciousness, but is generally suggested by the whole. Mr. Morell speaks as if we could be immediately conscious of our own annihilation, by a direct intuition of the infinite. Both theories are inadequate to prove the intended conclusion. That of Schleiermacher virtually amounts to a confession that the infinite is not a positive object of consciousness, but a mere negation suggested by the direct presence of the finite. That of Mr. Morell saves the intuition of the infinite, but annihilates itself; for if in any act of consciousness the subject becomes absolutely nothing, the consciousness must vanish with it; and if it stops at any point short of nothing, the object is not infinite.

NOTE XV. p. 83.

That this is the legitimate result of Schleiermacher's theory, may be gathered from a remarkable passage in *Der Christliche Glaube*, § 8, in which the polytheistic and monotheistic feelings of piety are compared together. The former, he says, is always accompanied by a sensible representation of its object, in which there is contained a germ of multiplicity; but in the latter, the higher consciousness is so separated from the sensible, that the pious emotions admit of no greater difference than that of the elevating or depressing tone of the feeling. This seems to imply that, in Schleiermacher's opinion, to worship a God of many attributes is equivalent to worshipping a plurality of Gods. And to those philosophers who make the Infinite in itself a direct object of religious worship, this identification is natural; for a God of many attributes cannot be conceived as infinite, and therefore in one sense partakes of the limited divinity of Polytheism. But, on the other hand, a God of no attributes is no God at all; and the so-called monotheistic piety is nothing but an abortive attempt at mystical self-annihilation. Some acute strictures on Schleiermacher's theory from this point of view will be found in Drobisch, *Grundlehren der Religionsphilosophie*, p. 84.

NOTE XVI. p. 84.

Schleiermacher himself admits (*Der Christliche Glaube*, §§ 33, 147) that the theory of absolute dependence is incompatible with the belief that God can be moved by any human action. He endeavours, however, to reconcile this admission with the duty of prayer, by maintaining that a right prayer can have no other object than that which lies within the order of God's pleasure; and that the prayer, though it cannot be regarded as the cause of the fulfilment, yet arises out of circumstances which belong to the conditions under which the result can effectually take place. A doctrine of this kind only explains away the language of Scripture to suit a human theory of the divine absoluteness.

NOTE XVII. p. 85.

Schleiermacher (*Der Chr. Glaube*, § 49) attempts, not very successfully, to meet this objection, by maintaining that even our free acts are dependent upon the will of God. This is doubtless true; but it is true as an article of faith, not as a theory of philosophy: it may be believed, but cannot be conceived, nor represented in any act of human consciousness. The apparent contradiction implied in the coexistence of an infinite and a finite will remains unsolved, and is most glaring in the theories of those philosophers who, like Schleiermacher (§ 54), maintain that God actually does all that he can do. The only solution is to confess that we have no true conception of the infinite at all. Schleiermacher himself is unable to avoid the logical consequence of his position. He admits (§ 80) that God's omnipotence is limited if we do not allow him to be the author of sin; though he endeavours to soften this monstrous admission by taking it in conjunction with the fact that God is also the author of grace.

NOTE XVIII. p. 87.

De Augmentis Scientiarum, l. III. c. 1. Compare Theophilus of Antioch, *Ad Autolycum*, I. 5. Καθάπερ γὰρ ψυχὴ ἐν ἀνθρώπῳ οὐ βλέπεται, ἀόρατος οὖσα ἀνθρώποις, διὰ δὲ τῆς κινήσεως τοῦ σώματος νοεῖται ἡ ψυχή, οὕτως ἔχοι ἂν καὶ τὸν Θεὸν μὴ δύνασθαι ὁραθῆναι ὑπὸ ὀφθαλμῶν ἀνθρωπίνων, διὰ δὲ τῆς προνοίας καὶ τῶν ἔργων αὐτοῦ βλέπεται καὶ νοεῖται.[g] And Athanasius, *Contra Gentes*, c. 35. Ἐκ γὰρ τῶν ἔργων πολλάκις ὁ τεχνίτης καὶ μὴ ὁρώμενος γιγνώσκεται, καὶ οἷόν τι λέγουσι περὶ τοῦ ἀγαλματοποιοῦ Φειδίου, ὡς τὰ τούτου δημιουργήματα ἐκ τῆς συμμετρίας καὶ τῆς πρὸς ἄλληλα τῶν μερῶν ἀναλογίας ἐμφαίνειν καὶ μὴ παρόντα Φειδίαν τοῖς ὁρῶσιν· οὕτω δεῖ νοεῖν ἐκ τῆς τοῦ κόσμου τάξεως τὸν τούτου ποιητὴν καὶ δημιουργὸν Θεόν, κἂν τοῖς τοῦ σώματος ὀφθαλμοῖς μὴ θεωρῆται. And Basil, Epist. ccxxxiv. Ἡμεῖς δὲ ἐκ τῶν ἐνεργειῶν γνωρίζειν λέγομεν τὸν Θεὸν ἡμῶν, τῇ δὲ οὐσίᾳ αὐτῇ προσεγγίζειν οὐχ ὑπισχνούμεθα· αἱ μὲν γὰρ ἐνέργειαι αὐτοῦ πρὸς ἡμᾶς καταβαίνουσιν, ἡ δὲ οὐσία αὐτοῦ μένει ἀπρόσιτος. On the other hand, Hegel, *Philosophie der Religion* (*Werke*, XII. p. 395), insists on the necessity of knowing God as He is, as an indispensable condition of all Theology.

NOTE XIX. p. 87.

Justin. Mart. *Apol.* II. c. 6. Τὸ δὲ Πατήρ, καὶ Θεὸς, καὶ Κτίστης, καὶ Κύριος, καὶ Δεσπότης, οὐκ ὀνόματά ἐστιν, ἀλλ' ἐκ τῶν εὐποιϊῶν καὶ τῶν ἔργων προσρήσεις· Clem. Alex., *Strom.* II. 16. Οὐχ ὡς ἔχει τὸ Θεῖον οἷόν τε ἦν λέγεσθαι· ἀλλ' ὡς οἷον τε ἦν ἐπαΐειν ἡμᾶς σαρκὶ πεπεδημένους, οὕτως ἡμῖν ἐλάλησαν οἱ προφῆται. Basil. *Adv. Eunom.* I. 12. Ὅλως δὲ τὸ οἴεσθαι τοῦ ἐπὶ πάντων Θεοῦ αὐτὴν τὴν οὐσίαν ἐξευρηκέναι, πόσης ὑπερηφανίας ἐστὶ καὶ φυσιώσεως ; ... ἐξετάσωμεν γὰρ αὐτὸν πόθεν αὐτῆς φησὶν ἐν περινοίᾳ γεγενῆσθαι ; ἆρ' ἐκ τῆς κοινῆς ἐννοίας ; ἀλλ' αὕτη τὸ εἶναι τὸ, Θεὸν, οὐ τὸ τί εἶναι ἡμῖν ὑποβάλλει· ἀλλ' ἐκ τῆς διδασκαλίας τοῦ Πνεύματος ; ποίας ; ἢ τῆς ποῦ κειμένης ; .... Τί δὲ τὸ σκεῦος τῆς ἐκλογῆς Παῦλος, ὁ λαλοῦντα ἔχων ἐν ἑαυτῷ τὸν Χριστόν, ὁ ἕως τρίτου ἁρπαγεὶς οὐρανοῦ .... τίνα ἡμῖν περὶ οὐσίας Θεοῦ διδασκαλίαν ἀφῆκεν ; .... Εἰ δὲ ταῦτα τοῖς εἰς τὸ τῆς Παύλου γνώσεως μέτρον ἐφθακόσιν ἀνέφικτα, πόσος ὁ τῦφος. τῶν ἐπαγγελλομένων εἰδέναι τοῦ Θεοῦ τὴν οὐσίαν ; Epist. ccxxxiv. πίστις δὲ αὐτάρκης εἰδέναι ὅτι ἔστιν ὁ Θεός, οὐχὶ τί ἐστι ; Gregor. Nyssen. *Contr. Eunom.* Orat. XII. Οὕτω καὶ τὸν ποιητὴν τοῦ κόσμου, ὅτι μὲν ἔστιν οἴδαμεν, τὸν δὲ τῆς οὐσίας λόγον ἀγνοεῖν οὐκ ἀρνούμεθα. Cyril. Hieros. *Catech.* VI. 2. Οὐ

[g] Compare a similar argument in Bishop Berkeley, *Minute Philosopher*, Dial. IV. § 4.

γὰρ τὸ τί ἐστι Θεός ἐξηγούμεθα· ἀλλ' ὅτι τὸ ἀκριβὲς περὶ αὐτοῦ οὐκ οἴδαμεν, μετ' εὐγνωμοσύνης ὁμολογοῦμεν. Ἐν τοῖς γὰρ περὶ Θεοῦ, μεγάλη γνῶσις τὸ τὴν ἀγνωσίαν ὁμολογεῖν. Chrysostom, *In II. Cor.* Homil. V. ἡμεῖς ὅτι μὲν ἔστι Θεὸς, ἴσμεν· τί δὲ τὴν οὐσίαν, οὐκέτι. *De Incompr. Dei Natura*, Hom. V. ἀρκεῖ πρὸς εὐσέβειαν τὸ εἰδέναι ὅτι ἔστιν ὁ Θεός. Pascal, *Pensées*, Partie II. Art. III. § 5. "Nous connaissons qu'il y a un infini, et nous ignorons sa nature. Ainsi, par exemple, nous savons qu'il est faux que les nombres soient finis: donc il est vrai qu'il y a un infini en nombres. Mais nous ne savons ce qu'il est. Il est faux qu'il soit pair; il est faux qu'il soit impair: car, en ajoutant l'unité, il ne change point de nature; cependant c'est un nombre .... On peut donc bien connaître qu'il y a un Dieu sans savoir ce qu'il est." Beveridge, *On the Articles*, p. 24. "Our understandings being themselves finite, they cannot apprehend what it is to be infinite; and as they are imperfect, they cannot conceive of any perfection as it is in God." The distinction is strongly repudiated by Hegel, *Werke*, XII., p. 396. Cf. IX. p. 19; XIV. p. 219. In the last of these passages, he goes so far as to say, that to deny to man a knowledge of the infinite is the sin against the Holy Ghost. The ground of this awful charge is little more than the repetition of an observation in Aristotle's Metaphysics, that God is not envious, and therefore cannot withhold from us absolute knowledge.

NOTE XX. p. 88.

Advancement of Learning, p. 128, ed. Montagu. Compare *De Augmentis*, III. 2.

NOTE XXI. p. 89.

This argument is excellently drawn out in Sir W. Hamilton's *Lectures on Metaphysics*, Lecture II. p. 30. So Mr. F. W. Newman observes, acutely and truly, "Nothing but a consciousness of active originating Will in ourselves suggests or can justify the idea of a mighty Will pervading Nature; and to merge the former in the latter is to sacrifice the Premise to the glory of the Conclusion."— *The Soul*, p. 40 (second edition).

NOTE XXII. p. 89.

Arist. *Metaph.* I. 5, Ξενοφάνης δὲ πρῶτος τούτων ἑνίσας .... τὸν ὅλον οὐρανὸν ἀποβλέψας τὸ ἓν εἶναί φησι τὸν θεόν. Cicero, *Acad. Quæst.* IV. 37. "Xenophanes dixit unum esse omnia, neque id esse mutabile, et id esse deum." Apuleius, *Asclepius Herm. Trimeg.*

c. 20. "Non enim spero totius majestatis effectorem omniumque rerum patrem vel dominum uno posse quamvis e multis composito nuncupari nomine: hunc vero innominem vel potius omninominem, si quidem is sit unus et omnia, ut sit necesse aut omnia esse ejus nomine aut ipsum omnium nominibus nuncupari." Lessing, as quoted by Jacobi, *Werke*, IV. p. 54. "Die orthodoxen Begriffe von der Gottheit sind nicht mehr für mich; ich kann sie nicht geniessen —Ἐν καὶ Πᾶν. Ich weiss nichts anders."—Schelling, *Bruno*, p. 185. "So ist die Allheit Einheit, die Einheit Allheit, beyde nicht verschieden, sondern dasselbe."

Note XXIII. p. 90.

Clemens Alex. *Strom.* V. 11. Εἰ τοίνυν ἀφελόντες πάντα ὅσα πρόσεστι τοῖς σώμασιν, καὶ τοῖς λεγομένοις ἀσωμάτοις, ἀπορρίψωμεν ἑαυτοὺς εἰς τὸ μέγεθος τοῦ Χριστοῦ, κἀκεῖθεν εἰς τὸ ἀχανὲς ἁγιότητι προΐοιμεν, τῇ νοήσει τοῦ παντοκράτορος ἀμηγέπῃ προσάγοιμεν, οὐχ ὅ ἐστιν, ὃ δὲ μή ἐστι γνωρίσαντες. Augustin. *Enarr. in Psalm.* lxxxv. 12. "Deus ineffabilis est; facilius dicimus quid non sit, quam quid sit." Beveridge, *On the Articles*, p. 24. "When we poor finite creatures set ourselves to consider of our infinite Creator, though we may apprehend something of Him by ascribing all perfections to Him, yet more by removing all imperfections from Him. We cannot so well apprehend what He is, as what He is not." Fichte, *Bestimmung des Menschen* (*Werke*, II. p. 305.) "Du *willst*, denn du willst, dass mein freier Gehorsam Folgen habe in alle Ewigkeit; den Act deines Willens begreife ich nicht, und weiss nur soviel, dass er nicht ähnlich ist dem meinigen."

Note XXIV. p. 90.

The distinction which I have expressed by the terms *speculative* and *regulative knowledge*[h] holds an important place, under a slightly different nomenclature, in the philosophy of Kant; but his mode of applying it is the exact reverse of that adopted in the text. According to Kant, the idea of the absolute or unconditional has a *regulative*, but not a *constitutive* value; does not determine any posi-

---

[h] Kant employs the expression *speculative cognition* (speculative Erkenntniss) to denote the representation in consciousness of an object which cannot be presented in any possible experience. But precisely because no experience is possible, we have no guarantee that such a cognition accurately represents the real nature of its object; and hence Kant regards such cognitions as having a *regulative* but not a *constitutive* value. But *cognition* in this sense does not

tive conception of the object as it must exist; but it serves to give unity and direction to the lower conceptions of the understanding; indicating the point to which they tend, though they never actually reach it. But the regulative character thus paradoxically assigned, not to thought, but to its negation, in truth belongs to the finite conceptions as actually apprehended, not to any unapprehended idea of the infinite beyond them. Every object of positive thought, being conceived as finite, is necessarily regarded as limited by something beyond itself; though this something is not itself actually conceived. The true purpose of this manifest incompleteness of all human thought, is to point out the limits which we cannot pass; not, as Kant maintains, to seduce us into vain attempts to pass them. If there is but one faculty of thought, that which Kant calls the Understanding, occupied with the finite only, there is an obvious end to be answered in making us aware of its limits, and warning us that the boundaries of thought are not those of existence. But if, with Kant, we distinguish the Understanding from the Reason, and attribute to the latter the delusions necessarily arising from the idea of the unconditioned, we must believe in the existence of a special faculty of lies, created for the express purpose of deceiving those who trust to it. In the philosophy of religion, the true regulative ideas, which are intended to guide our thoughts, are the finite forms under which alone we can think of the infinite God; though these, while we employ them, betray their own speculative insufficiency and the limited character of all human knowledge.

NOTE XXV. p. 90.

" Diese Bemerkungen .... sollen nur bemerklich machen, dass im weitern Fortschritt der Untersuchungen die Frage nicht seyn kann, was und wie beschaffen Gott an sich sey, sondern nur, *wie wir ihn in Beziehung auf uns und die ganze sittlichnatürliche Welt zu denken haben.* Denn wenn durch den Glauben nicht das Seyn Gottes theoretisch erkannt wird, sondern nur sich *für uns als zur Sittlichkeit bestimmte Wesen sein Daseyn in der bestimmten Beziehung auf den sittlichen Weltzweck offenbart* (was in doppelter Hinsicht, nämlich durch die Beschränkung auf eine bestimmte Beschaffenheit des erkennenden Subjects und durch die bestimmte Beziehung des Erkannten eine

answer to *knowledge* as used above, p. 90, which implies an apprehension of the real nature of its object. Hence the term *speculative knowledge*, as used in the above passage, is not equivalent to Kant's *speculative cognition*, but answers more nearly to what he calls the *constitutive use* of such cognition.

blos relative Erkenntniss und eben darum keine Erkenntniss eines absoluten Seyns ist), so kann auch nicht von der Erkenntniss des Wesens, der Qualität eines Seyenden, sondern nur von einer nähern Bestimmung der *Idee* Gottes die Rede seyn, wie *wir* sie auf dem uns angewiesenen Standpunkte auszubilden haben; mit andern Worten: wir werden Gott nur durch *Relationen* zu denken haben."—Drobisch, *Grundlehren der Religionsphilosophie*, p. 189. " Was wir daher *Eigenschaften Gottes* (attributa divina) nennen, sind nur Vorstellungen, durch welche wir die Idee Gottes in und für unser beschränktes Bewusstseyn entwickeln; wodurch also nicht bestimmt wird, was Gott an sich sei, sonden nur, was er für uns sei."—Krug, *Philos. Lexikon* v. *Gott*. " The Scripture intimates to us certain facts concerning the Divine Being: but conveying them to us by the medium of language, it only brings them before us darkly, under the signs appropriate to the thoughts of the human mind. And though this kind of knowledge is abundantly instructive to us in point of sentiment and action; teaches us, that is, both how to feel, and how to act, towards God;—for it is the language that we understand, the language formed by our own experience and practice;—it is altogether inadequate in point of Science."—Hampden, *Bampton Lectures*, p. 54 (second edition). " We should rather point out to objectors that what is revealed is *practical*, and not speculative;—that what the Scriptures are concerned with is, not the philosophy of the Human Mind in itself, nor yet the philosophy of the Divine Nature in itself, but (that which is properly *Religion*) the *relation* and connection of the two Beings;—what God is *to us*,—what He has done and will *do* for us,—and what *we* are to be and to do, in regard to Him."—Whately, *Sermons*, p. 56 (third edition). Compare Berkeley, *Minute Philosopher*, Dial. VII. § 11.

LECTURE V.

Note I. p. 95.

Analogy, Part I. ch. VI.

Note II. p. 96.

" When he (the Sceptic) awakes from his dream, he will be the first to join in the laugh against himself; and to confess that all his objections are mere amusement, and can have no other tendency than to show the whimsical condition of mankind, who must act, and reason, and believe; though they are not able, by their most diligent inquiry, to satisfy themselves concerning the foundation of these operations, or to remove the objections which may be raised against them."—Hume, *Essay on the Academical Philosophy*, Part II.

Note III. p. 96.

See Plato, *Parmenides*, p. 129, *Philebus*, p. 14, *Sophistes*, p. 251, *Republic*, VII. p. 524. The mystery is insoluble, because thought cannot explain its own laws; for the laws must necessarily be assumed in the act of explanation. Every object of thought, as being one object, and one out of many, all being related to a common consciousness, must contain in itself a common and a distinctive feature; and the relation between these two constitutes that very diversity in unity, without which no thought is possible.

Note IV. p. 97.

"Das *commercium* zwischen Seele und Körper ist eine wechselseitige Dependenz der Bestimmung. Wir fragen demnach zuerst: Wie ist ein solches *commercium* zwischen einem denkenden Wesen und einem Körper möglich? . . . . Der Grund, die Schwierigkeit dieses *commercii* einzusehen, beruht darauf: Die Seele ist ein Gegenstand des innern Sinnes, und der Körper ist ein Gegenstand des äussern Sinnes. An dem Körper werde ich nichts Innerliches und an der Seele nichts Aeusserliches gewahr. Nun lässt es sich durch keine Vernunft begreifen, wie das, was ein Gegenstand des innern

Sinnes ist, ein Grund seyn soll, von dem, was ein Gegenstand des äussern Sinnes ist."—Kant's *Vorlesungen über die Metaphysik* (1821), p. 224.

NOTE V. p. 97.

" Quand on examine l'idée que l'on a de tous les esprits finis, on ne voit point de liaison nécessaire entre leur volonté et le mouvement de quelque corps que ce soit; on voit au contraire qu'il n'y en a point, et qu'il n'y en peut avoir."—Malebranche, *Recherche de la Vérité*, L. VI. Part II. ch. 3. "L'homme est à lui-même le plus prodigieux objet de la nature; car il ne peut concevoir ce que c'est que corps et encore moins ce que c'est qu'esprit, et moins qu'aucune chose comment un corps peut être uni avec un esprit. C'est là le comble de ses difficultés, et cependant c'est son propre être."—Pascal, *Pensées*, Partie I. Art. vi. § 26. "Ich bin freilich genöthigt zu glauben, das heisst, zu handeln, als ob ich dächte—dass durch mein Wollen meine Zunge, meine Hand, mein Fuss in Bewegung gesetzt werden könnten; wie aber ein blosser Hauch, ein Druck der Intelligenz auf sich selbst, wie der Wille es ist, Princip einer Bewegung in der schweren irdischen Masse seyn könne, darüber kann ich nicht nur nichts denken, sondern selbst die blosse Behauptung ist vor dem Richterstuhle des betrachtenden Verstandes reiner baarer Unverstand."—Fichte, *Bestimmung des Menschen* (*Werke*, II. p. 290). Spinoza, *Ethica*, III. 2, denies positively that such commerce can take place. " Nec corpus mentem ad cogitandum, nec mens corpus ad motum, neque ad quietem, nec ad aliquid (si quid est) aliud determinare potest."

NOTE VI. p. 98.

The theory of Divine Assistance and Occasional Causes was partially hinted at by Descartes, and more completely elaborated by his followers, De La Forge and Malebranche. See Descartes, *Principia*, L. II. § 36. De La Forge, *Traité de l'Esprit de l'Homme*, Ch. XVI. Malebranche, *Recherche de la Vérité*, L. VI. P. II. ch. 3; *Entretiens sur la Métaphysique*, Ent. VII. Cf. Hegel, *Geschichte der Phil.* (*Werke*, XV. p. 330). For Leibnitz's theory of a Pre-established Harmony, see his *Systéme nouveau de la Nature*, § 12-15, *Opera*, ed. Erdmann, p. 127; *Troisième Éclaircissement*, *Ibid.* p. 134; *Théodicée*, § 61, *Ibid.* p. 520. A brief account of these two systems, together with that of Physical Influx, which is rather a statement of the phenomenon, than a theory to account for it, is given by Euler,

Lettres à une Princesse d'Allemagne, Partie II. Lettre 14. ed. Cournot; and by Krug, *Philos. Lexikon*; Art. *Gemeinschaft der Seele und des Leibes*. The hypothesis, that the commerce of soul and body is effected by means of a Plastic Nature in the soul itself, is suggested by Cudworth, *Intellectual System*, B. I. ch. III. § 37, and further developed by Leclerc, *Bibliothèque Choisie*, II. p. 113, who supposes this plastic nature to be an intermediate principle, distinct from both soul and body. See Mosheim's note in Harrison's edition of Cudworth, vol. i. p. 248. See also Leibnitz, *Sur le Principe de Vie, Opera*, ed. Erdmann, p. 429; Laromiguière, *Leçons de Philosophie*, P. II. l. 9.

Note VII. p. 98.

These two analogies between our natural and spiritual knowledge are adduced in a remarkable passage of Gregory of Nyssa, *Contra Eunomium*, Orat. XII. Of the soul, and its relation to the body, he says: "Ὅθεν ἐν ἀγνοίᾳ πάντων διάγομεν, πρῶτον ἑαυτοὺς ἀγνοοῦντες, οἱ ἄνθρωποι, ἔπειτα δὲ καὶ τὰ ἄλλα πάντα. Τίς γάρ ἐστιν ὃς τῆς ἰδίας αὐτοῦ ψυχῆς ἐν καταλήψει γεγένηται; τίς ὁ ἐπιγνοὺς αὐτῆς τὴν οὐσίαν; ὑλική τις ἔστιν ἢ ἄϋλος; καθαρῶς ἀσώματος, ἢ τί καὶ σωματοειδὲς περὶ αὐτήν; πῶς γίνεται; πῶς κιρνᾶται; πόθεν εἰσκρίνεται; πῶς ἀφίσταται; τί τὸ συνδεσμοῦν καὶ μεσιτεῦον ἔχει πρὸς τὴν τοῦ σώματος φύσιν"; κ. τ. λ. (*Opera*, Paris, 1615. Vol. II. p. 321.) Of body, as distinguished from its attributes, he says: 'Ἐὰν γάρ τις τῷ λόγῳ τὸ φαινόμενον εἰς τὰ ἐξ ὧν σύγκειται διαλύσῃ, καὶ ψιλώσας τῶν ποιοτήτων, ἐφ' ἑαυτοῦ κατανοῆσαι φιλονεικήσῃ τὸ ὑποκείμενον, τί καταλειφθήσεται τῇ θεωρίᾳ οὐ συνορῶ. ὅταν γὰρ ἀφέλῃ τοῦ σώματος τὸ χρῶμα, τὸ σχῆμα, τὴν ἀντιτυπίαν, τὸ βάρος, τὴν πηλικότητα; τὴν ἐπὶ τόπου θέσιν, τὴν κίνησιν τὴν παθητικήν τε καὶ ἐνεργητικήν, τὸ πρός τι πως ἔχειν, ὧν ἕκαστον οὐδὲν ἐφ' ἑαυτοῦ σῶμά ἐστί, περὶ δὲ τὸ σῶμα τὰ πάντα, τί λοιπὸν ἔσται ὃ τὸν τοῦ σώματος δέχεται λόγον; οὔτε δι' ἑαυτῶν συνιδεῖν ἔχομεν, οὔτε παρὰ τῆς γραφῆς μεμαθήκαμεν. ὁ δὲ ἑαυτὸν ἀγνοῶν, πῶς ἄν τι τῶν ὑπὲρ αὐτὸν ἐπιγνοίη; *Ibid.* p. 422.

Note VIII. p. 98.

Essay on the Academical Philosophy (Philosophical Works, vol. iv. p. 182).

Note IX. p. 98.

The difficulty is ingeniously stated by Pascal, *Pensées*, Partie I. Art. II. "Car qu'y a-t-il de plus absurde que de prétendre qu'en divisant toujours un espace, on arrive enfin à une division telle qu'en la divisant en deux, chacune des moitiés reste indivisible et sans aucune étendue ? Je voudrais demander à ceux qui ont cette idée s'ils conçoivent nettement que deux indivisibles se touchent : si c'est partout, ils ne sont qu'une même chose, et partant les deux ensemble sont indivisibles ; et si ce n'est pas partout, ce n'est donc qu'en une partie ; donc ils ont des parties, donc ils ne sont pas indivisibles."

NOTE X. p. 101.

Kant's theory, that we know phenomena only, not things in themselves, is severely critised by Dr. M'Cosh, *Method of the Divine Government*, p. 536 (4th edition). I have before observed that Kant has, in two points at least, extended his doctrine beyond its legitimate place ; first, in maintaining that our knowledge of the personal self is equally phenomenal with that of external objects, and secondly, in dogmatically asserting that the thing in itself *does not* resemble the phenomenon of which we are conscious. Against the first of these statements it may be fairly objected, that my personal existence is identical with my consciousness of that existence ; and that any other aspect of my personality, if such exists in relation to any other intelligence, is in this case the phenomenon to which my personal consciousness furnishes the real counterpart. Against the second, it may be objected, that if, upon Kant's own hypothesis, we are never directly conscious of the thing in itself, we have no ground for saying that it is unlike, any more than that it is like, the object of which we are conscious ; and that, in the absence of all other evidence, the probability is in favour of that aspect which is at least subjectively true. But when these deductions are made, the hypothesis of Kant, in its fundamental position, remains unshaken. It then amounts to no more than this ; that we can see things only as our own faculties present them to us ; and that we can never be sure that the mode of operation of our faculties is identical with that of all other intelligences, embodied or spiritual. Within these limits, the theory more nearly resembles a truism than a paradox, and contains nothing that can be regarded as formidable, either by the philosopher or by the theologian.

In the same article, Dr. M'Cosh criticises Sir William Hamilton's cognate theory of the relativity of all knowledge. With the highest respect for Dr. M'Cosh's philosophical ability, I cannot help thinking that he has mistaken the character of the theory which he censures, and that the objection which he urges is hardly applicable. He attempts to avail himself of Sir W. Hamilton's own theory of the veracity of consciousness. He asks, "Does not the mind in sense-perception hold the object to be a real object?" Undoubtedly; but reality in this sense is not identical with absolute existence, if by the latter term is meant the nature of the thing as it exists out of all relation to a percipient mind, or as it must manifest itself to all possible intelligences under all possible laws of apprehension. Man can conceive reality, as he conceives other objects, only as the laws of his faculties permit; and in distinguishing reality from appearance, he is not distinguishing the related from the unrelated. Both appearance and reality must be given in consciousness, to be apprehended at all; and the distinction is only between some modes of consciousness, such as those of a dream, which are regarded as delusive, and others, as in a waking state, which are regarded as veracious. But consciousness, whatever may be its veracity, can tell us nothing concerning the identity of its objects with those of which we are not conscious. The relativity of our knowledge, as maintained by Sir W. Hamilton, does not, if I understand him rightly, imply any other limitation than this.

Dr. M'Cosh, in the above criticism, also classes Professor Ferrier as a representative of the same school with Kant and Hamilton. The resemblance is, I believe, merely accidental. Professor Ferrier's system more nearly approaches to the Philosophy of the Absolute than to that of the Relative. He himself distinctly announces that he undertakes "to lay down the laws, not only of *our* thinking and knowing, but of *all* possible thinking and knowing."[a] Such an undertaking, whether it be successful or not, is in its conception the very opposite of the system which maintains that our knowledge is relative to our faculties.

Note XI. p. 101.

See above, Lecture IV. note 25.

Note XII. p. 102.

"Il en est de même des autres Mystères, où les esprits modérés trouveront toujours une explication suffisante pour croire, et jamais autant qu'il en faut pour comprendre. Il nous suffit d'un certain ce que c'est (τί ἐστι); mais le *comment* (πῶς) nous passe, et ne nous est point nécessaire."—Leibnitz, *Théodicée, Discours de la conformité de la Foi avec la Raison*, § 56.

---

[a] *Institutes of Metaphysic*, p. 55.

Note XIII. p. 102.

"It is plain, that, in any communication from an infinite Being to creatures of finite capacities, one of two things must happen. Either the former must raise the latter almost to His own level; or else He must suit the form of His communication to their powers of apprehension. . . . If we turn to Scripture, however, we shall see how the matter is decided. In God's dealings with men we find 'wrath,' 'jealousy,' 'repentance,' and other affections, ascribed to the Divine Being. He is described as 'sitting on a throne;' His 'eyes' are said 'to behold the children of men;' not to mention other instances, which must suggest themselves to every one, in which God condescends to convey to us, not the very reality indeed, but something as near the reality as He sees it expedient for us to know."—Professor Lee, *The Inspiration of Holy Scripture*, pp. 63, 64 (second edition).

Note XIV. p. 104.

Plato, *Sophistes*, p. 242. Τὸ δὲ παρ' ἡμῖν Ἐλεατικὸν ἔθνος, ἀπὸ Ξενοφάνους τε καὶ ἔτι πρόσθεν ἀρξάμενον, ὡς ἑνὸς ὄντος τῶν πάντων καλουμένων οὕτω διεξέρχεται τοῖς μύθοις.—Sextus Empiricus, *Pyrrh. Hyp.* I. 225. Ἐδογμάτιζε δὲ ὁ Ξενοφάνης παρὰ τὰς τῶν ἄλλων ἀνθρώπων προλήψεις ἓν εἶναι τὸ πᾶν. Arist. *Metaph.* II. 4. 30. Τὸ γὰρ ἕτερον τοῦ ὄντος οὐκ ἔστιν, ὥστε κατὰ τὸν Παρμενίδου λόγον συμβαίνειν ἀνάγκη ἓν ἅπαντα εἶναι τὰ ὄντα καὶ τοῦτο εἶναι τὸ ὄν.—Plato *Parmenides*, p. 127. Πῶς, φάναι, ὦ Ζήνων, τοῦτο λέγεις; εἰ πολλά ἐστι τὰ ὄντα, ὡς ἄρα δεῖ αὐτὰ ὅμοιά τε εἶναι καὶ ἀνόμοια, τοῦτο δὲ δὴ ἀδύνατον . . . . οὐχ οὕτω λέγεις; Οὕτω, φάναι τὸν Ζήνωνα.—Arist. *Soph. Elench.* 10. 2. οἷον ἴσως τὸ ὂν ἢ τὸ ἓν πολλὰ σημαίνει, ἀλλὰ καὶ ὁ ἀποκρινόμενος καὶ ὁ ἐρωτῶν Ζήνων ἓν οἰόμενος εἶναι ἠρώτησε, καὶ ἔστιν ὁ λόγος ὅτι ἓν πάντα.—Arist. *De Cœlo*, III. 1. 5. Οἱ μὲν γὰρ αὐτῶν ὅλως ἀνεῖλον γένεσιν καὶ φθοράν· οὐθὲν γὰρ οὔτε γίγνεσθαί φασιν οὔτε φθείρεσθαι τῶν ὄντων, ἀλλὰ μόνον δοκεῖν ἡμῖν, οἷον οἱ περὶ Μέλισσόν τε καὶ Παρμενίδην. Diog. Laert. ix. 24. (De Melisso). Ἐδόκει δὲ αὐτῷ τὸ πᾶν ἄπειρον εἶναι, καὶ ἀναλλοίωτον, καὶ ἀκίνητον, καὶ ἕν, ὅμοιον ἑαυτῷ, καὶ πλῆρες· κίνησίν τε μὴ εἶναι, δοκεῖν δὲ εἶναι.—Cf. Plato *Theætetus*, p. 183. Compare Karsten, *Parmenidis Reliquiæ*, pp. 157, 194. Brandis, *Conmentationes Eleaticæ*, pp. 213, 214.

Note XV. p. 104.

Plato, *Theæt.* p. 152. Ἐγὼ ἐρῶ καὶ μάλ' οὐ φαῦλον λόγον, ὡς ἄρα ἓν μὲν αὐτὸ καθ' αὑτὸ οὐδέν ἐστιν, οὐδ' ἄν τι προσείποις ὀρθῶς οὐδ' ὁποιονοῦν τι, ἀλλ' ἐὰν ὡς μέγα προσαγορεύῃς, καὶ σμικρὸν φανεῖται, καὶ ἐὰν βαρύ, κοῦφον, ξύμπαντά τε οὕτως, ὡς μηδενὸς ὄντος ἑνὸς μήτε τινὸς μήτε ὁποιουοῦν. ἐκ δὲ δὴ φορᾶς τε καὶ κινήσεως καὶ κράσεως πρὸς ἄλληλα γίγνεται πάντα ἃ δή φαμεν εἶναι, οὐκ ὀρθῶς προσαγορεύοντες. ἔστι μὲν γὰρ οὐδέποτ' οὐδὲν, ἀεὶ δὲ γίγνεται. καὶ περὶ τούτου πάντες ἑξῆς οἱ σοφοὶ πλὴν Παρμενίδου συμφερέσθων, Πρωταγόρας τε καὶ 'Ηράκλειτος καὶ 'Εμπεδοκλῆς. Diogenes Laert. ix. 51. Ἔλεγέ τε (ὁ Πρωταγόρας) μηδὲν εἶναι ψυχὴν παρὰ τὰς αἰσθήσεις. Aristot. *De Xenophane, Zenone et Gorgia*, c. 5. (De Gorgia.) Οὐκ εἶναί φησιν οὐδέν· εἰ δ' ἔστιν, ἄγνωστον εἶναι· εἰ δὲ καὶ ἔστι καὶ γνωστόν, ἀλλ' οὐ δηλωτὸν ἄλλοις. Καὶ ὅτι μὲν οὐκ ἔστι, συνθεὶς τὰ ἑτέροις εἰρημένα, ὅσοι περὶ τῶν ὄντων λέγοντες τἀναντία, ὡς δοκοῦσιν, ἀποφαίνονταί αὐτοῖς, οἱ μὲν ὅτι ἓν καὶ οὐ πολλά, οἱ δὲ αὖ ὅτι πολλὰ καὶ οὐχ ἕν. "What we call a *mind*, is nothing but a heap or collection of different perceptions, united together by certain relations, and supposed, though falsely, to be endowed with a perfect simplicity and identity."—Hume, *Treatise of Human Nature*, Part IV. sect. 2. "'Tis confessed by the most judicious philosophers, that our ideas of bodies are nothing but collections formed by the mind of the ideas of the several distinct sensible qualities, of which objects are composed, and which we find to have a constant union with each other. . . . The smooth and uninterrupted progress of the thought . . . readily deceives the mind, and makes us ascribe an identity to the changeable succession of connected qualities."—*Ibid.* sect. 2.

NOTE XVI. p. 105.

"Il faut venir maintenant à la grande Question que M. Bayle a mis sur le tapis depuis peu, savoir, si une Vérité, et surtout une Vérité de Foi, pourra être sujette à des objections insolubles. . . . Il croit que la doctrine de la Prédestination est de cette nature dans la Théologie, et celle de la composition du *Continuum* dans la Philosophie. Ce sont en effet les deux Labyrinthes, qui ont exercé de tout tems les Théologiens et les Philosophes. Libertus Fromondus, Théologien de Louvain, qui a fort travaillé sur la Grâce, et qui a aussi fait un Livre exprès intitulé *Labyrinthus de compositione Continui*, a bien exprimé les difficultés de l'un et de l'autre : et le fameux Ochin a fort bien représenté ce qu'il appelle *les Labyrinthes de la Prédestination*." Leibnitz,—*Théodicée; Discours de la conformité de la Foi avec la Raison*, § 24. Compare Sir W. Hamilton's *Discussions*, p. 632.

Note XVII. p. 105.

See Bishop Browne's criticism of Archbishop King, *Procedure of the Understanding*, p. 15. "He hath unwarily dropped some such shocking expressions as these, *The best representations we can make of God are infinitely short of Truth*. Which God forbid, in the sense his adversaries take it; for then all our reasonings concerning Him would be groundless and false. But the saying is evidently true in a favourable and qualified sense and meaning; namely, that they are infinitely short of the real, true, internal Nature of God as He is in Himself." Compare *Divine Analogy*, p. 57. "Though all the Revelations of God are *true*, as coming from Him who is Truth itself; yet the truth and substance of them doth not consist in this, that they give us any new set of ideas, and express them in a language altogether unknown before; or that both the conceptions and terms are so immediately and properly adapted to the *true and real nature* of the things revealed, that they could not without great impropriety and even profaneness be ever applied to the things of this world. But the *truth* of them consists in this; that whereas the *terms* and *conceptions* made use of in those Revelations are strictly proper to things worldly and obvious; they are from thence *transferred analogically* to the correspondent objects of another world with as much *truth* and *reality*, as when they are made use of in their first and most *literal* propriety; and this is a solid foundation both for a *clear* and *certain knowledge*, and for a *firm* and well grounded *Faith*." See also Alliott, *Psychology and Theology*, pp. 144, 178.

Note XVIII. p. 106.

Augustin. *Confess.* I. XIII. c. 16. "Nam sicut omnino tu es, tu scis solus, qui es incommutabiliter, et scis incommutabiliter, et vis incommutabiliter. Et essentia tua scit et vult incommutabiliter, et scientia tua est et vult incommutabiliter, et voluntas tua est et scit incommutabiliter. Nec videtur justum esse coram te, ut quemadmodum se scit lumen incommutabile, ita sciatur ab illuminato commutabili."

Note XIX. p. 106.

See Hegel, *Philosophie der Geschichte*, *Werke*, IX. p. 238, 298; *Philosophie der Religion*, *Werke*, XI. p. 356, XII. p. 119. Schleiermacher substantially admits the same facts, though he attempts to connect them with a different theory.[b] He considers that there is a pantheistic and a personal element united in all religions; and this is perhaps true of heathen religions subjected to the philosophical analysis of a later age; though it may be doubted whether both elements are distinctly recognised by the worshipper himself. But even from this point of view, the Jewish religion stands in marked contrast to both Eastern and Western heathenism. In the latter forms of religion, the elements of personality and infinity, so far as they are manifested at all, are manifested in different beings: this is observable both in the subordinate emanations which give a kind of secondary personality to the Indian Pantheism, and in the philosophical abstraction of a supreme principle of good, which connects a secondary notion of the infinite with the Grecian Mythology. The Jewish religion still remains distinct and unique, in so far as in it the attributes of personality and infinity are united in one and the same living and only God.

NOTE XX. p. 109.

"Et Patrem quidem invisibilem et indeterminabilem, quantum ad nos est, cognoscit suum ipsius Verbum, et cum sit inenarrabilis, ipse enarrat eum nobis: rursus autem Verbum suum solus cognoscit Pater: utraque autem hæc sic se habere manifestavit Dominus. Et propter hoc Filius revelat agnitionem Patris per suam manifestationem. Agnitio enim Patris est Filii manifestatio: omnia enim per Verbum manifestantur. Ut ergo cognosceremus, quoniam qui advenit Filius, ipse est qui agnitionem Patris facit credentibus sibi, dicebat discipulis: 'Nemo cognoscit Patrem nisi Filius, neque Filium nisi Pater, et quibuscunque Filius revelaverit;' docens semetipsum et Patrem, sicut est, ut alterum non recipiamus Patrem, nisi eum qui a Filio revelatur." Irenæus, *Contr. Hæres.* IV. 6, 3. Οὐκοῦν ἀκολούθως ὁ τοῦ Θεοῦ Λόγος σῶμα ἀνέλαβε, καὶ ἀνθρωπίνῳ ὀργάνῳ κέχρηται, ἵνα καὶ ζωοποιήσῃ τὸ σῶμα, καὶ ἵν' ὥσπερ ἐν τῇ κτίσει διὰ τῶν ἔργων γνωρίζεται, οὕτω καὶ ἐν ἀνθρώπῳ ἐργάσηται, καὶ δείξῃ ἑαυτὸν πανταχοῦ, μηδὲν ἔρημον τῆς ἑαυτοῦ θειότητος καὶ γνώσεως καταλιμπάνων· Athanasius, *De Incarn. Verbi,* c. 45. "In qua ut fidentius ambularet ad veritatem, ipsa Veritas Deus Dei Filius, homine assumpto, non Deo consumpto, eamdem constituit atque fundavit fidem, ut ad hominis Deum iter esset homini per hominem Deum. Hic est enim mediator Dei et

---

[b] *Reden über Religion* (*Werke,* I. pp. 401, 441).

hominum homo Christus Jesus. Per hoc enim mediator, per quod homo; per hoc et via . . . Sola est autem adversus omnes errores via munitissima, ut idem ipse sit Deus et homo: quo itur, Deus; qua itur, homo." Augustin. *De Civ. Dei*, XI. 2.

NOTE XXI. p. 109.

"Qui credimus Deum etiam in terris egisse, et humani habitus humilitatem suscepisse ex causa humanæ salutis, longe sumus a sententia eorum qui nolunt Deum curare quidquam." Tertullian, *Adv. Marc.* II. 16.

NOTE XXII. p. 109.

It is only a natural consequence of their own principles, when the advocates of a philosophy of the Absolute maintain that the Incarnation of Christ has no relation to time. Thus Schelling says: "Die Menschenwerdung Gottes in Christo deuten die Theologen eben so empirisch, nämlich, dass Gott in einem bestimmten Moment der Zeit menschliche Natur angenommen habe, wobey schlechterdings nichts zu denken seyn kann, da Gott ewig ausser aller Zeit ist. Die Menschenwerdung Gottes ist also eine Menschenwerdung von Ewigkeit. Der Mensch Christus ist in der Erscheinung nur der Gipfel und in so fern auch wieder der Anfang derselben, denn von ihm aus sollte sie dadurch sich fortsetzen, dass alle seine Nachfolger Glieder eines und desselben Leibes wären, von dem er das Haupt ist. Dass in Christo zuerst Gott wahrhaft objectiv geworden, zeugt die Geschichte, denn wer vor ihm hat das Unendliche auf solche Weise geoffenbaret?"[c] Hegel, in his Lectures on the Philosophy of History,[d] thus comments on the language of St. Paul: "*Als die Zeit erfüllet war, sandte Gott seinen Sohn*, heisst es in der Bibel. Das heisst nichts Anderes als: das Selbstbewusstseyn hatte sich zu denjenigen Momenten erhoben, welche zum Begriff des Geistes gehören, und zum Bedürfniss, diese Momente auf eine absolute Weise zu fassen." This marvellous *elucidation* of the sacred text may perhaps receive some further light, or darkness, from the obscure passages of the same author, quoted subsequently in the text of this Lecture: and such is the explanation of his theory given by Baur, *Christliche Gnosis*, p. 715: "Auf dem Standpunct des

---

[c] *Vorlesungen über die Methode des Academischen Studium*, p. 192. Fichte speaks to the same effect, *Anweisung zum seligen Leben* (Werke, V. p. 482).

[d] *Werke*, IX. p. 338.

speculativen Denkens ist die Menschwerdung Gottes keine einzelne, einmal geschehene, historische Thatsache, sondern eine ewige Bestimmung des Wesens Gottes, vermöge welcher Gott nur insofern in der Zeit Mensch wird (in jeden einzelnen Menschen) sofern er von Ewigkeit Mensch ist. Die Endlichkeit und leidensvolle Erniedrigung, welcher sich Christus als Gottmensch unterzog, trägt Gott zu jeder Zeit als Mensch. Die von Christus vollbrachte Versöhnung ist keine zeitlich geschehene That, sondern Gott versöhnt sich ewig mit sich selbst, und die Auferstehung und Erhöhung Christi ist nichts anders, als die ewige Rückkehr des Geistes zu sich und zu seiner Wahrheit. Christus als Mensch, als Gottmensch, ist der Mensch in seiner Allgemeinheit, nicht ein einzelnes Individuum, sondern das allgemeine Individuum." It is no wonder that, to a philosophy of these lofty pretensions, the personal existence of Christ should be a question of perfect indifference.° From a similar point of view, Marheineke says: "Die Menschwerdung Gottes, begriffen in ihrer Möglichkeit, ist zunächst die wirkliche Menschlichwerdung der göttlichen Wahrheit, welche nicht nur das Denken Gottes, sondern zugleich sein Wesen ist, und Gottliches und Menschliches, obwohl noch unterschieden, doch nicht mehr von einander getrennt." *Grundlehren der Christlichen Dogmatik*, § 312. It is difficult to see what distinction can be made, in these theories, between the Incarnation of Christ as Man, and His eternal Generation as the Son of God; and indeed these passages, and those subsequently quoted from Hegel, appear intentionally to identify the two.

NOTE XXIII. p. 111.

Encyklopädie, § 564, 566. For the benefit of any reader who may be disposed to play the part of Œdipus, I subjoin the entire passage in the original. The meaning may perhaps, as Professor Ferrier observes of Hegel's philosophy in general, be extracted by *distillation*, but certainly not by literal translation.

"Was Gott als Geist ist,—Dies richtig und bestimmt im Gedanken zu fassen, dazu wird gründliche Speculation erfordert. Es sind znnächst die Sätze darin enthalten: Gott ist Gott nur in sofern er sich selber weiss; sein sich Sich-wissen ist ferner sein Selbstbe-

---

° For a criticism of these pantheistic perversions of Christianity, see Drobisch, *Grundlehren der Religionsphilosophie*, p. 247. The consummation of the pantheistic view may be found in Blasche, *Philosophische Unsterblich-keitlehre*, § 51-53. Here the eternal Incarnation of God is exhibited as the perpetual production of men, as phenomenal manifestations of the absolute unity.

wusstseyn im Menschen, und das Wissen des Menschen *von* Gott, das fortgeht zum Sich-wissen des Menschen *in* Gott.

"Der absolute Geist in der aufgehobenen Unmittelbarkeit und Sinnlichkeit der Gestalt und des Wissens, ist dem Inhalte nach der an-und-für-sich-seyende Geist der Natur und des Geistes, der Form nach ist er zunächst für das subjective Wissen der *Vorstellung*. Diese giebt den Momenten seines Inhalts einerseits Selbstständigkeit und macht sie gegen einander zu Voraussetzungen, und *zu einander folgenden* Erscheinungen und zu einem Zusammenhang *des Geschehens* nach *endlichen Reflexionsbestimmungen*; andererseits wird solche Form endlicher Vorstellungsweise in dem Glauben an den Einen Geist und in der Andacht des Cultus aufgehoben.

"In diesem Trennen scheidet sich die *Form* von dem *Inhalte*, und in jener die unterschieden Momente des Begriffs zu *besondern Sphären* oder Elementen ab, in deren jedem sich der absolute Inhalt darstellt,—a) als in seiner Manifestation bei sich selbst bleibender, Ewiger Inhalt;—β) als Unterscheidung des ewigen Wesens von seiner Manifestation, welche durch diesen Unterschied die Erscheinungswelt wird, in die der Inhalt tritt;—γ) als unendliche Rückkehr und Versöhnung der entäusserten Welt mit dem ewigen Wesen, das Zurückgehen desselben aus der Erscheinung in die Einheit seiner Fülle."

The passage which, though perhaps bearing more directly on my argument, I have not ventured to attempt to translate, is the following, § 568.

"Im Momente der *Besonderheit* aber des Urtheils, ist dies concrete ewige Wesen das *Vorausgesetzte*, und seine Bewegung die Erschaffung der *Erscheinung*, das Zerfallen des ewigen Moments der Vermittlung, des einigen Sohnes, in den selbstständigen Gegensatz, einerseits des Himmels und der Erde, der elementarischen und concreten Natur, andererseits des Geistes als mit ihr im *Verhältniss* stehenden, somit *endlichen* Geistes, welcher als das Extrem der in sich seyenden Negativität sich zum Bösen verselbstständigt, solches Extrem durch seine Beziehung auf eine gegenüberstehende Natur und durch seine damit gesetzte eigene Natürlichkeit ist, in dieser als denkend zugleich auf das Ewige gerichtet, aber damit in äusserlicher Beziehung steht."

Görres, in the preface to the second edition of his *Athanasius*, p. ix., exhibits a specimen of a new Creed on Hegelian principles, to be drawn up by a general council composed of the more advanced theologians of the day. The qualifications for a seat in the council are humorously described, and the creed itself contains much just and pointed satire. It will hardly, however, bear quotation; for a caricature on such a subject, however well intended, almost unavoidably carries with it a painful air of irreverence.

Note XXIV. p. 111.

See especially *Phänomenologie des Geistes*, Werke, II. p. 557; *Philosophie der Geschichte*, Werke, IX. p. 387; *Philosophie der Religion*, Werke, XII. p. 247; *Geschichte der Philosophie*, Werke, XIV. p. 222, XV. p. 88.

Note XXV. p. 111.

The indecision of Hegel upon this vital question is *satisfactorily* accounted for by his disciple, Strauss. To a philosophy which professes to exhibit the universal relations of necessary ideas, it is indifferent whether they have actually been realized in an individual case or not. This question is reserved for the Critic of History. See *Streitschriften*, Heft III. p. 68. Dorner too, while pointing out the merits of Hegel's Christology, admits that the belief in a historical Christ has no significance in his system; and that those disciples who reject it carry out that system most fully. See *Lehre von der Person Christi*, p. 409.

Note XXVI. 112.

Philosophie der Religion, Werke, XII. p. 286. In another passage of the same work, p. 281, the Atonement is *explained* in the following language: "Die Möglichkeit der Versöhnung ist nur darin, dass gewusst wird die *an sich seyende Einheit der göttlichen und menschlichen Natur*; das ist die nothwendige Grundlage; so kann der Mensch sich aufgenommen wissen in Gott, insofern ihm Gott nicht ein Fremdes ist, er sich zu ihm nicht als äusserliches Accidenz verhält, sondern wenn er nach seinem Wesen, nach seiner Freiheit und Subjectivität in Gott aufgenommen ist; diess ist aber nur möglich, insofern *in Gott selbst diese Subjectivität der menschlichen Natur ist*. Compare also, p. 330, and *Phänomenologie des Geistes*, Werke, II. p. 544, 572; *Philosophie der Geschichte*, Werke, IX. p. 405; *Geschichte der Philosophie*, Werke, XV. p. 100.

Note XXVII. p. 112.

Grundlehren der Christlichen Dogmatik, § 319, 320.

Note XXVIII. p. 113.

Ibid. § 325, 326. A similar theory is maintained, almost in the same language, by Rosenkranz, *Encyklopädie der theologischen Wissenschaften,* § 26, 27. The substance of this view is given by Hegel himself, *Werke,* IX. p. 394, 457; XV. p. 89. Some valuable criticisms on the principle of it may be found in Dr. Mill's *Observations on the application of Pantheistic Principles to the Criticism of the Gospel,* pp. 16, 42.

Note XXIX. p. 114.

Leben Jesu, § 151, English Translation, Vol. III. p. 437. The passage has also been translated by Dr. Mill in his *Observations on the application of Pantheistic Principles,* &c. p. 50. I have slightly corrected the former version by the aid of the latter. A sort of anticipation of the theory may be found in Hegel's *Phänomenologie des Geistes, Werke,* II. p. 569.

Note XXX. p. 114.

"Nur das Metaphysische, keinesweges aber das Historische, macht selig." Fichte, *Anweisung zum seligen Leben* (*Werke,* V. p. 485). With this may be compared the language of Spinoza, Ep. XXI. "Dico, ad salutem non esse omnino necesse, Christum secundum carnem noscere; sed de æterno illo filio Dei, hoc est Dei æterna sapientia, quæ sese in omnibus rebus, et maxime in mente humana, et omnium maxime in Christo Jesu manifestavit, longe aliter sentiendum."

LECTURE VI.

NOTE I. p. 121.

SEE above, Lecture IV. p. 87, and note 19.

NOTE II. p. 121.

Christliche Lehre von der Sünde, II. p. 156, third Edition (English Translation, II. p. 126). The doctrine that the Divine Essence is speculatively made known through Christ, is a common ground on which theologians of the most opposite schools have met, to diverge again into most adverse conclusions. It is substantially the opinion of Eunomius;[a] and it has been maintained in modern times by Hegel and his disciple Marheineke, in a sense very different from that which is adopted by Müller. See Hegel, *Philosophie der Geschichte, Werke* IX. p. 19. *Philosophie der Religion, Werke*, XII. p. 204, and Marheineke, *Grundlehren der Christlichen Dogmatik*, § 69.

NOTE III. p. 122.

See L. Ancillon, in the *Mémoires de l'Académie de Berlin*, quoted by Bartholmèss, *Histoire des Doctrines religieuses*, I. p. 268. On the parallel between the mystery of Causation and those of Christian doctrines, compare Magee on the Atonement, Note XIX. See also Mozley, *Augustinian Doctrine of Predestination*, p. 19, and the review of the same work by Professor Fraser, *Essays in Philosophy*, p. 274.

NOTE IV. p. 122.

Seven different theories of the causal nexus, and of the mode of our apprehension of it, are enumerated and refuted by Sir W. Hamilton, *Discussions*, p. 611. His own, which is the eighth, can hardly be regarded as more satisfactory. For he resolves the causal judgment itself into the inability to conceive an absolute commencement of phenomena, and the consequent necessity of thinking that what appears to us under a new form had previously existed under others. But surely a cause is as much required to account for the

---

[a] See Neander, vol. iv. p. 60, ed. Bohn.

change from an old form to a new, as to account for an absolute beginning. On the defects of this theory I have remarked elsewhere—See *Metaphysics*, p. 271, and *Prolegomena Logica*, 2nd edition, note C. It has also been criticised by Dr. M'Cosh, *Method of the Divine Government*, p. 529, fourth edition; by Professor Fraser, *Essays in Philosophy*, p. 170 sqq.; by Mr. Tyler, *Progress of Philosophy*, p. 174; and by Mr. Calderwood, *Philosophy of the Infinite*, p. 139 sqq.

Note V. p. 122.

That Causation implies something more than invariable sequence, though what that something is we are unable to determine, is maintained, among others, by M. Cousin, in his eloquent Lectures on the Philosophy of Locke. " Par cela seul," he says, " qu'un phénomène succède à un autre et y succède constamment, en est-il la cause? est-ce là toute l'idée que vous vous formez de la cause? Quand vous dites, quand vous pensez que le feu est la cause de l'état de fluidité de la cire, je vous demande si vous ne croyez pas, si le genre humain tout entier ne croit pas qu'il y a dans le feu *je ne sais quoi, une propriété inconnue* qu'il ne s'agit pas ici de déterminer, à laquelle vous rapportez la production du phénomène de la fluidité de la cire."—*Histoire de la Philosophie au XVIIIe. siècle*, Leçon xix. Engel speaks to the same effect in almost the same words. " Dans ce que nous appelons, par exemple, force d'attraction, d'affinité, ou même d'impulsion, la seule chose connue, (c'est-à-dire représentée à l'imagination et aux sens), c'est l'effet opéré, savoir, le rapprochement des deux corps attirés et attirant. Aucune langue n'a de mot pour exprimer ce *je ne sais quoi* (*effort, tendance, nisus*), qui reste absolument caché, mais que tous les esprits conçoivent nécessairement comme ajouté à la représentation phénoménale."[b] Dr. M'Cosh (*Method of the Divine Government*, p. 525) professes to discover this *je ne sais quoi*, in *a substance acting according to its powers or properties*. But, apart from the conscious exercise of free will, we know nothing of *power* or *property* save as manifested in its effects. Compare Berkeley, *Minute Philosopher*, Dial. VII. § 9. Herder, *Gott, Werke*, viii. p. 224.

Note VI. p. 122.

That the first idea of Causation is derived from the consciousness of the exercise of power in our own volitions, is established, after a

[b] *Mémoires de l'Académie de Berlin*, quoted by Maine de Biran, *Nouvelles Considérations*, p. 23.

hint from Locke,[e] by Maine de Biran, and accepted by M. Cousin.[d] To explain the manner in which we transcend our own personal consciousness, and attribute a cause to all changes in the material world, the latter philosopher has recourse to the hypothesis of a necessary law of the reason, by virtue of which it disengages, in the fact of consciousness, the necessary element of causal relation, from the contingent element of our personal production of this or that particular movement. This Law, the Principle of Causality, compels the reason to suppose a cause whenever the senses present a new phenomenon. But this Principle of Causality, even granting it to be true as far as it goes, does not explain what the idea of a Cause, thus extended, contains as its constituent feature: it merely transcends personal causation, and substitutes an unknown *something* in its room. We do not attribute to the fire a consciousness of its power to melt the wax: and in denying consciousness, we deny the only positive conception of power which can be added to the mere juxtaposition of phenomena. The *cause*, in all sensible changes, thus remains a *je ne sais quoi*. On this subject I have treated more at length in another place. See *Prolegomena Logica*, pp. 135, 309 (2nd edition, pp. 146, 348).

And even within the sphere of our own volitions, though we are immediately conscious of the exercise of power, yet the analysis of the conception thus presented to us carries us at once into the region of the incomprehensible. The finite power of man, as an originating cause within his own sphere, seems to come into collision with the infinite power of God, as the originating Cause of all things. Finite power is itself created by and dependent upon God; yet, at the same time, it seems to be manifested as originating and independent. Power itself acts only on the solicitation of motives; and this raises the question, Which is prior? does the motive bring about the state of the will which inclines to it; or does the state of the will convert the coincident circumstances into motives? Am I moved to will, or do I will to be moved? Here we are involved in the mystery of endless succession. On this mystery there are some able remarks in Mr. Mozley's *Augustinian Theory of Predestination*, p. 2, and in Professor Fraser's *Essays in Philosophy*, p. 275.

[e] *Essay*, B. II. Ch. 21, §§ 4, 5. A similar view is taken by Jacobi, *David Hume, oder Idealismus und Realismus* (*Werke*, II. p. 201).
[d] See De Biran, *Œuvres Philosophiques*, IV. pp. 241, 273; Cousin, *Cours de l'Histoire de la Philosophie*, Deuxième Série, Leçon 19; *Fragments Philosophiques*, vol. IV. Préface de la Première Edition.

Note VII. p. 123.

De Ordine, II. 18. Compare *Ibid.* II. 16, " de summo illo Deo, qui scitur melius nesciendo."

Note VIII. p. 123.

Enarratio in Psalmum LXXXV. 12. Compare *De Trinitate*, VIII. c. 2.

Note IX. p. 123.

F. Socinus, *Tractatus de Deo, Christo, et Spiritu Sancto* (*Opera*, 1656, vol. I. p. 811). "Ceterum vel ex eo solo, quod Deus unus esse aperte traditur, merito concludi potest, eum non esse nec trinum, nec binum. Opposita sunt enim inter se Unus et Trinus, sive Unus et Binus. Ita ut, si Deus sit trinus aut binus, non possit esse unus." Priestley, *Tracts in Controversy with Bishop Horsley*, p. 78. "They are therefore both *one* and *many* in the same respect, viz., in each being *perfect God*. This is certainly as much a contradiction as to say that Peter, James, and John, having each of them everything that is requisite to constitute a complete man, are yet, all together, not *three men*, but only *one man*."—F. W. Newman, *Phases of Faith*, p. 48. "If any one speaks of *three men*, all that he means is, 'three objects of thought, of whom each separately may be called man.' So also, all that could possibly be meant by *three Gods* is, 'three objects of thought, of whom each separately may be called God.' To avow the last statement, as the Creed does, and yet repudiate Three Gods, is to object to the phrase, yet confess to the only meaning which the phrase can convey."

Note X. p. 123.

Schleiermacher (*Der Christliche Glaube*, § 171) has some objections against the Catholic doctrine of the Holy Trinity, conceived in the thorough spirit of Rationalism. In the same spirit Strauss observes (*Glaubenslehre*, I. p. 460), "Wer das *Symbolum Quicunque* beschworen hatte, der hatte die Gesetze des menschlichen Denkens abgeschworen." The sarcasm comes inconsistently enough from a disciple of Hegel, whose entire philosophy is based on an abjuration of the laws of thought. In one respect, indeed, Hegel is right; namely, in maintaining that the laws of thought are not applicable to the Infinite. But the true conclusion from this concession is not, as the Hegelians maintain, that a philosophy can be constructed independently of those laws; but that the Infinite is not an object of human philosophy at all.

Note XI. p. 124.

Paradise Lost, B. II. 667. In this vague abstraction of Being in general, Malebranche endeavours to discover a positive conception of the Infinite. See *Recherche de la Vérité*, l. III. p. ii. ch. 8, l. VI. p. i. ch. 5: *Entretiens sur la Métaphysique*, Ent. II. VIII. But this is really tantamount to a confession that the Infinite is inconceivable; for an object can be conceived only by distinction from other objects.

Note XII. p. 125.

The parallel between a plurality of persons in the Divine Unity, and a plurality of Attributes in the Divine Nature, with the corresponding difficulty in the conception of each, has been noticed by Boyle, in his 'Advices in judging of Things said to transcend Reason,' (*Works*, vol. iv. p. 454, ed. 1772). "I should not much scruple to say, in favour of the Christian Religion, that divers tenets granted both by Christians, Jews, and Heathens, as parts of natural theology, to me seem as difficult to be conceived as divers of those mysteries that for their unintelligibleness are fiercely opposed in revealed theology. I will not take upon me to judge of others; but, for my part, I confess, I do not much better understand how an intellect, and a will, and affections, are distinctly existent in God, in such sort as they are wont to be attributed to Him, than how in Him there can be a Trinity, stated, not as some schoolmen explicate, or rather darken it, but as the Gospel delivers it." The true mode of dealing with such difficulties is excellently declared in the words of Anselm, *De Fide Trinitatis*, c. 7. "At si negat tria dici posse de uno, et unum de tribus: ut tria non dicantur de invicem; sicut in his tribus personis et uno Deo facimus, quoniam hoc in aliis rebus non videt, nec in Deo intelligere valet; sufferat paulisper aliquid, quod intellectus ejus penetrare non possit, esse in Deo, nec comparet naturam, quæ super omnia est, libera ab omni lege loci et temporis et compositionis partium, rebus quæ loco aut tempore clauduntur, aut partibus componuntur; sed credat aliquid in illa esse, quod in istis esse nequit, et acquiescat auctoritati Christianæ, nec disputet contra illam."

Note XIII. p. 125.

See the objections raised against this doctrine by Mr. F. W. Newman, *Phases of Faith*, p. 84. "The very form of our past participle (*begotten*)," he tells us, "is invented to indicate an event in past time." The true difficulty is not grammatical, but metaphysical.

If ordinary language is primarily accommodated to the ordinary laws of thought, it is a mere verbal quibble to press its literal application to the Infinite, which is above thought.

Note XIV. p. 125.

The parallel here pointed out may be exhibited more fully by consulting Bishop Pearson's Exposition of this Doctrine, *On the Creed*, Art. I. and the authorities cited in his notes.

Notes XV. p. 126.

On this ground is established a profound and decisive criticism of Hegel's system, by Trendelenburg, *Logische Untersuchungen*, c. 2. "Das reine Sein," he says, "ist Ruhe; das Nichts—das sich selbst Gleiche—ist ebenfalls Ruhe. Wie kommt aus der Einheit zweier ruhenden Vorstellungen das bewegte Werden heraus." M. Bartholmèss in like manner remarks, "En convertissant ainsi l'abstraction en réalité, ce système attribue tacitement à l'être abstrait des vertus, des qualités qui ne conviennent qu'à un être concret et individuel, c'est-à-dire à un être seul capable d'action spontanée et réfléchie, d'intelligence et de volonté. Il lui accorde tout cela, dans le temps même qu'il le représente, et avec raison, comme un être impersonnel. Cet être abstrait produit des êtres concrets, cet être impersonnel produit des personnes: il produit les uns et les autres, parce qu'ainsi l'ordonne le système!"—*Histoire des Doctrines religieuses*, II. p. 277.

Note XVI. p. 126.

Schelling, *Bruno*, p. 168. "Im Absoluten ist alles absolut; wenn also die Volkommenheit seines Wesens im Realen als unendliches Seyn, im Idealen als unendliches Erkennen erscheint, so ist im Absoluten das Seyn wie das Erkennen absolut, und indem jedes absolut ist, hat auch keines einen Gegensatz ausser sich in dem andern, sondern das absolute Erkennen ist das absolute Wesen, das absolute Wesen das absolute Erkennen."

Note XVII. p. 127.

Aquinas, *Summa*, P. I. Qu. XXXII. Art. I. "Impossibile est per rationem naturalem ad cognitionem trinitatis divinarum personarum pervenire. Ostensum est enim supra quod homo per rationem naturalem in cognitionem Dei pervenire non potest, nisi ex creaturis. Creaturæ autem ducunt in Dei cognitionem sicut effectus in causam. Hoc igitur solum ratione naturali de Deo cognosci potest, quod competere ei necesse est, secundum quod est omnium rerum principium: et hoc fundamento usi sumus supra in consideratione Dei. Virtus autem creativa Dei est communis toti trinitati: unde pertinet ad unitatem essentiæ, non ad distinctionem personarum. Per rationem igitur naturalem cognosci possunt de Deo ea quæ pertinent ad unitatem essentiæ, non autem ea quæ pertinent ad distinctionem personarum." This wise and sound limitation should be borne in mind, as a testimony against that neoplatonizing spirit of modern times, which seeks to strengthen the evidence of the Christian Doctrine of the Trinity, by distorting it into conformity with the speculations of Heathen Philosophy. The Hegelian Theory of the Trinity is a remarkable instance of this kind. Indeed, Hegel himself expressly regards coincidence with neoplatonism as an evidence in favour of an idealist interpretation of Christian doctrine.[e] A similar spirit occasionally appears in influential writers among ourselves.

Note XVIII. p. 127.

For the objection, see *Catech. Racov.* De Persona Christi, Cap. I. (Ed. 1609. p. 43.) "Rationi sanæ repugnat. *Primo* quod duæ substantiæ proprietatibus adversæ coire in unam personam nequeant, ut sunt mortalem et immortalem esse; principium habere et principio carere; mutabilem et immutabilem existere: *deinde* quod duæ naturæ personam singulæ constituentes in unam personam convenire itidem nequeant: nam loco unius, duas personas esse oporteret, atque ita duos Christos existere, quem unum esse, ut unam ipsius personam, omnes citra omnem controversiam agnoscunt." Spinoza, *Epist. XXI.* "Ceterum quod quædam ecclesiæ his addunt, quod Deus naturam humanam assumpserit, monui expresse, me quid dicant nescire; imo, ut verum fatear, non minus absurde mihi loqui videntur, quam si quis mihi diceret, quod circulus naturam quadrati induerit." Similar objections are urged by F. W. Newman, *The Soul*, p. 116, and by Theodore Parker, *Critical and Miscellaneous Writings*, p. 320, *Discourse of Matters pertaining to Religion*, p. 234.

Note XIX. p. 128.

One half of this dilemma has been exhibited by Sir W. Hamilton, *Discussions*, p. 609, sqq. It is strange however that this great

---

[e] *Philosophie der Geschichte, Werke*, IX. p. 402.

thinker should not have seen that the second alternative is equally inconceivable; that it is as impossible to conceive the creation as a process of evolution from the being of the Creator, as it is to conceive it as a production out of nothing. This double impossibility is much more in harmony with the philosophy of the conditioned, than the hypothesis which Sir W. Hamilton adopts. Indeed, his admirable criticism of Cousin's theory (*Discussions*, p. 36) contains in substance the same dilemma as that exhibited in the text. For some additional remarks on this point, see above, Lecture II. note 33.

Note XX. p. 128.

Pensées, Partie II. Art. I. § I.

Note XXI. p. 130.

Greg, *Creed of Christendom*, p. 248, sqq. Compare the cognate passages from other Authors, quoted above, Lecture I. note 21.

Note XXII. p. 131.

For some remarks connected with this and cognate theories, see above, Lecture I. notes 21, 22, 23, Lecture III. notes, 16, 18.

Note XXIII. p. 132.

" Cum enim longe aliud sit universe, rei *impossibilitatem* intelligere, aliud *possibilitatem* rei *non* intelligere; tum maxime in iis quæ tam vehementer ignoramus, sicut ea quæ sensui exposita non sunt, haud profecto impossibilia sunt continuo, quorum possibilitas, modus ac facultas a nobis non perspicitur. Ergo, ut his utamur, philosophum non decet, universe negare divinam in condito mundo efficientiam, seu pro certo dicere, Deum ipsum (immediate) nihil quicquam conferre vel ad rerum naturalium consecutionem, veluti conservationem partis cujusque et speciei, quam genus animalium aut plantarum amplectitur, vel ad morales mutationes, ut animi humani emendationem, aut fieri omnino non posse, ut revelatio aliave eventa extraordinaria divinitus effecta fuerint." — Storr, *Annotationes quædam Theologicæ*, p. 5.

Note XXIV. p. 132.

" Certainement il faut une plus grande étendue d'esprit pour faire une montre qui, selon les lois des mécaniques, aille toute seule et réglément, soit qu'on la porte sur soi, soit qu'on la tienne suspendue, soit qu'on lui donne tel branle qu'on voudra, que pour en faire une qui ne puisse aller juste, si celui qui l'a faite n'y change à tous moments quelque chose, selon les situations où on la met.... Donc, établir des lois générales et choisir les plus simples, et en même temps les plus fécondes, est une manière d'agir digne de celui dont la sagesse n'a point de bornes ; et au contraire, agir par des volontés particulières, marque une intelligence bornée et qui ne peut comparer les suites ou les effets des causes les moins fécondes."—Malebranche, *Réponse au Livre des vrais et des fausses Idées*, Ch. iv. § 7. "Nam quum virtus et potentia naturæ sit ipsa Dei virtus et potentia, leges autem et regulæ naturæ ipsa Dei decreta, omnino credendum est, potentiam naturæ infinitam esse, ejusque leges adeo latas, ut ad omnia, quæ et ab ipso divino intellectu concipiuntur, se extendant. Alias enim, quid aliud statuitur, quam quod Deus naturam adeo impotentem creaverit, ejusque leges et regulas adeo steriles statuerit, ut sæpe de novo ei subvenire cogatur, si eam conservatam vult et ut res ex voto succedant. Quod sane a ratione alienissimum esse existimo."—Spinoza, *Tractatus Theologico-Politicus*, cap. VI. "Hi nimirum (Supernaturalistæ) Deum sumunt res humanas naturali ordine in universum regere, et, ubi hic naturalis ordo voluntati ipsius haud amplius satisfacere possit, miraculis patrandis ipsi quasi opem ac medicinam ferre: illi vero (Rationalistæ) Deum statuunt ab æterno omnes res continua serie secuturas tam sapienter disposuisse, ut quæ v. c. ante plura jam sæcula evenerint, id quod nunc evenit, præpararent et efficerent, nec opus esset miraculis quibusdam quasi intercalaribus." Wegscheider, *Instit. Theol.* § 12. From an opposite point of view to that of Spinoza, Herbart arrives at a similar conclusion. "Es fördert die Religion, dass derjenige, der als Vater für die Menschen gesorgt hat, jetzt in tiefsten Schweigen die Menschheit sich selbst überlässt, als ob er keinen Theil an ihr habe ; ohne Spur aller solchen Empfindung, welche der menschlichen Sympathie, vollends dem Egoismus gleichen könnte."[f] The simile of the calculating engine, acting by its own laws, is adduced by Mr. Babbage (*Ninth Bridgewater Treatise*, ch. 2), "to illustrate the distinction between a system to which the restoring hand of its contriver is applied, either frequently or at distant intervals, and one which had received at its first formation the impress of the will of its author, foreseeing the varied but yet necessary laws of its action throughout the whole of its existence;" and to shew "that that for which, after its original adjustment, no

---

[f] *Lehrbuch zur Einleitung in die Philosophie*, § 155 (*Werke*, 1. p. 278).

superintendence is required, displays far greater ingenuity than that which demands, at every change in its law, the direct intervention of its contriver." Mr. Jowett, though rejecting the analogy of the machine, uses similar language: "The directing power that is able to foresee all things, and provide against them by simple and general rules, is a worthier image of the Divine intelligence than the handicraftsman ' putting his hand to the hammer,' detaching and isolating portions of matter from the laws by which he has himself put them together."[g]

Note XXV. p. 133.

" The reason why, among men, an artificer is justly esteemed so much the more skilful, as the machine of his composing will continue longer to move regularly without any further interposition of the workman, is, because the skill of all *human* artificers consists only in composing, adjusting, or putting together certain movements, the principles of whose motion are altogether independent upon the artificer..... But with regard to *God*, the case is quite different; because He not only composes or puts things together, but is himself the Author and continual Preserver of their original forces or moving powers. And consequently it is not a diminution, but the true glory of his workmanship, that *nothing* is done without his *continual government* and *inspection*."—Clarke, *First Reply to Leibnitz*, p. 15.

Note XXVI. p. 133.

"I do not believe," says Theodore Parker, "there ever was a miracle, or ever will be; every where I find law,—the constant mode of operation of the infinite God."—*Some account of my Ministry*, appended to *Theism, Atheism, and Popular Theology*, p. 263. Compare the same work, pp. 113, 188; and Atkinson, *Man's Nature and Development*, p. 241. The statement is not at present true, even as regards the material world: it is false as regards the world of mind: and were it true in both, it would prove nothing regarding the "infinite God;" for the conception of law is, to say the least, quite as finite as that of miraculous interposition. Professor Powell, in a recent work, though not absolutely rejecting miracles, yet adopts a tone which, compared with such passages as the above, is at least painfully suggestive. "It is now perceived by all inquiring minds, that the advance of true scientific principles, and

---

[g] *Epistles of St. Paul*, vol. II. p. 412.

the grand inductive conclusions of universal and eternal law and order, are at once the basis of all rational theology, and give the death-blow to superstition."—*Christianity without Judaism*, p. 11.

NOTE XXVII. p. 133.

This point has been treated by the author at greater length in his *Prolegomena Logica*, p. 135 (2nd edit. p. 146), and in his *Metaphysics*, p. 270.

NOTE XXVIII. p. 135.

See M'Cosh, *Method of the Divine Government*, pp. 162, 166. The quotations which the author brings forward in support of this remark, from Humboldt and Comte, are valuable as showing the concurrence of the highest scientific authorities as to the facts stated. The religious application of these facts is Dr. M'Cosh's own, and constitutes one of the most instructive portions of his valuable work. The fact itself has been noticed and commented on with his usual sagacity by Bishop Butler, *Analogy*, Part II. ch. 3. "Would it not have been thought highly improbable, that men should have been so much more capable of discovering, even to certainty, the general laws of matter, and the magnitudes, paths, and revolutions of the heavenly bodies, than the occasions and cures of distempers, and many other things, in which human life seems so much more nearly concerned, than in astronomy?"

NOTE XXIX. p. 135.

"There are domains of nature in which man's foresight is considerably extended and accurate, and other domains in which it is very limited, or very dim and confused. Again, there are departments of nature in which man's influence is considerable, and others which lie altogether beyond his control, directly or indirectly. Now, on comparing these classes of objects, we find them to have a cross or converse relation to one another. Where man's foreknowledge is extensive, either he has no power, or his power is limited; and where his power might be exerted, his foresight is contracted. . . . . He can tell in what position a satellite of Saturn will be a hundred years after this present time, but he cannot say in what state his bodily health may be an hour hence. . . . . . We are now in circumstances to discover the advantages arising from the mixture of uniformity and uncertainty in the operations of nature. Both serve most important ends in the government of God.

The one renders nature steady and stable, the other active and accommodating. Without the certainty, man would waver as in a dream, and wander as in a trackless desert; without the unexpected changes, he would make his rounds like the gin-horse in its circuit, or the prisoner on his wheel. Were nature altogether capricious, man would likewise become altogether capricious, for he could have no motive to steadfast action: again, were nature altogether fixed, it would make man's character as cold and formal as itself."
—M'Cosh, *Method of the Divine Government*, pp. 172, 174 (4th edition).

NOTE XXX. p. 136.

The solution usually given by Christian writers of the difficulty of reconciling the efficacy of prayer with the infinite power and wisdom of God, I cannot help regarding, while thoroughly sympathizing with the purpose of its advocates, as unsatisfactory. That solution may be given in the language of Euler. "Quand un fidèle adresse à présent à Dieu une prière digne d'être exaucée, il ne faut pas s'imaginer que cette prière ne parvient qu'à présent à la connaissance de Dieu. Il a déjà entendu cette prière depuis l'éternité; et puisque ce père miséricordieux l'a jugée digne d'être exaucée, il a arrangé exprès le monde en faveur de cette prière, en sorte que l'accomplissement fût une suite du cours naturel des événements."[a] In other words, the prayer is foreseen and foreordained, as well as the answer. This solution appears to assume that the conception of law and necessity adequately represents the absolute nature of God, while that of contingence and special interposition is to be subordinated to it. The arrangements of God in the government of the world are fixed from all eternity, and if the prayer is part of those arrangements, it becomes a necessary act likewise. It is surely a more reverent, and probably a truer solution, to say that the conception of general law and that of special interposition are equally human. Neither probably represents, as a speculative truth, the absolute manner in which God works in His Providence; both are equally necessary, as regulative truths, to govern man's conduct in this life. In neither aspect are we warranted in making the one conception subordinate to the other. A similar objection may be urged against the theory which represents a miracle as the possible manifestation of a higher and unknown law. There is nothing in

---

[a] *Lettres à une Princesse d'Allemagne*, vol. i. p. 357, ed. Cournot. Compare M'Cosh, *Method of the Divine Government*, p. 222.

the conception of *law* which entitles it to this pre-eminence over other human modes of representation.

NOTE XXXI. p. 136.

Kant, though he attaches no value to miracles as evidences of a moral religion, yet distinctly allows that there is no sufficient reason for denying their possibility as facts, or their utility at certain periods of the history of religion.[1] This moderation is not imitated by his disciple, Wegscheider, who says, " Persuasio de *supernaturali* et *miraculosa* eademque *immediata* Dei revelatione haud bene conciliari videtur cum idea Dei æterni, semper sibi constantis, omnipotentis, omniscii, et sapientissimi."[k] Strauss, in like manner, assumes that the absolute Cause never disturbs the chain of secondary causes by arbitrary acts of interposition; and therefore lays it down as a canon, that whatever is miraculous is unhistorical.[l]

NOTE XXXII. p. 137.

See, on the one side, Babbage, *Ninth Bridgewater Treatise*, ch. 8; Hitchcock, *Religion of Geology*, p. 290. The same view is also suggested as probable by Butler, *Analogy*, Part II. ch. 4. On the other side, as regards the limitations within which the idea of law should be applied to the course of God's Providence, see M'Cosh, *Method of the Divine Government*, p. 155. Kant, *Religion innerhalb, u. s. w.*, p. 102, maintains, with reason, that, from a human point of view, a law of miracles is unattainable.

NOTE XXXIII. p. 139.

Sir William Hamilton, *Discussions*, p. 625.

---

[1] *Religion innerhalb der Grenzen der blossen Vernunft*, p. 99, edit. Rosenkranz.

[k] *Instit. Theol.* § 12.
[l] *Leben Jesu*, § 16.

LECTURE VII.

Note I. p. 141.

The Moral and Religious Philosophy of Kant, which is here referred to, is chiefly contained in his *Metaphysik der Sitten*, first published in 1785, his *Kritik der praktischen Vernunft*, in 1788, and his *Religion innerhalb der Grenzen der blossen Vernunft*, in 1793. For Kant's influence on the rationalist theology of Germany, see Rosenkranz, *Geschichte der Kant'schen Philosophie*, p. 323 sqq.; Amand Saintes, *Histoire du Rationalisme en Allemagne*, L. II. ch. xi.; Rose, *State of Protestantism in Germany*, p. 183 (2nd edition); Kahnis, *History of German Protestantism*, pp. 88, 167 (Meyer's translation).

Note II. p. 142.

See *Metaphysik der Sitten*, pp. 5, 31, 52, 87, 92; *Kritik der praktischen Vernunft*, p. 224 (ed. Rosenkranz).

Note III. p. 142.

A similar view of the superiority of the moral consciousness over other phenomena of the human mind, as regards absolute certainty, seems to be held by Mr. Jowett. In reference to certain doubts connected with the Doctrine of the Atonement, he observes, "It is not the pride of human reason which suggests these questions, but the moral sense which He himself has implanted in the breast of each one of us."[a] It is difficult to see the force of the antithesis here suggested. The "moral sense" is not more the gift of God than the "human reason;" and the decisions of the former, to be represented in consciousness at all, require the cooperation of the latter. Even as regards our own personal acts, the intellectual conception must be united with the moral sense in passing judgment; and in all general theories concerning the moral nature of God or of man, the rational faculty will necessarily have the larger share.

[a] *Epistles of St. Paul*, vol. ii. p. 468.

NOTE IV. p. 142.

Kritik der reinen Vernunft, p. 631, ed. Rosenkranz; *Metaphysik der Sitten*, p. 31; *Religion innerhalb u. s. w.* p. 123.

NOTE V. p. 142.

Religion u. s. w. p. 123.

NOTE VI. p. 142.

Ibid. p. 122, 184.

NOTE VII. p. 142.

Ibid. pp. 123, 133. Compare *Streit der Facultäten*, p. 304.

NOTE VIII. p. 143.

See above, Lecture III. p. 59.

NOTE IX. p. 144.

On the existence of necessary truths in morals, comparable to those of Mathematics, see Reid, *Intellectual Powers*, Essay VI. ch. 6 (pp. 453, 454, ed. Hamilton).

NOTE X. p. 145.

Compare Jacobi, *An Fichte, Werke*, III. pp. 35, 37. "So gewiss ich Vernunft besitze, so gewiss besitze ich mit dieser meiner menschlichen Vernunft *nicht* die Vollkommenheit des Lebens, *nicht* die Fülle des Guten und des Wahren; und so gewiss ich dieses mit ihr *nicht* besitze, *und es weiss;* so gewiss *weiss* ich, es ist ein *höheres* Wesen, und ich habe in ihm meinen Ursprung. . . . . Ich gestehe also, dass ich das *an sich Gute,* wie das *an sich Wahre,* nicht kenne, dass ich auch von ihm nur eine ferne *Ahndung* habe." That the moral providence of God cannot be judged by the same standard as the actions of men, see Leibnitz, *Théodicée, De la Conformité,* &c. § 32 (*Opera,* ed. Erdmann, p. 489).

NOTE XI. p. 145.

" Wherefore inasmuch as our actions are conversant about things beset with many circumstances, which cause men of sundry wits to be also of sundry judgments concerning that which ought to be done; requisite it cannot but seem the rule of divine law should herein help our imbecility, that we might more infallibly understand what is good and what evil. The first principles of the Law of Nature are easy; hard it were to find men ignorant of them. But concerning the duty which Nature's law doth require at the hands of men in a number of things particular, so far hath the natural understanding even of sundry whole nations been darkened, that they have not discerned, no not gross iniquity to be sin."—Hooker, *E. P.* I. xii. 2.

Note XII. p. 146.

This corresponds to the distinction drawn by Leibnitz, between *eternal* and *positive* truths of the reason. See *Théodicée, Discours de la Conformité,* &c., § 2. (*Opera,* Erdmann, p. 480.) The latter class of truths, he allows, may be subservient to Faith, and even opposed by it, but not the former.

Note XIII. p. 148.

That it is impossible to conceive the Divine Will as absolutely indifferent, is shown by Müller, *Christliche Lehre von der Sünde,* I. p. 128. But on the other hand, we are equally unable to conceive it as necessarily determined by the laws of the Divine Nature. We cannot therefore conceive absolute morality either as dependent on, or as independent of, the Will of God. In other words, we are unable to conceive absolute morality at all.

Note XIV. p. 149.

See above, Lecture I. note 14.

Note XV. p. 149.

" Sin *contains* its own retributive penalty, as surely and as naturally as the acorn contains the oak. . . . . It is ordained to follow guilt by God—not as a Judge, but as the Creator and Legislator of the universe. . . . . We can be redeemed from the punishment of sin only by being redeemed from its commission. Neither *can* there be any such thing as vicarious atonement or punishment. . . . . If the foregoing reflections are sound, the awful, yet wholesome conviction, presses upon our minds, that *there can be no forgiveness of sins.*"—Greg. *Creed of Christendom,* p. 265. " I believe God is a just God, rewarding and punishing us exactly as we act well or ill. I believe that such reward and punishment follow necessarily from His will as revealed in natural law, as well as in the Bible. I believe that as the highest justice is the highest mercy, so He is a merciful God. That the guilty should suffer the measure of penalty which their guilt has incurred, is justice."—Froude, *Nemesis of Faith*, p. 69.

NOTE XVI. p. 149.

See above, Lecture I. note 13.

NOTE XVII. p. 149.

See above, Lecture I. note 12.

NOTE XVIII. p. 149.

See Newman, *Phases of Faith*, p. 8. Compare Wegscheider, *Instit. Theol.* § 141. On the inadequacy of all these *à priori* objections to the Atonement as *improbable*, some excellent remarks will be found in W. A. Butler's *Sermons*, first series, p. 263.

NOTE XIX. p. 149.

"Expiation, at the very moment of pardon, recognises the guilt of the transgressor, and does homage to the offended majesty of law. Simple forgiveness, on the other hand, seems to have a plain tendency to blunt the perception of guilt, and so to paralyse conscience and convert the law into a dead letter—a set of enactments made only to be rescinded. And in proportion as the sense of guilt and the respect for law diminished, would the mercy exhibited in forgiving sins seem also to diminish; till pardon became too much a matter of course to command gratitude or love, till it was regarded not as grace but as debt, not as that which man might hope from God's mercy, but that which he might demand as his right."—Macdonnell's *Donnellan Lectures*, p. 199. In like manner Mr. Rigg justly observes of the theory of immediate forgiveness, as substituted for the Christian Atonement, "Let all men be told that 'God cannot be angry with any,' and that whatever may have been a man's sins, if he will but repent, there is no hindrance to God's freely forgiving him all, without the infliction of any punishment whatever, and without the need of any atonement or intercession. What would be the effect of such a proclamation? Would it make sin appear 'exceedingly sinful'? Would it enhance our idea of the holiness of God? Would it not make sin appear a light and trivial thing, tolerated too easily by a 'good-natured' God, to be held as of much

x

account by man?"[b] Wegscheider indeed actually urges this argument against the Christian doctrine, which it suits his purpose to represent as a scheme of unconditional forgiveness. "Experientia docet, persuasionem hominum de peccatorum remissione absoluta a nequissimo quoque facillime obtinenda, maximum semper veræ virtuti et probitati detrimentum attulisse."—*Instit. Theol.* § 140.

Note XX. p. 150.

Such is in fact the theory of Kant. See *Religion innerhalb der Grenzen der blossen Vernunft*, p. 84. He does not however carry his principle consistently out, but admits a kind of vicarious suffering in a symbolical sense; the penitent being morally a different individual from the sinner. Even this metaphorical conceit is utterly out of place, according to the main principles of his system.

Note XXI. p. 150.

Some excellent remarks on this point will be found in M'Cosh's *Method of the Divine Government*, p. 475 (4th edition).

Note XXII. p. 151.

"This natural indignation is generally moderate and low enough in mankind, in each particular man, when the injury which excites it doth not affect himself, or one whom he considers as himself. Therefore the precepts to *forgive* and to *love our enemies*, do not relate to that general indignation against injury and the authors of it, but to this feeling, or resentment, when raised by private or personal injury."—Butler, Sermon IX., *On Forgiveness of Injuries.*

Note XXIII. p. 151.

Thus Mr. Froude exclaims, "He! to have created mankind liable to fall—to have laid them in the way of a temptation under which He knew they would fall, and then curse them and all who were to come of them, and all the world for their sakes!"—*Nemesis of Faith,* p. 11. This author omits the whole doctrine of the redemption, and treats the fall and the curse as if they were the sole manner of God's dealing with sinners. His objection, stripped of its violent language, is but one form of the universal riddle—the existence of Evil. A similar objection is urged by Mr. Parker, *Theism, Atheism, and the Popular Theology*, p. 64; and by Mr. Atkinson, *Letters on the Laws of Man's Nature and Development*, pp. 173, 174.

[b] *Modern Anglican Theology*, p. 317.

Note XXIV. p. 151.

Aristotle, *Eth. Nic.* V. 10. Τοῦ γὰρ ἀορίστου ἀόριστος καὶ ὁ κανών ἐστιν, ὥσπερ καὶ τῆς Λεσβίας οἰκοδομῆς ὁ μολίβδινος κανών· πρὸς γὰρ τὸ σχῆμα τοῦ λίθου μετακινεῖται καὶ οὐ μένει ὁ κανών.

Note XXV. p. 152.

On this spirit of universal criticism, Augustine remarks: "Sunt autem stulti qui dicunt, Non poterat aliter Sapientia Dei homines liberare, nisi susciperet hominem, et nasceretur de femina, et a peccatoribus omnia illa pateretur? Quibus dicimus: Poterat omnino, sed si aliter faceret, similiter vestræ stultitiæ displiceret."—*De Agone Christiano*, c. 11.

The following passage from the *Eclipse of Faith*, p. 125, is an excellent statement of the versatility of the "moral reason," or "spiritual insight," when set up as a criterion of religious truth. "Even as to that fundamental position,—the existence of a Being of unlimited power and wisdom (as to his unlimited *goodness*, I believe that nothing *but* an external revelation will absolutely certify us), I feel that I am much more indebted to those inferences from *design*, which these writers make so light of, than to any *clearness* in the imperfect intuition; for if I found—and surely this is the true test—the traces of design less conspicuous in the external world, confusion there as in the moral, and in both greater than is now found in either, I extremely doubt whether the faintest surmise of such a Being would have suggested itself to me. But be that as it may; as to their other cardinal sentiments,—the nature of my relations to this Being—his placability if offended, the terms of forgiveness, if any,—whether, as these gentlemen affirm, he is accessible to all, without any atonement or mediator:—as to all this, I solemnly declare, that, apart from external instruction, I cannot by interrogating my racked spirit, catch even a murmur. That it must be faint, indeed, in *other* men; so faint as to render the pretensions of the certitude of the internal revelation, and its independence of all external revelation, perfectly preposterous, I infer from this,—that they have, for the most part, arrived at diametrically opposite conclusions from those of these interpreters of the spiritual revelation. As to the articles, indeed, of man's immortality and a future state, it would be truly difficult for *my* 'spiritual insight' to verify *theirs*; for, according to Mr. Parker, his 'insight' affirms that man *is* immortal, and Mr. Newman's 'insight' declares nothing about the matter! Nor is my consciousness, so far as I can trace it, mine only. This painful uncertainty has been the confession of multitudes of far greater minds; they have been so far from contending that we have naturally a clear utterance on these great questions, that they have acknowledged the necessity of an external revelation; and mankind *in general,* so far from thinking or feeling such light superfluous, have been constantly *gaping* after it, and adopted almost anything that but *bore the name.*

"What, then, am I to think of this all-sufficient revelation from *within?*"

NOTE XXVI. p. 152.

For the Socinian theory of a limited foreknowledge in God, see F. Socinus, *Prælect. Theol.* c. 8; 'Crellius, *De Deo ejusque Attributis,* c. 24; Wolzogen, *In Evang. Matth.* c. 4, Append. I. Compare Müller, *Christliche Lehre von der Sünde,* II. pp. 276, 288; Davison, *Discourses on Prophecy,* pp. 360, 367. A similar view is held by Rothe, *Theol. Ethik,* vol. i. p. 118; and by Drobisch, *Grundlehren der Religionsphilosophie,* p. 209. For the opposite necessitarian theory, see Calvin, *Inst.* L. II. c. 4, § 6; Edwards, *On the Freedom of the Will,* Part II. Sect. xii. quoted above, Lect. II. Note 7; and the authorities cited by Wegscheider, *Inst. Theol.* § 65.

NOTE XXVII. p. 152.

That God's knowledge is not properly *foreknowledge,* as not being subject to the law of time, is maintained by Augustine, *De Civ. Dei,* XI. 21, *De Div. Quæst. ad Simpl.* L. II. Qu. 2, § 2, and by Boethius, *De Consol. Phil.* L. V. Pr. 3-6. A similar view is taken by Wegscheider, *Inst. Theol.* § 65. As a speculative theory, this view is as untenable as the opposite hypothesis of an absolute foreknowledge and predestination. We can only say that we do not know that the Divine Consciousness is subject to the law of succession; not that we know that it is not. As a means of saving the infinity of God's knowledge, consistently with the free agency of man, the hypothesis becomes unnecessary, the instant we admit that the infinite is not an object of human conception at all. If this is once conceded, we need no hypothesis to reconcile truths which we cannot certainly know to be in antagonism to each other. We cannot assume the simultaneity of the divine consciousness; for we know nothing of the infinite, either in itself or in its relation to time. Nor, on the other hand, could we deduce the necessity of human actions from the fact of God's foreknowledge, even if the latter could be assumed as absolutely true; for we know not whether the conception of necessity itself implies a divine reality, or merely a human mode of representation.

NOTE XXVIII. p. 152.

Wegscheider (*Inst. Theol.* § 50) denies the possibility of prophecy, on the ground that a prediction of future events is destructive of human freedom. In this he follows Kant, *Anthropologie,* § 35.

NOTE XXIX. p. 153.

"As it is certain that prescience does not destroy the liberty of man's will, or impose any necessity upon it, men's actions being not therefore future, because they are foreknown, but therefore foreknown, because future; and were a thing never so contingent, yet upon supposition that it will be done, it must needs have been future from all eternity: so is it extreme arrogance for men, because themselves can naturally foreknow nothing but by some causes antecedent, as an eclipse of the sun or moon, therefore to presume to measure the knowledge of God Almighty according to the same scantling, and to deny him the prescience of human actions, not considering that, as his nature is incomprehensible, so his knowledge may be well looked upon by us as such too; that which is past our finding out, and too wonderful for us." Cudworth, *Intellectual System,* ch. V. (vol. iii. p. 19, ed. Harrison). " *We* may be unable to conceive how a thing not necessary in its nature can be foreknown—for *our* foreknowledge is in general limited by that circumstance, and is more or less perfect in proportion to the fixed or necessary nature of the things we contemplate: . . . but to subject the knowledge of God to any such limitation is surely absurd and unphilosophical, as well as impious." Copleston, *Enquiry into the Doctrines of Necessity and Predestination,* p. 46.

NOTE XXX. p. 153.

Origen, apud Euseb. *Præp. Evang.* VI. 11. 36. Καὶ εἰ χρὴ λέγειν οὐ τὴν πρόγνωσιν αἰτίαν τῶν γινομένων, (οὐ γὰρ ἐφάπτεται τοῦ προεγνωσμένου ἁμαρτησομένου ὁ Θεὸς, ὅταν ἁμαρτάνῃ,) ἀλλὰ παραδοξότερον μὲν ἀληθὲς δὲ ἐροῦμεν, τὸ ἐσόμενον αἴτιον τοῦ τοιάνδε εἶναι τὴν περὶ αὐτοῦ πρόγνωσιν. Lebnitz, *Théodicée,* § 37. "Il est fort aisé de juger que la prescience en elle-même n'ajoute rien à la détermination de la vérité des futurs contingens, sinon que cette détermination est connue: ce qui n'augmente point la détermination, ou la *futurition* (comme on l'appelle) de ces événemens, dont nous sommes convenus d'abord." Clarke, *Demonstration of the Being and Attributes of God*, p. 96. "The certainty of Foreknowledge does not cause the certainty of things, but is itself founded on the reality of their existence. Whatever now is, it is *certain* that it is; and it was yesterday and from eternity as *certainly* true, that the thing *would be* to-day, as 'tis now *certain* that it *is*. This *certainty of events* is equally the same, whether it is supposed that the thing could be foreknown, or not."

NOTE XXXI. p. 153.

See above, Lecture VI. p. 133, and note 27.

NOTE XXXII. p. 154.

This question is discussed at some length by Euler, *Lettres à une Princesse d'Allemagne*, vol. i. p. 360, ed. Cournot.

NOTE XXXIII. p. 155.

"Peccata finita sunt; inter finitum et infinitum nulla est proportio; ergo pœnæ quoque debent esse finitæ." Sonerus apud Leibnitz. *Præf.*[c]

The same argument is used by Blasche, *Philosophische Unsterblichkeitlehre*, § 4; as well as by Mr. Newman, *Phases of Faith*, p. 78, and by Mr. Froude, *Nemesis of Faith*, p. 17. The latter however entirely misrepresents Leibnitz's reply to the objection.

NOTE XXXIV. p. 155.

Thus Leibnitz replies to the objection of Sonerus. "Etiamsi igitur concederemus ipsi, nullum peccatum per se infinitum esse, revera tamen dici potest, damnatorum infinita numero peccata esse; quoniam per totam æternitatem in peccando perseverant." The same argument is repeated in the *Théodicée*, § 74, 133, 266. The reply which Mr. Froude attributes to Leibnitz; namely, that sin against an Infinite Being contracts a character of infinity, is merely noticed by him as "la raison vulgaire," urged, among others, by Ursinus. With Leibnitz's language may be compared that of Müller, "Und wenn nun die Erfahrung zeigt, dass viele dem heiligsten Werk der göttlichen Liebe *wirklich widerstreben*, warum soll es unmöglich sein, dass dieses Widerstreben gegen Gott sich auch jenseits des irdischen Lebens immer wieder erneuere, und so in

---

[c] Published by Lessing in his tract, *Leibnitz von den ewigen Strafen*. (*Lessing's Schriften*, ed. Lachmann, vol. ix. p. 154.)

endlose Zeiten fortsetze." *Christliche Lehre von der Sünde*, II. p. 601.

NOTE XXXV. p. 155.

Thus Mr. Newman says, "I saw that the current orthodoxy made Satan eternal conqueror over Christ. In vain does the Son of God come from heaven and take human flesh and die on the cross. In spite of him, the devil carries off to hell the vast majority of mankind, in whom not misery only, but *Sin* is triumphant for ever and ever."[d] And Mr. Parker, to the same effect, remarks, "I can never believe that Evil is a finality with God."[e] The remarks of Müller, in answer to similar theories, are worthy of consideration. "Es scheint nach der Bemerkung, von der wir eben ausgingen, undenkbar, dass die Weltentwickelung mit einem *unaufgelösten Zwiespalt* abschliesse, dass der Gegensatz gegen den göttlichen Willen in dem Willen irgend welches Geschöpfes sich behaupte. Diesen Knoten löst indessen zunächst schon ein richtiger Begriff der *Strafe*. Der Gegensatz gegen den göttlichen Willen behauptet sich eben nicht, sondern ist ein schlechterdings überwundener, wenn der ganze Zustand der Wesen, in denen er ist, Strafzustand ist, so dass das gebundene Böse den reinen Einklang der zum göttlichen Reiche verklärten Welt durchaus nicht mehr zu stören vermag."[f]

NOTE XXXVI. p. 156.

See a short treatise by Kant, *Ueber das Misslingen aller philosophischen Versuche in der Théodicée* (*Werke*, VII. p. 385). For a more detailed account of various theories, see Müller, *Christliche Lehre von der Sünde*, B. II. An able review of the difficulties of the question will be found in Mr. Mozley's *Augustinian Doctrine of Predestination*, p. 262 seq.

NOTE XXXVII. p. 156.

The theory which represents evil as a *privation* or a *negation*,—a theory adopted by theologians and philosophers of almost every shade of opinion, in order to reconcile the goodness of God with the apparent permission of sin, can only be classed among the numerous necessarily fruitless attempts of metaphysicians to explain the primary facts of consciousness, by the arbitrary assumption of a principle of which we are not and cannot be conscious, and of whose

---

[d] *Phases of Faith*, p. 78.
[e] *Some Account of my Ministry.* See *Theism, Atheism*, &c. p. 261.
[f] *Christliche Lehre von der Sünde*, II. p. 599.

truth or falsehood we have therefore no possible guarantee. Moral evil, in the only form in which we are conscious of it, appears as the direct transgression of a law whose obligation we feel within us; and thus manifested, it is an act as real and as positive as any performed in the most rigid compliance with that law. And this is the utmost point to which human research can penetrate. Whether, in some absolute mode of existence, out of all relation to human consciousness, the phenomenon of moral evil is ultimately dependent on the addition or the subtraction of some causative principle, is a question the solution of which is beyond consciousness, and therefore beyond philosophy. To us, as moral agents capable of right and wrong acts, evil is a reality, and its consequences are a reality. What may be the nature of the cause which produces this unquestionably real fact of human consciousness, is a mystery which God has not revealed, and which man cannot discover.

NOTE XXXVIII. p. 157.

Analogy, Part II. chap. 5. In another significant passage (Part I. ch. 2), Butler exhibits the argument from analogy as bearing on the final character of punishment. "Though after men have been guilty of folly and extravagance *up to a certain degree*, it is often in their power, for instance, to retrieve their affairs, to recover their health and character; at least in good measure; yet real reformation is, in many cases, of no avail at all towards preventing the miseries, poverty, sickness, infamy, naturally annexed to folly and extravagance *exceeding that degree* . . . So that many natural punishments are final to him who incurs them, if considered only in his tempora capacity." Compare Bishop Browne, *Procedure of the Understanding*, p. 351. "The difficulty in that question, *What proportion endless torments can bear to momentary sins?* is quite removed, by considering that the punishments denounced and threatened are not in themselves sanctions entirely arbitrary, as it is in punishments annexed to human laws; but they are withal so many previous warnings or declarations of the *inevitable* consequence and *natural* tendency of Sin in itself to render us miserable in another world."

NOTE XXXIX. p. 158.

Kant (*Religion, u. s. w., Werke*, X. p. 45) objects to the doctrine of inherited corruption, on the ground that a man cannot be responsible for any but his own acts. The objection is carried out more fully by Wegscheider, who says, " Nec benignitas Dei concedere potest, ut per unius hominis peccatum universa hominum natura corrumpatur atque depravetur; nec sapientia pati, ut opus Dei ab initio præstantissimis instructum dotibus paullo post ob causam levissimam in aliam plane deterioremque conditionem transformetur." (*Inst. Theol.* § 117.) The learned critic does not seem to be aware that the principle of one of these arguments exactly annihilates that of the other; for if we concede to the first that every man is born in the state of pristine innocence, we must admit, in opposition to the second, that God's work is destroyed by slight causes, not once only, but millions of times, in every man that sins. The only other supposition possible is, that sin itself is part of God's purpose,— in which case we need not trouble ourselves to establish any argument on the hypothesis of the divine wisdom or benevolence.

NOTE XL. p. 158.

Aristotle, *Eth. Nic.* VII. 2. ’Απορήσειε δ’ ἄν τις πῶς ὑπολαμβάνων ὀρθῶς ἀκρατεύεταί τις. Ἐπιστάμενον μὲν οὖν οὔ φασί τινες οἷόν τε εἶναι· δεινὸν γὰρ ἐπιστήμης ἐνούσης, ὡς ᾤετο Σωκράτης, ἄλλο τι κρατεῖν καὶ περιέλκειν αὐτὸν ὥσπερ ἀνδράποδον. Σωκράτης μὲν γὰρ ὅλως ἐμάχετο πρὸς τὸν λόγον, ὡς οὐκ οὔσης ἀκρασίας· οὐθένα γὰρ ὑπολαμβάνοντα πράττειν παρὰ τὸ βέλτιστον, ἀλλὰ δι’ ἄγνοιαν.

NOTE XLI. p. 159.

For sundry rationalist objections to the doctrine of Justification by Faith, see Wegscheider, §§ 154, 155. He declares the whole doctrine to be the result of the *anthropopathic* notions of a rude age.

NOTE XLII. p. 159.

"Unser Begriff von Freiheit schliesst ja ubrigens niemals Motiven des Bewussten Handelns aus; Motiven aber sind nicht Zwangsveranstaltungen, sondern werden immer nur erst durch den Willen wirksam; Motiven für den menschlichen Willen können also auch von Gott ausgehen, ohne dass dadurch der Mensch gezwungen, ohne dass er unfrei, ein blindes Werkzeug der höhern Macht wird." Drobisch, *Grundlehren der Religionsphilosophie*, p. 272. In like manner, Mr. Mozley, in his learned and philosophical work on the Augustinian Doctrine of Predestination, truly says, "What we have to consider in this question, is not what is the abstract idea of freewill, but what is the freewill which we really and actually have. This actual freewill, we find, is not a simple but a complex thing; exhibiting oppositions and inconsistencies; appearing on the one side to be a power of doing anything to which there is no physical hindrance, on the other side to be a restricted 'faculty" (p. 102). Neither the Pelagian theory on the one side, nor the Augustinian on the other, took sufficient account of the actual condition of the human will in relation to external influences. The question was argued as if the relation of divine grace to human volition must consist wholly in activity on the one side, and passivity on the other;—in the will of its own motion accepting the grace, or the grace by its irresistible force overpowering the will. The controversy thus becomes precisely analogous to the philosophical dispute between the advocates of freewill and determinism: the one proceeding on the assumption of an absolute indifference of the will; the other maintaining its necessary determination by motives.

Mr. Mozley has thrown considerable light on the true bearings of the predestinarian controversy; and his work is especially valuable, as vindicating the supreme right of Scripture to be accepted in all its statements, instead of being mutilated to suit the demands of human logic. But it cannot be denied that his own theory, however satisfactory in this respect, leaves a painful void on the philosophical side, and apparently vindicates the authority of revelation by the sacrifice of the laws of human thought. He maintains that where our conception of an object is indistinct, contradictory propositions may be accepted as both equally true; and he carries this theory so far as to assert of the rival doctrines of Pelagius and Augustine, "Both these positions are true, if held together, and both false, if held apart."[g]

Should we not rather say that the very indistinctness of conception prevents the existence of any contradiction at all? I can only know two ideas to be contradictory by the distinct conception of both; and, where such a conception is impossible, there is no evidence of contradiction. The actual declarations of Scripture, so far as they deal with matters above human comprehension, are not in them-

---

[g] P. 77. To the same effect are his criticisms on Aquinas, p. 260, in which he says, "The will as an original spring of action is irreconcilable with the Divine Power, a second first cause in nature being inconsistent with there being only one First Cause." This assumes that we have a sufficient conception of the nature of Divine Power and of the action of a First Cause; an assumption which the author himself in another passage repudiates, acknowledging that "As an unknown premiss, the Divine Power is no contradiction to the fact of evil; for we must know what a truth is before we see a contradiction in it to another truth" (p. 276). This latter admission, consistently carried out, would have considerably modified the author's whole theory.

selves contradictory to the facts of consciousness: they are only made so by arbitrary interpretation. It is nowhere said in Scripture that God so predestines man as to take from him all power of acting by his own will:—this is an inference from the supposed nature of predestination: an inference which, if our conception of predestination is indistinct, we have no right to make. *Man* cannot foreknow unless the event is certain; nor predestine without coercing the result. Here there is a contradiction between freewill and predestination. But we cannot transfer the same contradiction to Theology, without assuming that God's knowledge and acts are subject to the same conditions as man's.

The contradictory propositions which Mr. Mozley exhibits as equally guaranteed by consciousness, are in reality by no means homogeneous. In each pair of contradictories we have a limited and individual fact of immediate perception,—such as the power of originating an action,—opposed to an universal maxim, not perceived immediately, but based on some process of general thought, such as that every event must have a cause. To establish these two as contradictory of each other, it should be shewn that in every single act we have a direct consciousness of being coerced, as well as of being free; and that we can gather from each fact a clear and distinct conception. But this is by no means the case. The principle of causality, whatever may be its true import and extent, is not derived from the immediate consciousness of our volition being determined by antecedent causes; and therefore it may not be applied to human actions, until, from an analysis of the mode in which this maxim is gained, it can be distinctly shewn that these are included under it.[h]

By applying to Mr. Mozley's theory the principles advanced in the preceding Lectures, it may, I believe, be shewn that, in every case, the contradiction is not real, but apparent; and that it arises from a vain attempt to transcend the limits of human thought.

Note XLIII. p. 159.

Analogy, Introduction, p. 10.

[h] I am happy to be able to refer, in support of this view, to the able criticism of Professor Fraser, in his review of Mr. Mozley's work. "The coexistence," he says, "of a belief in causality with a belief in moral agency, is indeed incomprehensible: but is it so because the two beliefs are known to be contradictory, and not rather because causality and Divine Power cannot be fathomed by finite intelligence?"— *Essays in Philosophy,* p. 271.

LECTURE VIII.

Note I. p. 164.

F. W. Newman, *Phases of Faith*, p. 199; *Reply to the Eclipse of Faith*, p. 11.

Note II. p. 164.

"Christianity itself has thus practically confessed, what is theoretically clear, that an authoritative *external* revelation of moral and spiritual truth is essentially impossible to man.—F. W. Newman, *The Soul*, p. 59.

Note III. p. 164.

"In teaching about God and Christ, lay aside the wisdom of the wise: forswear History and all its apparatus: hold communion with the Father and the Son in the Spirit: from this communion learn all that is essential to the Gospel, and still (if possible) retain every proposition which Paul believed and taught. Propose them to the faith of others, *to be tested by inward and spiritual evidence only;* and you will at least be in the true apostolic track."—F. W. Newman, *The Soul*, p. 250.

Note IV. p. 164.

"This question of miracles, whether true or false, is of no religious significance. When Mr. Locke said the doctrine proved the miracles, not the miracles the doctrine, he admitted their worthlessness. They can be useful only to such as deny our internal power of discerning truth."—Parker, *Discourse of matters pertaining to Religion*, p. 170. Pascal, with far sounder judgment, says, on the other hand, "Il faut juger de la doctrine par les miracles, il faut juger des miracles par la doctrine. La doctrine discerne les miracles, et les miracles discernent la doctrine. Tout cela est vrai; mais cela ne se contredit pas. . . . . Jésus Christ guérit l'aveugle-né, et fit quantité de miracles au jour du sabbat, par où il aveuglait les pharisiens, qui disaient qu'il fallait juger des miracles par la doctrine." . . . . "Les pharisiens disaient: *Non est hic homo a Deo, qui sabbatum non custodit.* Les autres disaient: *Quomodo potest homo peccator hæc signa facere?* Lequel est le plus clair?"[a] In like manner Clarke observes, "'Tis indeed the miracles only, that prove the doctrine; and not the doctrine, that proves the miracle. But then in order to this end, that the miracles may prove the doctrine, 'tis always necessary to be first supposed that the doctrine be such as is in its nature capable of being proved by miracles. The doctrine must be in itself *possible* and *capable to be proved*, and then miracles will prove it to be *actually and certainly* true.[b] The judicious remarks of Archbishop Trench are to the same effect, "When we object to the use often made of these works, it is only because they have been forcibly severed from the whole complex of Christ's life and doctrine, and presented to the contemplation of men apart from these; it is only because, when on his head are 'many crowns,' one only has been singled out in proof that He is King of kings and Lord of lords. The miracles have been spoken of as though they borrowed nothing from the truths which they confirmed, but those truths everything from the miracles by which they were confirmed; when indeed the true relation is one of mutual interdependence, the miracles proving the doctrines, and the doctrines approving the miracles, and both held together for us in a blessed unity, in the person of Him who spake the words and did the works, and through the impress of highest holiness and of absolute truth and goodness, which that person leaves stamped on our souls;—so that it may be more truly said that we believe the miracles for Christ's sake, than Christ for the miracles' sake."[c]

Note V. p. 165.

Foxton, *Popular Christianity*, p. 105. On the other hand, the profound author of the *Restoration of Belief*, with a far juster estimate of the value of evidence, observes, "Remove the supernatural from the Gospels, or, in other words, reduce the evangelical histories, by aid of some unintelligible hypothesis (German-born) to the level of an inane jumble of credulity, extravagance, and myth-power (whatever this may be), and then Christianity will go to its place, as to any effective value, in relation to humanizing and bene-

---

[a] *Pensées*, Partie II. Art. xvi. § 1, 5, 10. Whatever may be thought of the evidence in behalf of the particular miracle on the occasion of which these remarks were written, the article itself is worthy of the highest praise, as a judicious statement of the religious value of miracles, supposing their actual occurrence to be proved by sufficient testimony.

[b] *Evidence of Natural and Revealed Religion*, Prop. xiv.

[c] *Notes on the Miracles of our Lord*, p. 94 (5th edition).

volent influences and enterprizes;—a place, say, a few degrees above the level of some passages in Epictetus and M. Aurelius. . . . . The Gospel is a FORCE in the world, it is a force available for the good of man, not because it is Wisdom, but because it is Power . . . . . But the momentum supplied by the Gospel is a force which disappears—which is utterly gone, gone for ever, when Belief in its authority, *as attested by miracles*, is destroyed," pp. 290, 291, 292. To the same effect are the excellent remarks with which Neander concludes his *Life of Jesus Christ*. "The end of Christ's appearance on earth corresponds to its beginning. No link in its chain of supernatural facts can be lost, without taking away its significance as a whole. Christianity rests upon these facts; stands or falls with them. By faith in them has the Divine life been generated from the beginning; by faith in them has that life in all ages regenerated mankind, raised them above the limits of earthly life, changed them from *glebæ adscripti* to citizens of heaven, and formed the stage of transition from an existence chained to nature, to a free, celestial life, far raised above it. Were this faith gone, there might, indeed, remain many of the *effects* of what Christianity had been; but as for Christianity in the true sense, as for a Christian Church, there could be none." (English Translation, p. 487.)

NOTE VI. p. 165.

Parker, *Some account of my Ministry*, appended to *Theism, Atheism, and the Popular Theology*, p. 258.

NOTE VII. p. 165.

"A doctrine may be very holy and good, and every way agreeable to the conceptions we have of God, and yet not be of Divine Revelation. The Philosophers among the Heathens uttered many such truths as might have become them, had they been really inspired; and yet we believe not, for this reason, that they *were* inspired, but that they spake merely from the dictates of their own reason and from the general consent of the wisest part of mankind; and so may any other man also, let the doctrine he teaches be never so just and holy, unless he produces somewhat beside the doctrine itself, to prove that it was revealed to him. For though the badness of any doctrine, and its disagreeableness to the eternal rules of right reason, be a certain sign that it did *not* come from God, yet the goodness of it can be no infallible proof that it did.—Atterbury, *Sermons on several Occasions*, vol. i. p. 211, ed. 1734. "But it must be premised, that from these internal proofs we do not pretend positively and directly to infer that any doctrine or system, the Scriptures of the New Testament for instance, are a Divine Revelation; but only that they may be."—Rogers, *The Necessity of Divine Revelation*, &c., Sermon III. p. 60. " As no evidence can prove a doctrine to come from God, if it be either impossible or wicked in itself; so, on the other hand, neither can any degree of goodness or excellency in the doctrine itself make it certain, but only highly probable, to have come from God, unless it has moreover some positive and direct evidence of its being actually revealed."—Clarke, *Evidence of Natural and Revealed Religion*, Prop. IX. " In my opinion, the reasonableness of a doctrine pretended to come immediately from God, is, of itself alone, no *proof*, but a *presumption* only of such its divine Original: because, though the excellence of a doctrine (even allowing it to surpass all other moral teaching whatsoever) may shew it to be worthy of God, yet from that sole *excellence* we cannot certainly conclude that it came immediately from Him; since we know not to what heights of moral knowledge the human understanding, unassisted by inspiration, may arrive."—Warburton, *Divine Legation*, B. IX. ch. 5. " Alle diese Kriterien sind die moralischen Bedingungen, unter denen allein, und ausser welchen nicht, eine solche Erscheinung von Gott, dem Begriffe einer Offenbarung gemäss, bewirkt seyn könnte; aber gar nicht umgekehrt,—die Bedingungen einer Wirkung, die bloss durch Gott diesem Begriffe gemäss bewirkt seyn könnte. Wären sie das letztere, so berechtigten sie durch Ausschliessung der Causalität aller übrigen Wesen zu dem Urtheile: das *ist* Offenbarung; da sie aber das nicht, sondern nur das erstere sind, so berechtigen sie bloss zu dem Urtheile: das *kann* Offenbarung seyn."—Fichte, *Versuch einer Kritik aller Offenbarung* (*Werke*, V. p. 146).

Note VIII. p. 166.

" Though it were to be granted that a perfect code of morality might possibly be framed by some well-educated philosopher, yet it may justly be stated to have been far beyond the power of a few unlettered fishermen of Galilee, to have invented, under those circumstances in which they were placed, that code, so pure and so sublime, which the Gospel brings before our view. The internal evidence, therefore, of the Christian religion may be sufficient to prove its superhuman origin, even though it were granted that *in other circumstances* a mere man might have invented it."—Penrose,

On the Evidence of the Scripture Miracles, p. 56. " A Revelation, *i.e.* a direct message from God to man*, itself bears in some degree a miraculous character; inasmuch as it supposes the Deity actually to present Himself before his creatures, and to interpose in the affairs of life in a way above the reach of those settled arrangements of nature to the existence of which universal experience bears witness. And as a Revelation itself, so again the Evidences of a Revelation may all more or less be considered miraculous. Prophecy is an evidence only so far as foreseeing future events is above the known powers of the human mind, or miraculous. In like manner, if the rapid extension of Christianity be urged in favour of its Divine origin, it is because such extension, under such circumstances, is supposed to be inconsistent with the known principles and capacity of human nature. And the pure morality of the Gospel, as taught by illiterate fishermen of Galilee, is an evidence, in proportion as the phenomenon disagrees with the conclusions of general experience, which leads us to believe that a high state of mental cultivation is ordinarily requisite for the production of such moral teachers. It might even be said that, strictly speaking, no evidence of a Revelation is conceivable which does not partake of the character of a Miracle; since nothing but a display of power over the existing system of things can attest the immediate presence of Him by whom it was originally established; or, again, because no event which results entirely from the ordinary operation of nature can be the criterion of one that is extraordinary."—J. H. Newman, *On the Nature and Uses of Miracles*, appended to the *Life of Apollonius Tyanæus*, in the *Encyclopædia Metropolitana*.

Note IX. p. 167.

Newman, *The Soul*, p. 58. Of a similar principle enunciated by Whitefoot in his manuscript *Dissertation on Future Punishment*, Barrow remarks, "Male applicata hæc regula totam pessundabit Theologiam" (*Works*, ed. Napier, vol. ix. p. 594).

Note X. p. 169.

Analogy, Part II. ch. 3.

Note XI. p. 173.

" Although some circumstances in the description of God's Firstborn and Elect, by whom this change is to be accomplished, may primarily apply to collective Israel, [many others will admit of no such application. Israel surely was not the child whom a virgin was to bear; Israel did not make his grave with the wicked, and with the rich in his death; Israel scarcely reconciled that strangely blended variety of suffering and triumph, which was predicted of the Messiah.]"—R. Williams, *Rational Godliness*, p. 56. In a note to this passage, the author adds, "I no longer feel confident of the assertion in brackets; but now believe that *all* the prophecies have primarily an application nearly contemporaneous." As a specimen of this application, we may cite a subsequent passage from the same volume, p. 169. " The same Isaiah sees that Israel, whom God had called out of Egypt, and whom the Eternal had denominated his first-born, trampled, captive, and derided: he sees the beauty of the sanctuary defiled, and the anointed priests of the living God degraded from their office, led as sheep to the slaughter, insulted by their own countrymen, as men smitten of God, cast off by Jehovah. Ah! he says, it is through the wickedness of the nations that Israel is thus afflicted; it is through the apostasy of the people that the priesthood is thus smitten and reviled; they hide their faces from the Lord's servant; nevertheless, no weapon that is formed against him shall prosper: it is a little thing that He should merely recover Israel, He shall also be a light to the Gentiles, and a salvation to the ends of the earth."

There are few unprejudiced readers who will not think the author's first thought on this subject preferable to his second. In the interpretation of any profane author, the perverse ingenuity which regards the Fifty-Third chapter of Isaiah (to say nothing of the other portions of the prophecy, which Dr. Williams has divorced from their context) as a description of the contemporaneous state of the Jewish people and priesthood, would be considered as too extravagant to need refutation. That such an interpretation should have found favour with thorough-going rationalists, determined at all hazards to expel the supernatural from Scripture, is only to be expected; and this may explain the adoption of this and similar views by a considerable school of expositors in Germany: but that it should have been received by those who, like Dr. Williams, hold fast the doctrine of the Incarnation of the Son of God, is less easily to be accounted for. If this greatest of all miracles be once conceded,— if it be allowed that "when the fulness of the time was come, God sent forth His Son, made of a woman;"—what marvel is it, that while the time was still incomplete, a prophet should have been divinely inspired to proclaim the future redemption? Once concede

Y

the possibility of the supernatural at all; and the Messianic interpretation is the only one reconcilable with the facts of history and the plain meaning of words. The fiction of a contemporaneous sense, whether with or without a subsequent Messianic application, is only needed to get rid of direct inspiration, and nothing is gained by getting rid of inspiration, so long as a fragment of the supernatural is permitted to remain. It is only when we assume *à priori*, that the supernatural is impossible, that anything is gained by forcing the prophetic language into a different meaning.

Note XII. p. 174.

Of this Eclectic Christianity, of which Schleiermacher may be considered as the chief modern representative, a late gifted and lamented writer has truly observed, "He could not effect the rescue of Christianity on these principles without serious loss to the object of his care. His efforts resemble the benevolent intervention of the deities of the classic legends, who, to save the nymph from her pursuer, changed her into a river or a tree. It may be that the stream and the foliage have their music and their beauty, that we may think we hear a living voice still in the whispers of the one and the murmurs of the other, yet the beauty of divine Truth, our heavenly visitant, cannot but be grievously obscured by the change, for 'the glory of the celestial is one, and the glory of the terrestrial is another.' Such ecclesiastical doctrines as contain what he regards as the essence of Christianity are received. All others, as being feelings embodied in the concrete form of dogmas, as man's objective conceptions of the divine, he considers as open to criticism. . . . Schleiermacher accounts as thus indifferent the doctrine of the Trinity, the supernatural conception of the Saviour, many of his miracles, his ascension, and several other truths of the same class. This one reply—'That doctrine makes no necessary part of our Christian consciousness,' stands solitary, like a Cocles at the bridge, and keeps always at bay the whole army of advancing queries. But surely it does constitute an essential part of our Christian consciousness whether we regard the New Testament writers as truthworthy or otherwise. If certain parts of their account are myths, and others the expression of Jewish prejudice, and we are bidden dismiss them accordingly from our faith, how are we sure that in what is left these historians were faithful, or these expositors true representatives of the mind of Christ? Our Christian consciousness is likely to become a consciousness of little else than doubt, if we give credit to the assertion,—Your sole informants on matters of eternal moment were, every here and there, misled by prejudice and imposed upon by faith."[d]

NOTE XIII. p. 175.

For the objections of modern Pantheism against the immortality of the soul, see Lecture III. note 27. Of the resurrection of the body in particular, Wegscheider observes, " Tantum vero abest ut resurrectio corporum cum sanæ rationis præceptis bene conciliari queat, ut plurimis gravissimisque impediatur difficultatibus. *Primum* enim dubitari nequit, quin hæc opinio e notionibus mancis et imperfectis hominum incultiorum originem traxerit, quippe qui, justa numinis divini idea destituti, vitam post mortem futuram e sola vitæ terrestris natura sibi fingere soleant; quo fit, ut apud complures gentes barbaras, itemque in Zoroastrica disciplina, e cujus fonte Judæi ipsi hausisse videntur, eadem illa deprehendatur. *Tum*. resurrectio corporum in ll. N. T. tradita, quæ inde ab ipsa apostolica ætate haud paucis improbata fuit, tam arcte conjuncta cernitur cum opinionibus de Messia mythicis et cum narratione de Jesu in vitam restituto, ut non alia ratione ac mythi isti judicari et explicari possit. . . . *Præterea* Deo sanctissimo benignissimoque aperte non convenit, quod homini, qui sine corpore vitam veram degere nequeat, post multa demum annorum millia hoc corpus reddere fingitur. . . . His et aliis ducti rationibus haud fere levioribus, vel Jesum, ubi doctrinam de resurrectione proposuisse perhibetur, popularium opinionibus indulsisse, vel potius discipulos ipsi tanquam Messiæ, cujus provinciam e vulgaribus Judæorum commentis atque certis ejusdem effatis allegoricis atque obscurioribus perperam judicarent, ejusmodi sententiam ex suis subjecisse censemus."[e] Concerning angels and spirits, one of the most significant specimens of modern Sadduceeism may be found in Dr. Donaldson's *Christian Orthodoxy reconciled with the conclusions of modern Biblical Learning*, p. 347 sqq. He holds with regard to intermediate Intelligences, the same view which Wegscheider suggests with regard to the Resurrection: namely, "that our Lord, in his dealings with the Jews, rather acquiesced in the established phraseology than sanctioned the prevalent superstitions."[f] He adds that " in many respects, our Lord

[d] *Essays and Remains of the Rev. Robert Alfred Vaughan*, vol. i. p. 93. Some excellent remarks on the same subject will also be found in Henry Rogers's *Essays*, vol. ii. pp. 329-334.

[e] *Institutiones Theologicæ*, § 195.
[f] P. 363. That is to say, it is boldly maintained that our Lord, in order to humour the prejudices of the Jews of that day, consented to lend His autho-

seems to have approved and recommended" the views of the Sadducees; though "he could not openly adopt a speculative truth, which was saddled with an application diametrically opposed to the cardinal verity of his religion."[g] It is obvious that, by this method of exposition, "Christian Orthodoxy" may mean anything or nothing: any doctrine which this or that expositor finds it convenient to reject, may be set aside as a concession to popular phraseology; and thus the teaching of Christ may be stripped of its most essential doctrines by men who profess all the while to believe in His immanent Divinity and Omniscience. Strauss arrives at a similar conclusion, though of course without troubling himself about Scriptural premises "Es ist also nicht genug, mit Schleiermacher, die Möglichkeit solcher Wesen, wie die Engeln sind, dahingestellt zu lassen, und nur so viel festzusetzen, dass wir weder in unserem Handeln auf sie Rücksicht zu nehmen, noch fernere Offenbarungen ihres Wesens zu erwarten haben: vielmehr, wenn die moderne Gottesidee und Weltvorstellung richtig sind, so kann es dergleichen Wesen überall nicht geben."[h] In the same spirit, Mr. Parker openly maintains that "Jesus shared the erroneous notions of the times respecting devils, possessions, and demonology in general;"[i]—a conclusion which is at least more logical and consistent than that of those who acknowledge the divine authority the Teacher, yet claim a right to reject as much as they please of his teaching.

NOTE XIV. p. 175.

Greg, *Creed of Christendom.* Preface, p. xii.

rity to the dissemination of a religious falsehood for the deception of posterity. This monstrous assertion is stated more plainly by Spinoza, *Tractatus Theologico-Polit.* c. 2. "Quod nempe suas rationes opinionibus et principiis uniuscujusque accommodavit. Ex. gr. quum Pharisæis dixit, *Et si Satanas Satanam ejicit, adversus se ipsum divisus est; quomodo igitur stare potest regnum ejus?* nihil nisi Pharisæos ex suis principiis convincere voluit, non autem docere, dari dæmones aut aliquod dæmonum regnum." In like manner, Schleiermacher (*Der Christliche Glaube,* § 42) asserts that Christ and his Apostles possibly adopted the popular representations, as we speak of fairies and ghosts. On the other side it is justly urged by Storr (*Doctrina Christiana,* § 52), that our Lord employed the same language privately with his disciples, as well as publicly with the people; *e.g.* Matt. xiii. 39, xxv. 41; Mark iv. 15; Luke xxii. 31. See also Mosheim's note, translated in Harrison's edition of Cudworth, vol. ii. p. 661; Neander, *Life of Christ,* p. 157 (Eng. Tr.); Lee, *Inspiration of Holy Scripture,* p. 69 (second edition).

[g] Pp. 372, 373.

[h] *Christliche Glaubenslehre,* § 49. To the same effect are his remarks on Evil Spirits, § 54. Among the earlier rationalists, the same view is taken by Röhr, *Briefe über den Rationalismus,* p. 35.

[i] *Discourse of matters pertaining to Religion,* p. 176.

NOTE XV. p. 175.

The theory which represents the human race as in a constant state of religious progress, and the various religions of antiquity as successive steps in the education of mankind, has been a favourite with various schools of modern philosophy. Hegel, as might naturally be expected, propounds a theory of the necessary development of religious ideas, as determined by the movements of the universal Spirit.[k] It is true that he is compelled by the stern necessities of chronology to represent the polytheism of Greece and Rome as an advance on the monotheism of Judea;[l] and perhaps, if we regard the Hegelian philosophy as the final consummation of all religious truth, this *retrograde progress* may be supported by some plausible arguments.[m] Another form of the same theory is that of Comte, who traces the progress of humanity, through Fetichism, Polytheism and Monotheism, to culminate at last in the Positive Religion, which worships the idea of humanity, including therein the auxiliary animals.[n] In theories of this kind, the distinction between progress and mere fluctuation depends upon the previous question, Whence, and Whither? What was the original state of religious knowledge in mankind, and what is the end

---

[k] See *Philosophie der Geschichte*, *Werke*, IX. p. 14. *Philosophie der Religion*, *Werke*, XI. p. 76, 78.

[l] See his *Philosophie der Religion*, *Werke*, XI. p. 82, XII. p. 45. The superiority of the Greek religion appears to consist in its greater acknowledgment of human freedom, and perhaps in being a step in the direction of Pantheism. See *Werke*, XII. 92, 125. Of the Roman Religion, he says that it contained in itself all the elements of Christianity, and was a necessary step to the latter. Its evils sprang from the depth of its spirit (XII. pp. 181, 184). The best commentary on this assertion may be found in Augustine, *De Civ. Dei*, Lib. VI.

[m] Among the *imperfections* of Judaism, Hegel includes the fact that it did not make men conscious of the identity of the human soul with the Absolute, and its absorption therein (Die Anschauung und das Bewusstseyn von der Einheit der Seele mit dem Absoluten, oder von der Aufnahme der Seele in den Schoos des Absoluten ist noch nicht erwacht, *Werke*, XII. p. 86). In another place (p. 161) he speaks of it as the religion of obstinate, dead understanding. Vatke (*Biblische Theologie*, p. 115) carries the absurdity of theory to its climax, by boldly maintaining that the later Judaism had been *elevated* by its conflict with the religions of Greece and Rome, and thus prepared to become the immediate precursor of Christianity. The Hegelian theory is also adopted by Baur, as representing the law of development of Christian doctrines. The historical aspects of the doctrine are to be regarded as phases of a process, in which the several forms are determined one by another, and all are united together in the totality of the idea. See especially his *Christliche Lehre von der Versöhnung*, p. 11, and the preface to the same work, p. vi.

[n] *Cours de Philosophie Positive*. Leçons 52, 53, 54. Compare *Catéchisme Positiviste*, pp. 31, 184, 243.

to which it is advancing? If Pantheism or Atheism is the highest form of religious truth, every step in that direction is unquestionably progressive: if otherwise, it is not progress, but corruption.

The previous question is clearly stated by Theodore Parker. "From what point did the human race set out,—from civilization and the true worship of one God, or from cannibalism and the deification of nature? Has the human race fallen or risen? The question is purely historical, and to be answered by historical witnesses. But in the presence, and still more in the absence, of such witnesses, the *à priori* doctrines of the man's philosophy affect his decision. Reasoning with no facts is as easy as all motion *in vacuo*." The analogy of the geological formation of the earth—its gradual preparation, so to say, for the reception of plants and animals, the ruder first, and then the more complex and beautiful, till at last she opens her bosom to man—this, in connection with many similar analogies, would tend to show that a similar order was to be expected in the affairs of men—development from the lower to the higher, and not the reverse. In strict accordance with this analogy, some have taught that man was created in the lowest state of savage life; his Religion the rudest worship of nature; his Morality that of the cannibal; that all of the civilized races have risen from this point, and gradually passed through Fetichism and Polytheism, before they reached refinement and true Religion. The spiritual man is the gradual development of germs latent in the natural man."[o]

It is to be regretted that Professor Jowett has partially given the sanction of his authority to a theory which it is to be presumed he would not advocate to the full extent of the above statement. "The theory of a primitive religion common to all mankind," he tells us, "has only to be placed distinctly before the mind, to make us aware that it is the baseless fabric of a vision; there is one stream of revelation only—the Jewish. But even if it were conceivable, it would be inconsistent with facts. The earliest history tells nothing of a general religion, but of particular beliefs about stocks and stones, about places and persons, about animal life, about the sun, moon, and stars, about the divine essence permeating the world, about gods in the likeness of men appearing in battles and directing the

---

[o] *Discourse of Matters pertaining to Religion*, pp. 68, 69. A similar view is advocated by Mr. Newman, *Phases of Faith*, p. 223, and by Mr. Greg, *Creed of Christendom*, p. 71. Mr. Parker does not distinctly adopt this view as his own, but he appears to regard it as preferable to the antagonist theory, which he speaks of as supported by a "party consisting more of poets and dogmatists than of philosophers."

course of states, about the world below, about sacrifices, purifications, initiations, magic, mysteries. These were the true religions of nature, varying with different degrees of mental culture or civilisation."[p] And in an earlier part of the same Essay, he says, "No one who looks at the religions of the world, stretching from east to west, through so many cycles of human history, can avoid seeing in them a sort of order and design. They are like so many steps in the education of mankind. Those countless myriads of human beings who know no other truth than that of religions coeval with the days of the Apostle, or even of Moses, are not wholly uncared for in the sight of God."[q]

It would be unfair to press these words to a meaning which they do not necessarily bear. We will assume that by the "earliest history," profane history alone is meant, in opposition to the Jewish Revelation; and that the author does not intend, as some of his critics have supposed, to deny the historical character of the Book of Genesis, and the existence of a primitive revelation coeval with the creation of man. Even with this limitation, the evidence is stated far too absolutely. But the words last quoted are, to say the least, incautious, and suggest coincidence in a favourite theory of modern philosophy, equally repugnant to Scripture and to natural religion. Two very opposite views may be taken of the false religions of antiquity. The Scriptures invariably speak of them as corruptions of man's natural reason, and abominations in the sight of God. Some modern writers delight to represent them as instruments of God's providence, and steps in the education of mankind. This view naturally belongs to that pantheistic philosophy which recognises no Deity beyond the actual constitution of the world, which acknowledges all that exists as equally divine, or, which is the same thing, equally godless; but it is irreconcilable with the belief in a personal God, and in a distinction between the good which He approves and the evil which He condemns. But men will concede much to philosophy who will concede nothing to Scripture. The sickly and sentimental morality which talks of the "ferocious" God of the popular theology,[r] which is indignant at the faith of Abraham,[s] which shudders over the destruction of the Canaanites,[t] which prides itself in discovering imperfections in the

[p] *Epistles of St. Paul*, vol. ii. p. 395.
[q] *Ibid.* p. 386.
[r] Parker, *Theism, Atheism, and the Popular Theology*, pp. 103, 104.
[s] Parker, *Discourse of Religion*, p. 214. Newman, *Phases of Faith*, p. 150.
[t] Parker, *Discourse*, p. 87. Newman, *Phases*, p. 151.

law of Moses,[a] is content to believe that the God who could not sanction these things, could yet create man with the morality of a cannibal, and the religion of a fetish-worshipper, and ordain for him a law of development through the purifying stages which marked the civilization of Egypt and Babylon and Imperial Rome. Verily this unbelieving Reason makes heavy demands on the faith of its disciples. It will not tolerate the slightest apparent anomaly in the moral government of God; but it is ready, when its theories require, to propound a scheme of deified iniquity, which it is hardly exaggeration to designate as the moral government of Satan.

We must believe, indeed, that in the darkest ages of idolatry God "left not himself without witness:" we must believe that the false religions of the world, like its other evils, are overruled by God to the purposes of His good Providence. But this does not make them the less evils and abominations in the sight of God. Those who speak of the human race as under a law of vegetable development, forget that man has, what vegetables have not, a moral sense and a free will. It is indeed impossible, in our present state of knowledge, to draw exactly the line between the sins and the misfortunes of individuals, to decide how much of each man's history is due to his own will, and how much to the circumstances in which he is placed. But though Scripture, like Philosophy, offers no complete solution of the problem of the existence of evil, it at least distinctly points out what the true solution *is not*. So long as it represents the sin of man as a fall from the state in which God originally placed him, and as a rebellion against a divine command; so long as it represents idolatry as hateful to God, and false religion as a declension towards evil, not as a progress towards good;— so long it emphatically records its protest against both the self-delusion which denies that evil exists at all, and the blasphemy which asserts that it exists by the appointment of God.

Note XVI. p. 177.

"If it have been proved and acknowledged that our principles are true (for instance, that God is perfectly veracious, and that Christian Religion hath His authority or attestation to it,) it will then be a part of absurd levity and inconsistency to question any particular proposition evidently contained therein . . . . . Our Religion then will allow (yea it invites and exhorts) an infidel to

---

[a] Parker, *Discourse*, pp. 204, 223. Greg, *Creed of Christendom*, p. 75.

consider and judge of its truth, although it will not allow a Christian to be so vain and inconstant as to doubt of any particular doctrine therein; seeing by so questioning a part, he in effect renounces the whole, and subverts the foundation of his faith; at least ceases thereby to be a steady Christian."—Barrow, *Sermons on the Creed*, Serm. XIII.

"It is an obvious snare, that many, out of such abundance of knowledge, should be tempted to forget at times this grand and simple point—that all *vital* truth is to be sought from Scripture alone. Hence that they should be tempted rather to combine systems for themselves according to some proportion and fancy of their own, than be content neither to add nor diminish anything from that which Christ and his Apostles have enjoined; to make up, as it were, a cento of doctrines and of precepts; to take from Christ what pleases them, and from other stores what pleases them (of course the best from each, as it appears to their judgment, so as to exhibit the most perfect whole); taking, *e.g.*, the blessed hope of everlasting life from JESUS CHRIST, but rejecting His atonement; or honouring highly His example of humanity, but disrobing Him of His divinity; or accepting all the comfortable things of the dispensation of the SPIRIT, but refusing its strictness and self-denials; or forming any other combination whatsoever, to the exclusion of the *entire* GOSPEL: thus inviting Christian hearers, not to the supper of the king's son, but to a sort of miscellaneous banquet of their own; 'using their liberty,' in short, 'as an occasion' to that *natural* disposition, which Christ came to correct and to repair.

"Now that by such methods, enforced by education and strengthened by the best of secondary motives, men may attain to an excellent proficiency in morals, I am neither prepared nor disposed to dispute. I am not desirous of disputing that they may possess therein an excellent religion, as opposed to Mahometanism or Paganism. But that they possess the true account to be given of their stewardship of that one talent, THE GOSPEL ITSELF, I do doubt in sorrow and in fear. I do doubt whether they 'live the life that now is,' as St. Paul lived it, 'by the faith of the SON OF GOD;' by true apprehension of the things that HE suffered for us, and of the right which HE has purchased to command us in all excellent qualities and actions; and, further, of the invisible but real assistance which he gives us towards the performance of them."— Miller, *Bampton Lectures*, p. 169 (third edition).

Note XVII. p. 178.

"Thus in the great variety of religious situations in which men are placed, what constitutes, what chiefly and peculiarly constitutes, the probation, in all senses, of some persons, may be the difficulties in which the evidence of religion is involved: and their principal and distinguished trial may be, how they will behave under and with respect to these difficulties."—Butler, *Analogy*, Part II. c. 6.

Note XVIII. p. 180.

I do not mean by these remarks to deny the possibility of any progress whatever in Christian Theology, such, for instance, as may result from the better interpretation of Holy Writ, or the refutation of unauthorized inferences therefrom. But all such developments of doctrine are admissible only when confined within the limits so carefully laid down in the sixth Article of our Church: "Holy Scripture containeth all things necessary to salvation: so that whatsoever is not read therein, nor may be proved thereby, is not to be required of any man, that it should be believed as an Article of the Faith, or be thought requisite or necessary to salvation." Within these limits the most judicious theologians have not hesitated to allow the possibility of progress, as regards at least the definite statement of Christian doctrine. Thus Bishop Butler remarks: "As it is owned the whole scheme of Scripture is not yet understood; so, if it ever comes to be understood, before the *restitution of all things*, and without miraculous interpositions; it must be in the same way as natural knowledge is come at: by the continuance and progress of learning and liberty; and by particular persons attending to, comparing, and pursuing intimations scattered up and down it, which are overlooked and disregarded by the generality of the world."[1] And a worthy successor to the name has pointed out the distinction between true and false developments of doctrine, in language based upon the same principle: "Are there *admissible developments* of doctrine in Christianity? Unquestionably there are. But let the term be understood in its legitimate sense or senses to warrant that answer; and let it be carefully observed how much, and how little, the admission really involves. All varieties of real development, so far as this argument is concerned, may probably be reduced to two general heads, *intellectual* developments,

---

[1] *Analogy*, Part II. ch. 3.

and *practical* developments, of Christian doctrine. By 'intellectual developments,' I understand *logical inferences* (and that whether for belief or practical discipline) from doctrines, or from the comparison of doctrines; which, in virtue of the great dialectical maxim, must be true, if legitimately deduced from what is true. 'Practical developments' are the *living, actual, historical results* of those true doctrines (original or inferential), when considered as influential on all the infinite varieties of human kind; the doctrines embodied in action; the doctrines modifying human nature in ways infinitely various, correspondently to the infinite variety of subjects on whom they operate, though ever strictly preserving, amid all their operations for effectually transforming and renewing mankind, their own unchanged identity . . . . In the former case, revealed doctrines may be compared with one another, or with the doctrines of 'natural religion;' or the consequences of revealed doctrines may be compared with other doctrines, or with their consequences, and so on in great variety: the combined result being what is called a System of Theology. What the first principles of Christian truth really are, or how obtained, is not now the question. But in all cases equally, no doctrine has any claim whatever to be received as obligatory on belief, unless it be either itself some duly authorized principle, or a logical deduction, through whatever number of stages, from some such principle of religion. Such only are legitimate developments of doctrine for the *belief* of man; and such alone can the Church of Christ—the Witness and Conservator of His Truth—justly commend to the consciences of her members. . . . . But in truth, as our own liability to error is extreme, especially when immersed in the holy obscurity ("the *cloud* on the mercy-seat") of such mysteries as these, we have reason to thank God that there appear to be few doctrinal developments of any importance which are not from the first drawn out and delivered on divine authority to our acceptance."[y]

It is impossible not to regret deeply the very different language, on this point, of a writer in many respects worthy of better things; but who, while retaining the essential doctrines of Christianity, has, it is to be feared, done much to unsettle the authority on which they rest. "If the destined course of the world," says Dr. Williams, "be really one of providential progress, if there has been such a thing as a childhood of humanity, and if God has been educating either a nation or a Church to understand their duty to Himself

---

[y] W. A. Butler, *Letters on the Development of Christian Doctrine*, pp. 55-58.

and to mankind; it must follow that when the fulness of light is come, there will be childish things to put away ... Hence, if the religious records represent faithfully the inner life of each generation, whether a people or a priesthood, they will all be, in St. Paul's phrase, *divinely animated,* or with a divine life running through them; and every writing, divinely animated, will be useful; yet they *may,* or rather they *must* be cast in the mould of the generation in which they were written; their words, if they are true words, will express the customs of their country, the conceptions of their times, the feelings or aspirations of their writers; and the measure of knowledge or of faith to which every one, in his degree, had attained. And the limitation, thus asserted, of their range of knowledge, will be equally true, whether we suppose the shortcoming to be, on an idea of *special* Providence, from a particular dictation of sentiment in each case; or whether, on the more reasonable view of a *general* Providence, we consider such things permitted rather than directed; the natural result of a grand scheme, rather than a minute arrangement of thoughts and words for each individual man. It may be, that the Lord writes the Bible, on the same principle as the Lord builds the city; or that He teaches the Psalmist to sing, in the same sense as He teaches his fingers to fight; thus that the composition of Scripture is attributed to the Almighty, just as sowing and threshing are said to be taught by Him; for every part played by man comes from the Divine Disposer of the scene."[z]

It is the misfortune of this sort of language, that it suggests far more than it directly asserts, and probably more than the author intends to convey. Dr. Williams probably does not mean to imply that we are no more bound by the authority of Scripture in matters of religion than by the primitive practice in sowing and threshing, or that we are as much at liberty to invent new theological doctrines as new implements of husbandry. But if he does not mean this, it is to be regretted that he has not clearly pointed out the respects in which his comparison does not hold good.

NOTE XIX. p. 180.

Summa, P. I. Qu. iii. Art. 2.

[z] *Rational Godliness,* pp. 291, 292. A similar view is maintained by Mr. Morell, *Philosophy of Religion,* p. 183, and is criticized by Professor Lee, *Inspiration of Holy Scripture,* p. 147.

NOTE XX. p. 181.

See Archbishop King's *Discourse on Predestination*, edited by Archbishop Whately, p. 10. A different, and surely a more judicious view, is taken by a contemporary Prelate of the Irish Church, whose earlier exposition of the same theory [a] probably furnished the foundation of the Archbishop's discourse. "Though," says Bishop Browne, "there are literally speaking no such passions in God as Love or Hatred, Joy or Anger, or Pity; yet there may be *Inconceivable Perfections* in Him some way *answerable* to what those passions are in us, under a due regulation and subjection to reason. It is sure that in God those perfections are not attended with any degree of natural disturbance or moral irregularity, as the passions are in us. Nay, Fear and Hope, which imply something *future* for their objects, may have nothing answerable to them in the divine Nature to which every thing is *present*. But since our reasonable affections are real dispositions of the soul which is composed of Spirit as well as Matter; we must conclude something in God *analogous* to *them*, as well as to our *Knowledge* or *Power*. For it cannot be a thought unworthy of being transferred to him, that he really *loves* a virtuous and *hates* a vicious agent; that he is *angry* at sinners; *pities* their moral infirmities; is *pleased* with their innocence or repentance, and *displeased* with their transgressions; though all these Perfections are in Him accompanied with the utmost *serenity*, and never-failing *tranquillity*."[b] With this may be compared the language of Tertullian (*Adv. Marc.* II. 16), " Quæ omnia patitur suo more, quo eum pati condecet, propter quem homo eadem patitur, æque suo more."

NOTE XXI. p. 183.

Compare the remarks of Hooker, *E. P.* I. 3, 2. "Moses, in describing the work of creation, attributeth speech unto God. . . . Was this only the intent of Moses, to signify the infinite greatness of God's power by the easiness of his accomplishing such effects, without travail, pain, or labour? Surely it seemeth that Moses had herein besides this a further purpose, namely, first to teach that

---

[a] In his Letter in answer to Toland's *Christianity not mysterious*.

[b] *Divine Analogy*, pp. 45, 46. King's Theory is also criticized more directly by the same author in the *Procedure of the Understanding*, p. 11. Mr. Davison (*Discourses on Prophecy*, p. 513) has noticed the weak points in King's explanation; but with too great a leaning to the opposite extreme, which reasons concerning the infinite as if it were a mere expansion of the finite.

God did not work as a necessary but a voluntary agent, intending beforehand and decreeing with himself that which did outwardly proceed from him: secondly, to shew that God did then institute a law natural to be observed by creatures, and therefore according to the manner of laws, the institution thereof is described, as being established by solemn injunction.

Note XXII. p. 183.

"But they urge, there can be no proportion or similitude between Finite and Infinite, and consequently there can be no analogy. That there can be no such proportion or similitude as there is between finite created Beings is granted; or as there is between any material substance and its resemblance in the glass: and therefore wherein the *Real Ground* of this analogy consists, and what the degrees of it are, is as incomprehensible as the real Nature of God. But it is such an analogy as he himself hath adapted to our intellect, and made use of in his Revelations; and therefore we are sure it hath such a foundation in the nature both of God and man, as renders our *moral* reasonings concerning him and his attributes, solid, and just, and true."—Bishop Browne, *Procedure of the Understanding*, p. 31. The practical result of this remark is, that we must rest satisfied with the belief in the analogical representation itself, without seeking to rise above it by substituting an explanation of its ulterior significance or real ground.

Note XXIII. p. 183.

I am glad to take this opportunity of expressing, in the above words, my belief in the purpose and authority of Holy Scripture; inasmuch as it enables me to correct a serious misunderstanding into which a distinguished writer has fallen in a criticism of my supposed views—a criticism to which the celebrity of the author will probably give a far wider circulation than is ever likely to fall to the lot of the small pamphlet which called it forth. Mr. Maurice, in the Preface to the second edition of his 'Patriarchs and Lawgivers of the Old Testament,' comments upon the distinction (maintained in the present Lectures and in a small previous publication) between *speculative* and *regulative* truths, in the following terms. "The notion of a revelation that tells us things which are not in themselves true, but which it is right for us to believe and to act upon as if they were true, has, I fear, penetrated very deeply into the heart of our English schools, and of our English world. It may be traced among persons who are apparently most unlike each other, who live to oppose and confute each other. . . . But their differences are not in the least likely to be adjusted by the discovery of this common ground. How the atmosphere is to be regulated by the regulative Revelation; at what degree of heat or cold this constitution or that can endure it; who must fix,—since the language of the Revelation is assumed not to be exact, not to express the very lesson which we are to derive from it,—what it does mean; by what contrivances its phrases are to be adapted to various places and times: these are questions which must, of course, give rise to infinite disputations; ever new schools and sects must be called into existence to settle them; there is scope for permissions, prohibitions, compromises, persecutions, to any extent. The despair which these must cause will probably drive numbers to ask for an infallible human voice, which shall regulate for each period that which the Revelation has so utterly failed to regulate."

Now I certainly believed, and believe still, that God is infinite, and that no human mode of thought, nor even of Revelation, if it is to be intelligible by the human mind, can represent the infinite, save under finite forms. And it is a legitimate inference from this position, that no human representation, whether derived from without or from within, from Revelation or from natural Religion, can adequately exhibit the absolute nature of God. But I cannot admit, as a further legitimate inference, that therefore " the language of the Revelation does not express the very lesson which we are to derive from it;" that it needs any regulation to adjust it to " this constitution or that;" that it requires " to be adapted to various places and times." For surely, if all men are subject to the same limitations of thought, the adaptation to their constitutions must be made already, before human interpretation can deal with the Revelation at all. It is not to the peculiarities which distinguish " this " constitution from " that," that the Revelation has to be adapted by man; but, as it is given by God, it is adapted already to the general conditions which are common to all human constitutions alike, which are equally binding in all places and at all times. I have said nothing of a revelation adapted to one man more than to another; nothing of limitations which any amount of intellect or learning can enable man to overcome. I have not said that the Bible is the teacher of the peasant rather than of the philosopher; of the Asiatic rather than of the European; of the first century rather than of the nineteenth. I have said only that it is the teacher of man as man; and that this is compatible with the possible existence of a more absolute truth in relation to beings of a higher intelligence. We must at any rate admit that man does not know God as God knows Himself; and hence that he does not know Him in the fulness of His Absolute Nature. But surely this admission is so far from implying that Revelation does not teach the very lesson which we are to derive from it, that it makes that lesson the more universal and the more authoritative. For Revelation is subject to no other limitations than those which encompass all human thought. Man gains nothing by rejecting or perverting its testimony; for the mystery of Revelation is the mystery of Reason also.

I do not wish to extend this controversy further; for I am willing to believe that, on this question at least, my own opinion is substantially one with that of my antagonist. At any rate, I approve as little as he does of allegorical, or metaphysical, or mythical interpretations of Scripture: I believe that he is generally right in maintaining that "the most literal meaning of Scripture is the most spiritual meaning." And if there are points in the details of his teaching with which I am unable to agree, I believe that they are not such as legitimately arise from the consistent application of this canon.

The above note remains as it stood in the first three editions; notwithstanding that Mr. Maurice has now indignantly rejected the proffered conciliation. His recent attack upon me, while it has convinced me that the differences between us are such as cannot be removed by any mere explanation of single passages, exhibits at the same time a tone and temper which make me comparatively indifferent about explanation or conciliation of any kind. But I retain the note in its original form; partly because it still expresses my opinion on the point in question; and partly as an evidence that Mr. Maurice's discourteous language towards me was not provoked by any previous discourtesy on my part.

Note XXIV. p. 185.

"There seems no possible reason to be given, why we may not be in a state of moral probation, with regard to the exercise of our understanding upon the subject of religion, as we are with regard to our behaviour in common affairs. . . . Thus, that religion is not intuitively true, but a matter of deduction and inference; that a conviction of its truth is not forced upon every one, but left to be, by some, collected with heedful attention to premises; this as much

constitutes religious probation, as much affords sphere, scope, opportunity, for right and wrong behaviour, as anything whatever does."
—Butler, *Analogy*, Part II. ch. 6.

Note XXV. p. 185.

Plato, *Rep.* VI. p. 486: Καὶ μὴν που καὶ τόδε δεῖ σκοπεῖν, ὅταν κρίνειν μέλλῃς φύσιν φιλόσοφόν τε καὶ μή. Τὸ ποῖον; Μή σε λάθῃ μετέχουσα ἀνελευθερίας· ἐναντιώτατον γάρ που σμικρολογία ψυχῇ μελλούσῃ τοῦ ὅλου καὶ παντὸς ἀεὶ ἐπορέξεσθαι θείου τε καὶ ἀνθρωπίνου· Cicero, *De Off.* II. 2: "Nec quidquam aliud est philosophia, si interpretari velis, quam studium sapientiæ. Sapientia autem est (ut a veteribus philosophis definitum est) rerum divinarum et humanarum, causarumque, quibus hæ res continentur, scientia."

Note XXVI. p. 185.

Plato, *Protag.* p. 343: Οὗτοι καὶ κοινῇ ξυνελθόντες ἀπαρχὴν τῆς σοφίας ἀνέθεσαν τῷ Ἀπόλλωνι ἐς τὸν νεὼν τὸν ἐν Δελφοῖς, γράψαντες ταῦτα ἃ δὴ πάντες ὑμνοῦσι, Γνῶθι σαυτὸν καὶ Μηδὲν ἄγαν. Compare Jacobi, *Werke*, IV.; Vorbericht, p. xlii.: "*Erkenne dich selbst*, ist nach dem Delphischen Gott und nach Socrates das höchste Gebot, und sobald es in Anwendung kommt, wird der Mensch gewahr: ohne göttliches Du sey kein menschliches Ich, und umgekehrt."

Note XXVII. p. 185.

Clemens Alex. *Pædag.* III. 1: Ἦν ἄρα, ὡς ἔοικε, πάντων μέγιστον μαθημάτων, τὸ γνῶναι αὑτόν. ἑαυτὸν γάρ τις ἐὰν γνῷη, Θεὸν εἴσεται.

Note XXVIII. 186.

"It is plain that there is a capacity in the nature of man, which neither riches, nor honours, nor sensual gratifications, nor any thing in this world, can perfectly fill up or satisfy: there is a deeper and more essential want, than any of these things can be the supply of. Yet surely there is a possibility of somewhat, which may fill up all our capacities of happiness; somewhat, in which our souls may find rest; somewhat, which may be to us that satisfactory good we are inquiring after. But it cannot be anything which is valuable only as it tends to some further end. . . . As our understanding can contemplate itself, and our affections be exercised upon themselves by reflection, so may each be employed in the same manner upon any other mind: and since the Supreme Mind, the Author and

Cause of all things, is the highest possible object to himself, he may be an adequate supply to all the faculties of our souls; a subject to our understanding, and an object to our affections."—Butler, Sermon XIV.

Note XXIX. p. 186.

"Christianity is not a religion for the religious, but a religion for man. I do not accept it because my temperament so disposes me, and because it meets my individual mood of mind, or my tastes. I accept it as it is suited to that moral condition in respect of which there is no difference of importance between me and the man I may next encounter on my path."—*The Restoration of Belief*, p. 325.

Note XXX. p. 186.

"The Scripture-arguments are arguments of inducement, addressed to the whole nature of man—not merely to intellectual man, but to thinking and feeling man living among his fellow-men;—and to be apprehended therefore in their *effect* on our *whole* nature."—Hampden, *Bampton Lectures*, p. 92. "There are persons who complain of the Word, because it is not addressed to some one department of the human soul, on which they set a high value. The systematic divine wonders that it is not a mere scheme of dogmatic theology, forgetting that in such a case it would address itself exclusively to the understanding. The German speculatists, on the other hand, complain that it is not a mere exhibition of the pure ideas of the true and the good, forgetting that in such a case it would have little or no influence on the more practical faculties. Others seem to regret that it is not a mere code of morality, while a fourth class would wish it to be altogether an appeal to the feelings. But the Word is inspired by the same God who formed man at first, and who knows what is in man; and he would rectify not merely the understanding or intuitions, not merely the conscience or affections, but the whole man after the image of God."—M'Cosh, *Method of the Divine Government*, p. 509.

THE END.

LONDON: PRINTED BY W. CLOWES AND SONS, DUKE STREET, STAMFORD STREET, AND CHARING CROSS.

ALBEMARLE STREET, LONDON,
September, 1868.

MR. MURRAY'S

GENERAL LIST OF WORKS.

ALBERT'S (PRINCE) SPEECHES AND ADDRESSES ON PUBLIC OCCASIONS; with an Introduction giving some Outlines of his Character. Portrait. 8vo. 10s. 6d.; or *Popular Edition*. Portrait. Fcap. 8vo. 1s.

ABBOTT'S (REV. J.) Philip Musgrave; or, Memoirs of a Church of England Missionary in the North American Colonies. Post 8vo. 2s.

ABERCROMBIE'S (JOHN) Enquiries concerning the Intellectual Powers and the Investigation of Truth. Fcap. 8vo. 6s. 6d.

——————— Philosophy of the Moral Feelings. Fcap. 8vo. 4s.

ACLAND'S (REV. CHARLES) Popular Account of the Manners and Customs of India. Post 8vo. 2s.

ÆSOP'S FABLES. A New Translation. With Historical Preface. By Rev. THOMAS JAMES. With 100 Woodcuts, by TENNIEL and WOLF. 50th *Thousand*. Post 8vo. 2s. 6d.

AGRICULTURAL (THE ROYAL) SOCIETY'S JOURNAL. 8vo. *Published half-yearly*.

AIDS TO FAITH: a Series of Theological Essays. By various Writers. Edited by WILLIAM THOMSON, D.D., Archbishop of York. 8vo. 9s.

AMBER-WITCH (THE). A most interesting Trial for Witchcraft. Translated from the German by LADY DUFF GORDON. Post 8vo. 2s.

ARMY LIST (THE). *Published Monthly by Authority*. 18mo. 1s. 6d.

ARTHUR'S (LITTLE) History of England. By LADY CALLCOTT. *New Edition, continued to* 1862. Woodcuts. Fcap. 8vo. 2s. 6d.

ATKINSON'S (MRS.) Recollections of Tartar Steppes and their Inhabitants. Illustrations. Post 8vo. 12s.

AUNT IDA'S Walks and Talks; a Story Book for Children. By a LADY. Woodcuts. 16mo. 5s.

AUSTIN'S (JOHN) LECTURES ON JURISPRUDENCE; or, the Philosophy of Positive Law. *New and Cheaper Edition*. 2 Vols. 8vo.

——————— (SARAH) Fragments from German Prose Writers. With Biographical Notes. Post 8vo. 10s.

B

BARBAULD'S (Mrs.) Hymns in Prose for Children. With 112 Original Designs. Small 4to. 5s.; or *Fine Paper*, 7s. 6d.

BARROW'S (Sir John) Autobiographical Memoir. From Early Life to Advanced Age. Portrait. 8vo. 16s.

———— (John) Life, Exploits, and Voyages of Sir Francis Drake. With numerous Original Letters. Post 8vo. 2s.

BARRY'S (Sir Charles) Life. By Alfred Barry, D.D. With Portrait, and Illustrations. Medium 8vo. 24s.

BATES' (H. W.) Records of a Naturalist on the River Amazons during eleven years of Adventure and Travel. *Second Edition.* Illustrations. Post 8vo. 12s.

BEAUCLERK'S (Lady Di) Summer and Winter in Norway. *Second Edition.* With Illustrations. Small 8vo. 6s.

BEES AND FLOWERS. Two Essays. By Rev. Thomas James. Reprinted from the "Quarterly Review." Fcap. 8vo. 1s. each.

BERTHA'S Journal during a Visit to her Uncle in England. Containing a Variety of Interesting and Instructive Information. *Seventh Edition.* Woodcuts. 12mo. 7s. 6d.

BERTRAM'S (Jas. G.) Harvest of the Sea: a Contribution to the Natural and Economic History of British Food Fishes. *Second and Cheaper Edition.* With 50 Illustrations. 8vo.

BICKMORE'S (Albert S., M.A.) Travels in the East Indian Archipelago. With Maps and Illustrations. 8vo. (*In preparation.*)

BIRCH'S (Samuel) History of Ancient Pottery and Porcelain: Egyptian, Assyrian, Greek, Roman, and Etruscan. With 200 Illustrations. 2 Vols. Medium 8vo. 42s.

BISSET'S (Andrew) History of the Commonwealth of England, from the Death of Charles I. to the Expulsion of the Long Parliament by Cromwell. Chiefly from the MSS. in the State Paper Office. 2 vols. 8vo. 30s.

BLAKISTON'S (Capt.) Narrative of the Expedition sent to explore the Upper Waters of the Yang-Tsze. Illustrations. 8vo. 18s.

BLOMFIELD'S (Bishop) Memoir, with Selections from his Correspondence. By his Son. *Second Edition.* Portrait, post 8vo. 12s.

BLUNT'S (Rev. J. J.) Undesigned Coincidences in the Writings of the Old and New Testament, an Argument of their Veracity: containing the Books of Moses. Historical and Prophetical Scriptures, and the Gospels and Acts. *Ninth Edition.* Post 8vo. 6s.

———— History of the Church in the First Three Centuries. *Third Edition.* Post 8vo. 7s. 6d.

———— Parish Priest; His Duties, Acquirements and Obligations. *Fourth Edition.* Post 8vo. 7s. 6d.

———— Lectures on the Right Use of the Early Fathers. *Second Edition.* 8vo. 15s.

———— Plain Sermons Preached to a Country Congregation. *Fifth and Cheaper Edition.* 2 Vols. Post 8vo.

———— Essays on various subjects. 8vo. 12s.

BOOK OF COMMON PRAYER. Illustrated with Coloured Borders, Initial Letters, and Woodcuts. A new edition. 8vo. 18s. cloth ; 31s. 6d. calf; 36s. morocco.

BORROW'S (GEORGE) Bible in Spain; or the Journeys, Adventures, and Imprisonments of an Englishman in an Attempt to circulate the Scriptures in the Peninsula. 3 Vols. Post 8vo. 27s.; or *Popular Edition*, 16mo, 3s. 6d.

—————— Zincali, or the Gipsies of Spain; their Manners, Customs, Religion, and Language. 2 Vols. Post 8vo. 18s.; or *Popular Edition*, 16mo, 3s. 6d.

—————— WILD WALES: its People, Language, and Scenery. *Third Edition*. With Introductory Remarks. Post 8vo. 6s.

—————— Lavengro ; The Scholar—The Gipsy—and the Priest. Portrait. 3 Vols. Post 8vo. 30s.

—————— Romany Rye; a Sequel to Lavengro. *Second Edition*. 2 Vols. Post 8vo. 21s.

BOSWELL'S (JAMES) Life of Samuel Johnson, LL.D. Including the Tour to the Hebrides. Edited by Mr. CROKER. Portraits. Royal 8vo. 10s.

BRACE'S (C. L.) History of the Races of the Old World. Post 8vo. 9s.

BRAY'S (MRS.) Life of Thomas Stothard, R.A. With Personal Reminiscences. Illustrated with Portrait and 60 Woodcuts of his chief works. 4to. 21s.

BREWSTER'S (SIR DAVID) Martyrs of Science; or, Lives of Galileo, Tycho Brahe, and Kepler. *Fourth Edition*. Fcap. 8vo. 4s. 6d.

—————— More Worlds than One. The Creed of the Philosopher and the Hope of the Christian. *Eighth Edition*. Post 8vo. 6s.

—————— Stereoscope : its History, Theory, Construction, and Application to the Arts and to Education. Woodcuts. 12mo. 5s. 6d.

—————— Kaleidoscope: its History, Theory, and Construction, with its application to the Fine and Useful Arts. *Second Edition*. Woodcuts. Post 8vo. 5s. 6d.

BRITISH ASSOCIATION REPORTS. 8vo.

York and Oxford, 1831-32, 13s. 6d.
Cambridge, 1833, 12s.
Edinburgh, 1834, 15s.
Dublin, 1835, 13s. 6d.
Bristol, 1836, 12s.
Liverpool, 1837, 16s. 6d.
Newcastle, 1838, 15s.
Birmingham, 1839, 13s. 6d
Glasgow, 1840, 15s.
Plymouth, 1841, 13s. 6d.
Manchester, 1842, 10s. 6d.
Cork, 1843, 12s.
York, 1844, 20s.
Cambridge, 1845, 12s.
Southampton, 1846, 15s.
Oxford, 1847, 18s.
Swansea, 1848, 9s.
Birmingham, 1849, 10s.

Edinburgh, 1850, 15s.
Ipswich, 1851, 16s. 6d.
Belfast, 1852, 15s.
Hull, 1853, 10s. 6d.
Liverpool, 1854, 18s.
Glasgow, 1855, 15s.
Cheltenham, 1856, 18s.
Dublin, 1857, 15s.
Leeds, 1858, 20s.
Aberdeen, 1859, 15s.
Oxford, 1860, 25s.
Manchester, 1861, 15s.
Cambridge, 1862, 20s.
Newcastle, 1863, 25s.
Bath, 1864, 18s.
Birmingham, 1865, 25s
Nottingham 1866, 21s.
Dundee, 1867, 26s.

BROUGHTON'S (Lord) Journey through Albania and other Provinces of Turkey in Europe and Asia, to Constantinople, 1809—10. *Third Edition*. Illustrations. 2 Vols. 8vo. 30s.

———————— Visits to Italy. *3rd Edition*. 2 Vols. Post 8vo. 18s.

BROWNLOW'S (Lady) Reminiscences of a Septuagenarian. From the year 1802 to 1815. *Third Edition*. Post 8vo. 7s. 6d.

BUBBLES FROM THE BRUNNEN OF NASSAU. By Sir Francis B. Head, Bart. 7th Edition, with Illustrations. Post 8vo. 7s. 6d.

BUNYAN (John) and Oliver Cromwell. Select Biographies. By Robert Southey. Post 8vo. 2s.

BURGON'S (Rev. J. W.) Christian Gentleman; or, Memoir of Patrick Fraser Tytler. *Second Edition*. Post 8vo. 9s.

———————— Letters from Rome. Post 8vo. 12s.

BURN'S (Col.) Dictionary of Naval and Military Technical Terms, English and French—French and English. *Fourth Edition*. Crown 8vo. 15s.

BUXTON'S (Charles) Memoirs of Sir Thomas Fowell Buxton, Bart. With Selections from his Correspondence. By his Son. Portrait. 8vo. 16s. Or *Popular Edition*. Fcap. 8vo. 2s. 6d.

———————— Ideas of the Day on Policy, Analysed and Arranged. *Third Edition*. 8vo. 6s.

BYRON'S (Lord) Life, Letters, and Journals. By Thomas Moore. Plates. 6 Vols. Fcap. 8vo. 18s.

———————— Life, Letters, and Journals. By Thomas Moore. Portraits. Royal 8vo. 9s.

———————— Poetical Works. *Library Edition*. Portrait. 6 Vols. 8vo. 45s.

———————— Poetical Works. Plates. 10 Vols. Fcap. 8vo. 30s.

———————— Poetical Works. 8 Vols. 24mo. 20s.

———————— Poetical Works. Plates. Royal 8vo. 9s.

———————— Poetical Works. (Pearl Edition.) Crown 8vo. 2s. 6d.

———————— Childe Harold. With 80 Engravings. Crown 8vo.

———————— Childe Harold. Vignettes. 16mo. 1s.

———————— Childe Harold. Portrait. 16mo. 6d.

———————— Childe Harold. 16mo. 2s. 6d.

———————— Tales and Poems. 24mo. 2s. 6d.

———————— Miscellaneous. 2 Vols. 24mo. 5s.

———————— Dramas and Plays. 2 Vols. 24mo. 5s.

———————— Don Juan and Beppo. 2 Vols. 24mo. 5s.

———————— Beauties. Portrait. Fcap. 8vo. 3s. 6d.

BURR'S (G. D.) Instructions in Practical Surveying, Topographical Plan Drawing, and on sketching ground without Instruments. *Fourth Edition.* Woodcuts. Post 8vo. 6s.

BUTTMAN'S LEXILOGUS; a Critical Examination of the Meaning of numerous Greek Words, chiefly in Homer and Hesiod. Translated by Rev. J. R. FISHLAKE. *Fifth Edition.* 8vo. 12s.

—— CATALOGUE OF IRREGULAR GREEK VERBS. With all the Tenses extant—their Formation, Meaning, and Usage, accompanied by an Index. Translated, with Notes, by Rev. J. R. FISHLAKE. *Fifth Edition.* Revised by Rev. E. VENABLES. Post 8vo. 6s.

CALLCOTT'S (LADY) Little Arthur's History of England. *New Edition, brought down to* 1832. With Woodcuts. Fcap. 8vo. 2s. 6d.

CAMPBELL'S (LORD) Lives of the Lord Chancellors and Keepers of the Great Seal of England. From the Earliest Times to the Death of Lord Eldon in 1838. *Fourth Edition.* 10 Vols. Crown 8vo. 6s. each.

—————— Lives of the Chief Justices of England. From the Norman Conquest to the Death of Lord Tenterden. *Second Edition.* 3 Vols. 8vo. 42s.

—————— Shakspeare's Legal Acquirements Considered. 8vo. 5s. 6d.

—————— Life of Lord Chancellor Bacon. Fcap. 8vo. 2s. 6d.

—————— (GEORGE) Modern India. A Sketch of the System of Civil Government. With some Account of the Natives and Native Institutions. *Second Edition.* 8vo. 16s.

—————— India as it may be. An Outline of a proposed Government and Policy. 8vo. 12s.

—————— (THOS.) Short Lives of the British Poets. With an Essay on English Poetry. Post 8vo. 3s. 6d.

CARNARVON'S (LORD) Portugal, Gallicia, and the Basque Provinces. From Notes made during a Journey to those Countries. *Third Edition.* Post 8vo. 3s. 6d.

—————— Recollections of the Druses of Lebanon. With Notes on their Religion. *Third Edition.* Post 8vo. 5s. 6d.

CASTLEREAGH (THE) DESPATCHES, from the commencement of the official career of the late Viscount Castlereagh to the close of his life. Edited by the MARQUIS OF LONDONDERRY. 12 Vols. 8vo. 14s. each.

CATHCART'S (SIR GEORGE) Commentaries on the War in Russia and Germany, 1812-13. Plans. 8vo. 14s.

CAVALCASELLE AND CROWE'S History of Painting in Italy, from the Second to the Sixteenth Century, from recent researches, as well as from personal inspection of the Works of Art in that Country. With 100 Illustrations. 3 Vols. 8vo. 63s.

—————— History of Painting in North Italy, including Venice, Lombardy, Padua, Vicenza, Verona, Parma, Friuli, Ferrara, and Bologna. With Illustrations. 2 Vols. 8vo. (*In preparation.*)

—————— Notices of the Lives and Works of the Early Flemish Painters. Woodcuts. Post 8vo. 12s.

CHILD (G. Chaplin, M.D.) Benedicite; or, Song of the Three Children; being Illustrations of the Power, Wisdom, and Goodness of the Creator. *New and Cheaper Edition*. Post 8vo.

CHURTON'S (Archdeacon) Gongora. An Historical Essay on the Age of Philip III. and IV. of Spain. With Translations. Portrait. 2 Vols. Small 8vo. 15s.

CICERO'S LIFE AND TIMES. With his Character viewed as a Statesman, Orator, and Friend, and a Selection from his Correspondence and Orations. By William Forsyth, Q.C. *New Edition*. With Illustrations. 8vo. 16s.

CLIVE'S (Lord) Life. By Rev. G. R. Gleig, M.A. Post 8vo. 3s. 6d.

COLCHESTER (The) PAPERS. The Diary and Correspondence of Charles Abbott, Lord Colchester, Speaker of the House of Commons, 1802-1817. Portrait. 3 Vols. 8vo. 42s.

COLERIDGE'S (Samuel Taylor) Table-Talk. *New Edition*. Portrait. Fcap. 8vo. 6s.

COLLINGWOOD'S (Cuthbert) Rambles of a Naturalist on the Shores and Waters of the China Sea. Being Observations in Natural History during a Voyage to China, Formosa, Borneo, Singapore, &c., during 1866—67. With Illustrations. 8vo. 16s.

COLONIAL LIBRARY. [See Home and Colonial Library.]

COOK'S (Canon) Sermons Preached at Lincoln's Inn Chapel, and on Special Occasions. 8vo. 9s.

COOKERY (Modern Domestic). Founded on Principles of Economy and Practical Knowledge, and adapted for Private Families. By a Lady. *New Edition*. Woodcuts. Fcap. 8vo. 5s.

CORNWALLIS (The) Papers and Correspondence during the American War,—Administrations in India,—Union with Ireland, and Peace of Amiens. *Second Edition*. 3 Vols. 8vo. 63s.

COWPER'S (Mary, Countess) Diary while Lady of the Bedchamber to Caroline Princess of Wales, 1714-20. Edited by Hon. Spencer Cowper. *Second Edition*. Portrait. 8vo. 10s. 6d.

CRABBE'S (Rev. George) Life and Poetical Works. Plates. 8 vols. Fcap. 8vo. 24s.; or Complete in 1 Vol. Plates. Royal 8vo. 7s.

CREE'S (E. D.) Portrait of the Primitive Church. Fcap. 8vo. 1s.

CROKER'S (J. W.) Progressive Geography for Children. *Fifth Edition*. 18mo. 1s. 6d.

———— Stories for Children, Selected from the History of England. *Fifteenth Edition*. Woodcuts. 16mo. 2s. 6d.

———— Boswell's Life of Johnson. Including the Tour to the Hebrides. Portraits. Royal 8vo. 10s.

———— Essays on the Early Period of the French Revolution. 8vo. 15s.

———— Historical Essay on the Guillotine. Fcap. 8vo. 1s.

CROMWELL (Oliver) and John Bunyan. By Robert Southey. Post 8vo. 2s.

CROWE'S AND CAVALCASELLE'S Notices of the Early Flemish Painters. Woodcuts. Post 8vo. 12s.

—————— History of Painting in Italy, from 2nd to 16th Century. Derived from Historical Researches as well as Inspection of the Works of Art in that Country. With 100 Illustrations. 3 Vols. 8vo. 21s. each.

—————————————————————— North Italy, including Venice, Lombardy, Padua, Vicenza, Verona, Parma, Friuli, Ferrara, and Bologna. With Illustrations. 2 Vols. 8vo. (*In preparation.*)

CUMMING'S (R. GORDON) Five Years of a Hunter's Life in the Far Interior of South Africa; with Anecdotes of the Chace, and Notices of the Native Tribes. *New Edition.* Woodcuts. Post 8vo. 5s.

CUNNINGHAM'S (ALLAN) Poems and Songs. Now first collected and arranged, with Biographical Notice. 24mo. 2s. 6d.

CURTIUS' (PROFESSOR) Student's Greek Grammar, for Colleges and the Upper Forms. Edited by DR. WM. SMITH. *Third Edition.* Post 8vo. 6s.

—————— Smaller Greek Grammar for the Middle and Lower Forms. 12mo. 3s. 6d.

CURZON'S (HON. ROBERT) ARMENIA AND ERZEROUM. A Year on the Frontiers of Russia, Turkey, and Persia. *Third Edition.* Woodcuts. Post 8vo. 7s. 6d.

—————— Visits to the Monasteries of the Levant. *Fifth Edition.* Illustrations. Post 8vo. 7s. 6d.

CUST'S (GENERAL) Warriors of the 17th Century—The Thirty Years' War—and the Civil Wars of France and England. 4 Vols. Post 8vo. 8s. each.

—————— Annals of the Wars—18th & 19th Century, 1700—1815. Compiled from the most Authentic Sources. With Maps. 9 Vols. Post 8vo. 5s. each.

DARWIN'S (CHARLES) Journal of Researches into the Natural History of the Countries visited during a Voyage round the World. Post 8vo. 9s.

—————— Origin of Species by Means of Natural Selection; or, the Preservation of Favoured Races in the Struggle for Life. *Fourth Edition, revised.* Post 8vo. 15s.

—————— Fertilization of Orchids through Insect Agency, and as to the good of Intercrossing. Woodcuts. Post 8vo. 9s.

—————— Variation of Animals and Plants under Domestication. With Illustrations. 2 Vols. 8vo. 28s.

—————— Fact and Argument for. By FRITZ MULLER. With numerous Illustrations and Additions by the Author. Translated from the German by W. S. DALLAS. 8vo. (*Nearly ready.*)

DAVIS'S (NATHAN) Visit to the Ruined Cities of Numidia and Carthaginia. Illustrations. 8vo. 16s.

—————— (SIR J. F.) Chinese Miscellanies: a Collection of Essays and Notes. Post 8vo. 6s.

DAVY'S (SIR HUMPHRY) Consolations in Travel; or, Last Days of a Philosopher. *Fifth Edition.* Woodcuts. Fcap. 8vo. 6s.

—————— Salmonia; or, Days of Fly Fishing. *Fourth Edition.* Woodcuts. Fcap. 8vo. 6s.

DELEPIERRE'S (OCTAVE) History of Flemish Literature. From the Twelfth Century. 8vo. 9s.

—— —— Historical Difficulties and Contested Events. Being Notes on some Doubtful Points of History. Post 8vo. 6s.

DENISON'S (E. B.) Life of Bishop Lonsdale, D.D. With Selections from his Writings. With Portrait. Crown 8vo. 10s. 6d.

DERBY'S (EARL OF) Translation of the Iliad of Homer into English Blank Verse. *Fifth Library Edition*, 2 vols. 8vo. 24s.; or *Seventh Edition*, with Translations from the Poets, Ancient and Modern. 2 Vols. Post 8vo. 10s.

*** Translations from the Poets, may be had separately. 8vo. 3s. 6d.

DE ROS'S (LORD) Memorials of the Tower of London. *Second Edition*. With Illustrations. Crown 8vo. 12s.

—— —— Young Officer's Companion; or, Essays on Military Duties and Qualities: with Examples and Illustrations from History. *New Edition*. Post 8vo.

DIXON'S (W. HEPWORTH) Story of the Life of Lord Bacon. *Second Edition*. Portrait. Fcap. 8vo. 7s. 6d.

DOG-BREAKING; the Most Expeditious, Certain, and Easy Method, whether great excellence or only mediocrity be required. With a Few Hints for those who Love the Dog and the Gun. By LIEUT.-GEN. HUTCHINSON. *Fourth Edition*. With 40 Woodcuts. Crown 8vo. 15s.

DOMESTIC MODERN COOKERY. Founded on Principles of Economy and Practical Knowledge, and adapted for Private Families. *New Edition*. Woodcuts. Fcap. 8vo. 5s.

DOUGLAS'S (SIR HOWARD) Life and Adventures. By S. W. FULLOM. Portrait. 8vo. 15s.

—————— Theory and Practice of Gunnery. *Fifth Edition*. Plates. 8vo. 21s.

—————— Military Bridges. *Third Edition*. Plates. 8vo. 21s.

—————— Naval Warfare with Steam. 8vo. 8s. 6d.

—————— Modern Systems of Fortification. Plans. 8vo. 12s.

DRAKE'S (SIR FRANCIS) Life, Voyages, and Exploits, by Sea and Land. By JOHN BARROW. *Third Edition*. Post 8vo. 2s.

DRINKWATER'S (JOHN) History of the Siege of Gibraltar, 1779-1783. With a Description and Account of that Garrison from the Earliest Periods. Post 8vo. 2s.

DU CHAILLU'S (PAUL B.) EQUATORIAL AFRICA, with Accounts of the Gorilla, the Nest-building Ape, Chimpanzee, Crocodile, &c. Illustrations. 8vo. 21s.

—————————— Journey to Ashango Land; and Further Penetration into Equatorial Africa. Illustrations. 8vo. 21s.

DUFFERIN'S (LORD) Letters from High Latitudes; an Account of a Yacht Voyage to Iceland, Jan Mayen, and Spitzbergen. *Fifth Edition*. Woodcuts. Post 8vo. 7s. 6d.

DYER'S (THOS. H.) History of Modern Europe, from the taking of Constantinople by the Turks to the close of the War in the Crimea. 4 Vols. 8vo.

EASTLAKE'S (SIR CHARLES) Italian Schools of Painting. From the German of KUGLER. Edited, with Notes. *Third Edition*. Illustrated from the Old Masters. 2 Vols. Post 8vo. 30s.

EDWARDS' (W. H.) Voyage up the River Amazon, including a Visit to Para. Post 8vo. 2s.

ELDON'S (LORD) Public and Private Life, with Selections from his Correspondence and Diaries. By HORACE TWISS. *Third Edition*. Portrait. 2 Vols. Post 8vo. 21s.

ELLESMERE'S (LORD) Two Sieges of Vienna by the Turks. Translated from the German. Post 8vo. 2s.

ELLIS'S (W.) Visits to Madagascar, including a Journey to the Capital, with notices of Natural History, and Present Civilisation of the People. *Fifth Thousand*. Map and Woodcuts. 8vo. 16s.

—— Madagascar Revisited. Setting forth the Persecutions and Heroic Sufferings of the Native Christians. Illustrations. 8vo. 10s.

—— (MRS.) Education of Character, with Hints on Moral Training. Post 8vo. 7s. 6d.

ELPHINSTONE'S (HON. MOUNTSTUART) History of India—the Hindoo and Mahomedan Periods. *Fifth Edition*. Map. 8vo. 18s.

ENGEL'S (CARL) Music of the Most Ancient Nations; particularly of the Assyrians, Egyptians, and Hebrews; with Special Reference to the Discoveries in Western Asia and in Egypt. With 100 Illustrations. 8vo. 16s.

ENGLAND (HISTORY OF) from the Peace of Utrecht to the Peace of Versailles, 1713—83. By LORD MAHON (now Earl Stanhope). *Library Edition*, 7 Vols. 8vo. 93s.; or *Popular Edition*, 7 Vols. Post 8vo. 35s.

—————— From the First Invasion by the Romans. By Mrs. MARKHAM. *New and Cheaper Edition, continued to 1863*. Woodcuts. 12mo. 4s.

—————— From the Invasion of Julius Cæsar to the Revolution of 1688. By DAVID HUME. Corrected and continued to 1858. Edited by WM. SMITH, LL.D. Woodcuts. Post 8vo. 7s. 6d.

—————— (Smaller History of). By WM. SMITH, LL.D. *New Edition, continued to 1865*. Woodcuts. 18mo. 3s. 6d.

—————— Little Arthur's. By LADY CALLCOTT. *New Edition, continued to 1862*. Woodcuts. 18mo. 2s. 6d.

ENGLISHWOMAN IN AMERICA. Post 8vo. 10s. 6d.

ESKIMAUX and English Vocabulary, for Travellers in the Arctic Regions. 16mo. 3s. 6d.

ESSAYS FROM "THE TIMES." Being a Selection from the LITERARY PAPERS which have appeared in that Journal. 2 vols. Fcap. 8vo. 8s.

ETHNOLOGICAL SOCIETY'S TRANSACTIONS. New Series. Vols. I. to VI. 8vo. 10s. 6d. each.

EXETER'S (BISHOP OF) Letters to Charles Butler, on his Book of the Roman Catholic Church. *New Edition*. Post 8vo. 6s.

FAMILY RECEIPT-BOOK. A Collection of a Thousand Valuable and Useful Receipts. Fcap. 8vo. 5s. 6d.

FARRAR'S (A. S.) Critical History of Free Thought in reference to the Christian Religion. Being the Bampton Lectures, 1862. 8vo. 16s.

―――― (F. W.) Origin of Language, based on Modern Researches. Fcap. 8vo. 5s.

FERGUSSON'S (JAMES) Palaces of Nineveh and Persepolis Restored. Woodcuts. 8vo. 16s.

―――――― History of Architecture in all Countries: from the Earliest Times to the Present Day. With 1200 Illustrations and an Index. Vols. I. and II. 8vo. 42s. each.

―――――― History of Architecture. Vol. III.—The Modern Styles. With 312 Illustrations, and an Index. 8vo. 31s. 6d.

―――――― Holy Sepulchre and the Temple at Jerusalem; being the Substance of Two Lectures delivered at the Royal Institution, 1862 and '65. Woodcuts. 8vo. 7s. 6d.

FISHER'S (REV. GEORGE) Elements of Geometry, for the Use of Schools. *Fifth Edition.* 18mo. 1s. 6d.

―――― First Principles of Algebra, for the Use of Schools. *Fifth Edition.* 18mo. 1s. 6d.

FLEMING (WM.) Student's Manual of Moral Philosophy. Post 8vo. 7s. 6d.

FLOWER GARDEN (THE). By REV. THOS. JAMES. Fcap. 8vo. 1s.

FONNEREAU'S (T. G.) Diary of a Dutiful Son. Fcap. 8vo. 4s. 6d.

FORBES' (C. S.) Iceland; its Volcanoes, Geysers, and Glaciers. Illustrations. Post 8vo. 14s.

FORSTER'S (JOHN) Arrest of the Five Members by Charles the First. A Chapter of English History re-written. Post 8vo.

―――――― Grand Remonstrance, 1641. With an Essay on English freedom under the Plantagenet and Tudor Sovereigns. *Second Edition.* Post 8vo. 12s.

―――――― Sir John Eliot: a Biography, 1590—1632. With Portraits. 2 Vols. Crown 8vo. 30s.

―――――― Biographies of Oliver Cromwell, Daniel De Foe, Sir Richard Steele, Charles Churchill, Samuel Foote. *Third Edition.* Post 8vo. 12s.

FORD'S (RICHARD) Gatherings from Spain. Post 8vo. 3s. 6d.

FORSYTH'S (WILLIAM) Life and Times of Cicero. With Selections from his Correspondence and Orations. *New Edition.* Illustrations. 8vo. 16s.

FORTUNE'S (ROBERT) Narrative of Two Visits to the Tea Countries of China, 1843-52. *Third Edition.* Woodcuts. 2 Vols. Post 8vo. 18s.

―――― Third Visit to China. 1853-6. Woodcuts. 8vo. 16s.

―――――― Yedo and Peking. With Notices of the Agriculture and Trade of China, during a Fourth Visit to that Country. Illustrations. 8vo. 16s.

FOSS' (Edward) Judges of England. With Sketches of their Lives, and Notices of the Courts at Westminster, from the Conquest to the Present Time. 9 Vols. 8vo. 126s.

———— Tabulæ Curiales; or, Tables of the Superior Courts of Westminster Hall. Showing the Judges who sat in them from 1066 to 1864; with the Attorney and Solicitor Generals of each reign. To which is prefixed an Alphabetical List of all the Judges during the same period. 8vo. 10s. 6d.

FRANCE (HISTORY OF). From the Conquest by the Gauls. By Mrs. MARKHAM. *New and Cheaper Edition, continued to* 1856. Woodcuts. 12mo. 4s.

———— From the Earliest Times to the Establishment of the Second Empire, 1852. By W. H. PEARSON. Edited by WM. SMITH, LL.D. Woodcuts. Post 8vo. 7s. 6d.

FRENCH (THE) in Algiers; The Soldier of the Foreign Legion— and the Prisoners of Abd-el-Kadir. Translated by Lady DUFF GORDON. Post 8vo. 2s.

FRERE'S (M.) Old Deccan Days; or, Hindoo Fairy Legends Current in Southern India. Collected from Oral Tradition. Illustrated by C. F. FRERE. With an Introduction and Notes, by SIR BARTLE FRERE. Crown 8vo. 12s.

GALTON'S (FRANCIS) Art of Travel; or, Hints on the Shifts and Contrivances available in Wild Countries. *Fourth Edition.* Woodcuts. Post 8vo. 7s. 6d.

GEOGRAPHY (ANCIENT). By Rev. W. L. BEVAN. Woodcuts. Post 8vo. 7s. 6d.

———— (MODERN). By Rev. W. L. BEVAN. Woodcuts. Post 8vo. *In the Press.*

———— Journal of the Royal Geographical Society of London. 8vo.

GERMANY (HISTORY OF). From the Invasion by Marius, to Recent times. By Mrs. MARKHAM. *New and Cheaper Edition.* Woodcuts. 12mo. 4s.

GIBBON'S (EDWARD) History of the Decline and Fall of the Roman Empire. *A New Edition.* Preceded by his Autobiography. And Edited, with Notes, by Dr. WM. SMITH. Maps. 8 Vols. 8vo. 60s.

———— (The Student's Gibbon); Being an Epitome of the above work, incorporating the Researches of Recent Commentators. By Dr. WM. SMITH. Woodcuts. Post 8vo. 7s. 6d.

GIFFARD'S (EDWARD) Deeds of Naval Daring; or, Anecdotes of the British Navy. Fcap. 8vo. 3s. 6d.

GLADSTONE'S (W. E.) Financial Statements of 1853, 60, 63, and 64; with Speeches on Tax-Bills and Charities. *Second Edition.* 8vo. 12s.

———— Speeches on Parliamentary Reform. *Third Edition.* Post 8vo. 5s.

GLEIG'S (G. R.) Campaigns of the British Army at Washington and New Orleans. Post 8vo. 2s.

———— Story of the Battle of Waterloo. Post 8vo. 3s. 6d.

———— Narrative of Sale's Brigade in Affghanistan. Post 8vo. 2s.

———— Life of Robert Lord Clive. Post 8vo. 3s. 6d.

———— Sir Thomas Munro. Post 8vo. 3s. 6d.

GOLDSMITH'S (OLIVER) Works. A New Edition. Edited with Notes by PETER CUNNINGHAM. Vignettes. 4 Vols. 8vo. 30s.

GONGORA; An Historical Essay on the Times of Philip III. and IV. of Spain. With Illustrations. By ARCHDEACON CHURTON. Portrait. 2 vols. Post 8vo. 15s.

GORDON'S (SIR ALEX. DUFF) Sketches of German Life, and Scenes from the War of Liberation. From the German. Post 8vo. 3s. 6d.

——————— (LADY DUFF) Amber-Witch: A Trial for Witchcraft. From the German. Post 8vo. 2s.

——————— French in Algiers. 1. The Soldier of the Foreign Legion. 2. The Prisoners of Abd-el-Kadir. From the French. Post 8vo. 2s.

GOUGER'S (HENRY) Personal Narrative of Two Years' Imprisonment in Burmah. *Second Edition.* Woodcuts. Post 8vo. 12s.

GRAMMARS (LATIN and GREEK). See CURTIUS; SMITH; KING EDWARD VITH., &c. &c.

GREECE (HISTORY OF). From the Earliest Times to the Roman Conquest. By WM. SMITH, LL.D. Woodcuts. Post 8vo. 7s. 6d.

——————— (SMALLER HISTORY OF). By WM. SMITH, LL.D. Woodcuts. 16mo. 3s. 6d.

GRENVILLE (THE) PAPERS. Being the Public and Private Correspondence of George Grenville, including his PRIVATE DIARY. Edited by W. J. SMITH. 4 Vols. 8vo. 16s. each.

GREY'S (EARL) Correspondence with King William IVth. and Sir Herbert Taylor, from November, 1830, to the Passing of the Reform Act in 1832. 2 Vols. 8vo. 30s.

——————— Parliamentary Government and Reform; with Suggestions for the Improvement of our Representative System. *Second Edition.* 8vo. 9s.

——————— (SIR GEORGE) Polynesian Mythology, and Ancient Traditional History of the New Zealand Race. Woodcuts. Post 8vo. 10s. 6d.

GRUNER'S (LEWIS) Terra-Cotta Architecture of North Italy, From careful Drawings and Restorations. With Illustrations, engraved and printed in Colours. Small folio. 5l. 5s.

GROTE'S (GEORGE) History of Greece. From the Earliest Times to the close of the generation contemporary with the death of Alexander the Great. *Fourth Edition.* Maps. 8 Vols. 8vo. 112s.

——————— PLATO, and the other Companions of Socrates. *Second Edition.* 3 Vols. 8vo. 45s.

——————— (MRS.) Memoir of Ary Scheffer. Post 8vo. 8s. 6d.

GUIZOT'S (M.) Meditations on Christianity, and on the Religious Questions of the Day. Part I. The Essence. Part II. The Present State. 2 Vols. Post 8vo. 20s.

——————— Meditations on Christianity. Part III. Its Relation to the State of Society and Progress of the Human Mind. Post 8vo. (*Nearly Ready.*)

HALLAM'S (HENRY) Constitutional History of England, from the Accession of Henry the Seventh to the Death of George the Second. *Seventh Edition.* 3 Vols. 8vo. 30s.

————— History of Europe during the Middle Ages. *Tenth Edition.* 3 Vols. 8vo. 30s.

————— The Student's Hallam. An Epitome of the History of Europe during the Middle Ages. With Additional Notes and Illustrations. By WM. SMITH, LL.D. Post 8vo. Uniform with the "Student's Hume." (*In Preparation.*)

————— Literary History of Europe, during the 15th, 16th and 17th Centuries. *Fourth Edition.* 3 Vols. 8vo. 36s.

————— Historical Works. Containing History of England,—Middle Ages of Europe,—Literary History of Europe. 10 Vols. Post 8vo. 6s. each.

————— (ARTHUR) Remains; in Verse and Prose. With Preface, Memoir, and Portrait. Fcap. 8vo. 7s. 6d.

HAMILTON'S (JAMES) Wanderings in North Africa. With Illustrations. Post 8vo. 12s.

HANNAH'S (REV. DR.) Bampton Lectures for 1863; the Divine and Human Elements in Holy Scripture. 8vo. 10s. 6d.

HART'S ARMY LIST. (*Quarterly and Annually.*) 8vo.

HAY'S (J. H. DRUMMOND) Western Barbary, its Wild Tribes and Savage Animals. Post 8vo. 2s.

HEAD'S (SIR FRANCIS) Horse and his Rider. Woodcuts. Post 8vo. 5s.

————— Rapid Journeys across the Pampas. Post 8vo. 2s.

————— Bubbles from the Brunnen of Nassau. Illustrations. Post 8vo. 7s. 6d.

————— Emigrant. Fcap. 8vo. 2s. 6d.

————— Stokers and Pokers; or, the London and North Western Railway. Post 8vo. 2s.

————— (SIR EDMUND) Shall and Will; or, Future Auxiliary Verbs. Fcap. 8vo. 4s.

HEBER'S (BISHOP) Journey through the Upper Provinces of India, from Calcutta to Bombay, with an Account of a Journey to Madras and the Southern Provinces. *Twelfth Edition.* 2 Vols. Post 8vo. 7s.

————— Poetical Works, including Palestine, Europe, The Red Sea, Hymns, &c. *Sixth Edition.* Portrait. Fcap. 8vo. 6s.

————— Hymns adapted to the Weekly Church Service of the Year. 16mo. 1s. 6d.

HERODOTUS. A New English Version. Edited, with Notes and Essays, historical, ethnographical, and geographical, by Rev. G. RAWLINSON, assisted by SIR HENRY RAWLINSON and SIR J. G. WILKINSON. *Second Edition.* Maps and Woodcuts. 4 Vols. 8vo. 48s.

FOREIGN HANDBOOKS.

HAND-BOOK—TRAVEL-TALK. English, French, German, and Italian. 18mo. 3s. 6d.

———————— NORTH GERMANY,—HOLLAND, BELGIUM, PRUSSIA, and the Rhine from Holland to Switzerland. Map. Post 8vo. 10s.

———————— SOUTH GERMANY, Bavaria, Austria, Styria, Salzberg, the Austrian and Bavarian Alps, the Tyrol, Hungary, and the Danube, from Ulm to the Black Sea. Map. Post 8vo. 10s.

———————— KNAPSACK GUIDE TO THE TYROL. Post 8vo. 6s.

———————— PAINTING. German, Flemish, and Dutch Schools. Woodcuts. 2 Vols. Post 8vo. 24s.

———————— LIVES OF THE EARLY FLEMISH PAINTERS. By CROWE and CAVALCASELLE. Illustrations. Post 8vo. 12s.

———————— SWITZERLAND, Alps of Savoy, and Piedmont. Maps. Post 8vo. 10s.

———————— KNAPSACK GUIDE TO SWITZERLAND. Post 8vo. 5s.

———————— FRANCE, Normandy, Brittany, the French Alps, the Rivers Loire, Seine, Rhone, and Garonne, Dauphiné, Provence, and the Pyrenees. Maps. Post 8vo. 12s.

———————— CORSICA and SARDINIA. Maps. Post 8vo. 4s.

———————— PARIS, and its Environs. Map and Plans. Post 8vo. 3s. 6d.

*** MURRAY'S PLAN OF PARIS, mounted on canvas. 3s 6d.

———————— SPAIN, Andalusia, Ronda, Granada, Valencia, Catalonia, Gallicia, Arragon, and Navarre. Maps. Post 8vo. (In the Press.)

———————— PORTUGAL, LISBON, &c. Map. Post 8vo. 9s.

———————— NORTH ITALY, Piedmont, Liguria, Venetia, Lombardy, Parma, Modena, and Romagna. Map. Post 8vo. 12s.

———————— CENTRAL ITALY, Lucca, Tuscany, Florence, The Marches, Umbria, and the Patrimony of St. Peter's. Map. Post 8vo. 10s.

———————— ROME AND ITS ENVIRONS. Map. Post 8vo. 9s.

———————— SOUTH ITALY, Two Sicilies, Naples, Pompeii, Herculaneum, and Vesuvius. Map. Post 8vo. 10s.

———————— KNAPSACK GUIDE TO ITALY. Post 8vo. 6s.

———————— SICILY, Palermo, Messina, Catania, Syracuse, Etna, and the Ruins of the Greek Temples. Map. Post 8vo. 12s.

———————— PAINTING. The Italian Schools. Edited by Sir CHARLES EASTLAKE, R.A. Woodcuts. 2 Vols. Post 8vo. 30s.

———————— LIVES OF ITALIAN PAINTERS, FROM CIMABUE to BASSANO. By Mrs. JAMESON. Portraits. Post 8vo. 10s. 6d.

———————— DENMARK, SWEDEN, and NORWAY. New Edition. Maps. Post 8vo. (In Preparation.)

HAND-BOOK—KNAPSACK GUIDE TO NORWAY. Map. Post 8vo. 5s.

——————— GREECE, the Ionian Islands, Albania, Thessaly, and Macedonia. Maps. Post 8vo. (*In preparation.*)

——————— TURKEY, Malta, Asia Minor, Constantinople, Armenia, Mesopotamia, &c. Maps. Post 8vo. (*In preparation.*)

——————— EGYPT, Thebes, the Nile, Alexandria, Cairo, the Pyramids, Mount Sinai, &c. Map. Post 8vo. 15s.

——————— HOLY LAND—SYRIA AND PALESTINE, Peninsula of Sinai, Edom, and Syrian Desert. Maps. 2 Vols. Post 8vo. 24s.

——————— INDIA.— BOMBAY AND MADRAS. Map. 2 Vols. Post. 8vo. 24s.

——————— RUSSIA, ST. PETERSBURGH, MOSCOW, POLAND, and FINLAND. Maps. Post 8vo. 15s.

ENGLISH HANDBOOKS.

HAND-BOOK—MODERN LONDON. Map. 16mo. 3s. 6d.

——————— WESTMINSTER ABBEY. Woodcuts. 16mo. 1s.

——————— KENT AND SUSSEX, Canterbury, Dover, Ramsgate, Sheerness, Rochester, Chatham, Woolwich, Brighton, Chichester, Worthing, Hastings, Lewes, Arundel, &c. Map. Post 8vo. 10s.

——————— SURREY AND HANTS, Kingston, Croydon, Reigate, Guildford, Winchester, Southampton, Portsmouth, and ISLE OF WIGHT. Maps. Post 8vo. 10s.

——————— WILTS, DORSET, AND SOMERSET, Salisbury, Chippenham, Weymouth, Sherborne, Wells, Bath, Bristol, Taunton, &c. Map. Post 8vo.

——————— DEVON AND CORNWALL, Exeter, Ilfracombe, Linton, Sidmouth, Dawlish, Teignmouth, Plymouth, Devonport, Torquay, Launceston, Truro, Penzance, Falmouth, &c. Maps. Post 8vo. 10s.

——————— BERKS, BUCKS, AND OXON, Windsor, Eton, Reading, Aylesbury, Uxbridge, Wycombe, Henley, the City and University of Oxford, and the Descent of the Thames. Map. Post 8vo. 7s. 6d.

——————— GLOUCESTER, HEREFORD, AND WORCESTER Cirencester, Cheltenham, Stroud, Tewkesbury, Leominster, Ross, Malvern, Kidderminster, Dudley, Bromsgrove, Evesham, Map. Post 8vo. 6s. 6d.

——————— CATHEDRALS OF GLOUCESTER, HEREFORD and WORCESTER. Illustrations. 2s. 6d. each, or in 1 Vol., Post 8vo. 8s. 6d.

——————— NORTH AND SOUTH WALES, Bangor, Carnarvon, Beaumaris, Snowdon, Conway, Menai Straits, Carmarthen, Pembroke, Tenby, Swansea, The Wye, &c. Maps. 2 Vols. Post 8vo. 12s.

——————— DERBY, NOTTS, LEICESTER, AND STAFFORD, Matlock, Bakewell, Chatsworth, The Peak, Buxton, Hardwick, Dove Dale, Ashborne, Southwell, Mansfield, Retford, Burton, Belvoir, Melton Mowbray, Wolverhampton, Lichfield, Walsall, Tamworth. Map. Post 8vo. 7s. 6d.

——————— YORKSHIRE, Doncaster, Hull, Selby, Beverley, carborough, Whitby, Harrogate, Ripon, Leeds, Wakefield, Bradford, Halifax, Huddersfield, Sheffield. Map and Plans. Post 8vo. 12s.

HAND-BOOK—DURHAM AND NORTHUMBERLAND, Newcastle, Darlington, Gateshead, Bishop Auckland, Stockton, Hartlepool, Sunderland, Shields, Berwick-on-Tweed, Morpeth, Tynemouth, Coldstream, Alnwick, &c. Map. Post 8vo. 9s.

———— WESTMORLAND AND CUMBERLAND—Lancaster, Furness Abbey, Ambleside, Kendal, Windermere, Coniston, Keswick, Grasmere, Carlisle, Cockermouth, Penrith, Appleby. Map. Post 8vo. 6s.

*** MURRAY'S MAP OF THE LAKES, on canvas. 3s. 6d.

———— EASTERN COUNTIES, Essex, Suffolk, Norfolk, and Cambridge. Map. Post 8vo. (*In the Press.*)

———— SCOTLAND, Edinburgh, Melrose, Kelso, Glasgow, Dumfries, Ayr, Stirling, Arran, The Clyde, Oban, Inverary, Loch Lomond, Loch Katrine and Trossachs, Caledonian Canal, Inverness, Perth, Dundee, Aberdeen, Braemar, Skye, Caithness, Ross, Sutherland, &c. Maps and Plans. Post 8vo. 9s.

———— IRELAND, Dublin, Belfast, Donegal, Galway, Wexford, Cork, Limerick, Waterford, the Lakes of Killarney, Coast of Munster, &c. Maps. Post 8vo. 12s.

———— EASTERN CATHEDRALS, Oxford, Peterborough, Norwich, Ely, and Lincoln. With 90 Illustrations. Crown 8vo. 18s.

———— SOUTHERN CATHEDRALS, Winchester, Salisbury, Exeter, Wells, Chichester, Rochester, Canterbury. With 110 Illustrations. 2 Vols. Crown 8vo. 24s.

———— WESTERN CATHEDRALS, Bristol, Gloucester, Hereford, Worcester, and Lichfield. With 50 Illustrations. Crown 8vo. 16s.

———— NORTHERN CATHEDRALS, York, Ripon, Durham, Carlisle, Chester, and Manchester. With Illustrations. Crown 8vo. (*In preparation.*)

HAND-BOOK OF FAMILIAR QUOTATIONS. From English Authors. *Third Edition.* Fcap. 8vo. 5s.

HESSEY (REV. DR.). Sunday—Its Origin, History, and Present Obligations. Being the Bampton Lectures for 1860. *Second Edition.* 8vo. 16s. Or *Popular Edition.* Post 8vo. 9s.

HICKMAN'S (WM.) Treatise on the Law and Practice of Naval Courts-Martial. 8vo. 10s. 6d.

HOLLWAY'S (J. G.) Month in Norway. Fcap. 8vo. 2s.

HONEY BEE (THE). An Essay. By REV. THOMAS JAMES. Reprinted from the "Quarterly Review." Fcap. 8vo. 1s.

HOOK'S (DEAN) Church Dictionary. *Ninth Edition.* 8vo. 16s.

———— (THEODORE) Life. By J. G. LOCKHART. Fcap. 8vo. 1s.

HOPE'S (A. J. B.) English Cathedral of the Nineteenth Century. With Illustrations. 8vo. 12s.

HOPE'S (T. C.) ARCHITECTURE OF AHMEDABAD, with Historical Sketch and Architectural Notes by T. C. HOPE, and JAMES FERGUSSON, F.R.S. With 2 Maps, 120 Photographs, and 22 Woodcuts. 4to. 5l. 5s.

———— BEJAPOOR, with Historical Sketch and Architectural Essay by Col. MEADOWS TAYLOR and JAS. FERGUSSON. With 2 Maps, 78 Photographs, and 13 Woodcuts. Folio. 10l. 10s.

———— DHARWAR and MYSORE. With Historical Sketch and Architectural Essay by Col. MEADOWS TAYLOR and JAS. FERGUSSON. With 2 Maps, 100 Photographs, and numerous Woodcuts. Folio. 12l. 12s.

HOME AND COLONIAL LIBRARY. A Series of Works adapted for all circles and classes of Readers, having been selected for their acknowledged interest and ability of the Authors. Post 8vo Published at 2s. and 3s. 6d. each, and arranged under two distinctive heads as follows:—

CLASS A.
HISTORY, BIOGRAPHY, AND HISTORIC TALES.

1. SIEGE OF GIBRALTAR. By JOHN DRINKWATER. 2s.
2. THE AMBER-WITCH. By LADY DUFF GORDON. 2s.
3. CROMWELL AND BUNYAN. By ROBERT SOUTHEY. 2s.
4. LIFE OF SIR FRANCIS DRAKE. By JOHN BARROW. 2s.
5. CAMPAIGNS AT WASHINGTON. By REV. G. R. GLEIG. 2s.
6. THE FRENCH IN ALGIERS. By LADY DUFF GORDON. 2s.
7. THE FALL OF THE JESUITS. 2s.
8. LIVONIAN TALES. 2s.
9. LIFE OF CONDE. By LORD MAHON. 3s. 6d.
10. SALE'S BRIGADE. By REV. G. R. GLEIG. 2s.
11. THE SIEGES OF VIENNA. By LORD ELLESMERE. 2s.
12. THE WAYSIDE CROSS. By CAPT. MILMAN. 2s.
13. SKETCHES OF GERMAN LIFE. By SIR A. GORDON. 3s. 6d.
14. THE BATTLE OF WATERLOO. By REV. G. R. GLEIG. 3s. 6d.
15. AUTOBIOGRAPHY OF STEFFENS. 2s.
16. THE BRITISH POETS. By THOMAS CAMPBELL. 3s. 6d.
17. HISTORICAL ESSAYS. By LORD MAHON. 3s. 6d.
18. LIFE OF LORD CLIVE. By REV. G. R. GLEIG. 3s. 6d.
19. NORTH - WESTERN RAILWAY. By SIR F. B. HEAD. 2s.
20. LIFE OF MUNRO. By REV. G. R. GLEIG. 3s. 6d.

CLASS B.
VOYAGES, TRAVELS, AND ADVENTURES.

1. BIBLE IN SPAIN. By GEORGE BORROW. 3s. 6d.
2. GIPSIES OF SPAIN. By GEORGE BORROW. 3s. 6d.
3 & 4. JOURNALS IN INDIA. By BISHOP HEBER. 2 Vols. 7s.
5. TRAVELS IN THE HOLY LAND. By IRBY and MANGLES. 2s.
6. MOROCCO AND THE MOORS. By J. DRUMMOND HAY. 2s.
7. LETTERS FROM THE BALTIC. By a LADY. 2s.
8. NEW SOUTH WALES. By MRS. MEREDITH. 2s.
9. THE WEST INDIES. By M. G. LEWIS. 2s.
10. SKETCHES OF PERSIA. By SIR JOHN MALCOLM. 3s. 6d.
11. MEMOIRS OF FATHER RIPA. 2s.
12. 13. TYPEE AND OMOO. By HERMANN MELVILLE. 2 Vols. 7s.
14. MISSIONARY LIFE IN CANADA. By REV. J. ABBOTT. 2s.
15. LETTERS FROM MADRAS. By a LADY. 2s.
16. HIGHLAND SPORTS. By CHARLES ST. JOHN. 3s. 6d.
17. PAMPAS JOURNEYS. By SIR F. B. HEAD. 2s.
18 GATHERINGS FROM SPAIN. By RICHARD FORD. 3s. 6d.
19. THE RIVER AMAZON. By W. H. EDWARDS. 2s.
20. MANNERS & CUSTOMS OF INDIA. By REV. C. ACLAND. 2s.
21. ADVENTURES IN MEXICO. By G. F. RUXTON. 3s. 6d.
22. PORTUGAL AND GALLICIA. By LORD CARNARVON. 3s. 6d.
23. BUSH LIFE IN AUSTRALIA. By REV. H. W. HAYGARTH. 2s.
24. THE LIBYAN DESERT. By BAYLE ST. JOHN. 2s.
25. SIERRA LEONE. By a LADY. 3s. 6d.

*** Each work may be had separately.

HORACE (WORKS OF.) Edited by DEAN MILMAN. With 100 Woodcuts. Crown 8vo. 7s. 6d.
——— (Life of). By DEAN MILMAN. Woodcuts, and coloured Borders. 8vo. 9s.
HOUGHTON'S (LORD) Poetical Works. Fcap. 8vo. 6s.
HUME (THE STUDENT'S) A History of England, from the Invasion of Julius Cæsar to the Revolution of 1688. Corrected and continued to 1858. Edited by DR. WM. SMITH. Woodcuts. Post 8vo. 7s. 6d.
HUTCHINSON (GEN.) on the most expeditious, certain, and easy Method of Dog-Breaking. *Fourth Edition*. Enlarged and revised, with 40 Illustrations. Crown 8vo. 15s.
HUTTON'S (H. E.) Principia Græca; an Introduction to the Study of Greek. Comprehending Grammar, Delectus, and Exercise-book, with Vocabularies. *Sixth Edition*. 12mo. 3s. 6d.
IRBY AND MANGLES' Travels in Egypt, Nubia, Syria, and the Holy Land. Post 8vo. 2s.
JAMES' (REV. THOMAS) Fables of Æsop. A New Translation, with Historical Preface. With 100 Woodcuts by TENNIEL and WOLF. *Fiftieth Thousand*. Post 8vo. 2s. 6d.
JAMESON'S (MRS.) Lives of the Early Italian Painters— and the Progress of Painting in Italy—Cimabue to Bassano. *New Edition*. With 50 Portraits. Post 8vo. 10s. 6d.
JENNINGS' (L. J.) Eighty Years of Republican Government in the United States. Post 8vo. 10s. 6d.
JESSE'S (EDWARD) Gleanings in Natural History. *Eighth Edition*. Fcp. 8vo. 6s.
JOHNS' (REV. B. G.) Blind People; their Works and Ways. With Sketches of the Lives of some famous Blind Men. With Illustrations. Post 8vo. 7s. 6d.
JOHNSON'S (DR. SAMUEL) Life. By James Boswell. Including the Tour to the Hebrides. Edited by MR. CROKER. Portraits. Royal 8vo. 10s.
——— Lives of the English Poets. Edited by PETER CUNNINGHAM. 3 vols. 8vo. 22s. 6d.
KEN'S (BISHOP) Life. By a LAYMAN. Portrait. 2 Vols. 8vo. 18s.
——— Exposition of the Apostles' Creed. Fcap. 1s. 6d.
——— Approach to the Holy Altar. Fcap. 8vo. 1s. 6d.
KENNEDY'S (GENERAL) Notes on the Battle of Waterloo. With a Memoir of his Life and Services, and a Plan for the Defence of Canada. With Map and Plans. 8vo. 7s. 6d.
KERR'S (ROBERT) GENTLEMAN'S HOUSE; OR, HOW TO PLAN ENGLISH RESIDENCES, FROM THE PARSONAGE TO THE PALACE. With Tables and Cost. Views and Plans. *Second Edition*. 8vo. 24s.
——— Ancient Lights; a Book for Architects, Surveyors, Lawyers, and Landlords. 8vo. 5s. 6d.
——— (R. MALCOLM) Student's Blackstone. A Systematic Abridgment of the entire Commentaries, adapted to the present state of the law. Post 8vo. 7s. 6d.
KING'S (REV. C. W.) Antique Gems; their Origin, Use, and Value, as Interpreters of Ancient History, and as illustrative of Ancient Art. *Second Edition*. Illustrations. 8vo. 24s.
KING EDWARD VITH's Latin Grammar; or, an Introduction to the Latin Tongue. *Seventeenth Edition*. 12mo. 3s. 6d.
——— First Latin Book; or, the Accidence, Syntax, and Prosody, with an English Translation. *Fifth Edition*. 12mo. 2s. 6d.

KING GEORGE THE THIRD'S CORRESPONDENCE WITH LORD NORTH, 1769-82. Edited, with Notes and Introduction, by W. BODHAM DONNE. 2 vols. 8vo. 32s.

KIRK'S (J. FOSTER) History of Charles the Bold, Duke of Burgundy. Portrait. 3 Vols. 8vo. 45s.

KUGLER'S Italian Schools of Painting. Edited, with Notes, by SIR CHARLES EASTLAKE. *Third Edition*. Woodcuts. 2 Vols. Post 8vo. 30s.

——— German, Dutch, and Flemish Schools of Painting. Edited, with Notes, by DR. WAAGEN. *Second Edition*. Woodcuts. 2 Vols. Post 8vo. 24s.

LAYARD'S (A. H.) Nineveh and its Remains. Being a Narrative of Researches and Discoveries amidst the Ruins of Assyria. With an Account of the Chaldean Christians of Kurdistan; the Yezedis, or Devil-worshippers; and an Enquiry into the Manners and Arts of the Ancient Assyrians. *Sixth Edition*. Plates and Woodcuts. 2 Vols. 8vo. 36s.

*** A POPULAR EDITION. With Illustrations. Post 8vo. 7s. 6d.

——— Nineveh and Babylon; being the Narrative of a Second Expedition to Assyria. Plates. 8vo. 21s.

*** A POPULAR EDITION. With Illustrations. Post 8vo. 7s. 6d.

LEATHES' (STANLEY) Short Practical Hebrew Grammar. With an Appendix, containing the Hebrew Text of Genesis i.—vi., and Psalms i.—vi. Grammatical Analysis and Vocabulary. Post 8vo. 7s. 6d.

LENNEP'S (REV. H. J. VAN) Missionary Travels in Asia Minor. With Illustrations. 2 Vols. Post 8vo. (*In preparation*.)

LESLIE'S (C. R.) Handbook for Young Painters. With Illustrations. Post 8vo. 10s. 6d.

——— Autobiographical Recollections, with Selections from his Correspondence. Edited by TOM TAYLOR. Portrait. 2 Vols. Post 8vo. 18s.

——— Life and Works of Sir Joshua Reynolds. Portraits and Illustrations. 2 Vols. 8vo. 42s.

LETTERS FROM THE BALTIC. By a LADY. Post 8vo. 2s.

——— MADRAS. By a LADY. Post 8vo. 2s.

——— SIERRA LEONE. By a LADY. Post 8vo. 3s. 6d.

LEVI'S (LEONE) Wages and Earnings of the Working Classes. With some Facts Illustrative of their Economic Condition. 8vo. 6s.

LEWIS (SIR G. C.) On the Government of Dependencies. 8vo. 12s.

——— Glossary of Provincial Words used in Herefordshire, &c. 12mo. 4s. 6d.

——— (M. G.) Journal of a Residence among the Negroes in the West Indies. Post 8vo. 2s.

LIDDELL'S (DEAN) History of Rome. From the Earliest Times to the Establishment of the Empire. With the History of Literature and Art. 2 Vols. 8vo. 28s.

——— Student's History of Rome, abridged from the above Work. With Woodcuts. Post 8vo. 7s. 6d.

LINDSAY'S (LORD) Lives of the Lindsays; or, a Memoir of the Houses of Crawfurd and Balcarres. With Extracts from Official Papers and Personal Narratives. *Second Edition*. 3 Vols. 8vo. 24s.

LISPINGS from LOW LATITUDES; or, the Journal of the Hon. Impulsia Gushington. Edited by LORD DUFFERIN. With 24 Plates. 4to. 21s.

LITTLE ARTHUR'S HISTORY OF ENGLAND. By LADY CALLCOTT. *New Edition, continued to* 1862. With 20 Woodcuts. Fcap. 8vo. 2s. 6d.

LIVINGSTONE'S (DR.) Popular Account of his Missionary Travels in South Africa. Illustrations. Post 8vo. 6s.

―――――― Narrative of an Expedition to the Zambezi and its Tributaries; and of the Discovery of Lakes Shirwa and Nyassa. 1858-64. Map and Illustrations. 8vo. 21s.

LIVONIAN TALES. By the Author of "Letters from the Baltic." Post 8vo. 2s.

LOCKHART'S (J. G.) Ancient Spanish Ballads. Historical and Romantic. Translated, with Notes. *New Edition*. Post 8vo. 2s. 6d.

―――――― Life of Theodore Hook. Fcap. 8vo. 1s.

LONDON (OLD). A series of Essays on its Archæology and Antiquities, by DEAN STANLEY; A. J. BERESFORD HOPE, M.P.; G. G. SCOTT, R.A.; R. WESTMACOTT. R.A.; E. FOSS, F.S.A.; G. T. CLARK; JOSEPH BURTT; REV. J. R GREEN; and G. SCHARF, F.S.A. 8vo. 12s.

LONDON'S (BISHOP OF) Dangers and Safeguards of Modern Theology. Containing Suggestions to the Theological Student under present difficulties. *Second Edition*. 8vo. 9s.

LONSDALE'S (BISHOP) Life. With Selections from his Writings. By E. B. DENISON, Q.C. With Portrait. Crown 8vo. 10s. 6d.

LOUDON'S (MRS.) Instructions in Gardening. With Directions and Calendar of Operations for Every Month. *Eighth Edition*. Woodcuts. Fcap. 8vo. 5s.

LUCAS' (SAMUEL) Secularia; or, Surveys on the Main Stream of History. 8vo. 12s.

LUCKNOW: a Lady's Diary of the Siege. Fcap. 8vo. 4s. 6d.

LYELL'S (SIR CHARLES) Elements of Geology; or, the Ancient Changes of the Earth and its Inhabitants as illustrated by Geological Monuments. *Sixth Edition*. Woodcuts. 8vo. 18s.

―――――― Principles of Geology; or, the Modern Charges of the Earth and its Inhabitants considered as illustrative of Geology. *Tenth Edition*. With Illustrations. 2 Vols. 8vo. 32s.

―――――― Geological Evidences of the Antiquity of Man. *Third Edition*. Illustrations. 8vo. 14s.

LYTTELTON'S (LORD) Ephemera. Post 8vo. 10s. 6d.

LYTTON'S (LORD) Poems. *New Edition*. Post 8vo. 10s. 6d.

―――――― Lost Tales of Miletus. *Second Edition*. Post 8vo. 7s. 6d.

MACPHERSON'S (MAJOR S. C.) Memorials of Service in India, while Political Agent at Gwalior during the Mutiny. With Portrait and Illustrations. 8vo. 12s.

MAHON'S (LORD) Works. See STANHOPE (Earl of).

McCLINTOCK'S (SIR L.) Narrative of the Discovery of the Fate of Sir John Franklin and his Companions in the Arctic Seas. *Twelfth Thousand*. Illustrations. 8vo. 16s.

McCULLOCH'S (J. R.) Collected Edition of RICARDO's Political Works. With Notes and Memoir. 8vo. 16s.

MacDOUGALL'S (COL.) Modern Warfare as Influenced by Modern Artillery. With Plans. Post 8vo. 12s.

MAINE (H. SUMNER) On Ancient Law: its Connection with the Early History of Society, and its Relation to Modern Ideas. 8vo. 12s.

MALCOLM'S (SIR JOHN) Sketches of Persia. Post 8vo. 3s. 6d.

MANSEL (CANON) Limits of Religious Thought Examined. Being the Bampton Lectures for 1858. Post 8vo. 8s. 6d.

MANSFIELD (SIR WILLIAM) On a Gold Currency for India. 8vo. 3s. 6d.

MANTELL'S (GIDEON A.) Thoughts on Animalcules; or, the Invisible World, as revealed by the Microscope. Plates. 16mo. 6s.

MANUAL OF SCIENTIFIC ENQUIRY. For the Use of Travellers. Edited by Sir J. F. HERSCHEL and Rev. R. MAIN. Maps. Post 8vo. 9s. (*Published by order of the Lords of the Admiralty.*)

MARKHAM'S (MRS.) History of England. From the First Invasion by the Romans, down to Recent Times. *New Edition, continued to 1863.* Woodcuts. 12mo. 4s.

——————— History of France. From the Conquest by the Gauls, to Recent Times. *New Edition, continued to 1856.* Woodcuts. 12mo. 4s.

——————— History of Germany. From the Invasion by Marius, to Recent Times. *New Edition.* Woodcuts. 12mo. 4s.

——————— (CLEMENTS R.) Travels in Peru and India. Maps and Illustrations. 8vo. 16s.

MARRYAT'S (JOSEPH) History of Modern and Mediæval Pottery and Porcelain. With a Description of the Manufacture. *Third and revised and enlarged Edition.* Plates and Woodcuts. 8vo. (*Nearly Ready.*)

——————— (HORACE) Jutland, the Danish Isles, and Copenhagen. Illustrations. 2 Vols. Post 8vo. 24s.

——————— Sweden and Isle of Gothland. Illustrations. 2 Vols. Post 8vo. 28s.

MARSH'S (G. P.) Student's Manual of the English Language. Post 8vo. 7s. 6d.

MAUREL'S (JULES) Essay on the Character, Actions, and Writings of the Duke of Wellington. *Second Edition.* Fcap. 8vo. 1s. 6d.

MAYNE'S (CAPT.) Four Years in British Columbia and Vancouver Island. Its Forests, Rivers, Coasts, and Gold Fields, and Resources for Colonisation. Illustrations. 8vo. 16s.

MELVILLE'S (HERMANN) Typee and Omoo; or, Adventures amongst the Marquesas and South Sea Islands. 2 Vols. Post 8vo. 7s.

MILLS' (REV. JOHN) Three Months' Residence at Nablus, with an Account of the Modern Samaritans. Illustrations. Post 8vo. 10s. 6d.

MILMAN'S (DEAN) Historical Works. Containing: 1. History of the Jews, 3 Vols. 2. History of Early Christianity, 3 Vols. 3. History of Latin Christianity, 9 Vols. Post 8vo. 6s. each.

——————— Annals of St. Paul's Cathedral. Portrait and Illustrations. 8vo. (*In preparation.*)

——————— Character and Conduct of the Apostles considered as an Evidence of Christianity. 8vo. 10s. 6d.

——————— Translations from the Agamemnon of Æschylus and Bacchanals of Euripides. With Illustrations. Crown 8vo. 12s.

——————— Works of Horace. With 100 woodcuts. Small 8vo. 7s. 6d.

——————— Life of Horace. Woodcuts. 8vo. 9s.

——————— Poetical Works. Plates. 3 Vols. Fcap. 8vo. 18s.

——————— Fall of Jerusalem. Fcap. 8vo. 1s.

——————— (CAPT. E. A.) Wayside Cross. A Tale of the Carlist War. Post 8vo. 2s.

MEREDITH'S (Mrs. Charles) Notes and Sketches of New South Wales. Post 8vo. 2s.

MESSIAH (THE): A Narrative of the Life, Travels, Death, Resurrection, and Ascension of our Blessed Lord. By the Author of "Life of Bishop Ken." Map. 8vo. 18s.

MICHIE'S (Alexander) Siberian Overland Route from Peking to Petersburg, through the Deserts and Steppes of Mongolia, Tartary, &c. Maps and Illustrations. 8vo. 16s.

MODERN DOMESTIC COOKERY. Founded on Principles of Economy and Practical Knowledge and adapted for Private Families. *New Edition.* Woodcuts. Fcap. 8vo. 5s.

MOORE'S (Thomas) Life and Letters of Lord Byron. Plates. 6 Vols. Fcap. 8vo. 18s.; or 1 Vol. Portraits. Royal 8vo. 9s.

MOTLEY'S (J. L.) History of the United Netherlands: from the Death of William the Silent to the Twelve Years' Truce, 1609. Embracing the English-Dutch struggle against Spain; and a detailed Account of the Spanish Armada. Portraits. 4 Vols. 8vo. 60s. Or *Popular Edition.* 4 Vols. Post 8vo. 6s. each.

MOUHOT'S (Henri) Siam, Cambojia, and Lao; a Narrative of Travels and Discoveries. Illustrations. 2 vols. 8vo. 32s.

MOZLEY'S (Rev. J. B.) Treatise on Predestination. 8vo. 14s.

——— Primitive Doctrine of Baptismal Regeneration. 8vo. 7s. 6d.

MUNDY'S (General) Pen and Pencil Sketches in India. *Third Edition.* Plates. Post 8vo. 7s. 6d.

MUNRO'S (General Sir Thomas) Life and Letters. By the Rev. G. R. Gleig. Post 8vo. 3s. 6d.

MURCHISON'S (Sir Roderick) Russia in Europe and the Ural Mountains. With Coloured Maps, Plates, Sections, &c. 2 Vols. Royal 4to. 5l. 5s.

——— Siluria; or, a History of the Oldest Rocks containing Organic Remains. *Fourth Edition.* Map and Plates. 8vo. 30s.

MURRAY'S RAILWAY READING. Containing:—

Wellington. By Lord Ellesmere. 6d.
Nimrod on the Chase. 1s.
Essays from "The Times." 2 Vols. 8s.
Music and Dress. 1s.
Layard's Account of Nineveh. 5s.
Milman's Fall of Jerusalem. 1s.
Mahon's "Forty-Five." 3s.
Life of Theodore Hook. 1s.
Deeds of Naval Daring. 3s. 6d.
The Honey Bee. 1s.
James' Æsop's Fables. 2s. 6d.
Nimrod on the Turf. 1s. 6d.
Art of Dining. 1s. 6d.
Hallam's Literary Essays. 2s.
Mahon's Joan of Arc. 1s.
Head's Emigrant. 2s. 6d.
Nimrod on the Road. 1s.
Croker on the Guillotine. 1s.
Hollway's Norway. 2s.
Maurel's Wellington. 1s. 6d.
Campbell's Life of Bacon. 2s. 6d.
The Flower Garden. 1s.
Lockhart's Spanish Ballads. 2s. 6d.
Taylor's Notes from Life. 2s.
Rejected Addresses. 1s.
Penn's Hints on Angling. 1s.

MUSIC AND DRESS. By a Lady. Reprinted from the "Quarterly Review." Fcap. 8vo. 1s.

NAPIER'S (Sir Chas.) Life; chiefly derived from his Journals and Letters. By Sir W. Napier. *Second Edition.* Portraits. 4 Vols. Post 8vo. 48s.

——— (Sir Wm.) Life and Letters. Edited by H. A. Bruce, M.P. Portraits. 2 Vols. Crown 8vo. 28s.

——— English Battles and Sieges of the Peninsular War. *Fourth Edition.* Portrait. Post 8vo. 9s.

NAUTICAL (THE) ALMANACK. Royal 8vo. 2s. 6d. (By Authority.)

NAVY LIST (THE). (Published Quarterly, by Authority.) 16mo. 2s. 6d.

NEW TESTAMENT (ILLUSTRATED). With Explanatory Commentary. Edited by ARCHDEACON CHURTON, M.A., and BASIL JONES, M.A. With 110 authentic Views of Places, from Sketches and Photographs taken on the spot. 2 Vols. Crown 8vo. 30s. cloth; 52s. 6d. calf; 63s. morocco.

NICHOLLS' (SIR GEORGE) History of the English, Irish and Scotch Poor Laws. 4 Vols. 8vo.

——— (Rev. H. G.) Historical Account of the Forest of Dean. Woodcuts, &c. Post 8vo. 10s. 6d.

NICOLAS' (SIR HARRIS) Historic Peerage of England. Exhibiting the Origin, Descent, and Present State of every Title of Peerage which has existed in this Country since the Conquest. By WILLIAM COURTHOPE. 8vo. 30s.

NIMROD On the Chace—The Turf—and The Road. Woodcuts. Fcap. 8vo. 3s. 6d.

OLD LONDON; Papers read at the London Congress of the Archæological Institute, July, 1866. By A. J. B. BERESFORD HOPE, M.P.; DEAN STANLEY, D.D.; G. T. CLARK, Esq.; G. GILBERT SCOTT. R.A.; PROFESSOR WESTMACOTT, R.A.; EDWARD FOSS, F.S.A.; JOSEPH BURTT, Esq.; REV. J. R. GREEN; GEORGE SCHARF, F.S.A. With Illustrations. 8vo. 12s.

OXENHAM'S (REV. W.) English Notes for Latin Elegiacs; designed for early Proficients in the Art of Latin Versification, with Prefatory Rules of Composition in Elegiac Metre. Fourth Edition. 12mo. 3s. 6d.

OXFORD'S (BISHOP OF) Popular Life of William Wilberforce. Portrait. Post 8vo. 10s. 6d.

PARIS' (Dr.) Philosophy in Sport made Science in Earnest; or, the First Principles of Natural Philosophy inculcated by aid of the Toys and Sports of Youth. Ninth Edition. Woodcuts. Post 8vo. 7s. 6d.

PARKYNS' (MANSFIELD) Life in Abyssinia: During a Three Years' Residence and Travels in that Country. New Edition, with Map and 30 Illustrations. Post 8vo. 7s. 6d.

PEEL'S (SIR ROBERT) Memoirs. Edited by EARL STANHOPE and Mr. CARDWELL. 2 Vols. Post 8vo. 7s. 6d. each.

PENN'S (RICHARD) Maxims and Hints for an Angler and Chess-player. New Edition. Woodcuts. Fcap. 8vo. 1s.

PENROSE'S (F. C.) Principles of Athenian Architecture, and the Optical Refinements exhibited in the Construction of the Ancient Buildings at Athens, from a Survey. With 40 Plates. Folio. 5l. 5s.

PERCY'S (JOHN, M.D.) Metallurgy of Fuel, Coal, Fire-Clays, Copper, Zinc, Brass, &c. Illustrations. 8vo. 21s.

——— Metallurgy of Iron and Steel. Illustrations. 8vo. 42s.

——— Metallurgy of Lead, Silver, Gold, Platinum, Nickel, Cobalt, Antimony, Bismuth, Arsenic, &c. Illustrations. 8vo. (In the Press.)

PHILLIPP (C. S. M.) On Jurisprudence. 8vo. 12s.

PHILLIPS' (JOHN) Memoirs of William Smith, (the Father of Geology). Portrait. 8vo. 7s. 6d.

——— Geology of Yorkshire, The Coast, and Limestone District. Plates. 4to. Part I., 20s.—Part II., 30s.

——— Rivers, Mountains, and Sea Coast of Yorkshire. With Essays on the Climate, Scenery, and Ancient Inhabitants. Second Edition, Plates. 8vo. 15s.

PHILPOTTS' (Bishop) Letters to the late Charles Butler, on his " Book of the Roman Catholic Church." *New Edition.* Post 8vo. 6s.

POPE'S (Alexander) Life and Works. *A New Edition.* Containing nearly 500 unpublished Letters. Edited, with a New Life, Introductions and Notes, by Rev. Whitwell Elwin. Portraits 8vo. *(In the Press.)*

PORTER'S (Rev. J. L.) Five Years in Damascus. With Travels to Palmyra, Lebanon and other Scripture Sites. Map and Woodcuts. 2 Vols. Post 8vo. 21s.

———— Handbook for Syria and Palestine: including an Account of the Geography, History, Antiquities, and Inhabitants of these Countries, the Peninsula of Sinai, Edom, and the Syrian Desert. Maps. 2 Vols. Post 8vo. 24s.

PRAYER-BOOK (Illustrated), with Borders, Initials, Vignettes, &c. Edited, with Notes, by Rev. Thos. James. Medium 8vo. 18s. cloth; 31s. 6d. calf; 36s. morocco.

PUSS IN BOOTS. With 12 Illustrations. By Otto Speckter. 16mo. 1s. 6d. or Coloured, 2s. 6d.

QUARTERLY REVIEW (The). 8vo. 6s.

RAMBLES among the Turkomans and Bedaweens of the Syrian Deserts. Post 8vo. 10s. 6d.

RANKE'S (Leopold) History of the Popes of Rome during the 16th and 17th Centuries. Translated from the German by Sarah Austin. 3 Vols. 8vo. 30s.

RAWLINSON'S (Rev. George) Herodotus. A New English Version. Edited with Notes and Essays. Assisted by Sir Henry Rawlinson and Sir J. G. Wilkinson. *Second Edition.* Maps and Woodcut. 4 Vols. 8vo. 48s.

———— Five Great Monarchies of the Ancient World, Chaldæa, Assyria, Media, Babylonia, and Persia. With Maps and 650 Illustrations. 4 Vols. 8vo. 16s. each.

———— Historical Evidences of the truth of the Scripture Records stated anew. *Second Edition.* 8vo. 14s.

REED'S (E. J.) Practical Treatise on Shipbuilding in Iron and Steel. With 250 Illustrations. 8vo. *(In the Press)*

REJECTED ADDRESSES (The). By James and Horace Smith. Fcap. 8vo. 1s.

RENNIE'S (D. F.) British Arms in Peking, 1860; Kagosima, 1862. Post 8vo. 12s.

———————— Peking and the Pekingese: Being a Narrative of the First Year of the British Embassy in China. Illustrations. 2 Vols. Post 8vo. 24s.

———————— Story of Bhotan and the Dooar War; including Sketches of a Residence in the Himalayas and Visit to Bhotan in 1865. Map and Woodcut. Post 8vo. 12s.

REYNOLDS' (Sir Joshua) Life and Times. Commenced by C. R. Leslie, R.A., continued and concluded by Tom Taylor. Portraits and Illustrations. 2 Vols. 8vo. 42s.

———— Descriptive Catalogue of his Works. With Notices of their present owners and localities. By Tom Taylor and Charles W. Franks. With Illustrations. Fcap. 4to. *(In the Press.)*

RICARDO'S (David) Political Works. With a Notice of his Life and Writings. By J. R. M'Culloch. *New Edition.* 8vo. 16s.

RIPA'S (Father) Memoirs during Thirteen Years' Residence at the Court of Peking. From the Italian. Post 8vo. 2s.

ROBERTSON'S (CANON) History of the Christian Church, from the Apostolic Age to the Death of Boniface VIII., A.D. 1122—1304. 3 Vols. 8vo.

ROBINSON'S (REV. DR.) Biblical Researches in Palestine and the Adjacent Regions; a Journal of Travels in 1838 and 1852. *Third Edition.* Maps. 3 Vols. 8vo. 42s.

——— Physical Geography of the Holy Land. Post 8vo. 10s. 6d.

ROME (STUDENT'S HISTORY OF). FROM THE EARLIEST TIMES TO THE ESTABLISHMENT OF THE EMPIRE. By DEAN LIDDELL. Woodcuts. Post 8vo. 7s. 6d.

——— (SMALLER HISTORY OF). By WM. SMITH, LL.D. Woodcuts. 16mo. 3s. 6d.

ROWLAND'S (DAVID) Manual of the English Constitution; Its Rise, Growth, and Present State. Post 8vo. 10s. 6d.

——— Laws of Nature the Foundation of Morals. Post 8vo. 6s.

RUNDELL'S (MRS.) Domestic Cookery, adapted for Private Families. *New Edition.* Woodcuts. Fcap. 8vo. 5s.

RUSSELL'S (RUTHERFURD) History of the Heroes of Medicine. Portraits. 8vo. 14s.

RUXTON'S (GEORGE F.) Travels in Mexico; with Adventures among the Wild Tribes and Animals of the Prairies and Rocky Mountains. Post 8vo. 3s. 6d.

SALE'S (SIR ROBERT) Brigade in Affghanistan. With an Account of the Defence of Jellalabad. By REV. G. R. GLEIG. Post 8vo. 2s.

SALLESBURY'S (EDWARD) "Children of the Lake." A Poem. Fcap. 8vo. 4s. 6d.

SANDWITH'S (HUMPHRY) Siege of Kars. Post 8vo. 3s. 6d.

SCOTT'S (G. GILBERT) Secular and Domestic Architecture, Present and Future. 8vo. 9s.

——— (Master of Baliol) University Sermons. Post 8vo. 8s. 6d.

SCROPE'S (G. P.) Geology and Extinct Volcanoes of Central France. Illustrations. Medium 8vo. 30s.

SHAW'S (T. B.) Manual of English Literature. Edited, with Notes and Illustrations, by DR. WM. SMITH. Post 8vo. 7s. 6d.

——— Specimens of English Literature. Selected from the Chief Writers. Edited by WM. SMITH, LL.D. Post 8vo. 7s. 6d.

SHIRLEY (EVELYN P.) on Deer and Deer Parks, or some Account of English Parks, with Notes on the Management of Deer. Illustrations. 4to. 21s.

SIERRA LEONE; Described in Letters to Friends at Home. By A LADY. Post 8vo. 3s. 6d.

SIMMONS (CAPT. T. F.) on the Constitution and Practice of Courts-Martial; with a Summary of the Law of Evidence. *Sixth and Revised Edition.* 8vo. (*In the Press.*)

SMITH'S (REV. A. C.) Attractions of the Nile and its Banks. A Journal of Travels in Egypt and Nubia. Woodcuts. 2 Vols. Post 8vo.

SOUTH'S (JOHN F.) Household Surgery; or, Hints on Emergencies. *Seventeenth Thousand.* Woodcuts. Fcp. 8vo. 4s. 6d.

SMILES' (SAMUEL) Lives of British Engineers; from the Earliest Period to the Present Time, with an account of their Principal Works; including a History of the Invention and Introduction of the Steam Engine. With 9 Portraits and 400 Illustrations. 4 Vols. 8vo. 21s. each.

——— Lives of George and Robert Stephenson. With Portraits and Illustrations. Medium 8vo. 21s. Or *Popular Edition*, with Woodcuts. Post 8vo. 6s.

——— Lives of Boulton and Watt. With Portraits and Illustrations. Medium 8vo. 21s.

——— Lives of Brindley and the Early Engineers. With Portrait and 50 Woodcuts. Post 8vo. 6s.

——— Life of Telford. With a History of Roads and Travelling in England. Woodcuts. Post 8vo. 6s.

——— Self-Help. With Illustrations of Character and Conduct. Post 8vo. 6s. Or in French. 5s.

——— Industrial Biography: Iron-Workers and Tool Makers. A sequel to "Self-Help." Post 8vo. 6s.

——— Huguenots in England and Ireland: their Settlements, Churches and Industries. *Third Thousand*. 8vo. 16s.

——— Workmen's Earnings—Savings—and Strikes. Fcap. 8vo. 1s. 6d.

SOMERVILLE'S (MARY) Physical Geography. *Fifth Edition*. Portrait. Post 8vo. 9s.

——— Connexion of the Physical Sciences. *Ninth Edition*. Woodcuts. Post 8vo. 9s.

——— Molecular and Microscopic Science. Illustrations. 2 Vols. Post 8vo. (*In the Press*.)

SOUTHEY'S (ROBERT) Book of the Church. *Seventh Edition*. Post 8vo. 7s. 6d.

——— Lives of Bunyan and Cromwell. Post 8vo. 2s.

SPECKTER'S (OTTO) Puss in Boots. With 12 Woodcuts. Square 12mo. 1s. 6d. plain, or 2s. 6d. coloured.

STANLEY'S (DEAN) Sinai and Palestine. Map. 8vo. 14s.

——— Bible in the Holy Land; being Extracts from the above Work. Woodcuts, Fcap. 8vo, 2s. 6d.

——— St. Paul's Epistles to the Corinthians. With Dissertations and Notes. 8vo. 18s.

——— History of the Eastern Church. Plans. 8vo. 12s.

——— Jewish Church. 2 Vols. 8vo. 16s. each.

——— Historical Memorials of Canterbury. Woodcuts. Post 8vo. 7s. 6d.

——— Memorials of Westminster Abbey. Illustrations. 8vo. 18s.

——— Sermons in the East. 8vo. 9s.

——— on Evangelical and Apostolical Teaching. Post 8vo. 7s. 6d.

——— ADDRESSES AND CHARGES OF BISHOP STANLEY. With Memoir. 8vo. 10s. 6d.

SMITH'S (Dr. Wm.) Dictionary of the Bible; its Antiquities, Biography, Geography, and Natural History. Illustrations. 3 Vols. 8vo. 105s.
——— Concise Bible Dictionary, for Families and Students. Illustrations. Medium 8vo. 21s.
——— Smaller Bible Dictionary, for Schools and Young Persons. Illustrations. Post 8vo. 7s. 6d.
——— Dictionary of Christian Antiquities: from the Times of the Apostles to the Age of Charlemagne. Illustrations. Medium. 8vo. (*In preparation.*)
——— Biblical Atlas. Folio. (*In preparation.*)
——— Greek and Roman Antiquities. Woodcuts. 8vo. 42s.
——— Greek and Roman Biography and Mythology. Woodcuts. 3 Vols. 8vo. 5l. 15s. 6d.
——— Greek and Roman Geography. Woodcuts. 2 Vols. 8vo. 80s.
——— Classical Atlas. Folio. (*In preparation.*)
——— Classical Dictionary, for the Higher Forms. With 750 Woodcuts. 8vo. 18s.
——— Smaller Classical Dictionary. With 200 Woodcuts. Crown 8vo. 7s. 6d.
——— Smaller Dictionary of Greek and Roman Antiquities. With 200 Woodcuts. Crown 8vo. 7s. 6d.
——— Copious and Critical English-Latin Dictionary. 8vo and 12mo. (*Nearly Ready.*)
——— Complete Latin English Dictionary. With Tables of the Roman Calendar, Measures, Weights, and Money. 8vo. 21s.
——— Smaller Latin-English Dictionary. 12mo. 7s. 6d.
——— Latin-English Vocabulary; for Phædrus, Cornelius Nepos, and Cæsar. 12mo. 3s. 6d.
——— Principia Latina—Part I. A Grammar, Delectus, and Exercise Book, with Vocabularies. *Sixth Edition*. 12mo. 3s. 6d.
——————————— Part II. A Reading-book of Mythology, Geography, Roman Antiquities, and History. With Notes and Dictionary. *Third Edition*. 12mo. 3s. 6d.
——————————— Part III. A Latin Poetry Book. Hexameters and Pentameters; Eclog. Ovidianæ; Latin Prosody, &c. *Second Edition*. 12mo. 3s. 6d.
——————————— Part IV. Latin Prose Composition. Rules of Syntax, with Examples, Explanations of Synonyms, and Exercises on the Syntax. *Second Edition*. 12mo. 3s. 6d.
——————————— Part V. Short Tales and Anecdotes for Translation into Latin. 12mo. 3s.
——— Student's Latin Grammar for the Higher Forms. Post 8vo. 6s.
——— Smaller Latin Grammar, for the Middle and Lower Forms. 12mo. 3s. 6d.
——— Initia Græca, Part I. An Introduction to Greek; comprehending Grammar, Delectus, and Exercise-book. With Vocabularies. 12mo. 3s. 6d.
——— Initia Græca, Part II. A Reading Book. Containing Short Tales, Anecdotes, Fables, Mythology, and Grecian History. Arranged in a systematic Progression, with a Lexicon. 12mo. 3s. 6d.
——— Initia Græca, Part III. Greek Prose Composition. Containing the Rules of Syntax, with copious Examples and Exercises. 12mo. (*In preparation.*)

SMITH'S (Dr. Wm.) Student's Greek Grammar for the Higher Forms. By Professor Curtius. Post 8vo. 6s.

————— Smaller Greek Grammar for the Middle and Lower Forms. 12mo. 3s. 6d.

————— Smaller History of England. With Illustrations. 16mo. 3s. 6d.

————— History of Greece. With Illustrations. 16mo. 3s. 6d.

————— History of Rome. With Illustrations. 16mo. 3s. 6d.

————— Classical Mythology. With Translations from the Ancient Poets. Illustrations. 12mo. 3s 6d.

————— Scripture History. With Woodcuts. 16mo. (In preparation.)

STUDENT'S HUME. A History of England from the Invasion of Julius Cæsar to the Revolution of 1688. By David Hume. Corrected and continued to 1858. Woodcuts. Post 8vo. 7s. 6d.

** Questions on the above Work, 12mo. 2s.

————— HISTORY OF FRANCE; from the Earliest Times to the Establishment of the Second Empire, 1852. By W. H. Pearson, M.A. Woodcuts. Post 8vo. 7s. 6d.

————— HISTORY OF GREECE; from the Earliest Times to the Roman Conquest. With the History of Literature and Art. By Wm. Smith, LL.D. Woodcuts. Crown 8vo. 7s. 6d.

** Questions on the above Work, 12mo. 2s.

————— HISTORY OF ROME; from the Earliest Times to the Establishment of the Empire. With the History of Literature and Art. By Dean Liddell. Woodcuts. Crown 8vo. 7s. 6d.

————— GIBBON; an Epitome of the Decline and Fall of the Roman Empire. Incorporating the Researches of Recent Commentators. Woodcuts. Post 8vo. 7s. 6d.

————— OLD TESTAMENT HISTORY; from the Creation to the Return of the Jews from Captivity. Maps and Woodcuts. Post 8vo. 7s. 6d.

————— NEW TESTAMENT HISTORY. With an Introduction connecting the History of the Old and New Testaments. Maps and Woodcuts. Post 8vo. 7s. 6d.

————— BLACKSTONE: a Systematic Abridgment of the Entire Commentaries. By R. Malcolm Kerr, LL.D. Post 8vo. 7s. 6d.

————— MANUAL OF ANCIENT GEOGRAPHY. By Rev. W. L. Bevan, M.A. Woodcuts. Post 8vo. 7s. 6d.

————— MODERN GEOGRAPHY. By Rev. W. L. Bevan. Woodcuts. Post 8vo. (In the Press.)

————— ECCLESIASTICAL HISTORY. Containing the History of the Christian Church from the Close of the New Testament Canon to the Reformation. Post 8vo. (In preparation.)

————— MORAL PHILOSOPHY. With Quotations and References. By William Fleming, D.D. Post 8vo. 7s.6d.

————— ENGLISH LANGUAGE. By Geo. P. Marsh. Post 8vo. 7s.6d.

————— ENGLISH LITERATURE. By T. B. Shaw, M.A. Post 8vo. 7s. 6d.

————— SPECIMENS OF ENGLISH LITERATURE. Selected from the Chief Writers. By Thomas B. Shaw, M.A. Post 8vo. 7s. 6d.

STANHOPE'S (EARL) History of England, from the Peace of Utrecht to the Peace of Versailles, 1713-83. *Library Edition.* 7 vols. 8vo. 93s. Or *Popular Edition.* 7 Vols. Post 8vo. 5s. each.
—————— British India, from its Origin till the Peace of 1783. Post 8vo. 3s. 6d.
—————— "Forty-Five;" a Narrative of the Rebellion in Scotland. Post 8vo. 3s.
—————— Spain under Charles the Second. Post 8vo. 6s. 6d.
—————— Historical and Critical Essays. Post 8vo. 3s. 6d.
—————— Life of Belisarius. Post 8vo. 10s. 6d.
—————— Condé. Post 8vo. 3s. 6d.
—————— William Pitt. With Extracts from his MS. Papers. Portraits. 4 Vols. Post 8vo. 24s.
—————— Miscellanies. Post 8vo. 5s. 6d.
—————— Story of Joan of Arc. Fcap. 8vo. 1s.
ST. JOHN'S (CHARLES) Wild Sports and Natural History of the Highlands. Post 8vo. 3s. 6d.
—————— (BAYLE) Adventures in the Libyan Desert and the Oasis of Jupiter Ammon. Woodcuts. Post 8vo. 2s.
STEPHENSONS' (GEORGE and ROBERT) Lives. By SAMUEL SMILES. With Portraits and 70 Illustrations. Medium 8vo. 21s. Or *Popular Edition* with Woodcuts. Post 8vo. 6s.
STOTHARD'S (THOS.) Life. With Personal Reminiscences. By Mrs. BRAY. With Portrait and 60 Woodcuts. 4to. 21s.
STREET'S (G. E.) Gothic Architecture in Spain. From Personal Observations during several journeys through that country. Illustrations. Medium 8vo. 50s.
SULLIVAN'S (SIR EDWARD) Princes, Warriors, and Statesmen of India; an Historical Narrative of the most Important Events, from the Invasion of Mahmoud of Ghizni to that of Nadir Shah. 8vo. 12s.
SUMNER (GEORGE HENRY), M.A. Principles at Stake, being Essays on the Church Questions of the day. By various Writers. 8vo. (*In the Press.*)
SWIFT'S (JONATHAN) Life, Letters, Journals, and Works. By JOHN FORSTER. 8vo. (*In Preparation.*)
SYBEL'S (VON) History of Europe during the French Revolution, 1789—1795. Translated from the German. By WALTER C. PERRY. Vols. 1 & 2. 8vo. 24s.
SYME'S (PROFESSOR) Principles of Surgery. *5th Edition.* 8vo. 12s.
TAIT'S (BISHOP) Dangers and Safeguards of Modern Theology, containing Suggestions to the Theological Student under Present Difficulties. 8vo. 9s.
TAYLOR'S (HENRY) Notes from Life—on Money, Humility and Independence, Wisdom, Choice in Marriage, Children, and Life Poetic. Fcap. 8vo. 2s.
THOMSON'S (ARCHBISHOP) Sermons, Preached at Lincoln's Inn. 8vo. 10s. 6d.
—————— Life in the Light of God's Word. Post 8vo. 6s.
THREE-LEAVED MANUAL OF FAMILY PRAYER; arranged so as to save the trouble of turning the Pages backwards and forwards. Royal 8vo. 2s.
TREMENHEERE (H. S.); The Franchise a Privilege and not a Right, proved by the Political Experience of the Ancients. Fcap. 8vo. 2s. 6d.
TRISTRAM'S (H. B.) Great Sahara, or Wanderings South of the Atlas Mountains. Map and Illustrations. Post 8vo. 15s.

TWISS' (HORACE) Life of Lord Chancellor Eldon, with Selections from his Correspondence. Portrait. *Third Edition.* 2 Vols. Post 8vo. 21s.

TYTLER'S (PATRICK FRASER) Memoirs. By REV. J. W. BURGON, M.A. 8vo. 9s.

VAMBERY'S (ARMINIUS) Travels in Central Asia, from Teheran across the Turkoman Desert on the Eastern Shore of the Caspian to Khiva, Bokhara, and Samarcand in 1863. Map and Illustrations. 8vo. 21s.

VAN LENNEP (HENRY J.) Missionary Travels in Little Known Parts of Asia Minor. With Map and Illustrations. 2 Vols. Post 8vo. (*In preparation.*)

VAUGHAN'S (REV. DR.) Sermons preached in Harrow School. 8vo. 10s. 6d.

WAAGEN'S (DR.) Treasures of Art in Great Britain. Being an Account of the Chief Collections of Paintings, Sculpture, Manuscripts, Miniatures, &c. &c., in this Country. Obtained from Personal Inspection during Visits to England. 4 Vols. 8vo.

WELLINGTON'S (THE DUKE OF) Despatches during his various Campaigns. 8 Vols. 8vo. 21s. each.

—————— Supplementary Despatches. Vols. I. to XII. 8vo. 20s. each.

—————— Civil and Political Correspondence. Vols. I. to III. 8vo. 20s. each.

—————— Selections from Despatches and General Orders. 8vo. 18s.

—————— Speeches in Parliament. 2 Vols. 8vo. 42s.

WHITE'S (HENRY) Massacre of St. Bartholomew. Preceded by a History of the Religious Wars in the Reign of Charles IX. Based on a Personal Examination of Documents in the Archives of France. With Illustrations. 8vo. 16s.

WHYMPER'S (FREDERICK) Travels and Adventures in Alaska and on the River Yukon, the Russian Territory, now ceded to the United States, and Visits to other parts of the North Pacific. With Illustrations. 8vo. (*In preparation.*)

WILKINSON'S (SIR J. G.) Popular Account of the Private Life, Manners, and Customs of the Ancient Egyptians. With 500 Woodcuts. 2 Vols. Post 8vo. 12s.

WILSON'S (BISHOP DANIEL) Life, Letters, and Journals. By Rev. JOSIAH BATEMAN. *Second Edition.* Illustrations. Post 8vo. 9s.

—————— (GENL. SIR ROBERT) Secret History of the French Invasion of Russia, and Retreat of the French Army, 1812. *Second Edition.* 8vo. 15s.

—————— Private Diary of Travels, Personal Services, and Public Events, during Missions and Employments in Spain, Sicily, Turkey, Russia, Poland, Germany, &c. 1812-14. 2 Vols. 8vo. 26s.

—————— Autobiographical Memoirs. Containing an Account of his Early Life down to the Peace of Tilsit. Portrait. 2 Vols. 8vo. 26s.

WOOD (SIR W. P.) On the Continuity of Scripture, as Declared by the Testimony of Our Lord and of the Evangelists and Apostles. *Second Edition.* Post 8vo. 6s.

WORDSWORTH'S (ARCHDEACON) Journal of a Tour in Athens and Attica. *Third Edition.* Plates. Post 8vo. 8s. 6d.

—————— Pictorial, Descriptive, and Historical Account of Greece. *New and Cheaper Edition.* With 600 Woodcuts. Royal 8vo.

www.ingramcontent.com/pod-product-compliance
Lightning Source LLC
Chambersburg PA
CBHW030542300426
44111CB00009B/829